INTERPERSONAL
COMMUNICATION

INTERPERSONAL
COMMUNICATION

Philip Emmert
University of Wyoming

Victoria J. Lukasko Emmert
University of Wyoming

ωcb
Wm. C. Brown Publishers
Dubuque, Iowa

wcb group

Wm. C. Brown Chairman of the Board
Mark C. Falb President and Chief Executive Officer

wcb

Wm. C. Brown Publishers, College Division
Lawrence E. Cremer President
James L. Romig Vice-President, Product Development
David Wm. Smith Vice-President, Marketing
David A. Corona Vice-President, Production and Design
E. F. Jogerst Vice-President, Cost Analyst
Marcia H. Stout Marketing Manager
Linda M. Galarowicz Director of Marketing Research
Marilyn A. Phelps Manager of Design
William A. Moss Production Editorial Manager
Mary M. Heller Visual Research Manager

Book Team

Judith A. Clayton Senior Developmental Editor
Moira Urich Production Editor
Carol M. Schiessl Visual Research Editor
Mavis M. Oeth Permissions Editor

Lisa Bogle cover designer/illustrator

Contents

Preface

Our intent in this book is to offer an intellectual understanding of the basic processes that occur within interpersonal communication systems. We believe, first, that the objectives of studying interpersonal communication ought to be to create effective interpersonal relationships and develop individual personal growth; second, that optimal personal growth in interpersonal communication occurs when cognitive, affective, and experiential learning reinforce one another. We are confident that understanding the basic processes of communication helps us increase our effectiveness in interpersonal communication. We also believe that affective learning best occurs through person-to-person interactions, and we hope that this book will be used in conjunction with classroom activities that enable students to develop those insights into the communication process which result from experience.

The book is aimed at the beginning student. We have assumed no prior knowledge of communication processes. New terminology is defined when used, and we have tried to avoid jargon. For example, we avoid systems theory terminology as much as possible even though the basic assumptions throughout the book come from that theoretical position, and the book attempts to help the student apply this theoretical approach to interpersonal communication.

Part 1 is an introduction to the basic motivational forces involved in interpersonal communication (chapter 1) and to the process of communication (chapter 2).

Part 2 covers the basic elements in interpersonal communication. In chapters 3 and 4 the focus is on the people involved in interpersonal communication. The influence of self-concept, self-esteem, the role of self-fulfilling prophecy, and person perception are discussed. Chapter 5 focuses on the use of words, or a formal language system. How can messages be understood more clearly? What are the important characteristics of word systems that can help and hinder communication? Chapter 6 considers nonverbal communication. What are the communicative effects of facial expressions, gestures, and vocal quality? Can we learn to communicate more effectively nonverbally? Chapter 7 deals with reception: listening and feedback — the part of the process that brings initiating communicator and responding communicator together. Discussion of conflict confrontation and negotiation in interpersonal communication in chapter 8 brings together previously discussed elements in the total process.

Part 3 focuses on two main contexts in which interpersonal communication occurs, the dyads (chapter 9) and small groups (chapter 10), and on the special context of interviews in the organizational setting (chapter 11).

This book is new but it grew out of a previous edition. Although the basic organization of the earlier edition has been retained, we have rearranged some material. For instance, discussions of perception of a relationship and dogmatism have been moved from chapter 8 to chapters 4 and 7, where the material could be oriented more to interpersonal communication. In response to users' suggestions, the last chapter has been changed from presentation of a diffuse view of organizational communication to a chapter on interviewing, with special emphasis on the employment interview. This material speaks to the concerns of the job seeker, with stress on the interactive influence of both parties in the interview.

Other major changes are in chapters 6, 7, 8, and 9. They have been updated and now have many more interpersonal examples and applications. Chapter 6 takes a much more functional approach to nonverbal communication and includes a section on how gender differences affect communication. Chapter 7 includes an expanded section on feedback and emphasizes interpersonal listening. Chapter 8 takes a more interpersonal approach to conflict and communication. Chapter 9, on the dyadic relationship, includes a section on terminating relationships through interpersonal communication.

The objectives at the beginning of each chapter and summaries at the end should help students organize their understanding of interpersonal communication at several levels.

Suggestions from users have helped us write this new edition. Please continue your interactions with us, however indirectly.

We would like to thank the persons who read, criticized, and made suggestions that improved the manuscript. They include:

John Countryman, University of Richmond, Richmond, Va.
Carrol Haggard, MacMurray College, Jacksonville, Ill.
Frank Junghaus, Certified Safety Professional Consultants, Inc., St. Paul, Minn.
Bernadette MacPherson, Emerson College, Boston, Mass.
Clark Olson, Macalester College, St. Paul, Minn.

Philip Emmert
Victoria J. Lukasko Emmert

INTERPERSONAL
COMMUNICATION

Introduction to Interpersonal Communication

1

You and Interpersonal Communication

1. To become aware of the amount of time and effort spent in interpersonal communication behavior.	**Objectives for the Reader**

1. To become aware of the amount of time and effort spent in interpersonal communication behavior.
2. To become aware of the survival function of interpersonal communication.
3. To learn a definition of interpersonal communication that differentiates interpersonal from other communication contexts.
4. To learn to classify needs and become more aware of the effect that needs have on interpersonal communication.
5. To develop an understanding of value systems and the relation of value systems to the individual's self-concept, goals, and interpersonal communication.

It is impossible for us to live our daily lives without engaging in interpersonal communication. To cooperate with the people with whom we live, we must communicate with them. Simply to get from home to school or work requires interpersonal communication to work out travel arrangements. At school or at work we often find ourselves in small groups trying to solve problems and work on projects. Those of us who stay at home find ourselves interacting with children, neighbors, and friends. When we return from school or work we interact with our family or roommates as we prepare for dinner, just as we interacted interpersonally when ordering lunch. We frequently eat meals in a small group in which we talk with one another. We then spend the rest of the evening watching television, reading, or listening to the radio, but constantly interacting with other people in a small group setting.

1. David K. Berlo, *The Process of Communication* (New York: Holt, Rinehart & Winston, 1960), 1.

We spend much of our time communicating interpersonally with other people. Communication generally takes up 70 percent of our time.[1] Most of that is interpersonal communication. That is a lot of time. Why do we spend this much time with other people communicating interpersonally?

THE IMPORTANCE OF INTERPERSONAL COMMUNICATION

Interpersonal communication is one of the most basic activities we perform — following breathing, eating, sleeping, and reproducing. It is even more basic than eating and reproducing in a sense because those two activities may be impossible for us until we master some aspects of interpersonal communication.

From the time we are born, it is necessary for us to communicate to satisfy our need for food. A baby cries to be fed. Mothers and fathers, through communication, learn the necessity of feeding babies regularly, and the baby has interpersonal communication to thank for getting its daily milk. In relations between men and women, we see a complex and subtle system consisting of a collection of behaviors designed to influence the opposite sex — ultimately, for sexual reasons. Certain ways males and females walk, stand, gesture, and use eye contact are systematic within a culture and serve as cues to members of the opposite sex when some sort of sexual relationship is desired. We suspect that the system is so subtle that those involved in it frequently are not consciously aware of their own behavior. Nevertheless, interpersonal communication between the sexes does occur, and it appears to be necessary for the reproduction of our species.

As we go to school, it is through the process of interpersonal communication that we learn how to count, add, subtract, read marks from a book, get along with our friends, and learn what behaviors we have to perform to be approved of by an authority figure called a "teacher." Even before we go to school, we learn from our parents many things we should and should not do to receive approval and be accepted by our friends and others in our community. This occurs through interpersonal communication. Later, as adults, we make friends, sell cars, obtain information, pass time, are caused to laugh, and cause others to laugh through the process of interpersonal communication. Is all of this important? We think so.

Apart from its day-to-day importance, interpersonal communication assumes incredible importance within some specific situations. As we just mentioned, males and females meet each other and establish romantic and sexual relationships through interpersonal communication. Likewise, after the courting relationship has culminated in some form of permanent relationship (marriage more often than not, despite today's changing norms), interpersonal

communication continues to play an important role. When a husband comes home from work at night, pours a beer, collapses into an easy chair, and hides himself behind a newspaper, he may be communicating a great deal. At bedtime when a wife says she has a headache, she has probably communicated more to her husband than the amount of pain in her head. Marriages are made and maintained through interpersonal communication. The success or failure of a marriage depends far more on the interpersonal communication skills of the partners than on any other single variable.[2] In effect, interpersonal communication skills are probably the most important behaviors people ever learn.

Speech is the most obvious form of interpersonal communication. Speech as an expression of but not the same thing as a language system is also the feature that distinguishes human beings from other animals.[3] Research with porpoises and chimpanzees has involved attempts to communicate with these animals and teach them language systems. Although there have been some successes of a limited sort in which chimpanzees have communicated at a fairly basic level, using little plastic objects or American Sign Language instead of spoken words, neither the porpoises nor the chimpanzees have ever managed to produce spoken communication. This appears to be a unique characteristic of human beings. We have the physiological mechanism for producing

Without effective interpersonal communication a couple's relationship may deteriorate.

2. Ben N. Ard, "Communication in Marriage," *Rational Living* 5 (1971):20–22; Harold L. Raush, William A. Barry, Richard K. Hertel, and Mary Ann Swain, . *Communication, Conflict and Marriage* (San Francisco: Jossey-Bass, 1974).

3. Frank E. X. Dance, "Speech Communication: The Sign of Mankind," in *The Great Ideas Today 1975* (Chicago: Encyclopaedia Britannica, 1975), 40–57.

speech and the mental capability of using abstract language through speech. These abilities are tied to our survival and development as a species. In fact, we would suggest that the primary function of interpersonal communication is survival — for the species as for individuals.

Survival and Interpersonal Communication

Millions of years ago our ancestors became part of a mystery that would have intrigued Sherlock Holmes, had his primary interest been the study of communication. That mystery still interests us as we attempt to understand what makes human beings the unique creatures they are and why they became what they are today. Evidence gathered by anthropologists and ethologists (specialists in animal behavior) suggests that once upon a time people were not unlike our closest relatives on the evolutionary tree, the anthropoid apes. The question that puzzles us today is what made people different from the apes? Many think a major factor was the ability of early humans to communicate using the spoken word.[4]

4. Harold J. Vetter, *Language Behavior and Communication* (Itasca, Ill.: F. E. Peacock, 1969), 16.

Although other animals can communicate at a basic level, one of the major differences between our communicative ability and that of other animals appears to be the complexity of our communication systems. We can even employ language to talk about language (sometimes referred to as **metacommunication**), feelings, past and future events, ideas, and so forth.

We are unique among all animal species in that through the use of language we have become **time-binding** creatures.[5] Every generation does not have to relearn important facts from its own experience, because each generation learns them verbally from the preceding generations. For instance, we do not have to experience a depression to know the hardships of economic poverty; nor do we need to thrust our hands into a fire to know the searing pain of heat. These things can be learned from mothers and fathers through interpersonal communication. This ability makes it possible for us to achieve at a higher level than other animals because each generation need not reinvent the wheel, it can build upon the accomplishments of previous generations.

5. Alfred Korzybski, *Science and Sanity* (Lakeville, Conn: Institute of General Semantics, 1968), 223–24.

Communication Origins

Human beings have developed, conquered, and controlled as has no other animal species. From tiny bands of brutish beings we developed civilizations which have produced art, literature, social systems, and machines. We believe an understanding of interpersonal communication today is easier to come by if we consider *why* people communicate — both today and in the past. Furthermore, we feel people communicate today for essentially the same reasons they did two or three hundred thousand years ago. We do this in a different

context, certainly, and within different and more complex cultures. Neverthe-less, reasons very similar to those that prompted our ancestors to make their first utterances very likely motivate us today.

An important clue as to why human beings first communicated appears to be our relative inability to defend ourselves against other predators. We do not have the speed of an antelope or the strength of a buffalo. We do not have the claws and fangs of a tiger. From most evidence we can conclude that our ancestors never did have these characteristics.[6]

Another clue that seems rather important is that our ancestors appear to have been meat eaters from very early prehistoric times. There is considerable evidence to suggest that, contrary to many of our more idealistic concepts, we have always eaten meat. Furthermore, we have always killed to get this meat. There is evidence suggesting that we could not have acquired the meat for eating through scavenging alone. Fossils indicate that humans very likely lived on a diet of meat provided by the killing of animals considerably larger and more dangerous than themselves.[7] We must wonder how, if we were relatively weak compared with other predators, we managed to acquire the meat that seems always to have been a staple in our diet.

Our ancestors survived through the use of interpersonal communication.

6. Robert Ardrey, *The Social Contract* (New York: Atheneum, 1970), 355.

7. Ibid., 337–49.

8. Ibid., 359-70.

Archeological evidence suggests that hundreds of thousands of years ago, humans managed to evolve a society. To kill animals on the hunt and to protect themselves from predators they probably engaged in considerable cooperative social activity.[8] They did not do this because they liked other people for any altruistic reasons, but rather because they had to. If humans were to survive as a species, cooperative behavior was a necessity. Without this cooperation they could never have killed the animals for food, and they very likely could not have protected themselves against the predators of prehistoric times.

From this, we can deduce that our ancestors probably developed the ability to communicate because they *had* to communicate to develop the social system that was necessary for survival. *People learned to communicate in order to survive.*[9]

9. Ibid.

When we talk about survival in prehistoric times, we are referring to both our physical survival as a species and our survival as individuals. Some ethologists believe that as a species we would not have survived had we not been able to evolve a communication system. Communication can be viewed as a tool to ensure our survival, just as a set of claws or fangs is such a tool. Whether we evolved the ability to speak so that we could act together and so survive, or whether the ability to speak was a biological inevitability that happened to result in our survival as a species, is a moot point. Interpersonal communication and survival are inseparable.

Why We Communicate Today

Today we communicate interpersonally for the same reason as in the past: to survive. Of course, by survival we are referring largely to other than immediate physical survival, although admittedly, the physical survival of our species still very much depends on our ability to communicate (about energy supplies, population explosions, war, pollution, and the like).

Instead of using interpersonal communication to organize a hunting party for the purpose of killing game, as was done in prehistoric times, we use it to acquire symbols that represent wealth, which we then exchange for food, clothing, shelter, and the like. We are still involved in the same old physical survival race, but we communicate not only to assure immediate and long-range physical survival, but to satisfy other needs as well. Males and females communicate to satisfy the need for love, and a company foreman may communicate to satisfy the need for power. Some people communicate simply to satisfy a need for identity — to know who and what they are. In a society as complex as ours, some people barely survive and some survive very well. One point should be clear: we began to communicate interpersonally because we had to in order to survive, and we continue to for the same reason: survival.

Self-Concept Survival

Central to our survival is the need to think well of ourselves. This need is discussed later in this chapter and in chapter 3, but here we want to bring out that self-concept is central to survival and that it is created by interpersonal communication.

How did you develop your self-image? How do you know who and what you are? How do you know whether you are good or bad at the things you do? How did you decide that you were a good person or not a good person? This kind of self-awareness and self-concept comes largely through the process of interpersonal communication, beginning at a very early age — at birth. When children are born, they can be treated in many different ways. Parents can treat them and talk to them in ways that make them feel valued, desired, and wanted or in ways that make them feel rejected, unwanted, and worthless. This kind of communication continues throughout our lives. People tell us every day how worthwhile they consider us — by the way they look at us; by how close they stand to us; by the way they initiate or do not initiate conversations with us. Every time we interact with someone the other person tells us how he or she regards us as an individual.

As this happens, we develop our sense of identity. If we have parents who praise us for the work we have done at school, the way we have played on the baseball team, our work in the drama club, or our accomplishments at cooking, we develop a positive perception of ourselves. Even when we have experienced failure, if a friend, parent, teacher, or minister pats us on the back and says, "That's OK, you gave it your best shot — you did your best and we're proud of you," we will think we are worthwhile and a valuable part of humanity. A positive interpersonal comment, insignificant though it may seem, can have quite an impact on someone. So can a statement like "Boy, did you louse it up!" Such a comment can make us feel worthless and reluctant to try again. These are simplistic examples, but no doubt like things you have experienced.

The more often people say positive things to us and about us, the more positive is the self-concept we develop. The less we experience positive interactions, the more negatively we think of ourselves. We have known intelligent, physically attractive people who believed they were incompetent and unattractive. This resulted from experiences throughout their lives in which their family, friends, and others communicated with them in a negative way, which ultimately contributed to their overall negative self-concept.

A parent who communicates supportively does much to help a child develop a positive sense of identity and a feeling of worth.

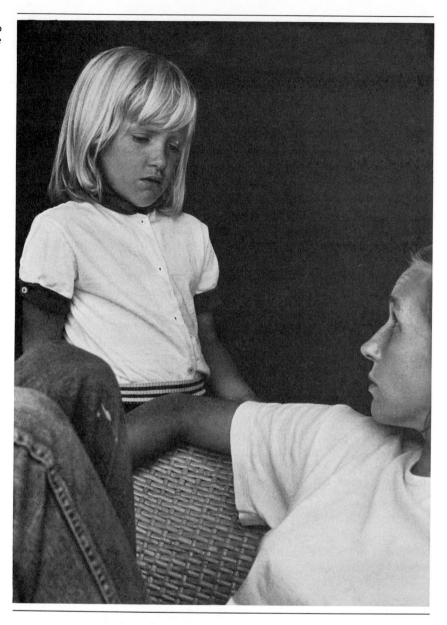

Since a positive self-concept is strongly related to our survival, it is important that we be aware that the way we communicate with other people has a profound effect on their self-concepts. A person who has a negative self-concept will not attempt new projects, initiate interactions with other people, or tackle difficult tasks. Because such people are unwilling to try these things, they frequently limit their careers severely and thus do not enjoy the kind of career they might otherwise have had. They frequently cut themselves off from contact with others — the social survival that seems necessary for well-adjusted personalities. It is even possible for a person whose self-concept has been systematically "beaten down" to develop abnormal perceptions of himself or herself and the people with whom they interact. Many psychological disorders for which people seek help from psychologists and counselors (or for which they must be institutionalized for treatment) result from abnormally negative self-concepts. Such an extreme negative self-concept can often be the result of ineffective interpersonal communication with family and friends. Most of us have developed our self-concepts, either positive or negative, through interpersonal communication — and we contribute to the development of the self-concept of others through the same process.

Social Survival

It is so necessary for human beings to be with other human beings that we have been called "the social animal." A person isolated completely from other people will, after a relatively short time, begin to hallucinate and lose touch with reality. We appear to acquire much of our perception of the world from the people around us. When we are isolated from people, we have a harder time accurately perceiving the world and surviving within it. Because we need people to survive physically, we seem to have developed a need simply to interact with others.

We have known many people who have indicated that "they don't need other people" and yet, with the exception of hermits, who are a special case, very few people manage to get along without others for very long. Even people who seem reclusive interact with others in many ways which they probably convince themselves are necessary — and which, incidentally, provide contact with other human beings.

While in college, one of us had a roommate who developed a bad infection in his throat. The throat specialist who treated him instructed the patient not to speak until the illness was gone. This went on for about five or six weeks. Although occasionally the patient whispered, by and large he simply wrote messages and did not talk during that time. This eliminated him from a great deal of interpersonal interaction. We recall that after some days of this kind of life he became irritable, nervous, and edgy. Finally, when the friend's throat had healed, we discussed the experience. He said at times he ''just wanted to scream.'' He needed to talk to people, even though he was something of a ''loner.'' Social survival and remaining well adjusted were difficult for him without speaking. Interpersonal communication is extremely important for the social survival of all of us because it is the only means to social relationships.

Career Survival

Effective interpersonal communication is critical to the performance of many jobs — perhaps most jobs. We know a highly skilled tool and die maker who for various reasons never developed effective interpersonal communication skills and is willing to talk about not getting along with people on the job. He will admit that he has not received the promotions that some of his colleagues have received simply because he did not ''butter up the boss'' or ''get along with the right people.'' This is another way of saying that his lack of interpersonal skills has hindered his career. Many people would not think of this kind of job as depending heavily upon interpersonal skills, but whatever the job, if you cannot get along with your fellow workers, you may not achieve at as high a level as others in promotions and pay increases. Many secretaries, contractors, bankers, lifeguards, teachers, police officers, janitors — the list could go on — do not progress well in their jobs and are not rewarded financially the way they feel they should be largely because they are ineffective at interpersonal communication. The letter to Ann Landers in figure 1.1 illustrates a physician's ineffective interpersonal communication. We know of no job that is totally divorced from a need for interpersonal communication skills. Even the artist who works alone ultimately interacts with a gallery director or potential customer — and how successfully he or she does so influences the attention and price placed on the artist's work.

The theme of this discussion has been survival. This is the primary goal, or purpose, of interpersonal communication — physical, social, self-concept, and career survival. To be sure, most people — in the Western World at least — no longer are as concerned with physical survival as they were hundreds of thousands of years ago, but concern for social, self-concept, and career survival has grown in importance for most of us — and thus plays a very large role in the interpersonal communication process. A greater awareness of the interpersonal communication process will contribute significantly to our survival in many ways. This book distinguishes the various components of interpersonal communication systems so that you can understand better what is occurring when people interact. With this increased understanding, you should be able to improve your own interpersonal communication competence.

ANN LANDERS

DEAR ANN LANDERS: Yesterday I had a complete physical that was required by a firm I started with recently. I am a healthy young woman (23) and this was my first thorough internal examination by a physician.

The doctor peered into every crevice with lights and poked with instruments. The exam lasted at least 20 minutes. He didn't say ONE word the whole time. After I put my clothes on he said I was very healthy and the results of the blood test and urinalysis would arrive in the mail.

This doctor is extremely competent and highly respected, but on a scale of 1 to 10, I would give him a 6. Why? Because he didn't utter one word throughout the entire examination. If he had said just a few phrases . . . "Everything is fine here" or, "No problem . . . looks excellent," he would have made me feel so much better. Silence during a physical examination can be terribly frightening to a patient.

Please print my letter, Ann. So many doctors need to know this, and it's something they don't teach in medical school.—I Live in Chicago

Dear Chic: I hope every person who has an appointment for a physical will clip this column and hand it to the doctor BEFORE going into the examining room. It's amazing how many competent physicians are insensitive or unaware of this critical aspect of patient care. Thanks for all the good you did today.

Figure 1.1

DEFINING INTERPERSONAL COMMUNICATION

Interpersonal communication is a process in which from two to twenty persons attempt to influence one another through the use of a common symbol system, in a situation permitting equal opportunity for all persons involved in the process to influence one another. Ideally, the process causes us to be aware of others as persons rather than as objects. To consider a dyad for a moment (a two-person communication system), "ideal" interpersonal communication occurs when both persons feel equally free to influence each other. If Charlie starts the interaction by saying something to Charlotte, then Charlotte should feel free to immediately influence him in response to his attempt to influence her. Charlotte's response to Charlie's initiating message is called **feedback.** Feedback is any message which is in response to someone else's message. Obviously, after an interaction is under way, all messages are feedback for someone. Feedback and its function in interpersonal communication are discussed in greater detail later in this chapter and in chapter 7.

10. Bernard Berelson and Gary A. Steiner, *Human Behavior* (New York: Harcourt, Brace & World, 1964), 325.

11. Daniel E. Costello, "Therapeutic Transactions: An Approach to Human Communication," in *Approaches to Human Communication,* Richard W. Budd and Grant D. Ruben, eds., (New York: Spartan Books, 1972), 428.

12. Bruce H. Westley and Malcolm S. MacLean, Jr., "A Conceptual Model for Communications Research," *Journalism Quarterly* (Winter 1957):31–38.

Persons involved in interpersonal communication interact using a language in which the symbols employed are those commonly accepted by people in the group. The numerical limits we place on the interpersonal situation are not arbitrary. When more than twenty people are involved, no longer can there be equal opportunity to influence one another.[10]

What interpersonal communication is *not* is as important to its definition as what it is. The communication process certainly occurs outside the interpersonal context but to go beyond that context would be beyond the scope of this text. Communication studies are subdivided into many disciplinary areas.[11] Small-group communication, organizational communication, public speaking, persuasion, dyadic communication, and mass communication are just some of these areas. These are not *different kinds* of communication but, rather, different **communication contexts** in which communication can occur. We feel that several of these contexts, while validly studied separately, fall under the heading of interpersonal communication.

We include *dyadic communication* (between two people), communication in *small groups* (numbering from three to twenty), and *interviewing,* a specialized form of dyadic communication, within the purview of interpersonal communication. However, organizational communication as such is not considered in this text, nor is public or mass communication.

A key criterion for determining whether or not a communication occurrence would be defined as interpersonal is related to the concept of feedback.[12] Within the communication process, do the individuals in a given situation have equal access to one another for the purpose of influencing one another? If they do, we consider the situation an interpersonal one. If they do not, the situation is not interpersonal. If the opportunity exists for immediate feedback, then there is nothing in the structure of the communication event to prevent equal access of all communicators to each other: two people in a face-to-face setting receive immediate feedback to their messages. However, a newscaster on television can receive only delayed feedback to his or her message, and this means that viewers of TV programs do not have the same access to broadcasters that broadcasters have to them. The equal opportunity to influence each other is not present in this situation, and thus it is not an interpersonal communication event. Likewise, a public speaking event would not be interpersonal communication, even though the speaker and audience are face-to-face. The accepted behaviors in a public speaking setting dictate that members of the audience delay all but their nonverbal feedback to the speaker until the speech is concluded. Again, there would not be equal opportunity for speaker and audience to influence each other, so the event would not be interpersonal.

Many contexts included under the heading of interpersonal communication have also been treated separately. This has probably occurred because the material and research within particular subareas is so vast as to merit intensive attention. Such is the case with respect to small-group and dyadic communication, for instance. However, such separate attention should not obscure the interpersonal nature of both of these communication contexts.

INTERPERSONAL MOTIVATION

Important to an understanding of how to communicate effectively with other people is an understanding of how we are motivated to do the things we do. What makes you brag? Why do you want to sit and talk with someone about a television show you saw last night? Why do you agree to get a drink of water for someone who asks you to? Why do you communicate the way you do? If we are to communicate effectively, we should know the answers to all these questions. All of them are based on our motivational systems.

The things that motivate us to communicate and to respond to messages include our need systems, our value systems, and our environment. These three elements combine to result in our desiring things and behaving in various ways. Understanding these three elements makes it possible for us to predict how people will respond to our messages and, furthermore, helps us to explain the messages we receive from other people.

Need Systems

Thus far we have referred to several kinds of needs. They can be grouped into four categories: physical, social, ego, and consistency needs.[13]

Physical Needs

Physical needs are what have been called physiological and safety needs[14] or security needs.[15] These are probably the needs that brought about communication originally. These include the physical needs of survival — food, sex, shelter, sleep, and physical security. People had to communicate with others cooperatively to defend their homes from outside attackers or to attack the homes of other people. Men and women had to communicate effectively to have sex, which ensures the survival of the human race (although we rarely think of it in that way at the time).

13. W. C. Langer, *Psychology in Human Living* (New York: Appleton-Century, 1943); Leon Festinger, *A Theory of Cognitive Dissonance* (Stanford, Calif.: Stanford University Press, 1957).

14. A. H. Maslow, *Motivation and Personality* (New York: Harper & Row, 1954), 80–92.

15. Ardrey, *Social Contract,* 108.

Our physical needs are actually rather few in number, and much of what we do today to satisfy those needs goes far beyond what is necessary. In fact, we might say that we often forget what our real physical needs are because of other, nonphysical, needs. It is intriguing to see persons working so long and hard to make money (which they think serves the purpose of taking care of their physical needs) that they earn many times what is necessary to satisfy actual physical needs. Very few of us really need homes as elaborate as we have, or the automobiles, or all the clothing in our closets and drawers. But before we condemn our materialism, we must remember that frequently the additional material things are meant to satisfy other than physical needs. Which brings us to our second need classification.

Social Needs

16. Maslow, *Motivation and Personality,* 80-92.

17. William C. Schutz, *The Interpersonal Underworld* (Palo Alto, Calif.: Science & Behavior Books, 1966), 18-25.

At this point we concern ourselves with **social needs** — needs to relate to other people. Such needs are variously called "love" or "belongingness" needs[16] or interpersonal needs. According to William Schutz,[17] these interpersonal needs include component needs for (1) **inclusion,** (2) **control,** and (3) **affection.** These terms refer to needs to: (1) "establish and maintain a satisfactory relationship with people with respect to interaction and association"; (2) "establish and maintain a satisfactory relationship with people with respect to control and power"; and (3) "establish and maintain a satisfactory relationship with people with respect to love and affection."

Interpersonal Needs and Messages   It is important to consider how the needs of other people affect their responses to our messages. It is also important to understand that our own needs affect the messages we produce. The level of our interpersonal needs for what Schutz called inclusion, affection, and control can cause us to overrespond, underrespond, or moderately respond to them in the messages we produce when interacting with other people.

For instance, if we have a high need for inclusion (to maintain satisfactory relationships with people in our interactions and associations), we might produce **undersocial messages** (deficient responses to our inclusion need); we might produce **oversocial messages** (excessive responses to our need for inclusion); or we might produce **social messages** (moderate responses to our needs). Undersocial persons are usually quiet and withdrawn and do not initiate a lot of interactions. In fact, undersocial persons frequently appear to be shy, or even antisocial sometimes, depending upon the way the person communicates nonverbally. The undersocial person responds to his or her need for inclusion with the defense mechanism of deciding not to try to initiate interaction for fear of being rejected or excluded from interactions. Many of the people we think of as quiet, who "don't like to talk" or have conversations, are people who would like that probably more than anyone else around.

Because of this it is often satisfying for them when someone does talk to them and tries to "draw them out." Oversocial persons, on the other hand, go out of their way to initiate interactions. Frequently they start talking before they even have something to talk about. They are the ones who are always inviting someone for a soda at the student union. They are the ones who wave to people across campus. Finally, social persons are able to initiate interactions moderately and are comfortable with themselves when no one else is around. In other words, they have moderate levels of the need for inclusion and moderately express the need. Their message behaviors would at any given time seem perfectly "normal."

In response to the need for affection, the excessive response is an **overpersonal message.** Overpersonal people constantly tell you how much they like you — how much you have in common — in messages that are never ending. We may feel almost suffocated by their attempt to communicate love to us. On the other hand, a deficient response to the need for affection results in **underpersonal messages.** The underpersonal person is perhaps one of the saddest of people because, although this person has a need for affection, he or she feels unlovable and, as a defense mechanism, denies liking people. Such people try to keep a "safe" distance from others. They rarely initiate loving relationships. Sometimes messages produced by these people, both verbal and nonverbal, are perceived by other people as somewhat cold. They seem to be detached from other persons. Because they act as though they do not want affectionate relationships, other people do not initiate affectionate relationships. This makes them feel the need even more, which in turn results in their becoming more defensive, and thus engaging in even more deficient responses to their needs. The ideal response to one's need for affection is to produce **personal messages.** Personal people are comfortable with close relationships with others and also with distant relationships, for they do not have to be close to everyone. They do not constantly tell people they love them, and yet, when such a relationship develops, they are very satisfied and comfortable with it.

Finally, there is the need for control. We all appear to need to feel some control of our lives as well as control over others in our interpersonal relationships. The deficient response to this need includes messages which typify **the abdicrat.** These people are especially noticeable in decision-making sessions. In chapter ten, dealing with small group communication, we mention that some people never wish to be in leadership positions in small groups. They feel that they do not have leadership ability. They feel that they are not in control of their lives even though they would like to be. Therefore they avoid all responsibility for taking control. Such people will almost always refuse leadership positions. They are afraid of failure. The opposite response, excessive need to control, results in messages which typify the **the autocrat,** the reverse of the abdicrat. This person attempts to grab control at every chance by assuming that he or she should always be in charge. This is the person who will nominate himself or herself for the chair of a committee. This is the person who tries to take leadership away from an already established leader in a small group. The ideal response to control needs is message behavior which typifies **the democrat.** This terminology means that a person can accept leadership or not, depending on the situation. In small group discussions this individual neither tries to wrest control from other people nor refuses control when other people recognize qualities in him or her that might be well suited to a leadership role.

These varying interpersonal needs result in varying kinds of message behavior. Observing other people should give us clues, then, to their interpersonal needs. Their messages should tell us whether they are over- or under-responding to needs for inclusion, affection, or control or showing balanced responses to those needs. Whatever the case, understanding the situation should suggest to us ways we can respond to people accordingly with messages that will appeal to their interpersonal needs.

All of us need to maintain some sort of interpersonal relationship with other people that is satisfactory to us. By this we mean that all of us need to love and be loved, to control others and have others control us, to relate to others and have them relate to us — and in each of these patterns we need to consider both the relationships and our positions in them to be "good." This basic need for interpersonal relationships is dramatically demonstrated by studies of orphan infants reared with and without affection. The infants who experienced affection were physically strong, healthy babies, whereas the infants who were not fondled and cuddled began to waste away physically.[18] This should indicate that we have these needs from the time we are born and that the need for affection may even be related to our physical survival.

Ego Needs

Ego needs of an individual can be significantly affected by one's experiences throughout life. These have been referred to as **self-esteem** and **self-actualization.**[19] Even animals are said to have a need for identity.[20] The need to think well of oneself, the self-esteem need, is an ego need. It might be achieved through making a series of bull's-eyes in archery, by learning how to ski successfully, or possibly by successfully memorizing a lengthy poem. In each case the person perceives his or her own accomplishments positively, and thus the need to think well of oneself is satisfied. If Charley is a carpenter, he has a basic need to think he is a good carpenter. It is equally important for Phyllis to feel she is a good doctor; or for Frank to feel he is a good cook. It is important for us to evaluate ourselves positively so we can accept ourselves as worthwhile human beings. According to many studies in counseling, psychology, and sociology, this is a strongly felt need.[21]

18. R. A. Spitz, "Hospitalism: An Inquiry into the Genesis of Psychiatric Conditions in Early Childhood," in O. Fenichel et al., eds., *The Psychoanalytic Study of the Child* (New York: International Universities Press, 1945), 53–74; Desmond Morris, *Intimate Behavior* (New York: Random House, 1971), 13–34.

19. Maslow, *Motivation and Personality,* 80–92.

20. Ardrey, *Social Contract,* 108–9.

21. John W. Kinch, "A Formalized Theory of the Self-Concept," in J. Manis and B. Meltzer, eds., *Symbolic Interaction,* 2d ed. (Boston: Allyn & Bacon, 1972), 245–52.

Likewise, we all have a need for **self-actualization.** That means we need to perform at the maximum level we think we are capable of. We suggested that individuals could enhance their self-esteem by learning how to ski. To "self-actualize," individuals would have to learn to ski as well as they thought they could. For one person to "self-actualize" through skiing, simply managing to get down an intermediate slope might be enough. For another person, cross-country skiing across the Rocky Mountains might be necessary. Different accomplishments are necessary for different people to "self-actualize" because they have different perceptions of their capabilities.

Some people appear to be bragging all the time. They constantly tell us how good they are or how well they do things. It may seem as if they are "stuck on themselves." However, they are very probably overcompensating for feelings of inadequacy,[22] and their bragging messages are parallel to the excessive responses to interpersonal needs discussed earlier, only these are excessive responses to ego needs. Frequently we engage in defensive behavior when we communicate. Often this takes the form of bragging to convince ourselves that we are good so that our own ego needs may be satisfied.[23]

22. Schutz, The Interpersonal Underworld, 25–32.

23. Alfred R. Lindesmith and Anselm L. Strauss, Social Psychology (New York: Holt, Rinehart & Winston, 1968), 328–30.

24. Maslow, Motivation and Personality, 80–92.

Maslow's Hierarchy of Needs

Abraham Maslow suggested that there is a **hierarchy of needs.**[24] The basic needs, he said, are physiological and security needs, or what we have been referring to as *physical needs.* Next, according to Maslow, are belongingness needs, which we are calling *social needs.* Finally come the needs of self-esteem and self-actualization, or what we are calling *ego needs.* Maslow maintained that unless people's physiological needs are met, they will not be concerned with their security needs or any other needs further up the hierarchy. "You can't preach ideology to a nation with an empty stomach" — i.e., overriding physical need such as hunger must be satisfied before people can be concerned with politics. Maslow suggested that once a lower-level need is satisfied, a person can attend to the next higher level of need.

Because needs are shaped by the events we experience during our developmental years, it is not unusual for interpersonal communication between generations to be adversely affected by differing need hierarchies. Many students in college today grew up during a time of turmoil, assassinations, riots in cities, confrontations between the U.S.A. and Russia, the Vietnam War, and the economic recession. All other things being equal, these events very likely had the effect of exaggerating the concern for security within their physical needs. It is common to find that many of these students are very concerned about getting a job, saving money, and planning/structuring their lives.

Many of their older brothers and sisters, however, who grew up during more peaceful times do not feel the same need for security. Many of these people went through their developmental years experiencing the security of relatively prosperous times, during which there was little societal conflict.

However, many of them also had parents who were working more than one job or heavily involved in community affairs, and thus, experienced minimal family interaction. These older brothers and sisters frequently have high interpersonal and social needs. They are concerned about developing close, meaningful relationships with others, belonging to clubs, and being a part of a movement.

It is often interesting to listen to these two generations talk. Their messages reflect the differences in need hierarchies.

> Older brother/sister: "Don't worry about getting a job. Don't worry about choosing a major in college that will prepare you for a job. The important thing is to learn how to relate to other people and form good friendships."
>
> Younger brother/sister: "You're crazy. This is a tough world we live in. I need to plan my life so I can survive in it. I need to make sure I can get a job and support myself. In this economy you really have to be ahead of the next guy."

In this example both people are communicating according to their own need systems, and in so doing, are talking "past each other." It is unlikely that either will understand the other so long as they communicate from their own needs. This highlights an important principle of interpersonal communication: you should not communicate according to your own needs, even though they may prompt you to communicate. Rather, your messages should be directed toward the needs of the person you wish to influence for maximum effectiveness.

The hierarchy-of-needs principle has been put to work in the business world. Willem James, who was in charge of an oil refinery in the Netherlands, wanted to improve production and morale. Having been exposed to Maslow's theories, James decided that physical needs were already being satisfied through good wages and working conditions, so he wanted to address needs higher up in the hierarchy. A number of problems in the operation of the refinery needed to be solved to ensure production, so he set the employees to the task of solving the problems in their own way. Through this approach he was attempting to enhance individual self-esteem by letting the workers know he had faith in them. He also gave them the opportunity to self-actualize by allowing them to solve problems at their highest possible level. The results were greatly improved morale and increased production, and thus increased profits.[25]

25. Ardrey, *Social Contract*, 181–86.

The consensus among those in management is that much more than satisfaction of physical needs is necessary for the maintenance of good employee morale. Many companies pay attention to interpersonal communication and need systems to try to satisfy needs beyond the physical level. They institute company magazines to recognize and publicize accomplishments of individual employees. Births are announced; results for company bowling leagues and

Interpersonal messages of recognition regarding an employee's efforts enhance the employee's self-esteem and foster good morale among all employees.

other sporting events are reported; prizes for suggestions that improve plant efficiency are publicized. Such activities and recognition provided by companies help satisfy their employees' social and ego needs.

Consistency Needs

While we can generally classify our needs as physical, social, and ego, there is also considerable evidence that we have strong **consistency needs.**[26] That means a need to have our ideas, values, perceptions, behaviors, and attitudes all consistent among themselves. If we disapprove of stealing, we cannot steal anything without being inconsistent with our own value system. We try to teach children that honesty is a value and then hope their behavior will remain consistent with that value. (We also apply punishment when they are dishonest, so children avoid dishonesty to be consistent with their physical need to avoid pain.)

Sometimes to maintain consistency we rationalize our behavior in devious ways. We can maintain honesty as a value and yet take pencils and paperclips home from the office. We tell ourselves that the company is so large and the

26. William J. McGuire, "The Current Status of Cognitive Consistency Theories," in Shel Feldman, ed., *Cognitive Consistency* (New York: Academic Press, 1966), 1–46; Charles A. Kiesler, Barry E. Collins, and Norman Miller, *Attitude Change* (New York: John Wiley & Sons, 1969), 155–237.

paper clips so small that it's really not stealing — and besides, it won't hurt anyone. This rationalization helps us restore consistency within our own minds. If, in fact, we perceived taking the pencils and paper clips as stealing, pure and simple, the inconsistency with our values would create pressure to restore consistency by leaving the things at the office.

This need for consistency has been given several names: **dissonance theory,**[27] **congruity theory,**[28] and **balance theory.**[29] It is common, when referring to people who are experiencing inconsistency, to say they are experiencing **dissonance.** In the preceding example, rationalization was used to reduce dissonance. Dissonance might also be used to bring about change. Here is an example. If Charlie is trying to get Bill to stop smoking, Charlie might say, "Bill, you really ought to stop smoking because it has been demonstrated that cigarette smoking is a cause of high blood pressure, heart attacks, and lung cancer." That message is Charlie's attempt to create dissonance in Bill's mind between Bill's (a) wanting to live a long time and (b) doing something that will prevent him from living a long time.

But that dissonance will not necessarily cause Bill to stop smoking. Bill may resolve the dissonance in other ways. For instance, he may forget the message. Or he may distort it by perceiving Charlie to have said, "Cigarette smoking *may be* [rather than is] a cause." Or Bill may rationalize his response to the message by thinking, "Well, that's only five to ten years off the end of my life, and I'm young now, so I'm not going to worry about it."

Although dissonance theory suggests a basic strategy we can use in interpersonal communication to try to bring about change, applying the strategy successfully is not necessarily easy. Nevertheless, some communication scholars advocate deliberately creating dissonance through messages as a means of effecting change. The communicator must then rely on the listener to choose change and not some other way to restore consistency.

Our need for consistency probably relates to the requirement of prediction for survival. Although we can only guess, it seems reasonable that to survive physically in the world, we must be able to predict events and the behavior of others. If people were totally inconsistent and unpredictable, how would we ever know how to approach anyone? It would be impossible. Society could not exist without some degree of order and consistency. Just as we need others to be consistent, they also need us to be consistent. It should be apparent that our need for consistency is related to our need and society's need to survive.

An Overview of Needs

The need categories as we have presented them in this discussion of our need systems are not as neat or mutually exclusive as we would like in a classification system. Certainly many of what we have referred to here as ego needs might be classified as social needs by some people. The view of our need systems

27. Festinger, *A Theory of Cognitive Dissonance.*

28. Charles E. Osgood and Percy H. Tannenbaum, "The Principle of Congruity in the Prediction of Attitude Change," *Psychological Review* 62 (1966):42–55.

29. Fritz Heider, *The Psychology of Interpersonal Relations* (New York: Science Editions, John Wiley & Sons, 1968).

just presented is useful for our discussion of interpersonal communication. It also helps us answer the original question we posed of why people began to communicate. We can see that they communicated to survive: to get food and to protect themselves. This need for immediate physical survival may have generated subsequent needs in humans, such as those we have been discussing. These then became layers of basic needs.

It is obvious that we must minimally satisfy our physical needs so that we (and our species) survive. If we do not eat, get enough sleep, maintain the correct body temperature, and avoid things like heavy falling objects, we die. If we do not reproduce, our species will cease to exist.

The need to think well of ourselves is less directly related to survival, but is related nevertheless. People who think too badly of themselves may develop defense mechanisms that prevent them from adequately coping with their environment. These people usually end up as mental incompetents, unable to care for themselves. Too many people unable to assure their own survival would indirectly threaten species survival. This is why the mental wellbeing of others should be a matter of concern to us. We need as many people as possible to be pulling their own weight at all times. Although the relationship may not seem direct, our ego needs must be satisfied for us and our species to survive.

The sexual need of men and women for each other may also be viewed as a physical need that evolved into what we would now call a social need, the need for love. Maybe at one time in our evolutionary history the social need was not a primary one, but certainly as humans evolved, this need to relate to other people became as basic as any of our other needs.[30]

Indeed, we have such strong social needs[31] that we will engage in some very unusual kinds of behavior to satisfy them. Peer-group influence of friends and members of groups we belong to, or aspire to belong to, is so great that we can be pressured to consider ourselves wrong even when we are right; to distort what we see with our own eyes; to change our attitudes about modes of behavior that are repugnant to us — simply to assure our acceptance by a group. Studies done over the last two or three decades repeatedly indicate this overpowering need for acceptance in interpersonal relationships with others.[32] We will say things we do not believe; wear clothes we do not like; drive cars that are unsafe; buy homes we cannot afford — to gain acceptance from groups whose approval we value.

It is probable that our need for acceptance by others is related to survival. In this case survival does not necessarily mean survival of the individual, but rather survival of the species. It may be, if we modify Darwin's theory of evolution, that behavioral characteristics that contribute to the survival of the species have been reinforced and perpetuated genetically in individuals, just as individuals, who, because of desirable physical traits contribute to the survival

30. Richard H. Walters and Ross D. Parke, "Social Motivation, Dependency, and Susceptibility to Social Influence," in Leonard Berkowitz, ed., Advances in Experimental Social Psychology, vol. 1 (New York: Academic Press, 1964), 1:231-76.

31. Ibid.

32. Serge Moscovici and Claude Faucheux, "Social Influence, Conformity Bias, and the Study of Active Minorities," in Leonard Berkowitz, ed., Advances in Experimental Social Psychology, vol. 6 (New York: Academic Press, 1972), 6:157-60.

of the species, are also favored. Thus, we might view a set of behaviors and codes of conduct developed by a larger group that contribute to the survival of that group as that group's culture.

For instance, strict standards of conduct regarding sexual behavior toward close relatives such as sisters, brothers, daughters, sons, mothers, and fathers — that is, incest prohibitions — exist in most cultures. Without debating any values and codes which hold that things are simply "right" or "wrong," we could consider the biological results of the mating of close relatives — fathers and daughters, brothers and sisters, first cousins, and so forth. We find a much higher incidence of defects that, cumulatively, would weaken the species as a group. Therefore it seems logical that the species would develop codes of conduct to prevent defects by encouraging mating behavior that produces stronger and more "survivable" individuals. In this case peer-group pressure, or cultural pressure, which may still be survival oriented, becomes "institutionalized" as a value.

There are "institutionalized" interpersonal communication behaviors also. For instance, it is important to know when it is our turn to talk during a conversation. We don't know simply because someone stops producing sound for a moment. Therefore, we have turn-taking norms we follow. A value we are taught as children is that we should not interrupt people. If we were not taught this, it would be difficult to carry on a conversation — everyone would be interrupting everyone else. Thus, the value placed on waiting one's turn in interpersonal communication has survival value for our species in that it enables us to communicate effectively, which, in turn, facilitates survival. It is through nonverbal communication behaviors that we learn when it is "our turn." This will be further discussed in chapter six.

We could think of values as cultural control over how needs are expressed. To use some terminology of an earlier age, the values by which we are "nurtured" define how we may respond to the needs of our "nature."

Sometimes what may once have been a survival-oriented behavior may decrease in importance because of changed conditions. For example, current values regarding sexual behavior may have resulted from the development of safe, effective methods of contraception, as well as effective treatment of venereal disease. If social stability no longer depends on past prohibitions concerning sex, the taboos associated with it may break down. On the other hand, if the increase in "superstrains" of gonorrhea continues, along with an epidemic of herpes, the older sexual values may be reestablished.

Likewise, past communication norms regarding male-female interaction patterns may have lost their value in a more advanced, complex society. If so, this would account for some of the changes we can observe in which women are refusing to "take a back seat" to men in interpersonal communication, as well as in other situations.

We have been discussing people's basic needs: physical, social, ego, and consistency needs, and how the satisfaction of these is related to survival. It should be evident that we need consistency in each of the other need areas. It is our feeling that much interpersonal communication behavior can be explained in terms of our need systems and the interaction of our needs and our values. To better understand how these are interrelated, we turn now to a discussion of values and interpersonal communication.

Value Systems

Thus far, we have discussed what many people consider the basic elements of motivation. Although the need systems discussed are of extreme importance, other motivational elements should also be kept in mind when we are trying to understand and explain interpersonal communication. **Value systems** are "larger" than our need systems, in the sense that they are based both on need systems and on something more. Rokeach defined a *value* as "an enduring belief that a specific mode of conduct or end-state of existence is personally or socially preferable to an opposite or converse mode of conduct or end-state of existence. A *value system* is an enduring organization of beliefs concerning preferable modes of conduct or end-states of existence along a continuum of relative importance."[33] This means that our choice to engage in one behavior or to pursue one goal rather than others depends on the continuum of ranked values we have in our minds. Value systems are distilled from the cultural **norms** that define what is accepted by most people as normal.

33. Milton Rokeach, *The Nature of Values* (New York: Free Press, 1973), 5.

How do we develop these values? Most of us learn our value systems as we are growing up, first from our parents, then our families, and finally people outside the family. One of the best ways to predict the belief and value systems of a person is to look very carefully at the belief and value systems of that person's parents. If you reflect for a while, you may find that you have more in common with your parents than you might think. This becomes more apparent as we get older. As we reach adulthood and our middle years and take on additional roles comparable to the range of our parents' roles, we become more like our parents than we were during our teenage years and early twenties. The people who communicate norms and values to us do so by virtue of the roles they fulfill.

Role is a term that describes the relationship and the prescribed behaviors and powers that exist for an individual as he or she relates to another person. We would be very hard pressed, for instance, as parents to rear children if we had not learned parent roles and children roles from our friends, family, and others. Each of us is like an actor playing a role that relates to other people's roles.[34] And each of us has many different roles at the same time and throughout a lifetime.

34. Alfred Kuhn, *The Study of Society* (Homewood, Ill.: Richard D. Irwin and The Dorsey Press, 1963), 245–47; Erving Goffman, *The Presentation of Self in Everyday Life* (Garden City, N.Y.: Doubleday Anchor Books, 1969), 17–76.

Even game-playing is important for teaching survival skills such as turn-taking behavior.

"Roles" govern what any character we play should and should not do; may or may not do. A president of the United States may do some things that a senator may not. A doctor should do some things that a nurse should not. A parent may do some things that a child may not. Likewise, in interpersonal communication, whatever our role—whether it be friend, mother, child, brother, minister, teacher, lawyer, or the like—it carries with it expectations about the types of messages we produce, the kinds of behaviors we engage in, even the clothes we wear.

Parents have a significant effect on the values, attitudes, and communication behaviors of their children.

It is also possible to trace our value development to the environment in which we live. People reared among what we might refer to as "Midwest values" apparently have value systems different from people reared in New York City or Los Angeles. Still different value systems exist in the southeastern United States. Most of us would not notice dramatic differences among people from these different areas. If we talk about a number of different subjects, however, we will begin to notice that someone from New York City values "not wasting time" more than someone from the South. Someone from the South may value interpersonal courtesies such as "gentlemanly" or "ladylike" behavior more than someone from New York. Someone from the Midwest may value hard work and "saving for a rainy day" more than someone from Los Angeles; and someone from Los Angeles may value open space, ease of transportation, and "doing your own thing" more. These are, obviously a collection of stereotypes about people from different parts of the country, but we think that some elements of these values — admittedly exaggerated for the sake of an example — can be found among people in those different environments.

Norms, values, and roles all serve a survival purpose for our species because they cause people to behave in relatively predictable ways. This predictableness enables us to know how to interact with other people. We know what the norms of our society are. We know how to formulate our messages in relation to the norms of the society and the role the other person is in. We know the messages we should or should not produce because of the roles we happen to be in.

For purposes of relating values to interpersonal communication, we will focus on the general concept of values and consider that all people have value systems, or a collection of individual values concerning preferable behaviors and preferable goals. These values can include things like making money; having a big home, television sets, and cars; and going to fancy restaurants. Value systems can be centered on the goal of having a close-knit family — a spouse and children — all enjoying one another's company. We may have an individual value of good workmanship as we build something. We may value close friendships and good times with our friends. We may value devotion to country or commitment to God. Any of these are values that can govern our goal-seeking behavior and our day-to-day behavior.

Every value we have contributes to either an avoidance or an attraction behavior on our part. If we value fine cooking, we are attracted to messages that promise us the opportunity to spend enjoyable evenings in gourmet restaurants. If we negatively value pain, then we may avoid messages that threaten pain. Thus values contribute to our responses to messages.

Our values concern either preferred end-states of existence, which Rokeach calls **terminal values,** or preferred modes of conduct, which Rokeach calls **instrumental values.**[35] The latter govern our modes of conduct, moral behavior, and relationships. Both types of values have a significant effect on

35. Rokeach, *The Nature of Values*, 5.

the way we communicate interpersonally. If we have an instrumental value of good social relationships, we will engage in behaviors and modes of conduct that are conducive to satisfactory interpersonal relationships. On the other hand, terminal values that concern end-states such as acquiring wealth, getting good grades, and "scoring" on a date will also have a significant effect on the way we interact with people.

Our terminal values, or desired end-states, can often be inferred from modes of conduct, or instrumental values. For instance, a person who wants lasting friendships (a terminal value) will probably communicate in a manner intended to satisfy the needs of his or her friends. In other words, the instrumental value of having satisfying interaction grows out of the longer-term terminal value of having lasting friendships.

Importance of Self-concept

Of considerable importance to us in interpersonal communication is the notion that values are relative, that they can be ranked. As with Maslow's hierarchy of needs, we can think of a **value hierarchy** of higher-order values and lower-order values — but the ranking of values, Rokeach suggested, *relates to our* **self-concept.**[36]

36. Ibid.

We value more highly those things that will reinforce and contribute to a positive **self-image.** Although many people express the thought that all persons should be able to have a job if they wish and earn a reasonable wage, on their continuum of values, this is probably a lower-order social value compared to a higher-order value of personal need satisfaction. If these people discover that they may lose some of their own opportunities when everyone has an equal opportunity for a job, they are less likely to value equal opportunities. Their own hierarchy of values may cause them to oppose such things as minimum-wage laws and affirmative action programs because the value of having a happy and comfortable life for themselves is closer to their self-concept and thus more important than society-oriented values such as equal rights for everyone.

As we continue our discussion of interpersonal communication, this concept of the centrality of self as it relates to values will become more evident. Self-concept is so important in interpersonal communication that we have devoted all of chapter 3 to this topic. We should pay close attention to the communication behavior of others to determine what they are saying about themselves. As people speak out in favor of or against some topic, this frequently will tell us much about how the topic relates to their own self-concepts. Even though at times it may seem people are discussing a topic "objectively," they subjectively relate the topic back to their own self-concepts. This occurs constantly in conversations and small group discussions.

If we are sensitive to what people indirectly say, we can relate our own messages to their self-concepts in reply so that our points reinforce their self-concepts, and thus are more acceptable.

Our concern with the effect of messages on self-concept becomes more important if we consider that a simple statement by us can have a profound effect upon someone else's self-concept. A critical comment about a particular make of automobile could have a negative effect on a friend's self-concept because of the way cars relate to that self-concept. Although the comment might seem objective to us, it may be perceived as negative by someone else. This could have a significant effect on the outcome of any interpersonal interaction.

The Value Component in Interpersonal Communication

Although it is interesting to discuss what values are, ultimately the question most students of interpersonal communication are concerned with is what the values do for us. Values serve as standards, as motivational forces, and enable us to formulate plans and determine our self-presentation.[37]

37. Ibid.

Because values serve as standards for us, they also determine the stands we take in our messages. For example, people who have been taught to value thrift are more likely to argue for balanced budgets in government, while someone who is taught to value fair treatment of human beings may support social programs funded by government.

Values determine the way we present ourselves to other people. In any interpersonal interaction people can be cold, warm, logical, or emotional, depending largely on whether they value warmth, logic, feelings, or friendship. If we value friendship above all other things, we may throw caution to the wind regarding logic but work very hard to communicate in ways to establish and maintain friendships. Actually, none of us ever communicates entirely according to one value, so it is often necessary to relate our messages to several values if the messages are to have the desired effect.

Finally, we are concerned with values in interpersonal communication because of their motivational characteristics. Because values are an outgrowth of the needs we discussed earlier, it is not surprising that values have a significant effect on our behaviors. Different values relate to various needs but, it should be obvious that many values that motivate us relate to the ego needs of self-esteem and self-actualization.

IMPROVING YOUR INTERPERSONAL SKILLS

This book has grown out of the belief that we can improve our interpersonal skills significantly through improved understanding and awareness of the interpersonal communication process. We feel it is a mistake to try to develop skills without understanding the basis for them. A carpenter cannot simply learn how to hammer nails and saw wood. It is necessary for a carpenter to learn principles of stress as well as various design principles to know how to build in the strongest possible way. In interpersonal communication it is desirable to practice and improve interpersonal skills along with learning the principles. Your instructor may provide exercises for you in class.

In the next chapter we discuss more fully the process of interpersonal communication and the various elements and contexts involved. We hope that as you study the discussions of self-concept, perception, the use of words, nonverbal communication, information reception, and interpersonal communication patterns you will be able to practice interpersonal communication skills in various contexts, such as dyads, small groups, and organizations. This increased understanding and greater sensitivity to the elements of the interpersonal communication process should make you more adept and skilled at interpersonal communication.

Summary

Interpersonal communication is a basic human behavior which is essential for the survival of human beings. Our ancestors survived as a species through the use of interpersonal communication. Today we continue to use this basic human process to pursue our careers, develop our self-concept, and achieve satisfying relationships with others. This process of mutual influence through a common symbol system is as necessary for our survival today as it was in the infancy of our species.

Today, as in the past, we employ interpersonal communication to satisfy our own needs and those of others — physical, social, ego, and consistency needs. The extent to which we feel any of these needs depends greatly on our past experiences and environment.

We communicate and respond according to our own and others' values. The enduring set of beliefs regarding our goals and ways of achieving these goals — our value system — operates in conjunction with our need system to influence how we communicate and how we respond to the messages of others. Especially important is how our personal value hierarchy relates to our self-concept. We value and accept those things that reinforce our self-concept, including, of course, messages from others.

2

The Process of Interpersonal Communication

INTERPERSONAL COMMUNICATION AS A SYSTEM

In this chapter we will discuss the components of interpersonal communication as a system and develop an overview of the system. It is not enough to understand interpersonal communication generally. We must understand the components and the way they relate to one another to understand how interpersonal communication functions.

Figure 2.1 The communication process.

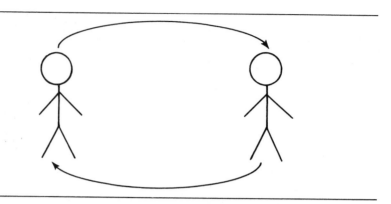

For centuries scholars have discussed communication as a **linear phenomenon.** The linear perspective implies that communication moves in one direction. People have typically thought of communication as proceeding from one individual to another — as something one *does to* someone else. This, however, is not how interpersonal communication occurs. Communication is a *process* in which the participants interact *with* one another.

Although Aristotle viewed communication as a process, this was not emphasized for centuries until contemporary communication scholars introduced the concept of *feedback*.[1] With the introduction of this concept, we became aware that not only does a message go from person A to person B, but also that there is a response from person B to person A. Following this line of thought, we began to discuss communication as a **circular** process rather than a linear phenomenon. Circular communication is communication in which messages travel from one person to another and then back. However, even the circular approach to communication understates the process nature of communication. Consider figure 2.1; the process is still unidirectional, beginning with one person, going to a second person, and returning.

Today we think of interpersonal communication as a system in which all persons involved mutually affect one another through messages. The **systems view** suggests that people interact with all individuals involved in the interaction influencing one another simultaneously. This view of interpersonal communication makes it almost impossible to single out one person at any given moment as the speaker or the listener. Both are simply interpersonal communicators, who communicate verbally and nonverbally through words, gestures, and the like. Each affects the other, constantly and simultaneously.

A student of ours once suggested in a description of public communication that the audience initiates the communication process. His reasoning was that, without an audience, a speaker would never begin speaking. In a way, his line of reasoning provides some insight into the interpersonal communication pro-

1. N. Wiener, *Cybernetics* (New York: John Wiley & Sons, 1948), 33.

cess because his description implies that the mere presence or absence of one or more individuals has an effect on other people in the communication setting.

Thus, in interpersonal communication there is a constant flow of verbal and nonverbal messages back and forth between and among all the participants. There is no beginning or end to which it is possible for us to trace communication, as all individuals in interpersonal communication are mutually affecting one another all the time. While you talk with a friend, the knowledge of who that person is and what the relationship is between you, as well as your observations of how that person is sitting or looking, affects what you are saying. At the same time, what you are saying affects your friend. It would be difficult indeed to determine an initiator and a concluder in an interaction, since there are multiple, simultaneous causes and effects of events at all times in any interpersonal relationship.

Although the systems view implies that all components of interpersonal communication should be considered simultaneously, that is impractical. As we examine the various components separately in this book, we hope you will reflect frequently on the interrelationships that may affect a specific component at any given moment. To do less and to consider one component at a time without attempting to explain interpersonal communication as a unified system would be to oversimplify the process and to mislead you.

The ideal goal of interpersonal communication is for the communicators to achieve mutual satisfaction of needs.

Characteristics of Interpersonal Communication Systems

Although interpersonal communication shares a great number of characteristics with communication in other contexts, it may prove instructive to consider the basic characteristics of interpersonal communication. None of these is necessarily unique to interpersonal communication; some can be found in other communication contexts as well.

Manipulation of the Environment

We engage in interpersonal communication to affect the behavior of others in such a way as to produce mutual satisfaction of needs. This principle was emphasized in chapter 1. Our species developed communication as a tool to aid in our survival in the world. Interpersonal communication is a tool for survival because it permits us to manipulate the world indirectly in such a way that we can make our environment more conducive to survival. If our species is distinct from other members of the animal kingdom, the major distinction is probably our manipulation of the world through communication rather than through some direct, physical means.

Our Past Environment

Interpersonal communication is never independent of past behavior. Because humans must learn to communicate throughout their developmental years and because the acquisition of language occurs within a specific environment, people can never be independent of those conditions under which they learn to communicate. Our attitudes have been formed as a result of a number of behavior characteristics that are rooted in our past environment.[2] Children who grow up in homes where parents constantly tell them how bad they are develop a low level of self-esteem that affects the way they communicate for the remainder of their lives. It is reasonable to suspect that the needs, fears, anxieties, desires, hopes, and dreams an individual has at any given moment in life are the product of previous influences.

This is not to suggest that we cannot rise above our environments. Someone who is deprived in childhood can rise to great heights in the business world, in politics, or in education, for example. However, even a person who rises above a poor early environment still communicates according to behavior patterns acquired in that environment. People react in many different ways to their environment because of individual and unique circumstances at any given time. The different behaviors we manifest during developmental years condition the way we acquire language, the kind of nonverbal behavior we consider appropriate to a situation, the attitudes and beliefs we develop, as

2. Arthur W. Staats, "Social Behaviorism and Human Motivation; Principles of the Attitude-Reinforcer-Discriminative Systems," in Anthony G. Greenwald, Timothy C. Brock, and Thomas M. Ostrom, eds., *Psychological Foundations of Attitudes* (New York: Academic Press, 1968), 33–66.

well as other communication habits regarding sentence structure, message organization, and so on.[3] All of these patterns affect our interpersonal communication in some way or another. It is, of course, possible to modify past behaviors at later points in our lives, but we must consider that the desire to modify them is also a result of our previous experience.

3. Leon Rappaport, *Personality Development* (Glenview, Ill.: Scott, Foresman, 1972), 234–35.

Verbal and Nonverbal Systems

Interpersonal communication depends on both verbal and nonverbal communication systems for maximal effectiveness. It almost seems a truism to say that we cannot communicate without spoken language. However, it is equally true that we need to communicate nonverbally.

Formal Language   A formal language system enables us to express very complex and abstract ideas, which in turn permit us to communicate about various machines, theories, formulas, and the like.[4] We are not passing judgment on the world in which we live and saying that this is the best of all possible worlds; however, the kind of world in which we live would be impossible without the formal system we call language. For us to exist without a formal symbol system would require that we regress to a very primitive form of existence. We could not live in our complex societies and have our sophisticated systems of medicine or entertainment without formal language.

4. John B. Carroll, "Work, Meaning, and Concepts: Part I, Their Nature," *Howard Educational Review* 34(1964):178–90.

If our unique characteristic is the use of communication to manipulate our environment, then one tool that makes this possible would have to be formal language. While other animals seem to possess the ability to communicate, none appears to have this ability to the degree that people do. Certainly, we lack evidence that even the highly communicative porpoise can manipulate symbols at a level as abstract as that achieved by a human child. Whether this is a strength or a weakness we leave to you to decide. We can, however, state that the use of a commonly accepted symbol system is a necessity for human beings if they are to engage in interpersonal communication for the purpose of affecting other individuals.

Nonverbal Communication   A formal language system, then, is imperative for effective interpersonal communication. Of equal importance, however, is nonverbal communication, our informal language system. It is through nonverbal communication that we manage to communicate emotions and subtleties of meaning that would be lost were we restricted solely to a verbal system.[5] The emotion of love is better communicated from one person to another nonverbally rather than through words. How often we complain of the inadequacy of words to express this emotion!

5. A. Mehrabian and S. R. Ferris, "Inference of Attitudes from Nonverbal Communication in Two Channels," *Journal of Consulting Psychology* 31(1967):248–52; A. Mehrabian and M. Wiener, "Decoding of Inconsistent Communications," *Journal of Personality and Social Psychology* 6(1967):109–14.

6. Ibid.

While research in the area of nonverbal communication is somewhat limited, it has been estimated that as much as 93 percent of our messages concerning feelings are communicated in a nonverbal manner.[6] Through nonverbal communication we manage to establish our roles, intent, and affection. It is very likely that through nonverbal communication parents communicate love and protection to a child. It is of no use to tell a child we love it if we do not caress the child and communicate love to the child nonverbally. This is especially true of young children who have not yet mastered language skills. When we consider that for the first two or three years of our lives we are restricted primarily to nonverbal communication for acquisition of information about the world and for manipulation of the world, we should not be surprised that researchers are becoming increasingly aware of the importance of this kind of communication.

People generally have become very sophisticated with verbal communication and are highly dependent on it to acquire the skills that are needed to survive in the world. However, as we become older and more skilled in the use of verbal language, we become less skilled in the use of nonverbal language. Exercises in sensitivity training are conducted for the purpose of re-teaching adults to communicate nonverbally as children do. Is it possible that we lose the skill to communicate nonverbally because we become dependent on language? At present we know of no study that suggests this conclusion, but from our own observations it would seem to be the case. More comments on nonverbal communication will be found in chapter 6.

Environment

7. J. Ruesch and G. Bateson, "Structure and Process in Social Relations," *Psychiatry* 12 (1949):105–24.

8. J. Ruesch, "Synopsis of The Theory of Human Communication," *Psychiatry* 10(1953):215–43.

The context of the interaction determines the nature of interpersonal communication. If our past environment and past behavior patterns continue to affect the process of interpersonal communication significantly, then the environment in which communication is occurring at any given moment must have at least as much effect.[7] We are conditioned by our role in any given situation.[8] In the office with our boss we communicate one way. At the bowling alley with friends we communicate another way. At a rock concert we communicate yet another way. What we are (in terms of role) in a given situation, who we are (in terms of socioeconomic level in society), how others perceive us, and how we perceive ourselves (in terms of our work as human beings) all condition and determine how we interact with other people.

Environmental factors that significantly affect interpersonal communication include role, physical setting, time, urgency or nonurgency in a situation, and number and status of people present. It would be impossible to enumerate all environmental factors in an interpersonal interaction, but it is safe to suggest that these environmental factors will affect the quality and nature of any interpersonal communication to a high degree.

Feedback Immediacy

Interpersonal communication provides the opportunity for direct communication among all parties in the communication process. This is probably the feature that distinguishes interpersonal communication from other forms of communication. Mass communication is primarily one-way, with extremely delayed feedback. It is very difficult for the receivers in mass communication to provide feedback directly to the initiating communicators. In public communication the same problem is true, although it would be possible for an audience to provide feedback to a speaker. The size of the audience in the public communication situation would generally prevent feedback as direct as is possible in the interpersonal situation. Thus we find that a distinguishing characteristic of interpersonal communication is the opportunity for communicators to affect one another mutually and immediately during the communication process.

Need Satisfaction

Ideally, interpersonal communication results in the mutual satisfaction of needs of the persons involved in the interaction. Admittedly, this statement reflects our personal value systems; if a positive relationship is the goal of any interaction (and we think it often is), then mutual satisfaction of needs is absolutely necessary. The result is the development of a positive relationship. If needs are not mutually satisfied, the outcome of the interaction very likely would be a negative relationship that would leave much hatred and/or enmity between the people involved.

Interpersonal Communication: Models and Elements

It is common to develop models of the phenomena we study. Communication models are developed to identify the elements in the communication system. Studying these models makes it easier for us not only to recognize the components in the system, but also to check out the relationships between and among the components. Models also provide us with plans of analysis we can use to approach any interpersonal communication situation in which problems have occurred. Models may suggest likely problem points in any interpersonal communication system. No one model identifies all the parts or explains all of the interacting relationships. The process is far too dynamic, the elements too numerous, and the interrelationships too complex to be represented with accuracy by a few line drawings or words in any one model. Nevertheless, models do help focus our attention on some parts of the process they represent.

Lasswell's Model

9. Harold Lasswell, "The Structure and Function of Communication in Society," in L. Bryson, ed., *The Communication of Ideas* (New York: Harper & Brothers, 1948), 37.

Lasswell's[9] model identifies five commonly accepted variables in the communication process: Who? Says what? In what channel? To whom? With what effect? All five of these variables have received considerable attention from researchers and textbook writers. Lasswell's model is a good example of a linear approach to communication. It is linear because it implies that messages go in one direction from one person(s) to another(others).

Schramm's Model

Wilbur Schramm's model as pictured in figure 2.2 introduced a concept that is of importance in interpersonal communication. The *source* is the brain of the person starting the communication process. It includes ideas the person desires to communicate. *Encoder* signifies a process by which the ideas are converted into symbols for transmission to another person. *Signal* signifies the message produced and transmitted. This could consist of the words uttered

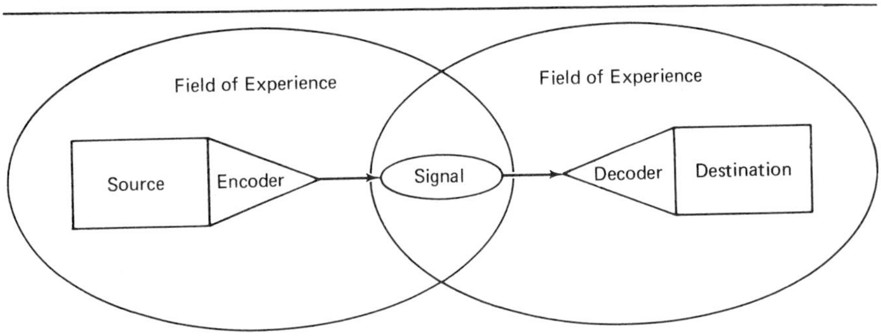

Figure 2.2 Schramm's Model of Communication.

by a person or any other physical stimuli produced by the communicator. *Decoder* signifies a process by which the stimuli received (such as spoken words) are converted into ideas by the recipient of the stimuli. (This is sometimes referred to as the *decoding process*.) *Destination* signifies the mind of the person to whom the message is directed. This is the person the initiating communicator wishes to influence.

Schramm's special contribution was his suggestion that each communicator has a personal **field of experience** that controls both the encoding and decoding processes and determines meaning in communication. For communication to occur between people, Schramm indicated that there must be some overlap in their fields of experience; nevertheless, his is a linear model. For us to understand other persons, or for others to understand us, we should have something in common in our backgrounds that enables us to perceive the stimuli or messages similarly. In chapter 5 we consider in greater detail the effect of our fields of experience on meaning.

Model of an Interpersonal Communication System

The model in figure 2.3 is an attempt to synthesize the models of Brooks and Emmert[10] and Emmert and Donaghy[11] to represent an interpersonal communication system. The major features of this model correspond to discussions in later chapters.

Environment Every interpersonal communication system occurs within an environment. The **environment** includes everything external to the components of the interpersonal communication system. If two people are talking, everything outside those two people is the environment in which their interpersonal communication is occurring. This could include things as diverse as the economy in which they live, culture, family, and schools. The environment is important to keep in mind because people within the communication system continually interact with it to some extent or are influenced by it. It is

10. William D. Brooks and Phillip Emmert, *Interpersonal Communication*, 2d ed. (Dubuque, Iowa: Wm. C. Brown, 1980), 27.

11. P. Emmert and W. C. Donaghy, *Human Communication* (Reading, Mass.: Addison-Wesley, 1981), 40.

Figure 2.3 Interpersonal
Communication System Model

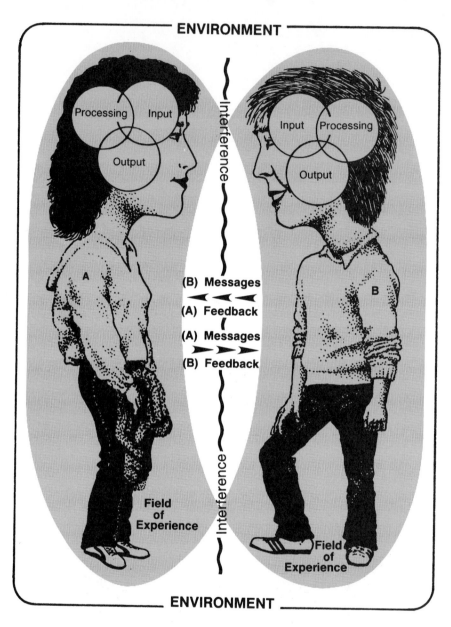

Figure 2.3 Interpersonal Communication System Model

Chapter 2

impossible, for instance, for a person to be part of an interpersonal communication system and ever completely lose the influence of his or her family. At all times we are affected by both our prior experiences and our awareness of what is presently going on in our environment.

Interpersonal communication cannot exist in isolation. It is affected by the environment as things filter through into the individual's internal processing system. To understand how another person is behaving, we may need to take into account the factors in the environment that are important enough to that person to have an effect on behavior. A way to think of the effect of environment on the persons in an interpersonal communication system is to imagine that persons are at all times surrounded by a context which we can call environment.

Field of Experience   Schramm introduced the idea of a person's **field of experience.** It includes all our education, accidents, interactions with others, and even our physiological makeup. In other words, all of our interactions with and experiences within our environment and other people in our environment in the past make up a ''bubble'' we carry around. Of course, it is not a physical bubble; it is something we have inside our minds. This field of experience significantly affects how we perceive, use language, and think. Note, that in our model, as in Schramm's, we have pictorially suggested that for communication to occur the fields of experience of the communicators must overlap, as in the shaded area of the model. In other words, we must have things in common in our fields of experience.

Input Subsystems   **Input subsystems** involve all reception processes in a human being. Input subsystems include the eyes, ears, nose, and nerves in our skin. These input subsystems allow us to receive messages and stimuli from outside and inside ourselves.

As part of our input system it would also be possible to include the perception process. This will be discussed in greater detail in chapter 4. In addition to physically receiving stimuli from the outside world, we must interpret them and make sense out of them. This interpreting process is called **perception.** Whether this is actually an input subsystem or a processing subsystem is questionable. It is probably a part of both subsystems.

It is important to remember that hearing and seeing are physical reception processes, but that if we do not *perceive* the aural or visual stimuli we may not respond to them. Sometimes people speak to us and we may physically hear them but we don't listen to them. Just because a message has been inputted does not necessarily mean that it will be processed and responded to.

Processing Subsystems   Processing in interpersonal communicators includes all of our thought processes. Reasoning, motivation, perception, and needs interact in ways that permit us to create messages in response to stimuli we have received. Our **processing subsystems,** or thought processes, are affected by all past experiences, illnesses, emotions, and the like, that we have ever experienced in our lives. Thus the way we interpret or create messages is determined in great part by what our prior experiences have been. We will be discussing the processing systems in detail in chapters 3, 4, and 7 as we discuss self-concept, perception, personal needs, and information reception.

Output Subsystems   The **output subsystem** of every interpersonal communicator includes all of the messages and behaviors produced at any given time. The output subsystem includes the production of speech, the use of gestures, eye contact, and facial expressions, as well as those other behaviors which, although not messages, become stimuli for other people who receive them. Our outputs obviously serve as inputs for persons involved in interpersonal communication with us. We will discuss communication output subsystems in chapters 5 and 6 when we discuss language and nonverbal communication. As you can see in figure 2.3, interpersonal communicators' input, processing, and output subsystems overlap, and the three subsystems mutually affect one another. Similarly the messages we receive have an effect on the way we think and feel; and the way we think and feel affects the way we perceive messages.

Messages   As we just discussed, the behaviors we produce may or may not be called **messages.** The distinction between a message behavior and a non-message behavior involves two major factors. First, was a commonly accepted symbol system a part of the behavior? A **symbol** is something we use to stand for something else. For example, we use the word "chair" to stand for a physical object we sit on. Thus "chair" is the symbol for the object. Commonly accepted symbol systems include all languages and also the facial expressions, gestures, and other nonverbal behaviors which follow cultural patterns (so that the meanings are similar for the people who interact within a culture group).

We are using the term *symbol* to include both arbitrary and natural symbols. The word *chair* is an arbitrary symbol for pieces of furniture we sit on. There is no "natural" connection between the symbol and the thing it stands for. In other words, we could use any word we want to stand for the piece of furniture we sit on. On the other hand, a clenched fist shaken at someone is a symbol for felt anger, aggressiveness, and hostility and is perhaps an extension of the act of hitting someone. In this case there is a "natural connection" between the nonverbal symbol of the clenched fist and the emotion it stands for.

The second factor which distinguishes a message behavior from a non-message behavior is intent to influence another person. As was mentioned in chapter 1, we define interpersonal communication as a situation in which people try to influence one another. It is difficult for us to imagine someone trying to influence another person unintentionally. Likewise, for a human being to engage in a symbolic process requires, in our eyes, intent on the part of the person using the symbol(s).

We would not suggest that all of our behavior is consciously intentional. Psychologists tell us that many of our actions are the result of unconscious motivations. In addition, some message behaviors are the result of past intentions which resulted in message habits that persist because they worked in the past. As discussed in chapter 6, many nonverbal behaviors especially are habits of this sort. Some behaviors which we perform to influence other people are so habitual we are no longer aware that we perform them. Other behaviors we acquired by imitating adults we saw when we were children. Unaware of even having observed these behaviors, we adopted them because we saw them work for valued adults in our environment. These behaviors were never in our conscious awareness and yet we use them to influence others.

Not all communication scholars agree that there must be symbolic behavior and intent to influence present for a behavior to be considered a message. Some authorities suggest that *all* behavior is communication if someone interprets it meaningfully.[12] We will refer to this viewpoint as the **unintentional,** or "receiver-oriented," approach to communication. We, and other scholars, believe the term "communication" should be reserved for those behaviors performed with intent to influence another person.[13] We will refer to this viewpoint as the **intentional,** or "sender-oriented," approach to interpersonal communication. Obviously, neither view is correct or incorrect. We have called your attention to the distinction between these two perspectives to emphasize that whether or not you interpret all behavior as communication is important, because of the possible effect your interpretation may have on your response to stimuli.

Although any behavior can have communicative implications, we should be cautious about inferring what that communicative intent is every time a behavior of someone appears to have meaning for us. First we must remember that there is usually no *inherent* connection between the behavior and a meaning, just as there is no *inherent* connection between any word and a meaning; any connection must be learned. Second, we must remember when we are inferring the meaning in someone else's behavior, that what we infer may or may not be what the other person was implying in that behavior. If we fail to realize that we are assigning meaning based on our own experiences, we may respond in a manner that is inappropriate and counterproductive. An example of this kind of situation can be found in job situations.

12. S. W. Littlejohn, *Theories of Human Communication,* 2d ed. (Belmont, Calif.: Wadsworth Publishing Co., 1983), 5–7.

13. Ibid.

If one person places a hand on the shoulder of another person, the intent can be, among others, either to show dominance or to show affection, as discussed in chapter 6. Also discussed in that chapter is the point that people with high status and high power are more likely to touch low status/low power persons than vice versa. In organizational settings it is not unusual for a superior to place a hand on the shoulder of a subordinate. This behavior can be interpreted very differently depending on whether the parties are both male, both female, or a male-female dyad.

If both persons are of the same sex, the touching behavior will probably signify a mixture of dominance and friendliness, and will probably be perceived that way by both parties. If a female superior should touch a male subordinate, however, the male may very well perceive the touching behavior as a sexual overture — even though the female superior means nothing different by the behavior than would a male superior. If the male subordinate responds to the sexual meaning he perceives, embarrassment could result for both parties, and possibly ill feelings that could adversely affect their working relationship in the future.

When the behavioral interaction is across cultures, the potential for misunderstanding grows enormously. Edward Hall, a pioneer in the study of nonverbal behavior and cross-cultural communication, often used Arab-American misunderstandings as examples:

> One Arab informant said that he was in constant hot water with Americans because of the way he looked at them without the slightest intention of offending. In fact, he had on several occasions barely avoided fights with American men who apparently thought their masculinity was being challenged because of the way he was looking at them. As noted earlier, Arabs look each other in the eye when talking with an intensity that makes most Americans highly uncomfortable.[14]

14. Edward T. Hall, *The Hidden Dimension* (Garden City, N.Y.: Doubleday Anchor Books, 1969), 161.

We are constantly engaged in trying to deduce or infer from observed stimuli something beyond those stimuli. All behavior can be interpreted meaningfully and can affect communication, even though what is intended is not what is perceived, or the intent to communicate may be absent. This means that all we can ever do is make inferences about the behaviors we observe.

This discussion is intended to call your attention to the fact that whether or not you interpret all behavior as intended messages is important because of the possible effect your interpretation may have on your response to what you receive as stimuli. If you perceive all behavior as intended messages, you may commit errors. It is our feeling that it is safer to assume all behaviors to be stimuli we can receive and interpret, but which do not have inherent meaning. And we should not necessarily assume them to be messages resulting from intent by the person producing them. Rather, we should pay close attention to all available stimuli and try to make inferences about them. It is important to remember that we are making inferences and should be prepared to readjust them at any moment. As long as we remember that the meanings we assign to behaviors are inferences and nothing more, it matters little whether we subscribe to the intentional or unintentional point of view.

We actually produce at least three types of behaviors. We produce **primary stimulus message** behaviors — those messages produced in response to our original need to communicate and communicated by whatever means seem most effective to us. Sitting in a car at a drive-in, we would probably choose the medium of speech as the most effective and produce the sounds ''I want a hot dog.'' This statement is our primary stimulus message because it is made in response to our hunger and transmitted via the medium we consider most efficient.

We also produce **complementary stimulus message** behaviors that are our responses to the original stimuli but are transmitted for the purpose of reinforcing the primary stimulus message. Any facial expressions, tones of voice, or gestures we might use to obtain better service at the drive-in would be complementary stimulus messages.

Finally, we emit **auxiliary behaviors** that are unrelated to the original stimulus to communicate but that nevertheless affect other people's perceptions of our messages. For example, if we look old, people perceive our messages one way; if we look young, they perceive our messages another way. All of these messages and/or behaviors can influence people to satisfy our needs or not.

Feedback   Throughout any kind of interaction, feedback exists. When person A provides a message which person B then responds to, person B's response is called **feedback.** It must be clear from the model in figure 2.3 that it is difficult to determine which is feedback and which is the message. When two people are interacting, feedback for one person is a message for another. To determine what is feedback in a communication interaction, it is useful to remember that feedback serves a **regulatory function.** All systems, be they communication systems or not, must be regulated to survive. Without order in the system, eventually complete chaos would result and the system could not continue to exist. In interpersonal communication systems this regulation is accomplished through response messages, or feedback. Feedback is not simply something that is ''nice'' to provide, it is *necessary* for our interpersonal communication system to survive.

If Joanne doesn't say ''I love you'' to John often enough to satisfy his needs for affection, John has the option of producing feedback (his own message). He may say something like ''You don't care about me anymore.'' This message would be an attempt by John to control Joanne's communication behavior.

Price list
short sleeve
0mo.-36mo.   5.00
2-8   5.50
10-16   6.00
long sleeve
0mo.-36mo.   6.00
2-8   6.50
10-16   7.00
short sleeve sets   8.00
long sleeve sets   9.00
women's short sleeve 8.50
women's long sleeve 10.00

People, noise, and activity can
all interfere in interpersonal
communication.

She might then say, ''I'm sorry but I've been busy lately. Actually, I love you
and need you more than ever.'' John's feedback has regulated Joanne's communication behavior.

As discussed in greater detail in chapter 7, feedback in any interpersonal
communication system is not simply desirable, it is essential to the survival of
any interpersonal communication relationship.

Interference   **Interference** can be any stimuli in the communication environment that can distort or alter messages. The model in figure 2.3 suggests that
all messages are distorted and come through finally as altered messages. If you
have ever tried to carry on a conversation when loud music was playing, you
know that the interference of the music made it difficult to hear and be heard.
There are also **interfering messages** present in communication situations not
produced by any of the persons who are communicating interpersonally.

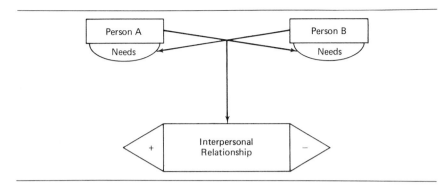

Figure 2.4 A satisfactory relationship

If two people having a conversation in a room overhear another conversation in the hall, the semantic content of the hall conversation would be an interfering message. The overheard conversation might influence the person who overhears it, but that would be an unintended effect, so we consider it an interfering message. Whether or not "communication" occurs as a result of an interfering message is a moot point. We do know the person who overhears will be influenced — intentionally or not.

Relationships   Two people who interact are relating to each other in a specified manner determined by their roles in relation to each other. Parent and child relate to each other differently than friend and friend, or lover and lover. Whenever we talk about an interpersonal communication system, it is important that we keep in mind the relationship of the people in the system. This is why the term *role* is used frequently throughout this book.

For you to understand the interpersonal relationship better, we offer a simple model. Figure 2.4 attempts to portray interpersonal communication as a *relationship,* with no individual designated as sender or receiver. In the case of two individuals, we would expect the goal of every interpersonal interaction to be a satisfactory *relationship.* As in figure 2.4, person A, in attempting to satisfy the needs of person B, experiences the mutual satisfaction of needs. This mutual satisfaction of needs, either directly through the interaction or indirectly through the outcome of the interaction, results in the development of a *relationship* between A and B. This relationship can be thought of as a new entity, as the mixing of hydrogen and oxygen creates a new entity, water. In addition, the relationship is unique.

In interpersonal communication we should keep in mind that often, as two people interact interpersonally, they begin to develop so many things in common that the relationship itself begins to exist as an entity. Two people can share so much that they reach a point where it is difficult for them to exist alone. This is not to say that neither one can exist alone but rather that it is simply "unnatural" to exist alone. If they were pulled apart, each one would cease to be the same person who was formerly interacting with the other person. This happens to many married couples when death, or other circumstances, separates the partners. The individual who remains ceases to be the same person as the one who was once involved in an interpersonal relationship.

CONTEXTS OF INTERPERSONAL COMMUNICATION

The three basic contexts of interpersonal communication are dyadic, small group, and interviewing contexts. The first two are discussed extensively in this book, the third is considered indirectly in the chapter on interviewing.

Dyadic communication involves the interaction of two people. We can define this context simply by the number of people involved. Whenever two people are interacting, we have an interpersonal dyadic communication system. Dyads result in communication characteristics that are different from other kinds of interpersonal communication settings. We focus on this context in chapter 9. We also discuss different types of dyadic relationships and the ways relationships are formed, maintained, and terminated.

Small-group communication causes us to expand our definition of interpersonal communication to include up to twenty people. The small group setting stimulates special behaviors by individuals that are worth consideration in and of themselves. Matters such as phases of interaction, leadership, and conformity are all of concern to people who work in small group settings. The small group context is discussed in chapter 10.

The *interviewing context* is not actually separate from the dyadic context, in that in both contexts two people are interacting. We cover the interviewing context in a separate chapter, however, for two reasons. First, the formal, structured nature of an interview raises concerns not present in other dyadic situations. Second, the feedback we have received from earlier editions of this book suggest that a chapter devoted to interviewing will be an asset to you in employment interviews as you prepare to enter your chosen profession.

Summary

This chapter presents the linear, circular, and systems perspectives on interpersonal communication and points out that the perspective in this book is systems oriented. The interrelatedness of elements of the communication process means that no communication behavior can occur independent of its environment; that a change in nonverbal behavior affects the meaning of the language that is used with it. The complexity and interrelatedness of interpersonal communication components are represented in a diagrammatic model.

In this chapter we suggest that not all behavior is necessarily communication. Further, for behavior to be a message, a commonly accepted symbol system must be used intentionally to change another's behavior. The importance of feedback as a regulatory mechanism in interpersonal communication is discussed. Finally, the different contexts of communication and their defining characteristics are discussed.

II

Elements of Interpersonal Communication

3

The Self in Communication: The Role of Self-Concept

Objectives for the Reader

1. To be able to define "self-concept" and describe five characteristics of a self-concept.
2. To be able to predict and explain the relationship between attitudes toward the concept of "self" and communication behavior.
3. To be able to differentiate between self-image and self-esteem and to explain how each is created from messages received from others.
4. To be able to analyze a self-concept identity crisis, its causes and effects, and possible resolutions.
5. To be able to gain greater control of your own self-fulfilling prophecies and to become more independent of others' self-fulfilling prophecies in order to create a healthier self-concept.
6. To be able to describe how positive and negative self-concepts affect the sending and receiving of messages.
7. To be able to predict the effects of communicator self-concept on communication behavior, satisfaction of interpersonal needs, and personal lifestyle.
8. To be able to increase your self-awareness, self-acceptance and self-actualization.
9. To be able to recognize and practice effective self-disclosure with others.

In his *Autobiography* Benjamin Franklin describes how as a young man he made a list of his strengths and deficits as a person. He made this list to get at the task of correcting his deficits and taking advantage of those assets he possessed. Indeed, Ben Franklin was a very wise man, and it would be equally wise for each of us to engage in the same kind of activity. This is the sort of honest self-appraisal we all need to go through every once in a while; moreover, we need to engage in genuine follow-up action, just as Franklin did. His specific procedure is a valid one for improving a person's self-concept.

Although there are many topics with which we will be concerned in this book, and although each of these topics may be of importance to our understanding of the communication process, the area that may have the greatest influence on one's behavior in interpersonal communication, as was suggested in chapter 1, is the perception of one's self, or one's self-concept. No matter how we view the world, interpersonal communication begins within the self, and effective, wholesome interpersonal communication is closely associated with a useful and realistic perception of self.

A DEFINITION OF SELF-CONCEPT

Self-concept can be defined as *the aggregate of those physical, social, and psychological perceptions of ourselves, that we have derived from our experiences and our interactions with others.* It is the awareness we have of being and functioning — of "ourself" as an object. It consists of those beliefs we have about ourselves — about our attractiveness or unattractiveness, our intellectual ability, attitudes, beliefs, values, the roles we play, and our expectations of how others see us and react to us in those roles.

Our self-concept is something we develop. We are not born with it. We must build our self-concept almost entirely on the outcome of our relationships with others. Nothing resembling the concept of a self could ever occur to a child who existed in isolation from others. Self can only be understood in terms of our relationships with others.

We have said that the self consists of the aggregate of our experiences in life. Many of our experiences are forgotten — that is, they are placed in our "unconscious" — but they are not lost. They can and do influence us, and sometimes they emerge suddenly into our consciousness, even surprising us. We consciously remember little of what occurred to us as a child, yet these experiences form the foundation of our self-concept. In this chapter, however, we are concerned mostly with the conscious self. It is not so much what we *are* but what we *think* we are that guides our acts and behavior.

If you think about it for a moment, you know that perception of self must be extremely important, because each of us spends considerable time thinking about ourselves — reflecting on the happenings, events, and interactions we have had with others — meditating on life, the meaning of it, where we are headed, and what we really want to do. Literature is filled with examples of thinking about self or of talking to one's self. Some excellent examples can be found in Eldridge Cleaver's *Soul on Ice,* in *Cool Cos: The Story of Bill Cosby,* and in Shakespeare's *Hamlet,* when Hamlet talks to himself, "O, what a rogue and peasant slave am I!"

How do you see yourself? Who are you? Do you like yourself? How do others see you? Who do they think you are? How do these things affect your interpersonal communication? The information we present in this chapter we hope will give you an understanding of what a self-concept is, of problems that sometimes arise relative to understanding and identifying the self, and of how these problems cause us to adopt certain strategies and behaviors in interpersonal communication. We identify the characteristics of a healthy self-concept, and suggest how one may go about improving the concept one already has of oneself.

We hope that as you read the remainder of this chapter you will apply it to yourself, because no other element in your interpersonal communication is more important than your perception of yourself. We tend to be what we think we are; we think we are whatever we say to ourselves; and much of what we say to ourselves is what we hear (or heard in the past) others saying about us or to us.

DEVELOPMENT OF AN INTEGRATED SELF-CONCEPT: THE MANY SELVES

We develop our concepts of self through communication with significant others (parents, siblings, friends, and teachers), through identification with groups (family, cliques, and clubs), and through comparing ourselves to others.[1] Notice that we said concept*s* of self. There are many selves. Not one of us is a single self. In fact, each of us plays many roles. We are parents, spouses, friends, professors, employees, strangers, and so on. The self varies for each relationship, for each role in which we find ourselves. Add to these selves those of private self, public self, physical self, emotional self, intellectual self, and spiritual self, and it is apparent that there are many selves.

One helpful exercise is to complete the phrase "I am . . ." with several responses that characterize yourself. After listing several phrases that complete "I am . . .," put each of those sentences describing yourself into one of the following categories: (1) *physical attributes* — such bodily characteristics as age, height, and weight; (2) *emotional attributes* — the feelings you possess: shy, happy, cynical, cheerful, frustrated, and so on; (3) *mental attributes* — intellectual characteristics: smart, average, or "dumb"; (4) *roles* — functions you fulfill relative to others: class level in school, whether you are single or married,

1. Leon Festinger, "A Theory of Social Comparison Processes," *Human Relations* 7(1954):117–40.

We all have "many selves" we display to the world and to ourselves, depending on the situation.

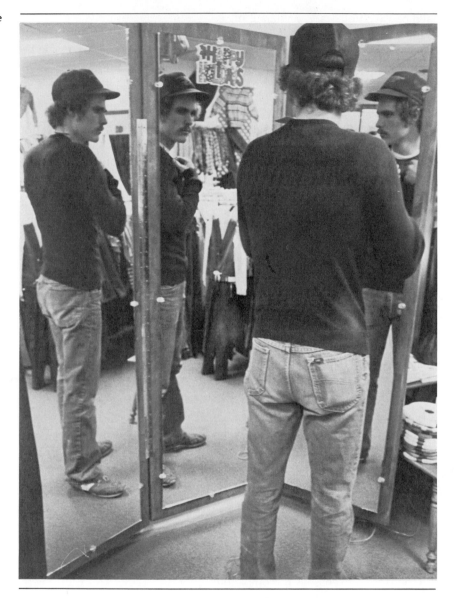

your major, your profession, and so on; (5) _relationships with others_ — the characteristic stance you take toward others: whether you are accessible and open, closed and withdrawn, or neutral and moderate.

As the preceding exercise illustrates, we are many selves. This multiplicity of selves can be a hindrance to effective communication, but also the means to effective communication. If we have accurate "self-awareness" (know who we are in all these relationships and situations), then we are able to express ourselves and to interact fully and effectively across a wide range of situations and persons. The person who has integrated these multiple selves can choose that self most appropriate to the unique communicative interaction. That person can be free, loving, and affectionate when that is appropriate, and in another situation can be controlled, logical, and intellectual when that is appropriate. In other words, the person can communicate flexibly and with some diversity.

An important part of our self-concept is our response to the idea that we have many selves.[2] Some individuals define their identities in terms of perceived internal, long-lasting personality characteristics. They guide their behavior almost solely on the basis of these perceived internal dispositions, moods, values, attitudes, and beliefs, and they are greatly concerned with being consistent with their "single self-concept" in every situation. These individuals are **"self-monitors"** because they look solely to themselves and their own perceptions in order to define themselves in each situation. Other individuals, who might be thought of as **"other"** or **"situation monitors,"** base much of their self-concept on the various roles they fill. These individuals are more concerned with interacting appropriately and are less affected in any given situation by their internal moods, attitudes, values, and beliefs. They perceive themselves as having many selves and choose the self which is most appropriate to the role they are currently engaged in. Most of us believe we are somewhere in between these two extremes. We perceive ourselves as having a relatively permanent self-concept. But we also perceive ourselves as very complex, with many roles to play and many selves which may not always be entirely consistent with one another. Whether individuals are self-monitors or situation-monitors will have a strong effect on their communication. Self-monitors demonstrate a greater convergence between their attitudes and their communication behavior; they are also more consistent over many situations. Situation/other-monitors are more skilled at reading the emotions and feelings of others. Because they are not distracted by their inner feelings, they are better able to intentionally express a wide range of emotions and feelings. They have a richer and larger repertoire of role behaviors and remember more information about the people with whom they interact. They are more flexible in their communication behavior and are more likely to lead and direct others.

2. Mark Snyder, "Self-Monitoring Processes," in Leonard Berkowitz, ed., *Advances in Experimental Social Psychology* 12(1979):85–128.

3. Based on Michael Argyle's discussion in *Social Interaction* (New York: Atherton Press, 1969), 356.

Now we want to take a close look at some important aspects of our self-concept. Two important aspects are our self-image and our self-esteem.[3] Our self-image(s) is composed of the pictures we have of ourselves. It includes our **body-image,** our picture of our physical self, and our **ideal self-concept,** the way we would like to be. While self-image refers to the sort of person we think we are, our **self-esteem** refers to the value we place on each of our images. Self-esteem is how well you like yourself, how good you think you are. Two individuals can have the same self-image — "not very athletic" — and one may experience lowered self-esteem for this reason while the other may not. Our self-image and self-esteem are both created through our interactions with others and exert a strong controlling effect on our communication behavior with others.

Self-Image

4. Ibid., 356–57.

Our self-image comes about to a great extent as a result of our interactions with others. More specifically, it comes about as a result of our being categorized by others.[4] This process of categorizing persons, for good or bad, is one of the basic and initial occurrences in interpersonal communication encounters. What is the first question asked about a newborn baby? "Is it a boy or a girl?" This is the first category we are placed in. Each of us does it, and everyone else does it to us — all of us place those others with whom we interact into categories. These categories, according to Argyle,[5] are established

5. Ibid., 357–60.

in terms of roles (mother, wife, husband, boss, male, female, playboy), positions (social class, religious affiliation, political affiliation, age), or personality traits (intelligent, neurotic, happy, superstitious, shy, humane). As we observe the reaction of others to us and as we are aware of how others categorize us, we develop an image of ourselves. We learn to predict how others will react to us and to anticipate how we will be categorized by others, and this becomes a part of our self-image and self-concept. We then behave in accordance with the image we have of ourselves.

6. H. A. Mulford and W. W. Salisbury, "Self-Conceptions in a General Population," *Sociology Quarterly* 5(1964):35–46.

Research[6] has shown that family roles are used most frequently in our categorization process (70 percent of the time); occupation is second (68 percent of the time); marital status is third (34 percent of the time); and religious affiliation, or religiosity, is fourth (30 percent of the time). Sounds familiar doesn't it? These are the questions you often ask when you first meet someone. Other roles are also used in the process of categorizing, however. Among these are racial, sexual, recreational and social roles. Women use family roles to categorize themselves more than do men. Men seem to use occupational and sexual roles for categorizing themselves more than women. And religious persons use religiosity and religious affiliation to a greater extent than do nonreligious persons for identifying themselves. Age appears to be used especially by younger and older people. The categories we most want to know about other people, or that we use to classify other people, are an indication of the categories which are personally important to us.

An important part of our self-image is our body image. Actually, this is the first self-image to be formed in a child's mind, and it continues to be a significant factor even for adults. Several researchers have found size to be an important dimension of body image. Males are most satisfied with their bodies when they are large; females are most satisfied with their bodies when they are smaller than normal.[7] Our body-image, like all our perceptions, is not always accurate. The prettier a high school senior's face is, the more likely she is to distort her body perception toward our cultural ideal.[8] Like all our self-images, our physical self-image is highly related to our self-esteem.

Self-Esteem

Self-esteem is another major component of self-concept. Like self-image, it comes about as a result of our interaction with others — but not by being categorized or described by others. Our self-esteem comes about by our being rewarded (or punished at times), by our being praised (or demeaned), and by our being accorded prestige for the categories we have been placed in. When others reward us, accord us prestige or worth, or praise and like us, then we like ourselves, value ourselves, and generally regard ourselves favorably. Social science researchers who have studied self-esteem identify high self-esteem as consisting of those favorable attitudes we have toward ourselves. Low self-esteem is the extent to which we have unfavorable or negative attitudes toward ourselves. Self-esteem is a powerful force inside us that affects our interpersonal communication behavior.

Several experiments have demonstrated this powerful effect of others on us. A dramatic illustration of the effect of others was reported by ABC television news in the documentary entitled "The Eye of the Storm." According to this documentary, in May 1970 Jane Elliott, an elementary school teacher in Iowa, demonstrated by an experiment how social role influenced the self-concept of the children in her third-grade class. She divided her class according to the color of their eyes and on the first day of the experiment blue-eyed children were declared "superior" and were "privileged." They could leave the room for a drink of water without requesting permission; they could stay outside for a longer recess; they went to lunch earlier; and they could sit anywhere in the room they pleased, even if it meant a brown-eyed child had to move. The brown-eyed children, who were not "privileged," began to think of themselves as "inferior" that day, and they scored lower than usual on card-recognition tests. The next day the teacher reversed the roles, making the brown-eyed children "privileged." That day, blue-eyed children began to view themselves as inferior, and their reading scores, which had been superior the day they were "privileged," declined dramatically.

7. P. A. Smith, "A Comparison of Three Sets of Rotated Factor Analytic Solutions of Self-Concept Data," *Journal of Abnormal and Social Psychology* 4(1967):326–33; S. M. Jourard and P. F. Secord, "Body-Cathexis and Personality," *British Journal of Psychology* 46(1960):130–38; C. R. Rogers and R. Dymond, *Psychotherapy and Personality Change* (Chicago: University of Chicago Press, 1954); and S. Fisher and S. S. Cleveland, *Body-Image and Personality* (Princeton: Van Nostrand, 1958).

8. Barbara Ford, "Who's beautiful to whom — and why?" *Science Digest,* January 1971, 9–15.

9. Sigmund Freud, *A General Introduction to Psychoanalysis* (New York: Simon & Schuster, 1969); Timothy Leary, *Interpersonal Diagnosis of Personality* (New York: Ronald Press, 1957); William C. Schutz, *FIRO: A Three-Dimensional Theory of Interpersonal Behavior* (New York: Holt, Rinehart & Winston, 1958); Robert R. Blake and Jane S. Mouton, *The Managerial Grid* (Houston: Gulf Publishing Co., 1964); D. Katz, N. Maccoby, G. Gurin, and L. G. Floor, *Productivity, Supervision and Morale Among Railroad Workers* (Ann Arbor, Mich.: Institute for Social Research, University of Michigan, 1951); and Maurice Lorr and D. N. McNair, "Expansion of the Interpersonal Behavior Circle," *Journal of Personality and Social Psychology* 2(1965):823-30.

10. Judee K. Burgoon and Thomas Saine, *The Unspoken Dialogue: An Introduction to Nonverbal Communication* (Boston: Houghton Mifflin, 1978), 172-93.

11. Don E. Hamachek, *Encounters with the Self* (New York: Holt, Rinehart & Winston, 1971), 108-27.

12. Ellen Berscheid, Elaine Walster, and George Bohrnstedt, "Body Image: The Happy American Body," *Psychology Today*, June 1973, 119-31.

13. G. W. Allport, *Patterns and Growth in Personality* (New York: Holt, Rinehart & Winston, 1965), 130-31.

14. Hamachek, 234-37.

The reactions of others which cause our self-esteem are for the most part distributed along two dimensions: (1) status and power, and (2) warmth and friendliness. The two dimensions have been labeled in various ways.[9] Terms equivalent or roughly equivalent to *status* and *power* are *dominance, authority, strength,* and *control.* Terms used in place of *warmth* and *friendliness* include *consideration, love, affection, concern for people, nurturance,* and *sociability.* Many of these rewards and punishments are delivered through nonverbal communication[10] and will be discussed later.

One of our self-images which is strongly rewarded in this way is our body image. When we look at someone admiringly or say someone is physically attractive we are attaching a value to the person's body and suggesting to them a value for their body-image. This perception of and acceptance or disapproval of one's body begins in babyhood and childhood. Parents often communicate their opinion of a child's body by praising the child for some physical skill, by expressing disappointment when the child cannot do something as well as they expect, or by commenting on how the child looks. How attractive we are and when we began developing as men and women influences our self-esteem. Late maturation is associated with a poorer self-concept for both males and females.[11] Researchers[12] have found that only 11 percent of people with a below-average body image have above-average self-esteem. This can be compared to individuals with an average or above-average body image; 50 percent of these individuals have above-average self-esteem. For both males and females, having an attractive face has the strongest effect on self-esteem. Being slim is second in importance for women and having a muscular chest is second for men.

Each self-image we have affects our self-esteem. We can think of our "ideal" self-concept as the self we would have to be in order to experience our maximum possible self-esteem. Figure 3.1 shows how **ideal self** or high self-concept is correlated with self-esteem and low self-concept — the person you do *not* want to be — is correlated with low self-esteem. Most of us experience low self-esteem to some degree. Less than 12 percent of the college students in one study reported that they did not have strong feelings of inferiority at some time.[13]

Individuals with low self-esteem have the following attitudes and behaviors.[14] They (1) are sensitive to criticism and often overreact to even the mildest criticism; (2) are over-responsive to praise and often perceive even the mildest approval as stronger than was intended; (3) are hypercritical of others; (4) are likely to blame others for their mistakes; (5) often feel that others do not like them; (6) are pessimistic about their ability to compete with others and win; (7) are often shy and high in communication apprehension. You may be able to think of someone you know who has these characteristics — a person who is supersensitive to criticism and who, you have learned, must be "handled with kid gloves" because he or she may explode, pout, or cry easily.

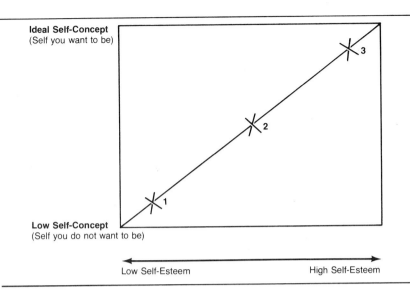

Figure 3.1 Self-concept and self-esteem.

Or perhaps you know someone who has only negative orientations. Such a person seldom has a happy word, a good word, a word of praise, or an expression of appreciation for anything or anyone. Rather, that person gripes, complains, criticizes, and debases. These characteristics of individuals with very negative self-concepts have a strong effect on their communication behavior, which we will discuss shortly.

THE UNINTEGRATED SELF: THE IDENTITY CRISIS

It is not always easy to integrate all our selves into a consistent, coherent, self-concept. We say that people with such integrated selves have a strong self-identity. We mean they know who they are; they know how others perceive them; they have a healthy acceptance of their many selves; and they understand their feelings and relationships with others.

But most of us sometimes feel we do not know who we "really" are. Most of us at various times throughout life go through **identity crises** of varying severity. Some identity crises are small ones and some are big ones. Most of us go through at least one period of difficult identity crisis in late adolescence.

With the onset of adolescence and continuing through high school and early college years, the relatively stable world of childhood becomes an unstable world of rapid change. The growth spurt and sexual development of this age create changes in identity. The physical body changes necessitate body-image changes. The new world, the adult world, that is almost upon us brings

During our teenage years, especially, we are experimenting with and searching for our identity.

increased concern and poses serious and important questions. There is an expectancy and an urge for adolescents to establish themselves as individuals — adult individuals. Most of us experience a strong desire to break away from the dependent relationship with our parents. Add to this the fact that several important and relatively final decisions are made during these years, and one can understand how an identity crisis can exist for a few months or even a few years during this time. Although the teenage years commonly bring an identity crisis for most of us, the quest for self-identity does not stop at age twenty-one or any other age. There is continued revision of the concept of self throughout life, for life is a process and is characterized by constant changes that require adjustments.[15]

15. Gail Sheehy, *Passages: Predictable Crises of Adult Life* (New York: Dutton, 1976).

An identity crisis can be triggered by many events. Rapid changes in our culture create rapid changes in the psychological climate in which we live. This in turn causes us to constantly question who we are. Alvin Toffler[16] focuses attention on this phenomenon. He calls it "future shock" and says it is a product of a tremendously accelerated rate of change occurring in our culture — changes in values, work, acquaintances, family, religion, sex, and almost all the other aspects of our culture.

16. Alvin Toffler, *Future Shock* (New York: Bantam Books, 1970).

In addition to the rapid changes in our physical and psychological environments that may cause identity problems and may give rise to responses such as those described by Toffler, there are other, perhaps slower-paced, causes of identity crises. First, any of us can experience conflicting elements of motivation. We may desire one thing very much and something else directly contrary to it just as much. For example, one can experience inconsistent ambitions — to be an artist or an attorney, to become an architect, or to stay in the family store.

A second possible cause of an identity crisis is failure to reconcile our self-image acquired in childhood with the fact of our adulthood. Some people find it difficult to grow up. They may be adults physically and in their work role, but the concept of themselves to which they cling is that created during their childhood. This situation almost guarantees the creation of an identity crisis.

A third possible cause of an identity crisis is failure to establish a central identity in terms of long-term goals and persistent striving around which we can integrate our many selves.

A fourth possible cause is unrealistic goals — establishment of goals that fail to relate to our abilities, wealth, or opportunities. When we cannot reach these goals we often experience a severe identity crisis and lowered self-esteem.

There are many possible responses to an identity crisis: becoming a playboy,[17] joining some frenetic group, or even schizophrenia. One of the responses used by some high-school- and college-age persons to deal with the identity crisis common to their time of life is to call a "moratorium."[18] This means that they postpone making those decisions that begin to define or identify them to themselves. Instead they experiment with a number of roles and behaviors. One role is taken today, but another tomorrow; one set of values or attitudes may be tested this month, but another set may be accepted later to guide one's adult life. Society leniently affords this age group greater opportunity for using the moratorium strategy as a means of coping with an identity crisis, of attempting to discover those values, goals, and behaviors that group members will select to define themselves and to create their self-identity. Adults, too, use the moratorium technique, although more as individuals than as a group. Adults may take a day off, or a weekend — even a year, when that is possible — simply to go away somewhere and "think things over." The moratorium technique, however, is not a permanent or effective solution. One cannot "go away" permanently, and it is difficult and unrewarding to go through life wearing a mask to hide one's identity. These are

17. J. E. Marcia, "Development and Validation of Ego-Identity Status," *Journal of Personality and Social Psychology* 3(1966):551–58.

18. E. H. Erickson, "The Problem of Ego Identity," *American Journal of Psychoanalysis* 4(1956):56–121.

not satisfactory substitutes for self-integration. There are, of course, persons in our world who try to hide permanently behind false identity masks, who have contradictory identities, who cling to unrealistic identities, or who form very tenuous and precarious identities. The objective toward which we ought to be moving, however, is a healthy concept of self — an integration of all our many selves. It requires no great insight to understand that self-identity is an important factor in interpersonal communication. When one is unsure of who one is, is doubtful of one's acceptability to others, or is unable to accept oneself — in short, when one is in an identity crisis about one's attitudes, beliefs, values, goals, and relationships with others with respect to various roles or selves one needs to be — one's interpersonal communication suffers.

RELATIONSHIP OF SELF-CONCEPT TO INTERPERSONAL COMMUNICATION

Our self-concept affects our interpersonal communication in several ways: (1) It is the basis of two types of **self-fulfilling prophecies.** (2) It determines our selection and use of messages. (3) It affects our attitude toward communicating — i.e., communication security versus communication apprehension.

Self-Concept: The Basis of Self-Fulfilling Prophecies About Ourselves

Each person behaves in a manner consistent with his or her self-concept. We often label ourselves and then act like the kind of person we perceive ourselves to be. The student who has said "I am a failure" can find plenty of excuses to avoid studying, reading, or participating in class discussion. Of course, at the end of the term that student usually receives the expected low grade. Similarly, the student who feels "Nobody likes me" will usually find that he or she is not liked. Such persons usually do not understand that it is their behaving in a manner consistent with a deprecated self-concept (sour expression, hostility, refusal to be friendly or to participate) that invites rejection by others.

According to Ellis,[19] one of the ways we lower our self-esteem is through the acceptance of a number of irrational beliefs about ourselves and the world. The first of these is that we should (must) perform perfectly. We label ourselves a complete failure if we achieve less than an A+ on a test, or make a less than perfect speech, or do not communicate perfectly in every interpersonal relationship and achieve perfect acceptance and total approval from all the significant other people in our lives. Since no one can achieve this unrealistic level of perfection, many individuals are unnecessarily labeling themselves as failures (are being hypercritical of themselves) and lowering their self-esteem. Achieving partial acceptance and approval from others may not be

19. Albert Ellis, "The Theory of Rational-Emotive Therapy," in Albert Ellis and John M. Whiteley, eds., *Theoretical and Empirical Foundations of Rational-Emotive Therapy* (Monterey, Calif.: Brooks/Cole, 1979), 33–60.

what we desire, but it may be all we can achieve because of circumstances other than our abilities and skills as a communicator.

We should pay close attention to the labels we give ourselves because they have a tremendous influence on who we become. If you label yourself as "no good in music" or a "poor public speaker," you may prove to be so. As Condon, a communication scholar, has stated: "Responding to such labels gives us direction, even if the direction is backwards; responding to such labels helps us decide what to do and what not to do, even if the choices are not the wisest."[20] For example, if you label yourself as "a loner," you will probably behave in a manner that is unfriendly. You will avoid opportunities to talk; you will refrain from smiling; you will seek seclusion rather than the company of others. It is quite important to use labels which will have a positive rather than a negative effect on our self-concept, since we tend to fulfill our own prophecies — that is, to become whatever we see ourselves as being.

20. John C. Condon, Jr., *Semantics and Communication* (New York: Macmillan, 1966), 60.

Others' Self-Fulfilling Prophecies About Us

Others can also label us and elicit behavior from us which fulfills their self-fulfilling prophecy about us. Even when there is no verbal communication of that expectation, the expectation may be communicated indirectly through nonverbal communication to us. Rosenthal, a psychologist, has discussed an interesting experiment in which elementary teachers were told that one group of children (the experimental group, selected randomly from the classroom) had scored exceptionally high on a test for "intellectual blooming." In reality, the children in the experimental group were no different from the control group regarding their real scores on the test, but the teachers believed they were different.[21] The teachers then labeled the experimental students as having high potential to bloom intellectually and responded to these students in such a way that they actually did become more accomplished. Other similar experiments, reviewed by Rosenthal, have the same findings.[22] We indeed live up to the labels others attach to us.

21. Robert Rosenthal, "Self-Fulfilling Prophecy," in *Readings in Psychology Today* (Del Mar, Calif.: CRM Books, 1967), 466-71.

22. Ibid.

This would not be a problem if the labels others applied to us always generated realistic and positive self-fulfilling prophecies about us. Unfortunately, one of the irrational beliefs others may hold about us[23] is that we should (must) perform perfectly, be completely sensitive to them, and treat them with their idea of perfect consideration and fairness. If we do anything less, they are likely to label us a complete failure and behave toward us in such a manner that we will have difficulty not living up to that label. When we are not able to articulate our feelings in a completely clear fashion during an argument, for example, the other person may label us as "naive and unknowing" about our inner selves. They may then sneer at our attempts to explain ourselves, make deprecating comments about the feelings we are trying to express, and begin to "analyze" us because they think we need help. When this occurs we will probably spend the rest of the conversation trying to explain what is missing

23. Ellis, 33-60.

in their analysis, becoming defensive about their attitude, and, in general, behaving exactly as they have predicted. At the conclusion of our conversation we may not be completely sure what happened. All we know is that somehow we failed and our self-esteem has been lowered. We have fulfilled their prophecy about us — but then, we may have had very little chance to do anything else.

We also hold many beliefs about others and create our own self-fulfilling prophecies for them. We will return to this type of self-fulfilling prophecy in the chapter on perception when we discuss how our perceptions affect the behavior of others.

Self-Concept Influences the Sending and Receiving of Messages

As sources and receivers, we use our self-concepts to direct our behavior relative to sending or encoding, receiving or decoding, and responding to messages. The process of encoding is influenced by our self-concept, since we are limited in encoding messages to our own experiences in life. It is not surprising, then, that the messages we send identify to others our perception of the world and our self-concept. Have you ever avoided small talk because you were afraid of the other person? Have you ever not taken sides in a controversy because you are uncomfortable in disagreeing with others? Or have you spoken up in an argument because you had knowledge or information on the subject? Our messages are affected by who we think we are — our self-concept. We tend to select messages to be sent that are consistent with our self-concept. Studies employing content analysis techniques have disclosed that certain types of persons utter certain types of statements.[24] Other studies have found that women, who consistently report lower levels of self-esteem than men,[25] use a communication style which projects this low self-concept.[26] Women are more likely to use a "tag question" at the end of their own opinions to request confirmation from the other person ("It's an interesting book, isn't it?"). Women also use more qualifiers when they speak ("sort of," "perhaps"); disclaimers ("I know this probably wouldn't work, but . . ."); and fillers ("uh," "you know," "well," "okay"). This style reflects the lack of confidence typical of someone with low self-esteem.

Similarly, "who one is" operates to create selective attention, so that only certain messages are selected to be received. A message that is inconsistent with our view of our self and of the world is often distorted or misinterpreted in decoding or is ignored entirely. Since our self-concept is our "perception" of ourself, it resists being changed. (See chapter 4 on perception, especially the discussion of the need for consistency in our perceptual structures.) Every time we change our self-concept, even if we are trying to improve our self-concept, we can expect to feel some tension and anxiety. To avoid this discomfort we use many strategies to protect our existing self-concept.[27] We

24. Mervin D. Lynch, "Stylistic Analysis" in Philip Emmert and William D. Brooks, eds., *Methods of Research in Communication* (New York: Houghton Mifflin, 1970), 315–42.

25. G. W. Allport, *Patterns of Growth in Personality* (New York: Holt, Rinehart & Winston, 1961), 130–31.

26. Barbara W. Eakins and R. Gene Eakins, *Sex Differences in Human Communication* (Boston: Houghton Mifflin, 1978), 23–56.

27. Hamachek, 17–28.

rationalize our behavior and the messages of others: "He didn't really understand what I was doing so his evaluation is not clear, not justified, lacks depth . . ." We can also repress our conscious awareness of certain aspects of our self-concepts. This is a kind of selective remembering: "He didn't say/mean that when I talked to him." We can choose to interact only with those who will support our self-concept[28]: "Well, if you think that about me, then we just won't speak to each other anymore." We dislike, disbelieve, and ignore people who disconfirm our self-concept. In communicating with others, we selectively attend to and distort information which does not confirm our self-concept.

28. Argyle, 386–88.

Self-Concept Affects Our Attitude Toward Communicating: Communication Security versus Communication Apprehension

One of the most serious communication problems concerns our attitude toward communicating with others. Individuals with low self-esteem are much more likely to describe themselves as "shy" and **"self-conscious."**[29] This is a common problem for high school and college age students; over 40 percent of these individuals call themselves "shy."[30] From 10 to 20 percent of all college students and adults suffer from extreme shyness or extreme **communication anxiety** or **apprehension.**[31] The percentages are even higher for secondary and elementary school students. According to several studies, a teacher can expect that one out of every four or five students has communication apprehension severe enough to be debilitating. Twenty-four percent of the students in one junior high school reported such problems.[32] Individuals with high communication apprehension have difficulty opening a conversation with a stranger, making small talk, extending conversations, following the point of a discussion and making pertinent contributions, and answering questions in the classroom and on the job — not because they lack the knowledge required but because they have difficulty phrasing and timing their messages.[33] These individuals will choose low status occupations with little monetary reward simply because these are also the occupations which require little communication with others.[34] They will also choose housing, apartments, and dormitories which place them away from high-communication areas. While they would like to date as often as others, they date less while they are in college. However, people with high communication apprehension are more likely to get married before they leave college. Since they find the dating process difficult, they may discover that it is easier to communicate in a permanent relationship. At the very least, they no longer need to initiate as many relationships with others.

People with high communication apprehension either withdraw from interaction with others or develop a very submissive communicator style. The low and timid voice, the avoidance of competitive play, the refusal to communicate with others, the submissive, noncontrolling style which demands that

29. M. Rosenberg, *Society and the Adolescent Self-Image* (Princeton, N.J.: Princeton University Press, 1965).

30. Paul A. Pilkonis, "The Behavioral Consequences of Shyness," *Journal of Personality* 45(1977):596–611.

31. James C. McCroskey, "Classroom Consequences of Communication Apprehension," *Communication Education* 26(1977):27–33.

32. Gerald M. Phillips, "Rhetoritherapy Versus the Medical Model: Dealing with Reticence," *Communication Education* 26(1977):34–43.

33. Ibid., 37.

34. James C. McCroskey, "Oral Communication Apprehension: A Summary of Recent Theory and Research," *Human Communication Research* 4(1977):78–96.

others choose the topics which will be discussed — these are the results of a poor self-concept as a communicator.

When we withdraw from others or respond only when they have initiated the conversation, chosen the topic, and determined how long we will be allowed to speak, we tell others very little about ourselves. As a consequence, even if they would like to meet our needs and develop a relationship with us, they will have difficulty doing so. People with high communication apprehension are often much more critical of their peers, their teachers, and their supervisors than are others,[35] and yet they do not seem to realize that one of the reasons these individuals have difficulty meeting their needs is that they have not allowed their needs to be known.

When an individual experiences unmet interpersonal needs over a long period of time, he or she will begin to mistrust others. This can lead to the individual becoming alienated from others. **Alienation** refers to being estranged or withdrawn from other persons. An alienated person holds negative attitudes toward other persons and has a feeling of ''aloneness.'' Alienation does not mean simple disagreement with another person.[36] Disagreeing with another is communication, but alienation is nonparticipation. It is withdrawing from purposeful interaction because we come to the conclusion that our communication is useless in meeting our needs. It is being apart from others.[37] Alienation cannot occur between a person and someone that person has never known. Rather, it is a withdrawing from a relationship — an estrangement. It can happen between two persons or between a person and a group (family, for example). Alienation between two persons is what we are most interested in here — breakdown of a relationship or change of a positive relationship into a negative one. Often alienation between two persons is partial; that is, one person feels he or she is denied the right to communicate with the other on certain topics — not on all topics — or has been made to understand that he or she cannot communicate at certain times or under certain conditions. Of course, if one is denied the opportunity to communicate on certain topics or at certain times, then some withdrawal from the relationship is a natural consequence. Alienation is the result of being denied, of being ignored, or of not having our needs met in our relationships with others. If this happens enough times and with many persons with whom we normally interact, then anomia-alienation sets in.

Anomia-alienation is a general unwillingness to communicate. It works against effective interpersonal communication in numerous ways[38] besides the obvious, simple nonoccurrence of effective communication. This type of alienation is counterproductive to trust, supportiveness, self-disclosure, helpfulness to others, the enhancing of self-concept, and virtually all the other variables related to interpersonal communication that we discuss in this text.

35. Ibid.

36. Kim Giffin and Bobby R. Patton, *Fundamentals of Impersonal Communication* (New York: Harper & Row, 1971), 186–88.

37. See David J. Burrows and Frederick R. Lapides, eds., *Alienation: A Case Book* (New York: Thomas Y. Crowell, 1969) for illustrative cases of alienation and its withdrawal characteristics.

38. Judee K. Burgoon and Michael Burgoon, ''Unwillingness to Communicate, Anomia-Alienation, and Communication Apprehension as Predictors of Small Group Communication,'' *Journal of Psychology* 88(1974):31–38.

"The truth is, Cauldwell, we never
see ourselves as others see us."

IMPROVING YOUR SELF-CONCEPT

The fully functioning self — the healthy integrated self — possesses at least four characteristics: (1) an awareness of who you are; (2) an acceptance of who you are; (3) a belief in your ability to actualize yourself, to come closer to your ideal self; and (4) an ability to appropriately self-disclose yourself to others.

Self-Awareness: "Who Am I?"

Before you can accept yourself or improve yourself, it is necessary to be aware of yourself. This is a necessary first step. Who are you? Of course, you are not identical to the person you were four years ago, nor are we the same people we were four years ago. Also, we recognize that we will be different people four years from now. We hope we will be better people — better in terms of having achieved more objectives we have for ourselves. The point is that each of us has an *historical self*. It is a part of us and is related to whatever we are at this time. Also, each of us has a *present self,* and each of us has a *future self* — a self we would like to become. Self-awareness consists of knowing the historical self, present self, and future self. As you investigate these areas, you can better answer the question "Who am I?" It may be helpful to take inventories of these three selves.

Historical self-inventory

1. What is my family tree?
2. Where have I lived? What were those places like?
3. Who were my first playmates? First friends?
   Make a list.
4. What games did I play as a child?
5. What chores did I do?
6. What trips did I take?
7. What were the best things that happened to me?
8. What were some of my sad times?
9. What were my goals?
10. What were my fears?

You can add other categories to help you become aware of your historical self.

Present self-inventory: my strengths and weaknesses

1. What kinds of manual tasks am I best/worst at? Typing? Tuning a car? Furniture repair? Gardening? Window washing? Lawn care?
2. What is my strongest special skill? Sculpting? Sewing? Macrame? Interior design? Cooking? Electronics? Auto mechanics? Wordwork? Knitting? Piano playing? Photography? Drama?
3. What sports or games do I perform best/poorest? Skiing? Bridge? Backpacking? Volleyball? Bowling? Hiking? Chess? Swimming? Motorcycling? Football? Driving? Softball? Soccer? Handball? Track? Basketball? Billiards? Wrestling? Hockey? Badminton?
4. Which school subjects are easiest/hardest for me? History? Physical education: Drama? Mathematics? Speech? Geology? Chemistry? Home economics? French? Philosophy? English? Business? Biology?
5. What do I do especially well/poorly as a communicator? Listen? Organize thoughts? Use effective language? Treat others as humans rather than as objects? Make others comfortable? Be myself? Understand others' ideas?
6. What are my strongest/weakest personal characteristics? Loyalty? Enthusiasm? Understanding? Leadership ability? Thoughtfulness? Cheerfulness? Tact? Even temper? Flexibility?

7. Whose love have I been able to return? Children? Parents? Sister(s)? Brother(s)? Boss? Steady date? Best friend? Spouse? Teacher? Grandparents? Other relatives?

This list of strengths and areas for possible improvement does not completely represent your present self. You can continue it, adding other categories.

Future self-inventory
1. What do I want to do vocationally?
2. What are three of my most important future goals?
3. What new experiences do I want to have?
4. Where do I want to live?
5. What do I want to change about myself?

Self-Acceptance

Another factor in improving self-concept is **self-acceptance.** When we begin to accept ourselves and to like ourselves, our total concept of self begins to improve. It is not enough for you to be aware of yourself — your strengths and weaknesses, your positive attitudes and your negative attitudes, your confidences and your fears. You must also accept yourself. This does not mean that you come to like the negative things about yourself, but it means that you do not allow those things to disable you. You are aware of them, but you accept the fact that everyone has weaknesses and that, therefore, not to be perfect is all right and quite normal. As you identify your strengths and develop new strengths, it is easier to accept yourself. If you develop a negative concept of self, if you cannot accept yourself much of the time, if you are unsure as to how acceptable you are to others, then the negative spiral of unacceptableness of self, low self-concept, and ineffective interpersonal communication is set in motion. But if you accept your feelings, beliefs, and relationships as "all right" — if you accept yourself and approve of yourself — you free yourself to a positive spiral of growth.

Harris, a psychologist, has identified four possible positions we can take relative to liking and accepting both ourselves and others.[39] The first such position is that of not accepting oneself or any other person. This is the "I'm not OK and you're not OK" position. This position is characterized by severe withdrawal from others and from self. Such a person is highly self-critical, anxious, insecure, depressed, cynical, and defensive.

A second possible position is "I'm not OK, but you're OK." A person with this attitude is fearful of his or her ability to live in the world, fearful of being inadequate for the challenges and problems of life. Such a person adopts strategies to hide and conceal the self, holds others in awe and is compliant and willing to allow others to control him because he feels inferior to others.

39. Thomas A. Harris, *I'm OK — You're OK* (New York: Harper & Row, 1967).

A third orientation is "I'm OK, but you're not OK." This creates a superiority attitude. Such a person rejects support and help from others, avoids getting involved with others, and is ultra-independent.

Finally, there is a fourth position, that of liking oneself and others. It is the "I'm OK and you're OK" orientation. This person accepts himself or herself and others, is free, can establish meaningful relationships with others, and is reinforcing and supportive in relations with others.

Hamachek, a psychologist, has characterized the person who likes and accepts himself or herself even more specifically and extensively than has Harris.[40] Hamachek identified eleven characteristics of the person who likes and accepts the self:

40. D. E. Hamachek, *Encounters with the Self* (New York: Holt, Rinehart & Winston, 1971), 248–51.

1. Has certain values and principles believed in strongly and is willing to defend them even in the face of strong group opinion; however, feels personally secure enough to modify them if new experience and evidence suggest an error.

2. Is capable of acting on own best judgment without feeling excessively guilty or regretful if others disapprove.

3. Does not spend undue time worrying about what is coming tomorrow or being upset by today's experience or fussing over yesterday's mistakes.

4. Retains confidence in ability to deal with problems, even in the face of failure or setbacks.

5. Feels equal to others *as a person* — neither superior nor inferior — irrespective of differences in specific abilities, family backgrounds, or attitudes of others.

6. Takes more or less for granted that he or she is a person of interest and value to others — at least to those with whom he or she chooses to associate.

7. Can accept praise without the pretense of false modesty . . . and compliments without feeling guilty.

8. Is inclined to resist the efforts of others to dominate, especially when they are peers.

9. Is able to accept (and admit to others) the capability of feeling a wide range of impulses and desires, from being very angry to being very loving, from being very sad to being very happy, from feeling deep resentment to feeling great acceptance.

10. Is able to genuinely enjoy a wide variety of activities, involving work, play, creative self-expression, companionship, or just loafing.

11. Is sensitive to the needs of others, to social customs, and particularly to the idea that one cannot, willy-nilly, go about "self-actualizing" oneself at the expense of others.

The fully functioning self is identified by these attitudes or behaviors of liking and accepting oneself, and by an extensive repertoire of communication skills which help him or her develop effective interpersonal relationships with others.

Self-Actualization

Self-acceptance does not mean that you cease trying to improve. But it does mean that you will make the most of your strengths. You are you, with strengths as well as weaknesses, and you accept yourself that way. You will also continue to improve yourself because you will see yourself as capable of meeting new challenges and fulfilling the requirements of being successful — i.e., you will have the ability to see yourself as actualized and confident in your intellectual, social, and physical abilities and as constantly developing and acquiring new strengths.

Self-actualization means making the "ideal self" real or actual. It is "becoming who you want to be," and that is the greatest thing that can happen to you. It involves growth. It comes about only from your own motivation and your own willingness to work to improve yourself. As you come to know yourself, you are aware of the things about yourself that you like and the things that you do not like very well. If you want to change your interpersonal relationships, you are going to have to take steps to make it happen. If you want to improve your interpersonal communication skills, to allow others to know you better, then you must make the effort to become more self-actualized.

Self-Disclosure: Sharing Your Self-Concept with Others

People cannot see into our minds. They do not hear our thoughts, experience our hurts, or sense the happy feelings that surge through us. How can they know these things if we do not tell them through our verbal or nonverbal communication? If we close ourselves off to others, we isolate ourselves, and that is what is happening to many people in our world. The opposite of closing oneself to others is opening oneself. We call this **self-disclosure.** It is sharing, disclosing, and revealing something about oneself to another person.

There are two dimensions to self-disclosure: depth and breadth.[41] Breadth of self-disclosure refers to how many topics we are willing to discuss and reveal ourselves on to any given person. Depth refers to the level of intimacy in our self-disclosure for any given topic. In any relationship that we have with another individual, we can have breadth but not depth and reveal ourselves impersonally on many topics; or we can have depth but not breadth and reveal ourselves intimately but only on a few topics. Our breadth and depth are never the same for any two relationships.

41. Irwin Altman and Dalmas A. Taylor, *Social Penetration: The Development of Interpersonal Relationships* (New York: Holt, Rinehart & Winston, 1973), 15–16.

We reveal ourselves differently to every person we interact with.

42. A. W. Gouldner, "The Norm of Reciprocity: A Preliminary Statement," *American Sociological Review* 25(1960):161-78.

We sometimes become uncomfortable with the depth of another's self-disclosure when we are conversing with them. This happens because there appears to be a "norm of reciprocity"[42] in our culture which obligates us to return a self-disclosure at the same, or similar, depth we receive from the other person. If someone is telling us something very intimate about himself or herself, we will not feel that we have been "fair" in the interaction unless we reciprocate. When this happens we may self-disclose ourselves more intimately than we wish and feel uncomfortable, or we may change the topic and substitute breadth of self-disclosure for depth of self-disclosure. One reason we are hesitant to make disclosures is that we fear rejection. When we reveal something new about ourselves to someone that is a significant part of us, we are fearful that the person may not accept it. We are afraid that the person may laugh or in other ways reject us. Or sometimes what we want to reveal is a negative feeling we have toward the person and yet do not want to hurt the person or cause the person to react negatively against us. Some research suggests that men and women have different fears concerning self-disclosure.[43] Men are more likely to report that they avoid self-disclosure because they do not want to lose control over the other person or over other relationships which might be affected by their self-disclosure in this relationship. Women avoid self-disclosure because they fear they will be personally

43. Lawrence B. Rosenfeld, "Self-Disclosure Avoidance: Why I am Afraid to Tell You Who I am," *Communication Monographs* 46(1967):63-74.

hurt by the other's reaction or that problems will develop which will hurt the relationship they have with that person. For any of these reasons, and others, it is often easier to cover up and to mask our true feelings and true selves.

Dropping False Masks

Too often we will not reveal ourselves but try instead to appear to be something else. Ours is a success-oriented society, and so we are taught to appear successful. We come to believe that we simply *must* appear intelligent, healthy, clean, and attractive to other persons. Thus most of the time when we are interacting with others we are trying to create the appearance of being *superpersons*. Too often what we offer is a sham rather than our real selves. We are fearful that other persons may not like us, so we spend our time and energy attempting to maintain that false front. We are afraid to risk exposing who we really are. The result is that a good many relationships are based on

The Self in Communication: The Role of Self-Concept

contact between two imitation selves. We attempt to show how smart, knowledgeable, and wonderful we are, while we hide our true feelings lest we expose our ignorance or unattractiveness. As in the Peanuts comic strip that illustrated this behavior, we may hide the fact that all we see is a ducky because we think we ought to be brilliant — that we ought to be seeing a famous painting or a sophisticated design.

When we pretend to be what we are not, three things can happen. First, we waste energy and concentration. Our attention is on our own performance rather than on the other person, so we miss the messages and clues which tell us what the other person is feeling and how that person is perceiving us.

Second, pretending to be who we are not is dangerous because we may not be good enough at acting to carry it off. In fact, such acts are almost impossible to carry off. The falsity in us sooner or later slips out. This "being caught in a false face" is damaging to us as communicators because we lose credibility. We hardly want those with whom we have interacted to go away saying, "What a stupid, tragic clown! What a phony!" When the other person discovers our falsity, that person cannot further depend on anything we have to say. Rather than creating confidence and trust, we engender doubt and suspicion.

Third, when we pretend to be what we are not, we do not allow others to know our real selves so they cannot possibly meet our real interpersonal needs. They will be attempting to meet the needs of the false person we are portraying. We are contributing to the failure of our relationship and should not be surprised when we are not satisfied or happy in that relationship.

One of the ways we avoid self-disclosure is through inappropriate use of silence and ritualized communication. It is true that both silence and ritual communication can serve constructively in interpersonal communication if used appropriately. It is the misuse of silence as an escape or hiding mechanism that is the problem. Such use of silence is seen by others as communicating indifference and/or an unwillingness to relate. For many people such silence may not really mean that they are indifferent or unwilling to relate. They may, in fact, desire companionship, but their fear of exposing themselves is so great that they sit mute. In any event, the other person interprets that kind of silence as unwillingness to relate and reacts by rejecting the silent person. This silence behavior is counterproductive and self-defeating.

Similarly, **ritualized communication,** pastimes, chit chat, and games can be used to avoid more open communication. One can hide in ritual. It is an easy way to avoid being ourselves. Ritualized conversations are often extremely shallow, carried on according to a kind of formula that avoids, almost entirely, honest communication. Being open is difficult because it means being vulnerable, but in human relationships vulnerability is a precondition of effective communication. We should increase our willingness to be vulnerable, to reveal ourselves. All this is *not* to suggest that there is just one "real" self, or

Figure 3.2 The Johari Window.

	Known to Self	Not Known to Self
Known to Others	I Free Area	II Blind Area
Not Known to Others	III Hidden Area	IV Unknown Area

that we should always reveal ourselves totally and immediately in every interpersonal communication situation. In fact, to try to be the same person in every situation and every encounter would be as harmful and counterproductive to effective interpersonal communication as to try to hide behind a known false image (and just as false, we might add). Every one of us is made up of various selves. The relationships and roles we each fulfill with our mothers, friends, bosses, and so on vary from person to person. We are not a single, absolute set of attitudes, behaviors, and relationships to all persons. The relationship we have with each is unique. The self we reveal in each of these encounters, however, needs to be an honest one — congruent with our feelings, meanings, and desired behaviors in that specific encounter — not knowingly false and sham. We must risk our real selves!

Seeking Out Trustworthy and Caring Persons

Before we can disclose, however, we need to seek out trustworthy and caring persons. We observed earlier in this chapter that our self-concept develops through interaction with others. To an extent, then, self-concept is related to the quality of the people with whom we interact. If we interact with people who will support our efforts to build a realistic and positive self-concept, we will find it easier to disclose ourselves because we will feel less vulnerable. But the primary responsibility for self-disclosure is our own.

There are yet two ideas we need to consider relative to self-disclosure: (1) how much should we disclose? and (2) what kinds of self-disclosure we should use.

Appropriate Self-Disclosure

Joseph Luft and Harry Ingham created a disclosure model, which they named for themselves. They called it the **Johari window**.[44] The Johari window has four panes, representing what you know about yourself and what the other person knows of you. It is illustrated in figure 3.2.

For purposes of self-disclosure, the free area (I) represents what you willingly reveal about yourself to the other person. The hidden area (III) represents what you could reveal but choose to keep hidden. The blind area (II) represents

44. Reprinted from Joseph Luft, *Group Processes: An Introduction to Group Dynamics* (Palo Alto, Calif.: Mayfield Publishing Co., 1970); Johari window also published in Joseph Luft, *Of Human Interaction* (Palo Alto, Calif.: National Press Books, 1969).

what the other person knows about you that you do not know about yourself. You are blind to it; it is not in your self-awareness. Similarly, the unknown area (IV) is not known to you or to the other person. The process of self-disclosure enlarges area I and decreases area III. Willingness to receive information from another about yourself can enlarge area I while decreasing area II.

You might draw Johari windows that picture your relationship with other persons — one to illustrate the relationship you have with your mother; another for your best friend; yet a third for the new person you met last week. These Johari windows would show how much you have shared and received from the other person in these dyadic relationships. As a person discloses more to the other person, the free area grows larger while the blind area and hidden area both decrease in size. Of course, the better you get to know someone and the greater the trust that develops in the relationship, the more self-disclosing and open you become in sharing feelings, opinions, and thoughts.

There are norms and rules for self-disclosure in most cultures. We do not tell a stranger our deepest, most intimate thoughts, nor do we disclose our perceived weaknesses to the waitress who serves us coffee in a restaurant. Identifying some of the different kinds of self-disclosure may help you to know what kind of disclosure is appropriate in a given situation. The type and depth of disclosure ought to be determined by the kind of relationship you have with the other person.

Impersonal Information   The safest or lowest level is probably that exchanged with strangers during the acquaintance process. We exchange demographic information, our names, where we live, what we do; we discuss people we might both know, places we have visited, events we might both have been to, and similar impersonal things. This sharing is an important beginning in an interpersonal relationship because it indicates a willingness to be open and friendly.

Personal Information   Another level of disclosure is the sharing of personal information. We begin to tell others what we think about some of the places, people, and events we have previously discussed impersonally. We begin to share some of our opinions. Recently a colleague was having an interesting and pleasant conversation with a clerk in a large department store. They were exchanging personal information while she was carrying out his business transaction, and she said in the midst of their joking, "You're a Virgo, aren't you?" He admitted that he was, and she said, "I knew it! You're friendly and have a great time!" Taking a shot in the dark, he replied, "And I'll bet you're a Virgo too!" She was, and she then proceeded to give her philosophy of work and fun. They had rapidly moved from "weather talk" to exchanges of personal information. That exchange, however, was not at the level of disclosing deep feelings or revealing frustrations, concerns, or fears, as one might in a more intimate relationship.

Disclosing Feelings   Another kind of sharing is the sharing of feelings. Of course, we can share our general feelings in conversations with acquaintances, classmates, persons with whom we work, and so on, but these feelings are often "polite," toned down, and even disguised and distorted. Genuine sharing of feelings is one of the most difficult kinds of self-disclosure. Even when we would like to share our feelings we are often afraid to do so or we feel it would be inappropriate to do so. Very often we simply do not tell others how we feel because we assume they should "just be able to know how I feel." In fact, very often people do not know how we feel unless we tell them. Tell the other person "I'm happy for you," "I'm sad for you," "I like what you did," or "What you did bothered me."

Sometimes we express our feelings incorrectly.[45] We hurt or anger the other person by accusing them, or labeling them, or being sarcastic, or shouting commands at them. The other person has to guess from our behavior what feeling is underneath. Sometimes it is fairly apparent that we are angry, but at other times we are so sophisticated and concealing that the other person has trouble knowing our true feeling.

We need to learn how to express our feelings in positive ways. Learning to express feelings constructively helps us in two ways:[46] (1) Finding the right words to express a feeling helps us identify and understand our feelings. (2) Constructive disclosure of our feelings can enable the other person to understand us and then to meet our needs. It can lead to a better relationship with the other person. We will examine the constructive expression of feelings further in chapter 7 when we discuss increasing your skill in delivering effective feedback to others.

If we desire to improve our relationships with other people, then effective self-disclosure must concern us. When we feel a commitment to a relationship and to another person, we will want to share our self-concept, to disclose ourselves to that person. In doing this we make a commitment to improve, to grow, and to actualize our potential as human beings.

45. David W. Johnson, *Reaching Out: Interpersonal Effectiveness and Self-Actualization* (Englewood Cliffs, N.J.: Prentice-Hall, 1972), 91–92.

46. Ibid.

Summary

Each of us has many self-concepts. Five aspects of our self-concept are discussed to help explain our multiplicity of "selves." Whether we are self-monitors or situation/other monitors will affect how we perceive our self-concept(s) and how we communicate to others.

Our self-concept consists of our self-image(s) and our self-esteem. Self-image is the result of being categorized by others; self-esteem results from being rewarded and punished by others. Individuals with a poor self-concept, low self-esteem, behave differently and have different attitudes toward themselves, toward others, and toward the communication process than do individuals with high self-esteem.

While we will need to redefine our self-concept many times during our lifetime, adolescence is commonly a time of identity crisis during which significant changes in self-concept occur for most of us.

Our self-concept is the basis for self-fulfilling prophecies we make for ourselves. Other people also affect our self-concept by eliciting behavior from us that fulfills their prophecies about us. Our self-concept determines which messages we receive accurately and which ones we distort. It affects how and what messages we send to others. Our concept concerning ourselves as "communicators" strongly affects the way we communicate to others.

We can improve our self-concept by becoming more aware of who we are and by learning to accept ourselves. Eleven characteristics of a healthy self-concept are identified. A healthy self-concept promotes individual growth and self-actualization.

Self-disclosure, the sharing of our self-concepts with others, is an important part of developing effective interpersonal relationships. Two aspects of self-disclosure, breadth and depth, are discussed. The importance of seeking out trustworthy and caring others, of following the norms for self-disclosure, and of dropping the false masks we wear when we are interacting with others is stressed. It is our responsibility to let others know us so they can meet our interpersonal needs.

4

Perceiving and Understanding Others

Objectives for the Reader

1. To be able to explain the difference between physically sensing stimuli and perceiving stimuli.
2. To be able to explain the structuralist and Gestalt approaches to perception.
3. To be able to relate the principles of the Gestalt approach to perception in interpersonal communication.
4. To be able to distinguish between the trait theory and the implicit personality theory of person perception.
5. To be able to explain the three components of interpersonal attraction.
6. To be able to explain the eight factors which have a significant effect on our perception of the interpersonal attractiveness of others.
7. To be able to explain why open, trusting, self-revealing messages can result in our being trusted more by those to whom we direct those messages.

As you read this book, what are you experiencing? We hope most of you experience the words and illustrations on the pages and, of course, the meanings we associate with these symbols. However, at any given time, you are experiencing considerably more. For instance, you may have a feeling of hunger if it has been a long time since you ate; or you could have a feeling of satiation if you just finished a meal.

Ordinarily we are not acutely conscious of such feelings when we are engaged in activities such as reading or talking with people, and yet we are experiencing them. We are experiencing other sensations too, such as the heat or cold of the room we are in. If we are not in a room, we may experience the feel of wind on our skin and in our hair. No matter where we are, we also detect lightness or darkness, depending on how our room is lighted or what the condition of the sky is. We also experience the sounds that come from heating systems, street traffic, fluorescent light fixtures, animals, and possibly conversations and/or radios or television sets outside or in our room. Rarely can we sit down and read a book and experience nothing but the book.

PERCEPTION CREATES OUR WORLD

If we stop to consider all the sensations we are experiencing at any given moment, it seems remarkable that we are not driven totally out of our minds by the chaotic bombardment of stimuli we receive. Yet, for most of us, this poses no problem because of the process known as **perception.** Very simply stated, *perception is a mental process in which we select, organize, and interpret the many stimuli that impinge on us at any given moment.*[1] It is very easy to overlook the hundreds of different sensations we experience every moment of our lives. It is not possible to list them all, but if you consider experiences by seeing, hearing, smelling, touching, and tasting, it must be obvious that we are receivers of a multitude of sensations.

It is important now to understand that there is a major difference between *sensing* stimuli and *perceiving* them. Experiencing sensation involves the physical reception of the stimuli.[2] If the temperature of the room in which you are reading this chapter is approximately sixty or sixty-five degrees, you experience a physical sensation in your feet, especially if you have no shoes or socks on. Without prior experience, it would be impossible to translate that particular physical sensation into a meaningful concept. The concept that has meaning for us is "cold," but to say that you experience "cold" is incorrect. You actually experience a certain arrangement and action of molecules, and then, given all the other sensations affecting you while reading this chapter, you select particular sets of physical sensations and interpret them as "cold."

In a room temperature of sixty or sixty-five degrees, you select from among the many stimuli available at the moment those that are important to you and exclude those that are not. We hope you are selecting among stimuli and organizing them so that sensations involving certain visual stimuli (books and notes) receive greater attention than the sensation you interpret as "cold."

The stimuli you select and organize for your attention are important to you because of your past experiences and needs. This would suggest, then, that as a result of our experiences with things, events, and people, *we learn to perceive.*[3]

1. Charles M. Butter, *Neuropsychology: The Study of Brain and Behavior* (Belmont, Calif.: Brooks Cole, 1968), 39.

2. Ibid.

3. John W. McDavid and Herbert Harari, *Social Psychology: Individuals, Groups, Societies* (New York: Harper & Row, 1968), 104–44.

If we could bring to mind the moment of our birth, we would say it must have been a very confusing and frightening time. A baby is born into a world in which there are unceasing sensations with little or no organization or meaning. This must be very disturbing indeed. It is no wonder babies sometimes cry when they are alone. The process of perception is not one we are necessarily equipped with at birth (at least not in the same way we have it throughout our lives). Certainly, at the moment of birth, we begin trying to select from and interpret the chaotic stimuli we receive. At some early point in our lives (whether it is prenatal or postnatal, we don't know), we learn to perceive through the experiences we have.

We are concerned with the process of perception in interpersonal communication because communication usually involves both visual and aural stimuli at least, and we must select, organize, and interpret these stimuli whenever we are in an interpersonal situation. We perceive what we think other people are communicating to us, and we also have perceptions of the communicators themselves.[4] Of course, we also perceive ourselves (as was discussed in chapter 3).

To understand the role of perception in interpersonal communication, it is necessary for us to consider some of the basic principles of perception. We cannot in the amount of space available in a book on interpersonal communication cover the process of perception in depth. However, we can cover

4. Fritz Heider, ``Consciousness, The Perceptual World Inc., and Communication With Others,'' in Ranao Tagiuri and Luigi Petrullo, eds., *Person Perception and Interpersonal Behavior* (Stanford, Calif.: Stanford University Press, 1958), 27–32.

those principles of perception that are especially relevant to an understanding of the basic process and how that process relates to interpersonal communication. That is the objective of the first section of this chapter. In the second section we apply these principles of perception to the way we see other people. In the third section we discuss perception as it affects interpersonal communication. The more you are able to ignore stimuli unrelated to the topics of interpersonal communication and perception so you can focus your attention on the text and your response to the text, the better you will understand perception and the role it plays in interpersonal communication.

Continuous Reception

One basic principle, to which we have already alluded, is that we constantly receive stimuli.[5] *The human being is an open and constant receptor.* Any individual has many receptors (related to the five senses of taste, smell, touch, hearing, and sight). The receptors are open at all times (if there is no physical impairment), so we constantly receive all physical stimuli present in our environment. This means that the world around us has a kind of immediacy.[6] Everything about us is received and translated into nerve impulses and transmitted through the nervous system.[7]

In interpersonal communication, it is especially important to realize that at any given moment, we are not only receiving stimuli from those with whom we are interacting, but we are also receiving other stimuli, any of which can affect our perception of the interpersonal situation.[8] At a party you may be talking with your date and yet also be experiencing the sights and sounds (and possibly the odors and touches) of other males and females in the room. Depending on how you perceive these other stimuli, you may or may not interact in a manner satisfactory to your date. Sometimes this results in a couple splitting up and going home with other persons. This example demonstrates how we receive stimuli continuously and also how interpersonal communication is affected by perception.

How Perception Works

How we receive and process the many different stimuli about us has been a source of concern in the social and behavioral sciences for many years. Several approaches have been taken. The assumptions made by different groups relate to their approach to the perception process. Two basic approaches, with differing assumptions, have been evident over time. These are the structuralist approach and the Gestalt approach.

5. David J. Schneider, Albert Hastorf and Phoebe C. Ellsworth, *Person Perception,* 2d ed. (Reading, Mass.: Addison-Wesley, 1979), 1–7.

6. Ibid.

7. Butter, *Neuropsychology,* 38.

8. Bruce H. Westley and Malcolm S. MacLean, Jr., "A Conceptual Model for Communications Research," *Journalism Quarterly* 35(1957):31–38.

Structuralist Approach

Scholars who take the **structuralist approach** have held that perception can be viewed as the process of combining all the sensations we receive through our different receptors into a single perception.[9] An assumption of the structuralist approach is that there are specific receptors programmed to receive specific stimuli.[10] A further assumption is that once the appropriate stimuli fall on the appropriate sensory receptors, the sensations received by all of them together can be added up to produce a perception. This is an additive approach. If we have a friend who is six feet tall, male, dresses in blue jeans and sweat shirts, likes symphonic music, drinks French wines, and is soft-spoken (we could add many other characteristics), it would be possible to say that our perception of that friend is the sum total of all the properties that our appropriate receptors received. This approach to perception is less in favor today, because many people suggest that a perception of an individual (or of any physical event) consists of a great deal more than the sum of the individual parts.[11]

Gestalt Approach

While Gestalt psychologists developed their approach to psychology quite independently, many of their views of the perceptual process represent some reaction to the structuralists.[12] Essentially, the **Gestalt approach** suggests that our perceptions are not the sum of many independent sensations; rather, we perceive perceptual wholes.[13]

While we may have many receptors constantly doing their job of receiving the many different stimuli present in our environment, our perception of physical events consists of more than a summation of parts.[14] It is almost impossible to explain our feelings for another person, for example, by cataloging his or her qualities or behaviors toward us.

The Gestalt approach — that we perceive something as a whole rather than as individual parts which we then put together — has resulted in some laws of perception that are accepted by most behavioral scientists today. Three of the **Gestalt principles of perception** have special relevance to interpersonal communication and, more specifically, to our perception of other people in interpersonal situations.

Proximity The first Gestalt principle of perception concerns what has been called the **principle of proximity** or *resemblance*.[15] It has also been referred to by communication scholars as the phenomenon of ''grouping.''[16] Things located and/or grouped together in close proximity with one another are perceived as a whole. From a purely visual point of view, two people who are standing next to each other in a room filled with many people will appear to

9. Julian E. Hochberg, *Perception* (Englewood Cliffs, N.J.: Prentice-Hall, 1964), 12.

10. Ibid.

11. Ibid.

12. Hochberg, *Perception*, 31–34.

13. McDavid and Harari, *Social Psychology*, 30.

14. S. Howard Bartley, *Principles of Perception* (New York: Harper & Row, 1958), 85.

15. William N. Dember, *The Psychology of Perception* (New York: Holt, Rinehart & Winston, 1966), 162.

16. Ronald L. Applbaum et al., *Fundamental Concepts in Human Communication* (San Francisco: Canfield Press, 1973), 21.

Figure 4.1

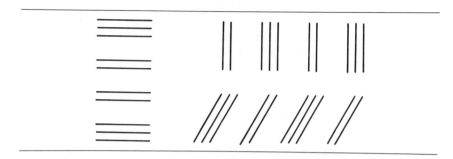

be "together." They are perceived as being a couple or as part of an interaction unit. Similarly, two people who look somewhat alike are paired or assumed to be relatives. Implications of this kind crop up frequently with brothers and sisters who bear family resemblances. If we see them together and we notice these resemblances, we perceive them as a "pair."

In figure 4.1, you can see examples of lines that can be perceived as units of a larger whole. We tend to perceive the lines as groups of two or three because of their physical closeness to one another. In like manner — even though this is impossible to represent on the printed page — we group sounds. For instance, Morse code symbols of long and short sounds are perceived in units because the symbols for individual letters come close together in time.

One of the effects of the principle of proximity or grouping is observable when communicators associate themselves, as they frequently do, with persons of high prestige in the expectation that with the resultant grouping, benefits of that high prestige will rub off on them. A kind of "gilt" by association occurs.[17] By the same token, some communicators suffer by being seen socially with someone of low status or low repute; then "guilt" by association occurs.

Good Form　Another principle of perception suggested by Gestaltists has been referred to as the **principle of good form.**[18] Good form, as it occurs within our environment, is a naturally perceived whole and involves closure. The dots in figure 4.2(a) can be perceived grouped as straight lines. If they are perceived in that way, the solid dots form a plus sign for us. What is meant by *common fate* is also shown in figure 4.2(a): the parts of each "line" appear in some respect to have the same directionality, to be going to the same place.

Similarly, in figure 4.2(b) what appear to be two semicircles are perceived as a complete circle. In this case the *symmetry* contributes to the perception.

Closure also occurs when we complete an incomplete figure without symmetry. In figure 4.3 we see the letters of the alphabet. All of them are incomplete yet enough of the patterns are there so that we know what the letters are and by acts of closure, we perceive wholes.

17. James C. McCroskey and Robert E. Dunham, "Ethos: A Confounding Element in Communication Research," *Speech Monographs* 32(1966):456–63.

18. James Deese, *General Psychology* (Boston: Allyn & Bacon, 1967), 277–311.

Figure 4.2

Figure 4.3

Whenever we "leave something to the imagination" of the people we are talking to, we are taking advantage of the closure phenomenon. Likewise, closure is frequently used in speaking. Whenever we say, "But you can guess the rest," we are relying on the listener to fill in what is missing. By causing our listeners to "fill in the blanks," we may well be more effective in our impact on them, since they are expending energy to complete our point.

Search for Order   The third basic Gestalt principle of perception (and a very important concept for us in interpersonal communication) is what is called the **search for order.**[19] We have previously discussed the chaotic world of sensations, in which we are constantly being bombarded by stimuli of many different sorts. The Gestaltists suggest that we have the need to determine some kind of consistency or order in all this chaos. It is as though the chaos itself represents a threat to our existence. If we can extend this notion a bit further and apply to it some of the material in chapter 1, it makes sense. People are actually trying to carve out some sort of niche for themselves in the world of random events about them.

One of the things necessary for us to do in meeting our needs, then, is to discern an orderliness in the world. Predictability is necessary because it enables us to manipulate the world.[20] Consider for a moment: if the world were random and had no order, it would be impossible to predict what would happen as a result of any of our behaviors. To manipulate the world (in order to control our environment), it is necessary for us to know various kinds of cause-and-effect relationships in the world, so we try to perceive whatever order we can. This appears to affect the way we perceive things.

19. Deese, *General Psychology,* 277–311.

20. Albert H. Hastorf, David J. Schneider, and Judith Polefka, *Person Perception* (Reading, Mass.: Addison-Wesley 1970), 1–10.

We can perceive whole pictures from unconnected dots.

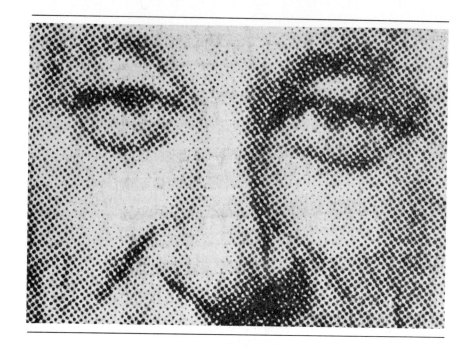

Bombarded by stimuli, we attempt to perceive order or organization among them. Thus, in figure 4.2(a), in which there are many dots, it is almost a natural inclination on our part to hunt for some kind of ordered perception among the available stimuli. We find a plus sign here, for all of the reasons suggested by the Gestalt perceptual principles. This search for order may account for our concern for organization in conversation. It could be a good reason always (even in informal situations) to put our thoughts in order before we attempt to communicate.

Because of this need for order,[21] Schneider, Hastorf, and Ellsworth suggest the existence of three perceptual responses to the chaotic world. In order to bring order into our world, we categorize stimuli, stabilize our perceptions, and attach meanings to our sensations. By doing these things we increase our perception of order in our world.

Categorization

We structure the world of sensations about us.[22] We are not satisfied with a random set of occurrences. We order things, assign priorities, categorize, take all the various incoming stimuli, and build a structure for ourselves. We do this through a **categorization** process that is greatly affected by our language and by our past history. We use language in this process.[23] We can categorize different kinds of organisms such as dogs, cats, and horses, and by so doing

21. Ibid.

22. Ibid.

23. J. S. Bruner, "The Course of Cognitive Growth," *American Psychologist* 19(1964):1–15; A. R. Luria, "The Directive Function of Speech in Development and Dissolution; Part 1, Development of the Directive Function of Speech in Early Childhood," *Word* 15(1959):341–52.

we establish an order among living creatures. By this process we create a system with which we can deal. (Language and its relationship to the physical world is discussed in greater detail in chapter 5.)

We go much further than the simple naming of things in our categorization system: we talk about cattle as food; we talk about dogs as man's best friend. We also categorize people, and this can have a significant impact on our interpersonal relationships. For instance, we categorize one group of people as very intelligent, another group as very crafty, and yet another group as dangerous. The problem is that this structure of the world which we develop to aid us in coping with the world becomes the filter through which we view it.[24]

We know some people who are anti-Semitic. Among their categorizations of the world is their classification of Jewish people as wealthy, clannish, and very different from "their own" kind of people. Some years ago, we were invited by some Jewish friends to spend Thanksgiving with them. We did so and experienced the usual traditional Thanksgiving of the sort that Norman Rockwell used to picture in the *Saturday Evening Post*. Upon hearing of this visit, these acquaintances reacted with "I didn't know Jews celebrated Thanksgiving." This was a very revealing statement because the categorizations, or the labels, that had been developed by these people for the purpose of structuring the world were operating to ensure that any future perceptions were in accord with their categorization system. This system would almost prevent these friends from perceiving Jews as ever being anything but very different from other people.

An interesting question is: Where do our category systems come from? The answer is they are an outgrowth of our past history. For example, research has shown that children who grow up in poor families perceive coins to be bigger than do children who grow up in wealthy families.[25] In fact, we are involved in a circular process: our language and our past history condition how we categorize the physical world,[26] and these categories then condition our perceptions.

Stabilizing Perceptions

In addition to categorizing the world of sensations in which we live, we also *attempt to impose consistency on our perceptions.*[27] We want our perceptions to be stable. As we stand in an airport and watch a plane land, the actual size of the plane that is being projected onto our retinal wall changes: when the plane is very distant and high, the image projected onto our retinal wall is small; as the plane nears the landing strip (and subsequently the terminal), the image actually projected on the retinal wall increases in size.

We all know perfectly well that the plane is not increasing in size. Consequently, through the process of perception (which is an interpretive process), we perceive the plane as remaining the same size but interpret the growth of the image on our retinal wall to mean that the plane is coming nearer to us.

24. Charles C. Spiker, "Verbal Factors in the Discrimination Learning of Children," *Monograph of the Society for Research in Child Development* 28 (1963):53–69.

25. J. S. Bruner and C. C. Goodman, "Value and Need as Organizing Factors in Perception," *Journal of Abnormal and Social Psychology* 42(1947):33–44.

26. Benjamin Lee Whorf, "Language Mind, and Reality," *Etc., a Review of General Semantics* 9(1952):167–88.

27. Schneider, Hastorf, and Ellsworth, *Person Perception.*

When the plane is distant, it is smaller; when it is nearer, it is larger. At no time do we actually begin to interpret that objects in the physical world outside literally grow in size as they come closer to us. In our perceptions, we impose consistency on the world and the objects about us, even though the physical stimuli we are receiving may be constantly varying in size, shape, sound, and color. We do this to preserve the order we have established in our initial world-view structure. This, of course, relates to the Gestalt principle of our search for order. By imposing consistency on our perceptions, we help preserve that order.

We also impose consistency on our interpersonal perceptions. How many times have you met someone you haven't seen for several years and been surprised at "how much they've changed"? Sometimes we have trouble adjusting to the fact that none of our friends and loved ones stay the same. We are all always changing; however, our need for order results in our stabilizing our perceptions. We can probably improve our interpersonal communication skills by remembering that people change even though our perceptions may not. We should then adjust our perceptions accordingly to improve our interpersonal accuracy and effectiveness.

Attaching Meanings to Sensations

28. Ibid.

We attach meaning to all the sensations we have.[28] In some communication texts this has been termed *decoding* (we receive physical stimuli and translate them into some sort of meaning for ourselves).[29] Actually, it is important in interpersonal communication to realize that the imposition of meaning on physical sensations involves a great deal more than simply associating a given meaning with a given stimulus.

29. David K. Berlo, *The Process of Communication* (New York: Holt, Rinehart & Winston, 1960), 31.

We were speaking earlier of the individual's need to structure the world. If such structuring of the world involves **micromeanings** (individual categorization of stimuli), then what we are talking about now should be considered **macromeaning.** We are concerned about relationships among different categories, different stimuli, and different structures.[30] This is a larger structure of the world that goes quite beyond the naming and categorization of things. It is as if we cannot stop at the creation of a simple structure. We also have to determine the relationships among the component parts of that structure. We cannot simply name dark clouds "rain clouds" and water that falls out of the sky "rain." Rather, to have an adequate predictive sense of the way things are in the world, we must establish the relationship between dark clouds and water that falls out of the sky and hits us on the face. The relationship becomes of paramount importance, just as the relationship between whistling and saying "Here, Spot" results in a little furry four-legged creature running to our feet. These relationships are part of our total perception of order in the world, and it is the perception of relationships that enables us to make predictions in

30. Schneider, Hastorf, and Ellsworth, *Person Perception*, 6–7.

the world. Being able to make predictions, in turn, makes it possible for us to manipulate the world in ways that satisfy our needs. Thus, when we perceive a physical stimulus we do not simply interpret a given object; we also interpret the relationship of that object to other objects about it.

To understand the approach just presented, picture a being from another planet happening onto one of our large athletic stadiums on a Saturday afternoon in the fall. That being would discover a tremendous number of people sitting on two sides of a rectangular field with white lines drawn all over it. (It is impossible to describe this situation without making use of some of the categories we have in our past history; but for the moment consider the plight of the extraterrestrial perceiving this and trying to understand it.)

First, it is necessary for our interplanetary visitor to structure the perceptions on a microlevel in which he, she, or it can classify people, the colors of uniforms, groups that appear to be near one another, and maybe even the existence of two different teams (because of the symmetry involved when the two are facing each other.) Although our visitor may be standing at one end of the field, with the teams running close and then far away, it is certainly possible for this observer to maintain observational consistency. Then, of course, to understand what is going on, it is necessary for the visitor to attach meaning to sensations received in terms of the relationships observed among the stimuli. As a matter of fact, we can think of no other way to explain what is going on in a football game than by considering the relationships among all the participants.

Note that in our interpersonal relationships we categorize at the micromeaning level when we call a person by name — for instance, Fred. We also categorize according to macromeanings when we use words like "friend," "pal," "sweetheart," "mother," and "father." Each of these words has relationship implications tied to it. Thus, when we talk, our language structures our perceptions of the objects, people, and things in our life and the relationships among them.

Perceiving the World: A Brief Summation

The view of perception presented here is derived from the Gestalt approach. In interpersonal communication we are concerned with perceptual wholes. Likewise, we are engaged in a search for order in our perceptions. As a result, we attempt to structure our perceptions of the world in a consistent manner so that our sensations are not left unordered. Finally, we impose upon our perceptions our own meanings and perceived relationships. All this enables us to perceive a more ordered, highly structured world; and that, in turn, enables us to predict more easily, which enables us to manipulate the world according to our needs because we are able to predict effects from causes — providing our perceptions are accurate.

HOW WE PERCEIVE PEOPLE

Up to this point we have been considering how people perceive stimuli generally. The research that has provided support for the statements we have been making was concerned with object perception—the perception of things—even though the applications presented have most often concerned people. Obviously, the primary concern in interpersonal communication is not with the perception of objects, but rather with the perception of people.

Try to remember the last time you met a new person. You were introduced to that person. You may have shaken hands and said a number of "nice things." That person probably did the same with you. As all this was going on, you were developing a total perception, or impression, of that person. What caused you to decide that you liked or did not like the person? What caused you to decide that you trusted or did not trust the person? What caused you to decide that the person was intelligent or unintelligent, emotional or unemotional, warm or cold?

These are the kinds of questions that have concerned behavioral scientists in an area of study usually referred to as **person perception.** The answers to these questions about how we see other people are very much related to the discussion we have just completed of the process of perception in general. Our perception of people parallels our perception of objects. We need to establish some sort of order in our perception of people, just as we do with objects. Likewise, it is important for us to develop some kind of meaning for people in terms of relationships.

Three Levels of Interpersonal Perception

Interpersonal perception is a very complex process because we do not perceive other people just as objects. We also perceive people as individuals who have perceptions of their own. Among the interpersonal perceptions which we think others have is a perception of us as we interact with them. We also recognize that they know we have an interpersonal perception of what they are thinking about the way we interact with them. These mutual "perceptions" of our interaction and our relationship can be broken down into three levels of interpersonal perception.[31]

31. R. D. Laing, H. Phillipson, and A. R. Lee, *Interpersonal Perception: A Theory and Method of Research* (New York: Harper & Row, 1972), 71.

The first, or **direct perspective,** is simply what each individual in the interaction really thinks—about the relationship, or some topic of discussion, or each other. For example, suppose you are talking to someone you have met on the street. You are in a hurry and need to leave because of an appointment elsewhere. Your direct perspective is that you need to bring the interaction to a close even though you might enjoy talking longer. The other person may not be in a hurry and might want to spend some time talking. Suppose the direct perspective of this other person is that a nice long chat would be enjoyable. If the two of you were to compare your direct perspectives, you could determine whether you *agreed or disagreed*.[32] In this case your direct perspectives would disagree.

32. Ibid., 80.

The second level of interpersonal perception, called a **metaperspective,** is the perception of each individual in an interaction of the other individual's direct perspective. To return to the preceding example, when you are interacting on the street with the other person, your metaperspective may be that the other person wishes to stop for a long chat. In this instance you would be correct and you would *understand* the other person. If the other person's metaperspective was that you too would like to have a long conversation, that other person would be incorrect and would *misunderstand* you. You would each need to compare your metaperspective with the other person's direct perspective in order to determine whether you correctly understood or misunderstood each other.

The third level of interpersonal perception, called a **meta-metaperspective,** is the perception of each individual in the interaction of the other individual's metaperspective. To return again to the example, your direct perception is that you want only a short conversation, your metaperspective is that the other person wishes to stop for a long conversation, and your meta-metaperspective is that the other person has a metaperspective that you would like a long conversation. In this case you will feel that you have been misunderstood. If your meta-metaperspective is that the other person has a metaperspective that you would like a short conversation, then you will feel understood, even though you have not been understood at all. Only by comparing your meta-metaperspective with the other individual's metaperspective can you correctly assess whether you are understood or misunderstood. Given these different levels of perception, it should be apparent why we often have difficulty communicating with one another. In our perceptions of one another we can agree, but fail to understand that we agree; or we can disagree and one of us may understand this, yet the other may fail to understand this. We may also fail to realize that we are understood, or that we are misunderstood, by the other person. The entire process of taking into consideration our perceptions (direct perspective), our perceptions of the other person's perceptions (metaperspective), and our perceptions of the other person's perceptions of our perceptions (meta-metaperspective) as we encode and decode the messages which we exchange is very complex. However, it is important that we at least try to understand our interpersonal perceptions at all three levels in order to improve our accuracy of interpersonal perception and communication.

Others' Intentions

One of the basic assumptions we apparently make about other people when we are developing our impressions of them is that they *intentionally* engage in whatever behaviors they exhibit.[33] In a way, that notion appears so obvious that it almost seems ludicrous to discuss it, yet it has important implications. We assume that someone who eats ice cream wants to eat it. That is a very simple example, yet we make inferences far more complex than this in the same manner. If someone smiles at us, we assume the person must like us and is being friendly toward us. Likewise, if someone does not speak to us, it is not unusual to decide that the person does not like us.

Inferences such as these are typical of all of us every day of our lives. We are constantly making our own decisions about people's motivations and intentions as a result of observations of some of their behaviors. Sometimes we are correct. Sometimes we are very wrong. We nevertheless do make these inferences because, as with objects, we are attempting to structure the sensations we have of other people, develop the consistency we need, and attach meaning to our sensations. With people, however, it is more difficult, because people are constantly changing. Therefore, we look for common ingredients among all the different behaviors we can observe.[34] In fact, it is always interesting to consider what causes us to make the judgments we do about other people. Have you ever decided that a person you have met is a prejudiced person? How did you arrive at that conclusion?

In all likelihood, something like the following occurred: the person you ultimately labeled as "prejudiced" made a statement or two about some group that would appear to be negative. For example, suppose someone makes the statement that property values in a neighborhood tend to decline after a black family moves into the neighborhood. That statement in and of itself may not necessarily be enough cause for you to perceive the person as prejudiced against blacks, but it might start you thinking that way. Actually, the person could make a statement of that sort on the basis of information from real estate agencies. We really do not know whether or not the person is prejudiced against blacks — yet.

Suppose, now, we are with this person at a banquet, and there is an empty chair very close to us that this person can sit in, and another empty chair a good distance away. A black person is sitting next to the chair nearest us, and the person we are observing walks the long distance to the chair between whites. At this point we have a couple of samples of behavior, and we may begin to infer that there were certain intentions and motivations underlying these behaviors.

If we can see a consistency among these different behaviors, we begin to use that to perceive, or explain, the person. In this case we might infer that the individual is prejudiced against blacks. If we are very careful in forming

33. Fritz Heider, *The Psychology of Interpersonal Relations* (New York: John Wiley & Sons, 1958), 100–101.

34. Leon Festinger, *A Theory of Cognitive Dissonance* (Stanford, Calif., Stanford University Press, 1957).

our opinions and our impressions and developing our inferences, we might demand more samples of behavior than that, but this is typical of the process we go through.

Unless we know the context it is sometimes difficult to anticipate the emotion in a particular situation.

Accuracy in Perceiving Others

For years social scientists have investigated the accuracy with which we judge other people's emotions and personalities. Our approach to the "prejudiced" person in the preceding section is one that would probably be taken by someone employing the structuralist view of perception. It is also possible to approach this question from a Gestaltist point of view, which is the way we will now try to do it.[35]

Most of the research conducted to this point appears to be inconclusive regarding the question of our accuracy in perceiving other people's emotions.[36] While it is true that some fairly reasonable percentages have been obtained (anywhere from 52 to 57 percent), the emotions identified by judges

35. Schneider, Hastorf, and Ellsworth, *Person Perception,* 204.

36. Nico H. Frijda, "Recognition of Emotion," in *Advances in Experimental Social Psychology* 35(1951):70–71; Nico H. Frijda, "Facial Expression and Situational Cues," *Journal of Abnormal and Social Psychology* 57(1958):149–54.

37. Ibid.

38. Schneider, Hastorf, and Ellsworth, *Person Perception,* 205-15.

39. H. D. Goldberg, "The Role of Cutting in the Perception of Motion Pictures," *Journal of Applied Psychology* 35(1951):70-71; Frijda, "Facial Expression," 149-54.

40. Michael Argyle, *Social Interaction* (Chicago: Aldine-Atherton, 1969), 158-64.

41. Ibid.

42. Argyle, 149-53.

43. Ibid.

44. Ibid.

have been general, and thus not useful in an interpersonal communication context.[37] It does seem possible, however, to be somewhat accurate in judging emotions such as surprise, happiness, fear, anger, disgust, and contempt.[38]

Of course, one of the reasons the research has been somewhat inconclusive in terms of emotion identification is that it is difficult for researchers to know which emotions are being portrayed and therefore which emotions are present to be recognized. Apparently, rather than there being any definite behavioral cues for us to recognize, we are very dependent on the *context* in which people behave before we determine what emotions are being expressed.[39] The research is incomplete on this point.

There is evidence suggesting that people differ in their ability to judge personality characteristics. This is true whether the judgment is one of intelligence or personality.[40] Many of our judgments of other people, however, appear to result from projections of our own characteristics onto someone else — an assumption that others are similar to ourselves.[41] One of the reasons we are sometimes accurate in assessing another person's personality may be because the individual concerned happens (fortunately) to be similar to us.

When we were discussing the perception of objects, one of the points we stressed was that background, history, and language systems significantly affect our perception of objects. This appears to be the case in terms of our perceptions of people, also. There are several factors that seem to affect the way we evaluate other people.

First, our own interpersonal attitudes appear to affect our judgment of other people's personalities significantly, because we are constantly looking for consistency within the world.[42] If we dislike another person, our judgment of that person's personality is very likely to be negative. If we meet person A and decide that we do not like that person, we may evaluate him or her as rude, hostile, cold, unfriendly, ignorant, and possessed of any other negative characteristics. That would be consistent with our negative interpersonal reaction.

Another factor that seems to affect our judgment of other people significantly is our role relations.[43] Given two persons, John and Fred, the role of each in relation to the other will significantly affect their perceptions of each other. If John is dependent on Fred for pay increases and promotions, it is very difficult for Fred to evaluate John's personality. Fred will never know whether John is being friendly because he really likes him or whether he is being friendly to get pay increases and promotions — just as John himself may not know.

It is also possible that a given set can affect our judgments of another person.[44] The kinds of information we have about an individual, whether true or not, will significantly affect the way we react to that person. This prior information can cause us to notice things we would not notice otherwise. It can cause us to interpret what we see differently from the way we would if we did not have the previous information. Of course, if the information tends toward the positive or the negative, it can cause us to try to bring everything else we think about the person into line with that tendency, simply to restore consistency in our perception.[45]

Our own moods and motivation at any given moment will also affect our perception of others.[46] If, for example, a young man who has not been on a date for months because he has been stationed in Antarctica meets a young lady of average looks and average to substandard personality, he may perceive her as an incredibly attractive young woman and possessed of a sparkling personality. His needs may have caused him to perceive her in a manner much different from the way he would under more normal circumstances.

45. Ibid.

46. Ibid.

Forming Impressions

Our own past experience also has a significant effect on how we form impressions of other people. The two main approaches among social and behavioral scientists interested in person perception are the **trait theory** approach and the **implicit personality theory** approach.

Trait Theory

The trait theory can be viewed either from a structuralist or a Gestalt point of view. The structuralist trait theory approach would consist, first, of our making separate judgments of different traits in an individual. Second, our impression of that individual would be the sum total of all the traits we have perceived. A Gestalt trait theory approach would be that our responses to each trait affect our responses to all other traits and, thus, the whole impression of an individual is equal to something greater than the sum of the individual traits. There is evidence in support of both of those approaches.

The classic research by Asch[47] supports both approaches. He gave to one group of subjects a set of adjectives describing a person which included the word "warm." Another set of subjects heard the same description, but instead of "warm" the word "cold" was included. Other than those two words, the lists were identical. The responses of the subjects indicated that their perceptions of this person were very different, depending on whether they were exposed to the word "warm" or the word "cold."

47. S. E. Asch, "Forming Impressions of Personality," *Journal of Abnormal and Social Psychology* 41(1946):258–90.

Some of Asch's further research suggested to him that "warm" and "cold" were what could be termed **central traits.** A central trait can be thought of as a characteristic that others perceive as a controlling and primary personality characteristic of the individual. Such adjectives had a greater effect on responses than many others might have had.[48] It is possible that one of the kinds of responses we have to people is in terms of traits we sum together into a total perception.

48. Ibid.

Implicit Personality Theory

The **implicit personality theory** is more Gestaltist in its orientation. This approach is probably more useful in terms of interpersonal communication, and there is research that supports it. Implicit personality theory predicts that when we meet someone, we generate a set of inferences about that person on the basis of whatever stimuli we are receiving.[49] In much the manner already discussed, we look for consistencies in behaviors, we infer motivations, and from that we develop some kind of implicit personality explanation for that individual. From that point on we make use of previously held personality expectations we have generated within ourselves over time.

For instance, if you meet someone you are able to classify as a gregarious personality, you then reach into your "storehouse" of implicit personality theories and find the things you tend to expect from people with gregarious personalities. If you associate someone who talks and laughs a lot with a gregarious personality, then you expect to see that kind of behavior from this individual. And you act accordingly.

It is important to note that our implicit personality theories are the result of a lifetime of hearing about different kinds of personalities from our friends and experiencing people with different kinds of personalities.[50] Sometimes the predictions we make and the implicit theories we carry around inside our heads are accurate. Sometimes they are not so accurate. We are not suggesting the formation of implicit personality theories as a goal. We are only presenting what many behavioral scientists believe to be a valid explanation of interpersonal perception.

Actually, it might be more simple to think of implicit personality theories as theories of stereotyped behaviors. We have certain stereotyped expectations for certain personalities. When we talk about implicit personality theories that people carry inside their heads, we are really talking about the stereotyped behaviors they expect from people who have specific personalities. If we expect a person with a gregarious personality to exhibit loud speaking behavior, expansive gestures, and great quantities of laughter, we have a **stereotype** in our heads of a gregarious person.

INTERPERSONAL ATTRACTION

How attractive we are perceived as being and how attractive we perceive others to be plays a significant role in any **interpersonal interaction.** The degree to which we are willing to accept what another person says to us and their willingness to accept our statements strongly relate to the perceived attraction we feel for each other. Notice that we have used the phrase "perceived attraction" instead of referring to *attractiveness* as a quality that resides

49. P. F. Secord, "Stereotyping and Favorableness in the Perception of Negro Faces," *Journal of Abnormal and Social Psychology* 59(1959):309–15; J. Wishner, "Reanalysis of Impressions of Personality," *Psychological Review* 67(1960):16–112.

50. D. M. Gilbert, "Stereotype Persistence and Change Among College Students," *Journal of Abnormal and Social Psychology* 46(1951):245–54.

The attractiveness of movie stars significantly affects our judgment about them as human beings, even though most of us lack the information necessary for that kind of judgment.

in a person. Unfortunately, in our society we have come to speak of "attractive people," "attractive features," "attractive ideas," and the like, as though the attractiveness resided in the people or ideas. However, this is not the case. Attractiveness is a quality that must be perceived in order to exist. The old cliché, "Beauty is in the eyes of the beholder," is more on target than many people realize.

How often have you heard someone make the following statement (or made it yourself): "I don't know what she(he) sees in him(her)"? We have all heard or made such a statement many times. The reason we frequently do not understand why someone finds a person to be attractive is because we are looking for an absolute quality of attractiveness in the person in question.

Perceiving and Understanding Others

Instead, we should be looking into ourselves and into the person who sees the attractiveness, because attractiveness can be perceived only from the perspective of one's background. Standards of attractiveness vary from culture to culture, from generation to generation, and from person to person. In spite of these differences in standards, we all appear to construct our perceptions of attractiveness with the same building blocks.

Components of Perceived Attractiveness

51. J. C. McCroskey and T. A. McCain, "The Measurement of Interpersonal Attraction," *Speech Monographs* 41(1974):261–66.

There are three components of perceived attractiveness: a **social-liking component,** a **task-respect component,** and a **physical appearance component.**[51] We will discuss each of these components to make more clear the role of perceived attractiveness in interpersonal communication.

Social-Liking Component

Whenever we make a statement such as "I like Becky," or "Mike is a great guy," we are expressing the *social-liking component* of perceived attractiveness. This component includes the degree to which we would like to have this person as a friend, how well we think we know the person, and how much we would like to meet the person. If you will think back to the discussion of social needs in chapter 1, you should recognize a parallel between this component and that set of needs. The social-liking component is, to a great degree, our response to our own social needs. We respond positively to a person who satisfies our social needs because of that component.

Task-Respect Component

This component involves a judgment about the expertise of an individual, most often relative to a given task. How qualified is the person to do a job? Do I want to work with this person? Can I depend on this person in a working relationship? These are the questions that are combined into a *task-respect response* to a person, and which, together, form one component of perceived attractiveness. Again, thinking back to our discussion of needs in chapter 1, you can see the parallel between this component and the ego needs discussed there. To respect another person, we evaluate that person in the light of our own self-perception, as was mentioned in chapter 3. Thus, the higher our own self-esteem, the more likely we are to perceive people positively on the task-respect component of perceived attractiveness.

Physical Appearance Component

When people talk of attractiveness, this is the component usually thought of. A person's physical characteristics are obvious to any observer and are the first stimuli we usually respond to when meeting a person for the first time. As will be discussed in greater detail in chapter 6, interpersonal communication is greatly affected by physical appearance. This is so, in great part, because the perceived attractiveness of a person is partially based on a judgment of *physical appearance*. This points up the importance of paying attention to appearance, not because it is the sole determiner of our success as a communicator, but because it is one of the building blocks of attractiveness.

Determinants of Attractiveness

Not all the determinants of our liking of another person lie within the other person; some of the causes and correlates of interpersonal attraction lie within ourselves and some lie within the situation itself. Although the characteristics and behavior of the other person play an important role in determining whether or not we find him or her attractive, researchers have found that liking often does lie in the eye of the beholder. What are the factors which affect our perceptions of others? Although it would be impossible to cover them all, we will now consider some of the factors which affect interpersonal attraction between people.

Accidental Happenings   One element that operates in interpersonal attraction is accidental happenings, either good or bad. Good happenings cause us to like the other person; bad happenings cause us to draw away from that person, even when what happens is beyond the person's control. There is evidence that we tend to like those who succeed (everybody likes a winner) and dislike those who fail. Reasons given in explanation for this phenomenon are that we want to believe that people get what they deserve; that people are responsible for their own fate; that the world is a just and predictable place. Walster's research reveals that persons who hear about an accident, for example, want to blame someone (often the victim) for the accident. Moreover, her research shows that the desire to hold the victim responsible increases proportionately with the severity of the consequences of the accident.[52]

A dramatic illustration of this phenomenon occurred a few years ago on the Wabash River at Lafayette, Indiana. Five men left Logansport, Indiana in two small boats to go downriver some thirty-five miles. One of the boats, with three men in it, ran out of gas, and when the engine stopped, the boat began to take on water. In the attempt to transfer one man to the other boat, both boats were upset, dumping all five men into the forty-six-degree flood waters.

52. E. Walster, "The Assignment of Responsibility for an Accident," *Journal of Personality and Social Psychology* 3(1966):73–79.

53. Lerner, M. J., "Evaluation of Performance as a Function of Performer's Reward and Attractiveness," *Journal of Personality and Social Psychology* 1(1965):355-60.

54. See K. E. Davis and E. E. Jones, "Changes in Interpersonal Perception as a Means of Reducing Cognitive Dissonance," *Journal of Abnormal and Social Psychology* 61(1960):402-10; J. Davidson, "Cognitive Familiarity and Dissonance Reduction," in Leon Festinger, ed., *Conflict, Decision, and Dissonance* (Stanford, Calif.: Stanford University Press, 1968), 45-60; D. C. Glass, "Changes in Liking as a Means of Reducing Cognitive Discrepancies Between Self-Esteem and Aggressiveness," *Journal of Personality* 32(1964):531-49; and T. C. Brock and A. H. Buss, "Effects of Justification for Aggression in Communication with the Victim on Post Aggressiveness Dissonance," *Journal of Abnormal and Social Psychology* 68(1964):403-12.

55. See G. C. Homans, *Social Behavior: Its Elementary Forms* (New York: Harcourt, Brace & World, 1961), 150; and J. W. Thibaut and H. H. Kelley, *The Social Psychology of Groups* (New York: John Wiley & Sons, 1959), 81-82.

56. See, for example, D. Landry and E. Aronson, "Liking of an Evaluation as Function of His Discernment," *Journal of Personality and Social Psychology* 8(1968):133-41; R. E. Brewer and M. B. Brewer, "Attraction and Accuracy of Perception in Dyads," *Journal of Personality and Social Psychology* 8(1968):188-93; and D. Byrne and W. Griffitt, "Similarity vs. liking: A Clarification," *Psychonomical Science* 6(1966):295-96.

Although people were on the scene of the accident almost immediately, only two of the men were saved, and not all of the bodies of the others had yet been found some three months later. It was a terrible tragedy, but the shocking thing to many people was the reaction of some persons. They not only blamed the victims for possible errors in judgment (standing in a boat, being out on a flooded river, overloading a boat, and so on), they also made statements to the effect that the victims deserved what they got. People try to convince themselves that chance occurrences really are deserved.[53] In this way we protect ourselves from feeling that we too are vulnerable and unable to always protect ourselves from something bad happening to us which is not our fault. So it is true that persons who win, who are successful, and to whom good things happen are valued and admired more than persons who lose, who fail, and who suffer unfortunate events.

Unjust Treatment   Another determinant of interpersonal attraction has to do with how we have treated the other person. Tacitus stated centuries ago: "It is a principle of human nature to hate those whom you have injured." Several recent experiments have demonstrated that when we behave in a cruel or in a generous way toward another, we tend to change our attitude toward that person so that it is consistent with our treatment of that person. A person who harms another tends to develop a dislike for the person harmed; and a person who does a favor for another tends to feel increased liking for the other.[54] Even if we did not *intend* to help or harm the other person, our attitudes change to match the consequences of our behavior.

Rewards   Liking may also be produced by the rewards provided us by others. We like those who reward us and dislike those who punish us. Several researchers have suggested that interpersonal relationships always cost us something along with giving us something, and that liking is a function of comparing the cost to the reward (reward − cost = profit).[55] If the relationship is profitable, or if mutually satisfying rewards are obtained each from the other, interpersonal attraction is high. When people praise us, our liking for them increases. If we find interpersonal communication with a person to be socially rewarding, enjoyable, or exciting, we will experience greater attraction to that person.[56] Conversely, if we make no effort to enjoy talking with others, we should not be surprised that we are not attractive to or liked by others. Again, we see the direct relationship between interpersonal communication and being likable. By improving our skills in interpersonal communicaiton, we can more easily discover others and help them discover us, and a mutually satisfying situation can be created. Reinforcing each other, each of us will come to like the other.

Stress Another factor is stress or anxiety. There is now considerable evidence indicating that when we are under stress we desire the presence of others, especially those who are in the same situation as we are, or those with whom we have had significant interaction previously.[57] Persons are often in a position to comfort and reassure one another. The mere presence of others appears to produce psychological and physiological responses helpful in reducing our anxiety. Combat studies of bomber crews have shown that the presence of others does reduce anxiety created by severe battle stress.[58] Anxiety and stress motivate people to seek out others and interact with them.

Social Isolation Social isolation is a fifth element which affects interpersonal attraction. There is ample evidence that isolation by itself creates a powerful desire for interpersonal contact and is a strong facilitator of subsequent interpersonal attraction. Man is a social creature, and social isolation for any prolonged period of time is a painful experience. As Schachter has pointed out, the autobiographical reports of criminals in solitary confinement in prison, of religious hermits, of prisoners of war, and of castaways clearly reveal that isolation is devastating.[59] One of the rewards another person can provide to the lonely or isolated person is simply sheer physical presence as a fellow human being.

Propinquity **Propinquity** (nearness in distance of persons) has been shown to influence choice of friends. Simply stated, the finding is that, other things being equal, the closer two individuals are geographically to one another, the more likely they will be attracted to each other. Studies supporting this finding are numerous and consistent. They have shown that proximity is directly related to friendship formation, to mate selection, and to a decrease in prejudice. Increased contact between white persons and black persons results in a reduction of prejudice, whether the contact is on the job,[60] in an integrated housing project,[61] in a university classroom,[62] or among policemen.[63]

People who live in apartments near stairways are better known and more popular than persons living in the other apartments in a building.[64] In classrooms, apartment houses, college dormitories, housing projects, and other situations, the finding of numerous studies is consistent — propinquity is directly related to liking. Persons in closer proximity (centrally located physically) tend to interact with others more, form social bonds more quickly, and experience greater attraction and liking. Conversely, persons on the edge or isolated from others tend to experience less interaction and less popularity. The implication of this finding for each of us ought to be clear. Liking and attraction comes more easily as we are in closer proximity to others, and it is more difficult to establish those relationships when we are not in proximity but are, instead, isolated from others. If we find it a little difficult to get acquainted with others or to talk with others, perhaps we ought to place ourselves in the

57. See S. Schachter, *The Psychology of Affiliation* (Stanford, Calif.: Stanford University Press, 1959); H. B. Gerard and J. M. Rabbis, "Fear and Social Comparisons," *Journal of Abnormal and Social Psychology* 62(1961):586–92; I. Sarnoff and P. G. Zimbardo, "Anxiety, Fear, and Social Affiliation," *Journal of Abnormal and Social Psychology* 62(1961):356–63; P. G. Zimbardo and R. Formica, "Emotional Comparison and Self-Esteem as Determinants of Affiliation," *Journal of Personality* 31(1963):141–62; and J. M. Darley and E. Aronson, "Self-Evaluation vs. Direct Anxiety Reduction as Determinants of the Fear-Affiliation Relationship," *Journal of Experimental Social Psychology* supplement 1(1966):66–79.

58. D. G. Mandlebaum, *Soldier Groups and Negro Soldiers* (Berkeley: University of California Press, 1952), 45–48.

59. Schachter, *Psychology of Affiliation,* 6.

60. E. B. Palmore, "The Introduction of Negroes into White Departments," *Human Origins* 14(1955):27–28.

61. M. Deutsch and M. E. Collings, "The Effect of Public Policy in Housing Projects upon Interracial Attitudes," in Eleanor Maccoby, T. M. Newcomb, and E. L. Hartley, eds., *Readings in Social Psychology,* (New York: Holt, Rinehart & Winston, 1958), 612–23.

62. J. H. Mann, "The Effect of Interracial Contact on Sociometric Choices and Perceptions," *Journal of Social Psychology* 50(1959):143–52.

63. See, for example, L. Festinger, S. Schachter, and K. Bork, "Social Pressures in Informal Groups" (New York: Hayes & Brothers, 1950); Mark Abrahamson, *Interpersonal Accommodation* (New York: Van Nostrand, Reinhold, 1966); and R. F. Priest and J. Lawyer, "Proximity and Peership: Bases of Balance in Interpersonal Attraction," *American Journal of Sociology* 72(1967):633–49.

64. Festinger, Schachter, and Bork, "Social Pressures."

65. E. E. Lett, W. Clark, and I. A. Altman, *A Propositional Inventory of Research on Interpersonal Distance* (Bethesda, Md.: Naval Medical Research Institute, Technical Report No. 1, 1969).

''middle of the action'' when we can. Certainly, going into the corner or as far away as we can will only serve to intensify our problem.

Liking and proximity tend to be reciprocally correlated; that is, as liking increases, persons come into closer proximity, just as, if proximity increases, liking tends to increase.[65] Perhaps you or someone you know has had occasion to move from one floor to another in a dormitory—or even from one house to another—so as to be nearer to a particular friend.

All these studies on proximity and liking may bring to mind the old saying ''Absence makes the heart grow fonder,'' which we may need to qualify by adding ''when no one else is around!'' However, there are variables other than proximity at work in interpersonal attraction; proximity is not the whole story. At the outset of this discussion on proximity we said, ''other things being equal,'' proximity determines interpersonal attraction. It is clearly true, however, that proximity is a powerful influence in bringing about liking, and liking is related directly to interpersonal communication. Liking facilitates interpersonal communication, and through more effective interpersonal communication, we all increase our own likableness and interpersonal attractiveness. It is an interactive process, and it is possible to influence the process so as to create an upward spiral—a mutual, positive, ever-improving situation.

66. See E. G. Beier, A. M. Rossi, and R. L. Garfield, ''Similarity Plus Dissimilarity of Personality: Basis for Friendship,'' *Psychology Report* 8(1961):3–8; and J. S. Broxton, ''A Test of Interpersonal Attraction Predictions Derived from Balance Theory,'' *Journal of Abnormal and Social Psychology* 63(1963):394–97.

67. N. Reader and H. B. English, ''Personality Factors in Adolescent Female Friendships,'' *Journal of Consulting Psychology* 11(1947):212–20.

Similarity of Personality   Another factor in liking and interpersonal attraction is similarity of personality. Friends perceive each other as being more similar in personality than do nonfriends.[66] However, do persons who are attracted to each other actually possess similar personality characteristics? Do ''birds of a feather flock together''? In fact, there does appear to be a significantly higher positive correlation between friends' personalities than between the personalities of those who are not friends.[67] This finding should not be surprising inasmuch as it is consistent with other findings relative to the similarity of friends—that friends are similar on dimensions such as attitudes, socioeconomic class, religion, values, and beliefs. It is not clear whether friends *become* similar as a result of their associating together, or whether they become friends *because* they are similar. Research findings on this question are contradictory.

Similarity of Attitudes   A final element which has a strong effect on interpersonal attraction is similarity of attitudes and beliefs. As is the situation with similarity of personality and attraction, so it is with similarity of attitudes and attraction—we do not know whether persons are attracted to each other because they have similar attitudes and beliefs or whether, as a result of their attraction and association, they come to develop similar attitudes and beliefs. Perhaps it is some of both. In any event, similarity of attitudes does have the strongest effect of any of the factors we have discussed on interpersonal attraction between people.[68] We like people with similar attitudes to our own and dislike those with different attitudes.

68. Donn Byrne, *The Attraction Paradigm* (New York: Academic Press, 1971).

Figure 4.4

In addition, there is a tendency to make our attitudes or orientations toward objects and ideas congruent with our attitudes toward a person in interpersonal communication. One of the best explanations of this phenomenon has been given by Heider.[69] His P-O-X **balance theory,** based on our need for consistency, explains how orientations held by each person toward the other are related in a balanced way to the orientations each holds toward the object of communication. In figure 4.4, *P*, a person, is talking to *O*, the other person, about *X*, an object of communication. If + indicates a positive attitude or evaluation toward the object of communication or a liking for the other person, and − indicates a negative attitude or evaluation toward the object of communication or a dislike of the other person, then "balanced situations" in which all the attitudes are congruent can be illustrated as is shown in figure 4.4.

For example, if the relationship between person *P* and the other person *O* is positive (+) and *P* has a positive attitude (+) toward an issue *X* (let us use euthanasia as an example), then the other person will probably have a positive attitude toward euthanasia too (fig. 4.4 *left*). Or, if persons *P* and *O* have a positive relationship with each other and one of them has a negative attitude toward the object, then the other one will probably also have a negative attitude toward the object (fig. 4.4 *center*). If the relationship between persons *P* and *O* is negative and P has a positive evaluation of X, then P assumes that O has a negative evaluation of X (fig. 4.4 *right*). The theory suggests that there is a tendency for people who like each other to share likes and dislikes and for people who dislike each other to disagree in likes and dislikes.

Heider's balance theory recognizes that attitudes between people as well as their attitudes toward common objects of social reality are important factors in interpersonal communication, and that the two factors are interrelated.

However, unbalanced orientations do occur, and would include situations such as those illustrated in figure 4.5. Figure 4.5 *left* shows two persons *P* and *O* who like each other or relate positively to each other, but *P* has a positive attitude toward *X* (euthanasia) while *O* believes that euthanasia is murder. The models in figure 4.5 *center* and *right* show persons who do not like each other and yet they agree perfectly on euthanasia, one pair approving euthanasia and the other pair disapproving euthanasia. In all three cases in figure 4.5 things are not the way they are "supposed to be" as far as the people involved are concerned.

69. Fritz Heider, *Psychology of Interpersonal Relations*, 208.

Figure 4.5

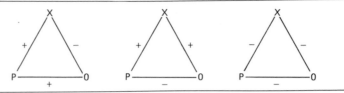

It is difficult for two people who strongly like one another to accept that they strongly hold opposing beliefs. It is also difficult to believe that someone you strongly dislike and think poorly of is smart enough to agree with you on an important issue — if someone you think is stupid agrees with you, maybe you've been wrong all along!

Therefore, through communication, people who are attracted to each other tend to try to bring their attitude and belief systems into balance, to preserve states of balance, or to resolve states of imbalance. Most of us have had the experience of hearing someone we like very much say something we could not agree with and did not like at all. Suppose you had a friend who spoke out against equal rights for women, and you were very much for it. When that happened, you probably experienced what is called dissonance — anxiety, stress, or discomfort due to a state of imbalance. What feelings did you have, and what did you do or think in order to resolve the situation for yourself? You may have found it very difficult to maintain your previous attitudes toward your friend and toward equal rights for women. Research findings suggest that some alteration of attitudes or beliefs is necessary in such a situation. We cannot maintain attitudes and beliefs that create a state of imbalance. In the example above, it would be possible for you to change your attitude toward your friend (you think less of your friend now); or you could change your attitude toward equal rights for women ("I didn't realize it meant all that!"). Another option is to get your friend to reconsider this orientation toward equal rights for women.

A different option you may select is to forget it, repress it, or remember to avoid bringing the subject up when talking with this person. In some instances we may have learned indirectly of a friend's attitude toward an object of communication; or, by inference from various related cues, we may suspect that our friend has an attitude opposite to ours on some topic. In such situations we may purposely avoid the topic. This option of "leaving the field" psychologically is often used by persons to avoid situations of imbalance; thereby a perception of a balanced situation is created.

We have discussed briefly eight factors which affect interpersonal attraction. When there are strong positive relationships between persons, there is a high probability that communication will be successful; but when there is a strong dislike between persons, communication will be severely handicapped and positive interpersonal relationships will fail to develop.

Effects of Stability

One of the primary characteristics of our perceptions of people is that those perceptions are stable. Of course, this fits in with our need for a consistent, well-ordered world. The reason we develop our ordered and structured perceptions in the first place is to have order and consistency within a random, chaotic world of stimuli. It is not very likely that we will lose sight of our perceptions. Consequently, we tend to avoid information that will upset or contradict those perceptions.[70] We tend to distort what we see to support our perceptions, or at least to avoid contradicting them.

If Professor Smith has developed the perception of one of his colleagues as a kind, well-mannered, thoughtful person, it is not very likely that he will easily cope with information suggesting that his colleague cheats on his wife, drinks to excess, and is sometimes irresponsible. Rather, he will try to rationalize or distort the information so that he can make it consistent with his previous perception. In fact, he will even avoid information that contradicts his previous perception of this person, if possible. Our perceptions are stable and remain relatively constant, and we do whatever we can to make them so.

Culture and Perception

Our perception of things is affected by our culture in many ways. Erickson suggested that there are at least three reasons our culture may cause us to perceive one object instead of another.[71] First, an object may have greater meaning because of cultural associations. Second, of two objects, the one that occurs more frequently is likely to be perceived more easily than the other. Finally, because of cultural association and/or previous associations, there may be a more pleasant association related to one object than to another.

A study of Hudson suggests that we actually see photographs differently according to the culture we grow up in.[72] Hudson administered photographs to white and black subjects; the former group attended school and the latter did not. He discovered that the subjects who attended school could see the pictures three dimensionally, whereas the subjects not attending school did not. Evidently, the people who did not attend school were culturally isolated from photographs and thus had not learned to perceive photographs three dimensionally. Thus, even the way we perceive a physical object can be affected by the kind of cultural experiences we have had.

70. Judson Mills, "Interest in Supporting and Discrepant Information," in Robert P. Ableson, Elliott Aronson, William J. McGuire, Theodore M. Newcomb, Milton J. Rosenberg, and Percy H. Tannenbaum, eds., *Theories of Cognitive Consistency: A Sourcebook* (Chicago: Rand McNally, 1968), 771-76.

71. C. W. Erickson, *Concepts of Personality* (Chicago: Aldine Press, 1963), 30-60.

72. W. Hudson, "Pictorial Depth Perception in Sub-Cultural Groups in Africa," *Journal of Social Psychology* 52(1960):183-208.

73. Leigh Triandis and William W. Lampert, "Source of Frustration and Targets of Aggression: A Cross Culture Study," *Journal of Abnormal and Social Psychology* 62(1961):640–48.

Also of interest to us in interpersonal communication is the effect of culture on our perception of emotions in other people. People from rural cultures perceive different emotions than do persons from urban cultures when looking at the same picture.[73] For example, when looking at pictures that show intense anger in arguments, rural people tend to perceive less tension in the photographs than do urban dwellers. Differences of this sort could significantly affect interaction between people, as our sensitivity to different emotions can vary according to our background.

Self-Fulfilling Prophecy

74. John W. Kinch, "A Formalized Theory of the Self-Concept," in J. Manis and B. Meltzer, eds., *Symbolic Interaction,* 2d ed. (Boston: Allyn & Bacon, 1972), 245–52.

One of the reasons our perceptions are stable is of importance in interpersonal communication. As discussed in chapter 3, it is possible to develop a self-image that in turn creates a self-fulfilling prophecy. We engage in behaviors that ensure that we will be what we perceive ourselves to be. Likewise, we can have self-fulfilling prophecies about the people with whom we communicate interpersonally.[74] Because of the self-fulfilling nature of our perceptions of other people, it appears that the following kind of relationship can frequently occur in interpersonal communication. Peggy develops a perception of Michelle in which Michelle is perceived as warm and friendly. Peggy's set of predictions for Michelle was suggested by her implicit personality theories. Therefore, Peggy communicates in a warm and friendly way with Michelle because she perceives Michelle as warm and friendly. As a result of Peggy's warm and friendly communication behavior, Michelle responds similarly, thus fulfilling Peggy's expectations.

This kind of self-fulfilling cycle can occur with other perceived communication behavior, such as hostility or stupidity, as well as with warm and friendly behavior. It is not unusual for a teacher to perceive a student in a class as intelligent. From that point on, the student can do no wrong in class; the teacher knows that the student is intelligent, thus the interactions with that student will be at such a level that the teacher will cause the student to engage in behaviors the teacher perceives as intelligent because of the self-fulfilling cycle. Horribly enough, the reverse can happen. That is to say, the teacher can have prior expectations of stupidity and slowness for a student and communicate in ways that will cause the student to confirm the teacher's expectations of ignorance or slowness.[75]

75. Ibid.

Openness in Communication

76. R. Wayne Pace and Robert R. Boren, *The Human Transaction* (Glenview, Ill.: Scott, Foresman, 1973); John R. Wenberg and William W. Wilmot, *The Personal Communication Process* (New York: John Wiley & Sons, 1973).

Many writers of interpersonal communication textbooks[76] suggest the value of open, trusting, and self-revealing communication. Sometimes this is simply called for as an absolute good. We suggest that open, honest, and revealing communication can be either effective or ineffective, depending on the context of the interaction. It can, for example, cause others to perceive us as trustworthy, honest, and open.[77] This, in turn, is likely to cause the others to communicate similarly. But this will not always work. Some communication contexts are competitive in nature, and in some such contexts there necessarily has to be a winner and a loser. In those situations it may not be possible to have completely open, honest communication between parties. However, for those situations in which we are trying to establish friendships and/or to continue them, the frank, open approach can certainly be effective communication behavior.

It is important to understand that a perception of **trust** between people is also based on predictability, which, in our estimation, is in keeping with and relates to a primary need for consistency in the world about us, discussed in chapter 1 and again in this chapter. We need to be able to predict behavior if we are to satisfy our needs. As we can predict behavior in other people, we trust them more because we are more able to satisfy our needs. Likewise, as they can predict our behavior, they trust us more for the same reason. Although predictability will not necessarily guarantee trust, it appears that trust is impossible without it. Thus, we can view predictability as a necessary ingredient for trust, even though it alone may not bring about trust.

It is entirely possible, then, that by constructing open, honest, and revealing messages about ourselves, we enable people to know us better, and this in turn gives them a kind of hold over us to the extent of ensuring the kind of behavior we will engage in. At least it enables them to predict our behavior better, and thus they should be able to trust us more. By having a trusting perception of us, they may respond to us in a more open manner.

Trust in communication will be discussed more fully in chapter 8, but a brief comment is in order at this time. It would appear that if we use open and revelatory messages to disclose more about ourselves to those with whom we are interacting, we would allow them to know us better, predict our behavior more accurately, and trust us more. We are not suggesting that you should constantly talk about yourself to everyone. However, it is possible to let others learn about you by engaging in open, nondefensive communication with them, through both verbal and nonverbal messages. We simply let others know how we really feel about ourselves, them, and the things we discuss. Thus, it is possible that open, honest, revelatory messages can in some contexts (which do not involve competition) result in an honest, trusting response from others.

77. Kinch, "Formalized Theory," 245–52.

Summary

At this point we hope you can see how important the process of perception is in interpersonal communication. It is through perception that others form their impression of us. These impressions subsequently condition the ways we behave toward one another, and the ways we behave toward one another reinforce our perceptions. Our perceptions are the result of our need to be able to predict and our need for consistency in the world. We will perceive whatever we need to perceive to ensure the consistency we need. Likewise, we hope it is now clear that a part of this consistency includes the necessity for explaining relationships and attaching meaning to those relationships. All this is a part of the perceptual process.

The process of perception and the discussion of it in this chapter should also dramatize the point that we do not ever "tell it like it is." We only "tell it the way we perceive it." We perceive according to our past histories, language systems, and categorization systems, with all our built-in biases and expectations. These condition the way we see, hear, feel, smell, and taste the world. Likewise, everything from our past conditions the way we communicate interpersonally, because it all conditions the way we perceive everything interpersonally.

5

Words and Meaning

---

1. To be able to explain the process by which words acquire meaning.
2. To be able to discuss the relationship of words to things.
3. To be able to differentiate between the denotative and connotative meanings of words.
4. To be able to demonstrate familiarity with the three components of meaning and the effect that past associations have on communication.
5. To be able to explain the Sapir-Whorf hypothesis about the relationship of language to thought.
6. To be able to discuss the possible cultural and subcultural differences of meaning for the same words.
7. To be able to explain the abstraction process in language in terms of both its advantages and disadvantages.
8. To be able to explain how words which seem ''innocent'' can sometimes be ''hidden antagonizers'' in our messages.

Objectives for the Reader

Probably the most important ability of human beings is the production of spoken language. From virtually the day we are born, we are confronted by other human beings making noises at us in an attempt to influence us. No doubt one of the things about us that would most impress an observer from another planet would be our speech behavior. The use of words in the communication process is so significant that Americans spend approximately twelve years in school (not including college) formally studying language usage.

One of the big events in every parent's life is that moment when a child utters the first word. Simply being able to speak a word is an important event in the lives of human beings. It should be, too, because words play an important role in our lives. It is very likely that the first spoken words were used to indicate the location of water and food and warn others of danger. Words were surely one of early mankind's most useful survival tools, and this remains true. Today we still employ words to obtain food and housing and to defend ourselves against other people. Although our present use of words probably works more indirectly in this defense and acquisition of food and housing, words are, if anything, more useful in survival behavior than in earlier times.

We make use of words in some very interesting ways. Some years ago former president Richard Nixon was the target of considerable criticism from many different groups because of fuel shortages. People were upset because of the shortages of gasoline and heating fuel. During a press conference, the president made the following statement: "The crisis is over, but we still have a problem." Essentially, he tried to change reality by changing the word used to describe it. The lines in front of gasoline stations, the shortage of heating fuel, and the higher cost of fuel continued, but the president was attempting to say that this situation no longer existed by calling it by a different name. Frequently this strategy will work, and many politicians use it effectively. Many people, because of their lack of awareness of how words can affect us, will accept that conditions have changed because the words relating to them have been changed.

How do words enable us to change someone's perception of reality? What is it about the words "love," "democracy," or "Communism" that permits us to build beautiful relationships, destroy a life, start a war, or work for peace? Why are words so powerful? These are not academic questions, any more than the question of how we live and breathe is academic. We are talking about a basic factor in our existence: the way we use a tool developed hundreds of thousands, possibly millions, of years ago to manipulate our environment and ensure our survival. To answer these and other questions, we will consider the nature of words and how we use and are affected by them in interpersonal communication.

Before we discuss the nature of words in interpersonal communication, we should consider the larger system of which words are a part — language. Although many people commonly use the terms *language* and *words* as if they were synonymous, linguists and psycholinguists point out that they are not. Rather, **language** is a processing system in which there are two subsystems interacting to produce meaning. The first is *syntax,* which consists of the rules that enable us to determine word order and relationships among units such as verbs, nouns, and adverbs, and permit us to interpret sentences in which words have been combined. This subsystem is sometimes also called **grammar.**[1] Second, there is our *vocabulary,* or meaningful units, or **words** we have learned.[2] This can be thought of as a storehouse of message units that need

1. Dan I. Slobin, *Psycholinguistics* (Glenview, Ill.: Scott, Foresman & Co., 1971), 15–20.

2. Ibid.

to be combined so that messages can be produced. Language, then, is a system for producing and interpreting messages. This is accomplished by using words and grammar together, because neither alone is sufficient for communication.

Grammar as studied by linguists and psycholinguists is at this time somewhat removed from the pragmatic contexts of interpersonal communication. On the other hand, the study of how words come to acquire meaning and how they can affect us in interpersonal communication can be quite useful. Although there is not complete agreement among all scholars about how words acquire meaning and how they affect us,[3] we will focus here upon some of the explanations of meaning we feel are of value in interpersonal communication.

3. Harold J. Vetter, *Language Behavior and Communication* (Itasca, Ill.: F. E. Peacock Publishers, 1969), 66.

THE NATURE OF WORDS

For the sake of simplicity, words can be thought of as *minimal units of meaning.* In addition, words are symbol behaviors people produce which are arbitrary in nature, can relate to some physical reality outside the person, and are used to change other people. Such symbols as words, Morse code, music notation, and even gestures refer to, or stand for, something else — something beyond themselves.[4] They suggest some reality relevant to the people using them. The "something else" may be events outside or inside the individual. *Words are **symbols** that indirectly make one thing stand for another.* We will be considering words as symbols used to refer to events, concepts, or feelings used to influence people in the interpersonal communication process.

4. Herbert Landar, *Language and Culture* (New York: Oxford University Press, 1966), 35.

Consider the word *book* — a symbol used to stand for the object you are looking at right now. Whenever we hear the word, we tend to think of objects that have many leaves of paper, printing or writing in them, consecutive numbering, and (sometimes) covers that are harder than the inside pages. Whether or not you think of the things just listed when you hear the word *book,* notice that the word is used to represent or refer to something else that does not have to be present for you to think of it when the word is used. This is essentially what words are all about. They are a means of being able to refer to something without actually having to have the something present.

We are talking about far more than just a reference process, however, because when we use the word *book,* what comes to mind will vary from person to person. One person may think of the Bible, another may think of a textbook, another may think of an erotic novel, and still another may think of betting on horses. It is this aspect of words that poses a problem for language theorists and language users alike. It is a rather simple matter to explain the process of reference — the process of how we make a symbol stand for something. It is another matter entirely to explain the notion of meaning, or how words cause responses in people.

Associations with a given word
vary from person to person.

Alan Weninger

The phenomenon of generating a variety of meanings in different people through the use of the same word is probably the most perplexing and intriguing aspect of language. What this really means for us is that we cannot simply use a word and always get the same response to it from different people, or even from the same person at different times. In addition to thinking of a word as a symbol for something, we should also think of a word or a symbol in any language as a stimulus we use and direct toward another person to produce a response.

In chapter 1 we defined communication as a process in which we were employing a commonly accepted symbol system to influence other people's behavior. That is the key to understanding words. If we want a glass of water, most of us say to someone who is near a faucet, "Would you please get me a drink of water?" We utter those words because we are under the impression that by doing so we can stir up responses and associations in the other person that cause them to comply with our request.

Most languages are the result of a long history and are identified closely with specific culture groups. People within a culture develop their own grammar and word meanings. It is interesting to note that we so identify people and their language that we often use the same word to designate both the people and their language. For example, the English speak English, and the French speak French. Because language systems have developed over time, they become almost sacred in the minds of the people who speak and write them — so much so that people are inclined to be highly critical of those who deviate from common practices in their use of language.

We should also note that there are a great number of different languages. The more obvious ones include the languages associated specifically with countries, such as French, German, Spanish, English, Russian, and Italian, to say nothing of the vast number of tribal and group languages emanating from smaller groups in various countries throughout the world. There also are languages of subcultures — such as, within the United States, those of blacks, Chicanos, and American Indians. We will discuss the relationship of language and culture later. In addition to languages, however, there are other kinds of communication systems that function in a similar manner except that they are not spoken. Morse code, which we alluded to earlier, consists of dots and dashes that are symbols for spoken words; semaphore codes consist of flags held at different angles to each other to symbolize letters; and road signs are a kind of pictographic symbolic form — to mention but a few.

THE NATURE OF MEANING IN WORDS

Meaning is Arbitrary

Lewis Carroll[5] caused Humpty Dumpty to define meaning and words when he wrote, " 'When I use a word,' Humpty Dumpty said in a very scornful tone, 'it means just what I choose it to mean — neither more nor less.' 'The question is,' said Alice, 'whether you can make words mean so many different things.' 'The question is,' said Humpty Dumpty, 'who is to be master, that's all.' " Thus Carroll pointed out that the meaning of a word is arbitrary.

Whatever meaning a word has is the meaning we give to it.[6] When we indicated earlier that words were symbols, and that a symbol was something that stood for something else, we were anticipating this idea. A symbol stands for something else — it has no meaning itself. It only *refers* to some other thing. Likewise, it should be clear that the person who makes it stand for something else is the person who uses it. Starting with Korzybski[7] through present-day general semanticists, we repeatedly find the statements "The word is not the thing" and "The map is not the territory."[8] Essentially, language scholars make the point that the meaning of words is in us, and that the word itself does not have any meaning. (The general semanticists frequently go considerably beyond this and suggest a philosophy that can be based on their approach to language, but that is not our concern here.) Our language merely refers to other things.[9] It is a map that represents some reality apart from itself.

5. Lewis Carroll, *Alice's Adventures in Wonderland, Through the Looking Glass, and The Hunting of the Snark* (New York: Modern Library, 1925), 246–47.

6. Charles E. Osgood, "The Nature and Measurement of Meaning," *Psychological Bulletin* 49(May 1952): 197–206.

7. Alfred Korzybski, *Science and Sanity* (Lakesville, Conn.: International Non-Aristotelian Library, 1947).

8. S. I. Hayakawa, *Language in Thought and Action*, 2d ed. (New York: Harcourt, Brace & World, 1964).

9. C. K. Ogden and I. A. Richards, *The Meaning of Meaning* (New York: Harcourt, Brace, 1946), 11.

If words actually contained meanings, it would be possible for any of us in one culture to communicate with someone in another culture without difficulty. Someone who speaks English would be able to communicate effectively with someone who speaks German because the words themselves would have meaning. This, of course, is not the case. If we wish to converse with someone from Germany about a table (unless that person has acquired a knowledge of our English language), we need to use the word *Tisch* rather than the word *table*. Also, it is not very likely that we will understand what the person from Germany is talking about when he or she says *Baum*. Of course, the German speaker will be frustrated because we do not recognize the reference to an object that is composed of wood, grows with roots in the ground, has leaves, and grows tall. This example should show that words of themselves do not contain meaning; it is, rather, we ourselves who are vessels of meaning.

It should be obvious that the meanings we have for words are totally arbitrary. We could just as easily use the word *giraffe* as the word *bicycle* to represent a two-wheeled object with pedals and handlebars that one sits upon and rides. As long as everyone agreed that the word would apply to the same

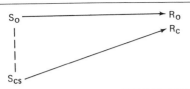

Figure 5.1

object, there would be no difficulty in using a word other than *bicycle* to represent the object. Many children develop their own language in which they substitute different words for those normally used. This is something of a game and they get a great kick out of it — and, of course, make fun of adults in so doing. They are also acting out the principle of arbitrary meaning.

Of course, Carroll also had another interesting point: who is to be the master? Will we control our words, or will our words control us? Later we will consider the effect of words on users as compared with our present discussion of how people use the words.

Meaning is Learned

Our position thus far has been that people acquire meanings for words. At this time, it is very difficult to say with certainty how we acquire meaning.[10] To answer this question with absolute assurance, we would need some way to open a person's brain and peer into it while he or she is acquiring meaning and actually look at the process (assuming there is a physical process to look at). This is not possible, so we cannot say for sure how meaning is acquired, although there are many theories about meaning from which to select.

There is fairly persuasive evidence, which we accept, explaining how word meaning develops. This approach to meaning is based on learning theory and relies on the stimulus-response paradigm in which we associate meanings (responses) with words (stimuli).[11]

This process is depicted in figure 5.1. The original stimulus (S_o), which produced an original response (R_o), is paired, or associated with, a conditioned symbol stimulus (S_{cs}). As a result of this association, the conditioned symbol stimulus (S_{cs}) will elicit a conditioned response (R_c), which is similar to the original response (R_o).[12]

A piece of meat that has been carved from a steer, placed on a charcoal-heated grill, and done to a sizzle produces a desire to eat, and perhaps even salivation. By pairing the word *steak* (S_{cs}) with the above-mentioned object (S_o) over time, the mouth-watering response that originally resulted from the original stimulus (R_o) can, through association, be elicited by the use of the word *steak*.

The simple process of association by itself will not completely explain all meaning; nor will it explain how we learn grammar.[13] However, it goes a long way toward explaining how we learn meaning, especially if we can think in

10. Slobin, *Psycholinguistics*, 68.

11. Charles E. Osgood, *Method and Theory in Experimental Psychology* (New York: Oxford University Press, 1953), 396.

12. Osgood, "Nature and Measurement of Meaning," 205.

13. Noam Chomsky, *Aspects of the Theory of Syntax* (Cambridge, Mass.: M.I.T. Press, 1965), 59.

Figure 5.2

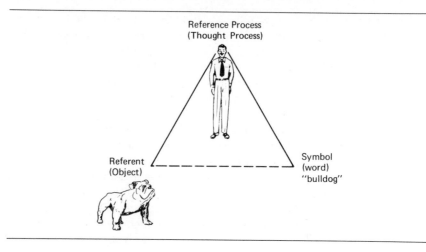

terms of complex groups of associations for each word. Imagine a *series of associations over time* as explaining our responses to words.

The word *mother* is one for which, when we hear it, we can have any number of responses. For many people the word *mother* refers to a warm female parent. It evokes many associations: the female parent as a source of comfort, as a provider of wholesome meals, as the one who was present at our special events, and so much more. All of these associations with the word *mother* have, over time, been acquired by many of us. To grasp fully what this means, it is necessary to try to imagine a complex combination of all these associations producing a single response, or a collection of responses, to the symbol *mother*.

This response is analogous to a cake. A cake is composed of many ingredients that are added at various times during preparation. The ultimate product bears little or no resemblance to the separate ingredients. Our response to words is very similar. Our separate individual associations and responses to a word are, like the ingredients of the cake, merged into a response-as-a-whole which bears little, if any, resemblance to the original ingredients — the associations and responses.

This is a complex process, difficult to pin down empirically, and yet some studies suggest that associating new experiences with a word can alter or change response to the word.[14] How this happens within our minds, we are not sure. We accept that it does happen, nevertheless.

One of the earlier attempts to diagram the process of meaning was that by Ogden and Richards.[15] They suggested that there is a **reference process** that occurs between a symbol and the thing symbolized. To represent this process, they created a *triangle of meaning* similar to that pictured in figure 5.2. The triangle of meaning includes the *referent* (the object referred to by

14. W. D. Mink, "Semantic Generalization as Related to Word Association," *Psychological Reports* 12(1963):59–67; Carolyn K. Staats and Arthur W. Staats, "Meaning Established by Classical Conditioning," *Journal of Experimental Psychology* 54(1957):74–80.

15. Ogden and Richards, *The Meaning of Meaning*, 11.

the symbol), the *reference process* (the thought process by which we form associations), and the *symbol*. The reference process is a mental process in which we connect the thing symbolized with the symbol itself. The dotted line between the symbol and the referent indicates that if there is a connection between the object and the symbol, it is the person who does the connecting. *There is no direct connection between the object and its symbol.* This is the point of our discussion of the arbitrary nature of word meaning. If there is a connection between the thing and the symbol, it is through a referential process that occurs within the mind of the individual acquiring the meaning; and this is probably the result of an association process.

This process results in each of us having a different meaning for every word we learn. This is evident with the word *broadcaster*. The word *broadcaster* elicits from most people a response having something to do with radio and television. In our communication classes we have asked students what the word *broadcaster* means to them. Students think of disc jockeys, announcers, and newscasters. But in most classes we also usually have one or two people who tentatively raise their hands and suggest that there might be another meaning for the word. They suggest that a broadcaster is a piece of machinery used to sow seed in gardens or on farms.

Both responses are correct. To some people broadcaster may well be a disc jockey because they have a series of associations concerning a person who works in radio and television. The association principle is just as true for a person who considers the word *broadcaster* to represent the machinery for sowing seed. Since meanings are learned through association, they are dependent upon our individual fields of experience.[16] If we have a field of experience that includes farming and farm practices, we will probably have associations for the word *broadcaster* that have to do with sowing seed.

16. Wilbur Schramm, "How Communication Works," in *The Process and Effects of Mass Communication,* ed. Wilbur Schramm, (Urbana, Ill.: University of Illinois Press, 1955), 6.

Denotative Meaning

Typically, language scholars have indicated that there is a kind of meaning for a word called **denotative meaning.** *Denotation* refers to what is commonly called the "dictionary meaning" of words. "Dictionary meanings" are simply a record of the ways most people use words. The first definition given in a dictionary reflects the most common usage of a word (and the most common associations), the second definition the next most common, and so on. Some people have even referred to this as "objective meaning," a meaning that includes properties of concepts but no emotional responses.[17]

17. John B. Carroll, *Language and Thought* (Englewood Cliffs, N.J.: Prentice-Hall, 1964), 26–28.

We can use a dictionary to gain an understanding of some of the associations people have for words so that we might more effectively employ words to which people will respond the way we expect. However, while we may learn something about the way words are used from a dictionary, we also must keep in mind that when the dictionary is published, it is already out of date. Individual words are constantly changing with respect to the way people use them. Although dictionaries can be a guide to meaning, they should always be regarded with some degree of caution.

Connotative Meaning

If we return to a consideration of the word *mother,* it must be obvious that not everyone has had warm experiences with his or her female parent. Some have experienced a female parent who is cold, unloving, and possibly even brutal. A person who has had this kind of childhood will have a response toward the word *mother* that is very different from that of someone who has known a warm, sensitive, loving female parent.

The emotional associations that affect responses to words result in what are called **connotative meanings** by many language scholars. The connotation of a word has typically been assumed to represent subjective responses to words. These include the emotional associations one person has with a word that no other person has.[18] These are the responses that are peculiar to each of us because of our own unique experiences and associations.

If we are to communicate effectively with another person, the primary concern regarding language should be to choose words which have similar connotations for the recipients of our message and for us. However, we should not assume that the way we learned a word is necessarily the way other people learned the word. Consequently, their responses to words will not necessarily be similar to our responses.

Dimensions of Meaning

It is difficult to discuss meaning adequately without considering what has become one of the classic approaches to meaning, developed by Charles Osgood and his associates. This approach was based on the associational view of meaning and has resulted in considerable amounts of empirical research.[19] Osgood, Suci, and Tannenbaum[20] presented evidence that indicated the existence of dimensions of meaning for words. Another way of thinking about these dimensions is to consider them the components, or building blocks, that make up meaning.

Osgood and his associates reasoned that if we ask someone what a word means, the person will usually try to define it by using many different words and associations he or she has for that given word. Many of the words used to define other words are adjectives. For instance, if you were asked to define *ice cream,* you might use adjectives like *cold, soft,* and *good.* Osgood, Suci, and Tannenbaum took defining through the use of adjectives a little further and made it more formal. They presented to their experimental subjects long lists of adjectives along with the words whose meaning they wanted to measure.

18. Joseph DeVito, *The Psychology of Speech and Language* (New York: Random House, 1970), 12–13.

19. Donald K. Darnell, "Semantic Differentiation," in Philip Emmert and William D. Brooks, eds., *Methods of Research in Communication* (Boston: Houghton Mifflin, 1970), 181.

20. Charles E. Osgood, George J. Suci, and Percy H. Tannenbaum, *The Measurement of Meaning* (Urbana, Ill.: University of Illinois Press, 1957).

Figure 5.3

Mother

Good	X	__	__	__	__	__	__	Bad
Fast	__	X	__	__	__	__	__	Slow
Valuable	X	__	__	__	__	__	__	Worthless
Hard	__	X	__	__	__	__	__	Soft
Passive	__	__	__	__	__	X	__	Active
Powerful	__	X	__	__	__	__	__	Weak

Good and *valuable* tap the evaluative component,
fast and *passive* the activity component, and
hard and *powerful* the potency component.

These adjectives were presented to the subjects as bipolar scales (as in fig. 5.3), which meant that every adjective had an opposite. If *cold* were used, its bipolar opposite was *hot*. If *soft* were used, so was *hard*. Subjects were asked to indicate on a seven-point scale the extent to which they thought the adjectives applied to the concept or word being rated. As a result of this kind of research, Osgood, Suci, and Tannenbaum discovered what they called three dimensions of meaning.

These dimensions of meaning include: an **evaluative component,** a **potency component,** and an **activity component.** The evaluative component in words involves a good-bad/valuable-worthless response to words. An element of meaning for every word we respond to is our positive-negative response to it. The potency component relates to strength and power. Part of our response to words has to do with how strong or weak we perceive the referents to be. The activity component involves the dynamism, or activity level, perceived in the referent of the word. This third part of our response to words is a perception of activeness-passiveness.

The meaning of any given word to us is a composite of these components, and each component reflects our previous experiences. As indicated earlier, our experiences provide us with associations for every word. Let us return to our example of the word *mother*. If our female parent were a person who did things for us when we were children, comforted us when we were hurt, dressed us warmly when it was cold, took us to movies, and had birthday parties for us (and other things desired by children), she was a person who satisfied our needs to a great extent. Thus, the evaluative component of our response to the word *mother* would probably be very positive (as marked in fig. 5.3). Likewise, if our female parent was somewhat dominant in our home, planned family activities, and generally "took charge," we would have developed a perception of strength as opposed to weakness within the potency component. If our female parent belonged to many organizations, rushed from meeting to meeting, and chauffeured us from place to place, we would probably have a perception of her as an active rather than passive person. Then the activity component of our response to the word *mother* would tend toward the active rather than the passive end of the active-passive continuum. Thus, our total response to the word *mother* would be that it means positiveness, strength, and activeness.

With this framework of three components of meaning, it is possible for us to compare our meanings with the meanings of others. Does our meaning include more positiveness? Less activeness? More strength? These components can become guidelines for us to follow in choosing words in interpersonal communication. Whenever we experience difficulty communicating, we may find we have used words that are too "strong" and "active" for the person we are trying to influence. While awareness of these components will not automatically provide answers to our problems, it can provide us with insight into probable responses to our words by others.

The findings of Osgood, Suci, and Tannenbaum have further practical implications. Their research made it possible to determine which of the components of meaning is predominant. Apparently, the *evaluative component* accounts for more of our response to words than the other two components combined.[21] This is important to us in interpersonal communication because it suggests that the meanings of words are, to a great extent, evaluative responses, and also that whenever we are using words in interpersonal communication, the people who are listening to us are having primarily positive-negative responses to our words. It is important for us, therefore, to understand the connotative meanings of words as they relate to those we wish to influence: what are positive and what are negative words for them? It does not make much sense to use language to which we know people are going to respond negatively because of their negative associations within the evaluative component of those words. Rather, if we are trying to be effective, it seems more reasonable to use words that have positive associations for our listeners so that their responses to our whole message will be positive.

There are, of course, situations for which we might choose words that people respond to negatively. That kind of situation would occur when we are trying to keep someone from doing something, or when we are trying to cause people to perceive some concept as negative. When that is the situation, we choose words that fall somewhere on the negative end of the evaluative continuum and try to associate those words with the concept we want our lis-

21. Darnell, "Semantic Differentiation," 183.

teners to reject. However, when we are trying to have people accept us and the concepts we are proposing, we want to associate words that are positively evaluated with ourselves and the concepts we support.[22]

22. Staats and Staats, "Meaning Established."

This frequently occurs in politics. A politician finds out (either through polling or through very sensitive listening to constituents) that voters perceive the word *busing* very negatively and the word *prosperity* very positively. Once an astute politician has discovered this, that person will take care in all public speeches and personal interactions to be verbally associated with prosperity, with its positive associations. Politicians assume that if they can associate themselves with prosperity, voters are more likely to accept them. Likewise, they will try to disassociate themselves verbally from the word *busing*, in the hope that they will become more acceptable to their constituents by avoiding a word that produces a negative response.

Another important finding of Osgood and his associates is that the multi-dimensionality of meaning crosses cultures.[23] Most of the research concerning the multiple components of meaning has been conducted in the United States with American subjects, but not all. Interestingly enough, the same components of meaning found to apply to English words in the United States apply also to the equivalents of those words in other languages and other cultures. It is rare in the behavioral sciences for findings to apply across cultures, but research on meaning with the Osgood, Suci, and Tannenbaum technique comes close to providing universal results. The components of meaning for words are as appropriate for Japanese as for American English. In every culture we can expect similar kinds of responses *in terms of the components people use to respond to words.*

23. Osgood, Suci, and Tannenbaum, *Measurement of Meaning.*

Brief Summary of Meaning

To arrive at the nature of meaning, we have considered four main points: (1) the meaning of a word is arbitrary — words do not have inherent meaning; (2) their meanings reside in people; (3) these meanings develop through a process of association that is complex, built up over years of conditioning to words and their referents; and (4) the meanings we associate with words are built up in terms of three components: evaluation, potency, and activity. Our responses to words along these dimensions are the result of the different experiences and associations we have had with the words and their referents and are combined into a total response to words that we call meaning. The principal dimension of meaning for words is the evaluative component, which suggests that people respond to words primarily along a positive-negative continuum.

WE PERCEIVE THROUGH WORDS:
THE SAPIR-WHORF HYPOTHESIS

An important question concerning the effect of words on us is related to what has been termed the **Sapir-Whorf hypothesis.** The Sapir-Whorf hypothesis was developed by Benjamin Lee Whorf, with considerable input by Edward Sapir, a linguist. Whorf himself was not a scholar in the formal sense. Yet, in addition to his career as an insurance engineer, he developed a theory about language that continues to stimulate scholars.[24] The hypothesis developed by Sapir-Whorf has been neither totally proved nor totally disproved[25] forty-some years after its formal statement.

The notion proposed in this theory is that our perception of reality and the world around us is determined by the thought processes we use and that these thought processes are determined by the language system we have learned.[26] For example, Eskimos have many different words for snow, whereas people who live in a southern climate in the United States may use only one, the word *snow*. According to the Sapir-Whorf hypothesis, a person from the south who has only one word for snow will see only one kind of physical reality when confronted with samples of frozen moisture falling out of the sky. However, an Eskimo, whose language differentiates among many different kinds of snow with many different words, will be able to see many different forms of snow. Skiers are able to distinguish and have words for somewhere up to about half-a-dozen different kinds of snow. For someone who grows up in the Midwest and is not a skier, however, there are usually only two types of snow: wet snow and dry snow. There is a corollary of the theory that the words we learn determine the reality we perceive: the environment in which our culture developed has shaped the language system our society later teaches us. Thus, we find ourselves faced with a circular process: the reality that faced our ancestors shaped the language, and, in turn, the language subsequently shapes the reality any of us perceive because we developed within and learned that language system.

This theory is consistent with the discussion in chapter 4 regarding the process of perception. In that chapter we indicated that some scholars believe it is necessary for us to categorize stimuli in order to perceive. We use a language system to categorize stimuli. This is what the Sapir-Whorf approach suggests: that as we are confronted with numerous stimuli, we select from, categorize, and attach meaning to stimuli according to our language system.

Students have sometimes complained to us that the first course in almost any discipline — whether it be communication, computer science, journalism, or management — consists of nothing but a lot of new words (and often these new words refer to familiar things). We would have to agree that this is probably the case. Beginning or introductory courses in most areas of study spend

24. Benjamin Lee Whorf, "The Relation of Habitual Thought and Behavior to Language," in John B. Carroll, ed., *Language, Thought and Reality: Selected Writings of Benjamin Lee Whorf* (Cambridge, Mass.: M.I.T. Press, 1956), 134–59.

25. Slobin, *Psycholinguistics*, 120–33.

26. Benjamin Lee Whorf, "Science and Linguistics," in Carroll, ed., *Language, Thought and Reality*, 107–19.

considerable time defining the jargon of the discipline. Every field appears to have its own words for talking about the phenomena studied in that particular field. It is our feeling that basic courses focus on providing to students beginning a discipline a new vocabulary because *it is necessary to have the language to discuss the concepts of that field effectively.* More specifically, it is not only necessary to have the new words to *discuss* the concepts, it may be necessary to have them in order to *perceive* instances of the concepts to which the words refer.

The term *feedback* has become a popular word in recent years. People in communication are happy to see the term become popular because it is so much a part of our discipline. We wonder whether others have not in recent years (in addition to learning and adopting the word *feedback*) also changed their perceptions of the way people relate and interact with one another because of use of the term. We cannot *prove* that use of the term *feedback* in recent years has caused a change in the way people interact, but we suspect that this new word, and other definitions and concepts associated with it, may have affected the way people perceive communication.

Probably the most acceptable interpretation of the Sapir-Whorf hypothesis uses a modified version of Whorf's original statement. Rather than suggesting that our thoughts are totally determined by our language, this version offers a facilitation approach that suggests that our language system makes it easier to think about some things than about other things.[27] This version of the Sapir-Whorf hypothesis does not say it is impossible for us to think certain thoughts or to perceive certain realities; rather, our language system makes it easier for us to perceive some realities and think certain thoughts. The words we learn, and the meanings associated with them, do have an effect on the way we perceive things. Likewise, the structure of the language we learn affects the way we think about things.

Most of us realize, to some extent, the effect our words can have on the perceptions of others. If you have not finished an assignment, which would you be more likely to say to your professor: "I haven't finished writing my paper"; or "My paper isn't finished yet"? It is a small difference, but notice that the second statement sounds less as though the speaker were at fault than does the first statement. If, as you learned the word *doctor* you associated it with an activity performed by males, how does that association affect your perception of a female who is introduced to you as "Doctor Smith"? Do you perceive her to be less qualified professionally because *doctor* is a "male term"? We think that is entirely possible.

In recent years there has been an effort to remove what are called sexist terms from job descriptions, textbooks, and even constitutions of various organizations. This is probably the result of a recognition that frequent use of terms like *he, him,* and *his* in association with terms like *president, sales manager,* and the like causes people to perceive the positions of sales manager

27. Slobin, *Psycholinguistics,* 125.

Words and Meaning   **133**

and president as jobs for men, not women. Likewise, if in a conversation you use the word *girl* to refer to an adult female, you probably perceive the person as "less mature," and you are more condescending than if you used the term *woman*. Our tendency to use words without regard to the possible effect on our own perceptions and those of others can distort perceptions and cause trouble.

What does this theory mean to us in interpersonal communication? Simply this: we have all grown up within a specific language system, and each person in any interpersonal situation may have grown up in more than one language system. (We all come from our own subcultures, in which we have learned our languages under different circumstances. Consequently, our language systems condition us to think differently about things, or at least facilitate our thinking about different things.) We should always be concerned with the nature of the language system of the persons with whom we communicate. Does their language system hinder thinking some thoughts? Does it lack certain words and prevent them from perceiving some things we perceive? The same questions should be applied to ourselves. Does the structure of our language hinder us in thinking in certain ways? Does our language lack certain words or concepts and thus prevent our perceiving some things that others perceive? If we begin to suspect this may be the case, it may be desirable to try to learn their language system, or at least try to understand it better. This may enable us to understand and resolve differences more easily.

HOW WORDS AFFECT INTERPERSONAL COMMUNICATION

Words and Culture

Excellent examples of the modified Sapir-Whorf hypothesis abound in the United States. We have many subcultural groups such as blacks, WASPs, males, females, Hispanics, Japanese-Americans, and American Indians. The culture of a person, be it a majority or minority culture, is significantly represented by language. Arabs have six thousand words for *camel*. Our category systems are very much bound up in our vocabularies.

Andrea Rich suggests that our symbol system can be viewed as an extension of culture.[28] We feel that words permit us to express those things that are of importance in our culture. Because, as discussed earlier, the weather is an important factor in the Eskimo culture, they have developed a vocabulary that reflects this and have many terms for ice and snow, whereas a person growing up in the Midwest may be able to distinguish only two kinds of snow. The difference is the result of the differing importance of snow in the cultures.

28. Andrea Rich, *Interracial Communication* (New York: Harper & Row, 1974), 129.

Rich concludes that "language, then, our conventionally agreed-on system of symbols, codes our experience; enables us to communicate that experience to others; structures our thoughts, perceptions, and actions; and serves both as an expression of and an influence on our culture".[29]

29. Ibid., 131.

The kind of problems that result from cultural differences in word meaning is made more clear by the experimental finding that Italians react to the words *thieves* and *criminals* as having a more successful and less foolish connotation than is the case for most Americans.[30] This may suggest a more generally positive perception of criminals in Italy than in the United States. Perhaps Italians and Americans, when communicating about criminal activities, have difficulty achieving understanding if they are unaware of this difference in the perception of these words.

30. Ephraim Rosen, "A Cross-Cultural Study of Semantic Profiles and Attitude Differences: (Italy)," *Journal of Social Psychology* 49(1959):137–44.

A similar problem exists between WASPs and ethnic minorities in our country. It has been suggested that many adult blacks function linguistically within the context of two or more different language systems: black language and white language.[31] Depending on the socioeconomic level of an individual black person in America, he or she may function in the context of at least three language systems: a language system referred to as standard American English; another language system common to blacks living in ghettos in America, and still another language system of middle- and upper-class blacks. It is possible, however, that the language system of middle- and upper-class blacks is more comparable to standard American English than to anything else.

31. David Lewit and Edward Abner, "Black-White Semantic Differences and Interracial Communication," *Journal of Applied Psychology* 1, no. 3(1971):276.

Members of different cultural groups in interpersonal communication need to take into consideration the possibility that they are responding differently to the same words. Lewit and Abner suggested that cooperation is possible when words mean the same to both whites and blacks.[32] Cooperation and trust may fail to be produced, however, in spontaneous, natural situations if one interacting person hears familiar words but infers meanings different from those of the speaker. This problem is present whenever members of two or more cultures or subcultures attempt to communicate with one another (especially if the communicators are unaware of these differences).

32. Ibid.

Of recent vintage, though possessing roots that reach far back into history, the women's movement has focused on the unequal treatment of women in our country. Women have been paid less for their work and have been denied jobs because of their sex. While that is what the movement has focused on, we would like to point out that in reality we have two very separate cultures: a male culture and a female culture existing side by side in the United States.[33]

33. Barbara W. Eakins and R. Gene Eakins, *Sex Differences in Human Communication* (Boston: Houghton Mifflin, 1978), 1–21.

This differentiation between the male and female worlds in this country can be defined by the various factors that constitute culture. Experiences of males and females differ to a marked extent in this country. The beliefs, values, and attitudes are very different. The meanings attached to a given word also differ greatly for males and females. Today there is a controversy over abortion.

Could a male and a female possibly perceive the meaning for the word *abortion* in the same way? Of course not; their experiences with it are different. It is something that happens to a woman. It does not happen to a man, who can be only indirectly involved in an abortion. Obviously, the same degree of personal involvement does not exist for males.

Likewise, if a male and a female have had sex together and some time later the female, upon discovering she is pregnant, says to the male, "I am pregnant," could we for a moment suggest that the word *pregnant* has the same meaning for the male as for the female? Again, it is not something that happens to a male. Many males often forget that the female experience is different from the male experience. Frequently males try to make decisions for females on matters that they cannot approach in the same way as females because they do not have the same point of view — they do not perceive the same meaning. Of course, the same thing holds true for the other side of the coin. As long as wars are fought by men, can *war* ever mean the same to males and females? We doubt it.

Many other words and concepts could be used to point out cultural communication differences. We suggest that you consider some of the different things different groups interact about and how their different cultures or subcultures could cause people to approach words differently.

Abstraction Process

A concept discussed by general semanticists for years, and which is of interest to us in interpersonal communication, is the abstraction process. The discussion of perception in chapter 4 stressed the chaotic nature of the world and the different stimuli impinging on us. Our only defense against this is the perception process, which consists of arranging the world into some kind of pattern so that we can impose order on the world.

Chapter 4 also presented the idea that we employ categories for the purpose of classifying the stimuli we perceive. There are numerous furry, four-legged, barking animals with tails that run around our neighborhoods. It is easier to deal with these animals if we can classify them and have some set of predictions for that classification. The classification we use is *dog*. There are any number of predictions we can make regarding what these animals might do on our lawns, what kinds of noises they might make under different circumstances, and whether they might or might not be friendly and thus either do us bodily damage or make us feel good under certain circumstances. This is the process of abstraction. To conceive of the category *dog*, it is necessary for us to abstract from each of these furry creatures those characteristics they all have in common. By noting those characteristics, we are able to depict a class of animal life. This class is an abstraction.

The word *dog* refers to both of these very different animals. *Dog* is an abstraction we may or may not agree about.

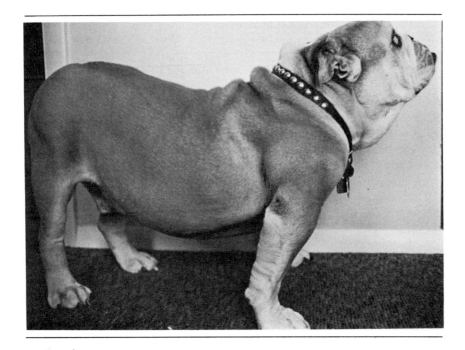

34. Alfred Korzybski, "The Role of Language in the Perceptual Processes," in Robert R. Blake and Glenn V. Ramsey, eds., *Perception: An Approach to Personality* (New York: Ronald Press, 1951).

The abstraction process not only includes noting similarities, it also involves overlooking differences.[34] It should be obvious that some very big differences must be overlooked. Our English bulldog is short, squat, very broad shouldered, has teeth that stick out, is bowlegged, and almost waddles when he walks. Our neighbor's black labrador is almost twice as tall as our bulldog, with long, silky hair, and a very long tail, as opposed to the bulldog's short curly tail. Our neighbor's dog is also incredibly graceful and able to jump great heights; our bulldog cannot jump. If all these differences were not over-looked — color, size, even the way the animals move — we might be inclined to question their being classified in the same category.

The two animals do have many characteristics in common. Their behavior patterns are quite similar, as are many of their apparent interests. Both are interested in chasing birds, barking at a stranger intruding upon their property at night, and playing with balls and sticks. We could also classify them in terms of their genetic similarities. They seem to have some common ancestry, per-haps discoverable if one checks back far enough. Thus, we classify them as *dog,* a creature that inevitably walks on four legs, has a tail, barks, and appears to be friendly more often than not toward people.

The abstraction or categorization process that we employ to handle in-coming stimuli in our day-to-day world could also be termed a *stereotyping process.* We stereotype dogs according to the characteristics they appear to have in common. Abstraction and stereotyping can be very useful, as was pointed out in chapter 4. It is impossible to handle every incoming stimulus individually and separately. Rather, it is necessary to have a system that per-mits predictions. If it were necessary for us to approach each dog as a totally different creature, without any basis for prediction (which we would have to do if we had no category or stereotype to guide our responses), we would probably go mad. Rather than do that, we employ abstractions and stereo-types, which provide us with some predictive ability.

If you had no ideas about a group of people called *doctors,* and what they can and cannot do, you would probably never go to one. If you did go to one, you would not know how to act in the presence of that person. How-ever, given the abstraction/stereotype most people have of medical doctors, you are able to choose to go to one when you consider yourself sufficiently ill to require such a person's services. You also have a basis for responding to the advice this person gives.

Although the abstraction process is useful, there are some real problems it can create in interpersonal communication. For example, we may assume that because we have an abstraction/stereotype of a given category, the char-acteristics of that category will necessarily hold true for every member. Using the category of *doctor,* it is quite possible for us to assume that if our abstrac-tion concerning doctors includes people who have a certain amount of train-ing and a certain amount of expertise and knowledge about the human body, then we may be inclined to accept blindly the advice given by any doctor, when, in fact, there are doctors who, for one reason of another, may be inadequate for our needs.

General semanticists have suggested that the abstraction process causes us to overlook the differences in people and things, simply because they are all in the same category.[35] (They suggested the same thing about stereotyping, because abstraction and stereotyping are similar processes.) Their implied warning is valid as applied to interpersonal communication, for if we respond to stereotypes and abstractions rather than to the person with whom we are trying to communicate, we can become very ineffective. Likewise, if the language employed by the other person is such that we respond to our stereotypes rather than observe that the other person may be expressing some idiosyncratically different meaning, we may respond to the wrong concept. We would be responding to our abstraction, not to the concept the other person intended.

35. Roger Brown, "How Shall a Thing Be Called?" *Psychological Review* 65, no. 1(1958):14–21.

General semanticists have suggested the devices of **indexing** and **dating** and the use of quotation marks to aid us in avoiding this kind of error.[36] We can index dogs by considering them "dog_1," "dog_2," and "dog_3" whenever we see a dog. This should remind us that all dogs are not necessarily friendly, and that we should test this assumption with each dog.

36. Korzybski, *Science and Sanity*, 1–18.

Likewise, we need to remember that the abstraction *mother* is one we may have developed some years back. We also need to remember that mother has probably changed in the intervening years; we live in a process world in which everything changes continually.[37] By employing dating procedures, we can remember that people and things change. $Mother_{1985}$ may not be the same as $Mother_{1965}$. Consequently, we need to respond to her differently. Terms change over time. Words and their meaning change over time. $Inflation_{1985}$ is not the same as $inflation_{1975}$. Thus when discussing inflation and ways to combat it, we may have to think in very different terms in 1985 from the way we did in 1975.

37. Korzybski, "Role of Language."

Finally, the use of mental quotation marks may remind us that the meaning we have for a word is an abstraction and can be very different from the meaning someone else has. For instance, when we are discussing the term *democracy,* it would be of use to keep in the backs of our minds imaginary quotation marks around that word because "democracy" for us may represent something very different from "democracy" for another person. If such is the case, we may at any time during a conversation simply stop the conversation and say, "Wait a minute. Tell me what you mean by 'democracy' and I'll explain what I mean by 'democracy.' " By going through that process, it may be possible to restore understanding.

We are not trying to say that the abstraction process in and of itself is necessarily bad. On the contrary, it should be obvious from the earlier discussion of perception that abstraction, categorization, and stereotyping are necessary for us to cope with a multitude of stimuli in the world. We are, however, cautioning that the abstraction process can cause us to use words in a way that leaves out characteristics. Thus, to communicate with one another and have common meanings and common responses to words, it is necessary for us to remember that the abstraction process occurs also with the person with whom we are communicating; therefore, we must always try to make sure that our responses to words are compatible with theirs.

Hidden Antagonizers

38. Hayakawa, *Language in Thought and Action*, 2d ed.

In *Language in Thought and Action,* S. I. Hayakawa[38] referred to the existence of "snarl words" and "purr words." He suggested that we use words that are in some respect similar to sounds issuing from animals, and more particularly the cat family. An example of snarl words would be, "You're a male chauvinist pig." A statement such as that is an indication of a feeling of hostility. The words do not necessarily indicate anything about the person to whom the comment is directed. What is being said is: "I feel very hostile toward you and so, consequently, I will snarl at you." Hence the expression **snarl words.**

Likewise, the comment "You're beautiful tonight" is not really as much about the person to whom the comment is directed as it is about feelings of the communicator toward the person who is receiving this utterance. In essence, what the communicator is saying is: "I love you and I feel good about you, and so, consequently, I am going to indicate my happiness to you." The person does this by using what Hayakawa referred to as **purr words.**

It is our feeling that we can go beyond Hayakawa's original comments about snarl words and purr words. It is rather obvious when we say hostile things like "You're a louse" or "I don't like you" that these are snarl words. But there is a different kind of word that merits attention and requires caution when we communicate. **Hidden antagonizers** are words perceived negatively by the recipient of our message because of the associations and connotations for that person. They are "hidden" antagonizers because the user is unaware that the words are snarl words to some people.

39. Lerone Bennett, Jr., "What's in a Name?", *ETC, A Review of General Semantics* 26, no. 4(1969):399–412.

In recent years a problem that has confronted many whites in this country is the question of what word should be used to refer to people of African ancestry with dark skin.[39] The terms *Negro* and *colored* have been rejected by many of these people. Other terms now in use include *black, Afro-American,* and *African* . The use of words such as *colored* or *Negro* in speaking to some of these persons produces a response very similar to what would result from the use of snarl words — an intense, extremely hostile response which is very difficult ever to atone for. The same kind of thing appears to be true for adherents of the women's movement with terms we will discuss later.

Some words that whites commonly use have intensely negative connotations for members of certain minority groups — not only blacks but also Hispanics, American Indians, and so on. Whites are frequently unaware of these negative connotations and use these hidden antagonizers with alarming regularity when interacting with members of other cultures. The responses obviously are negative, and the possibility of cooperation and trust is destroyed — if it ever existed in the first place. Certainly cooperation and trust are not created when words are employed this way.

It is also evident that whites are not the only cultural group that uses these hidden antagonizers. One study revealed that words which blacks frequently employ, such as *honky,* seem to be far more threatening to whites than blacks intend them to be. On the other hand, when whites employ derogatory terms toward blacks, such as *nigger,* the response of blacks to those terms is very close to the response expected.[40]

It is not clear why this is so. Perhaps blacks have been subjected to so much abuse by whites for so many years that they do not perceive it as an unusual thing to be at the receiving end of derogatory messages; thus, they do not react as intensely as whites under the same or similar circumstances. For white society in America today to find itself on the receiving end of insults is something of a new experience; so possibly whites react more intensely to a derogatory term than minority groups, such as blacks, would predict. Our past experience is what determines the meanings the words hold for us and how we respond to those words. It should be obvious that the past experiences of people in different cultural groups are considerably different.

While conducting a communication workshop once, we used the term *women's lib* during discussion. After uttering the term, we found ourselves being attacked verbally by a woman for having used it. Evidently the term *women's lib* was a snarl word for this person, which we had not anticipated. Finally, after some interaction, we and the woman managed to reach an understanding, and the ultimate outcome was that we refrained from using that term for the balance of the conference and began using the term *feminist movement.* It took this encounter for us to become aware of some very negative connotations associated with the term *women's lib* that are not associated with the term *feminist movement* for some women. However, the term women's movement seems to have become more preferable now.

Many of our words can become snarl words for someone else without our ever intending them to be so. While Hayakawa referred to the use of snarl words as a manifestation of hostility on the part of the communicator, it seems legitimate to suggest that, by the same token, the listener's role in converting seemingly innocent words into snarl words (even though the talker did not intend them that way) is a manifestation of the listener's hostility. In recent years hidden antagonizers have become talked about more and referred to more often. Words that label various ethnic groups, such as *Polack* and *Jap,* have received publicity, thanks in no small measure to a former vice-president's use of them. The use of male pronouns to refer to both sexes in textbooks has been attacked by members of the woman's movement for the effect it has upon young girls. Blacks, Hispanics, and Indians have pointed out many terms that are offensive to them.

40. Daniel J. Roadhouse, "Analysis of Interracial Differences Toward Derogatory Terms," term paper, University of Wyoming, Department of Communication, 1974.

Some terms have been hidden antagonizers for years. The recent focus on them is probably the result of an increased willingness to talk about ethnic problems and interracial interaction in the United States. The problem is very real, and one that is deceptive. It is possible for a communicator to think, "Well, I didn't mean anything derogatory or hostile when I used that term." This is quite beside the point. Former Vice-President Agnew used the term *Polack* during a press conference. A controversy immediately followed, and many letters were addressed to Mr. Agnew. His response was that he had not intended any slight when he used the term. Our point here is that it did not matter whether he intended the slight or not; the response of the listener to the words we use is all that really matters, because that response is the one we have to deal with. If we have used hidden antagonizers in our communication (even though they were hidden from us) and they antagonize someone listening to our message, our ability to continue the relationship with the person to whom we are speaking may be completely destroyed. There may be no way we can go back and pick up the relationship, regardless of the meanings we intended.

What do we do regarding hidden antagonizers? Because they are hidden from our awareness, we obviously do not know we are about to use them when we do. The only advice we can give is based on common sense. Listen to people around you, and read about different ethnic, religious, and special-interest groups. Find out what is offensive, unacceptable, and would antagonize people with whom you may interact. Remember, the hidden antagonizers are not ones that are necessarily obvious, nor are they words everyone will be aware of as being hidden antagonizers. Try to get to know better the people with whom you communicate, so you will know what words they are sensitive to.

Remember, the meanings for the listeners of the words you use in interpersonal communication will be determined by their fields of experience. You will have your own meaning, but this will be almost irrelevant, because your concern in interpersonal communication is with the effect you have on the other person. Thus, your first concern must be the field of experience of the other person, and the possible responses that person may have to words you use.

Of course, the concept of hidden antagonizers really refers to how people respond to the evaluative component of meaning in words. Recall that the primary response of people to words is to the evaluative component.

Reaching Agreement

Since words can provoke hostile responses, words can keep us from ever reaching agreement with people to whom we are speaking. Likewise, words can facilitate agreement. It is impossible for us to reach agreement on any matter so long as we and the people we are talking to are reacting to words

How do we define *freedom of speech?*

differently. If we are discussing freedom of speech, it is imperative that we and the person we are talking to have similar referents for the abstraction *freedom of speech.* If one of us means by this the freedom to express any political philosophy in a public forum and the other person means the showing of pornographic films, it may be very difficult to come to an understanding. Though we use the same word, our referents for the word are different. For us to reach agreement in any discussion, it would appear necessary for us to agree about the meaning of the language we are using in the discussion. How can we do this?

Let us return to Lewis Carroll and the conversation between Alice and Humpty Dumpty. The first part was omitted in the earlier presentation. It went like this: " 'I don't know what you mean by glory,' Alice said. Humpty Dumpty smiled contemptuously. 'Of course you don't — till I tell you.' "[41]

The interesting thing about this interaction is the way Alice approached Humpty Dumpty. He had used a word, *glory,* in a way that did not make sense to her, so she asked him what he meant. He then defined it for her as "a nice

41. Carroll, *Through the Looking Glass,* 246-47.

knock-down argument." Simplistic though it may seem, it is not a bad idea in interpersonal communication to simply ask, for instance, "What do you mean by *freedom of speech*?" Rather than continuing an argument on whether or not freedom of speech should be permitted, it would make sense to find out whether what the participants are arguing about is the same for both.

It is entirely possible that a simple definition of the term *freedom of speech* will not be adequate. Recall the comments earlier on the abstraction process, and remember that *freedom of speech* is a very abstract phrase and can refer to many different concrete events. Likewise, it is necessary to keep in mind that a definition for *freedom of speech* may itself be somewhat abstract and far removed from the concrete events it is being used to represent.

It may be necessary to say something like this to the person with whom you are talking: "Well, I think I understand your verbal definition. Let me see if the following example is what you mean." And then you give a concrete example, such as, "Do you mean freedom of speech to include the right to shout 'Fire!' in a public place when there is no fire?" At this point the other person can say, "Well, no, I don't intend freedom of speech to include that." Then it is possible for you to say, "Then *freedom of speech* doesn't really mean *absolute* freedom of speech and it does not include all examples of speech." It would be possible to go through some kind of exchange of this sort, using examples and definitions to pinpoint more accurately how each of you is using the term. If you can determine what the concrete reality is that the other person is using his or her words to represent, it is then possible to reach some sort of agreement on (1) the words we are using and what we intend them to mean; and (2) what the point of discussion is.

It is important to note also that one of the ways we can help someone else understand what we mean by a word is by attempting to describe our own field of experience so the other person can come to understand how we learned the word and, thus, our meaning for it. Conversely, it would help us understand another person's meaning for a word if we could determine what associations the other person has for his or her words and how they were acquired (through what field of experience). Having this background, we might better understand why such persons are sensitive to a word we are not sensitive to.

We have a daughter who, when she was between two and three years old, experienced a very severe infection in her throat, cheek, and mouth. Her cheek, jaw, and throat were very swollen and painful. Several doctors and dentists had to touch and probe the infected area and take samples for analysis. Not only was all this extremely painful it could not be adequately explained to a little girl. This experience was one of the most dramatic of her life to that point and became associated in her mind with the phrase *doctor's office*. Well into her teenage years she was tense in a doctor's office. If she were told that it was necessary for someone to look into her mouth or take a throat culture, the tension turned to fear. Although this is an extreme example, it shows how understanding a person's field of experience can help us understand the person's response to words and phrases we may use in interaction.

Of course, the maximum agreement can be reached when people find similar experiences to which they can relate the words they are using. It is probably a good idea whenever there is word disagreement to search for common elements in the respective fields of experience.[42]

42. Schramm, "How Communication Works," 3–26.

Summary

In this chapter we discussed meaning in words and its arbitrary nature. Meaning is very likely acquired through a complex association process, which results from a person's field of experience. This process creates meanings for words that can be analyzed into three components: evaluation, potency, and activity. The primary component of meaning is evaluative, and we are constantly responding to words in positive or negative ways. The Sapir-Whorf hypothesis is that language either determines how we think and perceive the world or (at least) makes easier certain ways of thinking and perceiving the world. This is, in turn, tightly bound to the cultural group within which someone learns that language.

Words are abstractions and sometimes have only a remote connection with any concrete referents. Words can be "hidden antagonizers," and it is important to be aware of how other people respond to our words. Much of what we know about language is very tentative at this point and needs to be tested. However, the concepts covered in this chapter, are based on research. Also, they are accepted by many scholars and have considerable practical significance for interpersonal communication. Keeping in mind these characteristics of language while we communicate should improve interpersonal effectiveness.

6

Nonverbal Communication: Influence Without Words

1. To be able to describe the complexity and importance of nonverbal communication.
2. To be able to explain the relationship of nonverbal to verbal communication.
3. To be able to predict how nonverbal attributes affect person perception and the reception of messages.
4. To be able to describe and use intentional manipulations of nonverbal communicative behavior.
5. To be able to encode and decode emotional expression more accurately:
   a. by explaining seven critical aspects of interpreting and displaying emotional expression;
   b. by discussing how nonverbal behaviors are combined to express complex attitudes toward others.
6. To be able to describe cultural differences in nonverbal communication which affect our understanding of one another.
7. To be able to predict differences in nonverbal communication between males and females in our culture which influence how we perceive and understand, or misunderstand, members of the opposite sex.

You have, no doubt, had the experience of meeting someone for the first time whom you liked immediately. Sometimes, too, you have experienced just the reverse — knowing nothing about a person on a first encounter and yet immediately disliking that person. Or you may have been in an interaction with someone and felt that something was "wrong" — the other person wasn't being entirely open or honest, or you just couldn't seem to interact smoothly with the other person. Whatever it is that causes us to respond with either like or dislike to another person or be comfortable or uncomfortable represents a combination of many things: the person's clothes; body movements; facial expressions; how close to us the person stands (or how far away); his or her relative physical attractiveness (or lack of it); and other nonverbal signs or messages which we exchange with the other person — to mention just a few. The number of nonverbal behaviors that can influence others is enormous.

Part of our nonverbal communication comes from the way we use our bodies: we gesture with our hands; nod our heads; gaze with our eyes; exhibit thousands of expressions on our faces; move our shoulders, arms, legs, and feet; and constantly change posture. We also communicate with one another through touch.

1. G. L. Trager, "Paralanguage: A First Approximation," *Studies in Linguistics* 13 (1958): 1–12.

Quality of voice also gives others an impression of us.[1] Our **pitch range** (the height and depth of our sound repertoire) and the **volume** (or loudness) of our voice are only two characteristics. We also speak with a **rhythm** (the way we phrase our words) and a **tempo** (the speed at which we deliver those words). Some of us speak with precision in our pronunciation — our **articulation** is careful. These vocal characteristics — such as pitch, volume, rhythm, tempo, articulation, even our pauses and silences as we speak — can communicate to others.

How we structure our spatial arrangements with others not only affects our communication, but also appears to communicate certain aspects of how we perceive our relationship to the other person. Even the way we use time communicates to others.

While we cannot radically change many aspects of our physical appearance, we do try to control them so they will communicate to others how we feel about ourselves and the communication contexts in which we are performing. We also use artifacts (or man-made objects) such as jewelry, furniture, or even the architectural design of a building to affect others and to "set the stage" for our communication performances. Sometimes we try to control our environment so it will be conducive to the type of communication we desire. The person who carefully arranges a candlelight dinner is doing more than just creating an effect, he or she is telling a companion what kind of communication is expected.

We use gestures, facial expressions, smiles, touching, space, and even eye contact (or lack of it) to communicate that we like or do not like someone. The clothes we wear can influence others. They way we wear our hair — even the kind of eyeglasses we select — can influence other people. These and many more behaviors can be deliberately employed as symbols to influence another person, just as we employ words to influence them. Males and females have recognized the importance of nonverbal cues from the beginning of man's history. The way a woman walks, the way a man moves, and the way they look at each other can determine how they will spend an evening — either in loneliness or in romantic companionship. Parents and children know how important nonverbal communication is. The way a parent raises or lowers the voice and the way a child manages to develop a tear in one eye can have far more to do with the outcome of an interaction than do the words spoken between them.

Most of us spend only ten to eleven minutes a day actually speaking.[2] Words uttered in the average sentence lasts for about two and a half seconds. We may spend hours involved in conversations, but the actual time each person spends uttering words is, nevertheless, only about ten or eleven minutes a day. It becomes obvious, then, that while we are involved in conversation a lot must be going on in addition to the speaking of words. What is going on is listening and a lot of nonverbal communication, during speaking as well as during silences.

Most of us receive formal instruction in the use of words throughout at least twelve years of schooling. But schools pay little attention to nonverbal communication. There are few courses in nonverbal communication comparable to our standard English courses, although more and more colleges and universities are beginning to develop such courses. It is apparent that we learn most of our nonverbal communication, as we learn language, during the early years of our lives. But we do not necessarily learn to use language well unless we have formal instruction. Likewise with nonverbal communication, many of us do not learn to use it well, or even understand it — even in our own cultural context, let alone any other cultural context. Is it any wonder that many of us fail so miserably in our attempts to influence other people in view of the lack of formal training in nonverbal communication? We have been placed in a situation in which much of our total communicative effort depends upon a skill for which few of us have received formal training. It is not surprising that we err in our communication efforts. It is more surprising when we succeed.

It is our intent to provide in this chapter some understanding of nonverbal communication, which we hope will whet your appetite for further study. Obviously we cannot do justice to the entire area in one chapter, but an introduction is better than nothing. We feel that, if you are at least aware of the important elements in nonverbal communication, you will be able to exercise greater control over your own nonverbal behavior and improve your nonverbal skills.

2. Mark L. Knapp, *Nonverbal Communication in Human Interacting,* 2d ed. (New York: Holt, Rinehart & Winston, 1978).

RELATIONSHIP OF NONVERBAL AND VERBAL COMMUNICATION

Nonverbal and verbal communication are not independent systems. They work together to make communication more complete. At least six relationships have been discovered between the verbal and nonverbal channels of communication.[3]

3. Paul Ekman "Communication Through Nonverbal Behavior: A Source of Information About an Interpersonal Relationship," in S. S. Thomkins and C. E. Izard, eds., *Affect, Cognition and Personality* (New York: Springer, 1965), 440–41.

Repetition

First, the nonverbal communication system may simply repeat the verbal message. This redundancy by **repetition** makes it easier for people to understand a particular message quickly. If you frown as you tell someone you are displeased with something, this makes it much more likely that the person will perceive the message more accurately.

Substitution

Second, a nonverbal message can be a **substitution** for a verbal message. Sometimes it is inconvenient or inappropriate to send a particular verbal message. Suppose you and a friend are at a party and you want to leave and don't want to tell your friend that you want to leave in front of the hostess. If the two of you are close friends, you may send your friend a message nonverbally: a glance, a lifting of the eyebrows, and a movement of the chin in the direction of the door. Frequently your friend will perceive this substitute message accurately, and the two of you will be able to leave without hurting the hostess's feelings. Many professions use nonverbal cues in place of verbal messages because verbal messages would be difficult to hear or would interrupt the activity which is occurring. Broadcasters, referees, auctioneers, and scuba divers have developed signals which they can use in place of verbal messages.

Emphasis

Third, nonverbal cues can also add **emphasis** to parts of the verbal message. We use vocal characteristics to emphasize the meaning of words.[4] As we become more excited or angry, or when we simply want to make a point more emphatic, we tend to increase the volume of our voice. As we wish to become more affectionate, considerate, and understanding in our speech, we tend to reduce the volume. Couples making love don't shout at each other. Romantic feeling appears to be most effectively communicated to another person through the use of a soft, breathy voice speaking barely above a whisper. Volume is an effective factor in communication. The rate at which we

4. Edward T. Hall, *The Silent Language* (Greenwich, Conn.: Fawcett Publications, 1959), 163–64.

Baseball umpires use nonverbal communication in place of words because it is difficult to be heard on a baseball diamond.

speak and the rhythm also have a significant effect on interpersonal communication.[5] As we increase our rate of speech, we change the listener's perception of the importance of what we are saying. Someone who is speaking rapidly tends to convey an impression of excitement and importance, whereas someone who speaks slowly conveys a relaxed atmosphere with no need for hurry or excitement. The rhythm with which we speak can vary. Some people speak in short spurts, while some tend to speak in a rather consistent fluent manner (although total fluency does not appear to exist with anyone). We also use our hands to emphasize certain parts of the message. For example, you can point your finger in a jabbing motion to emphasize what you are saying in the verbal channel of communication.

5. W. B. Pearce and F. Conklin, "Nonverbal Vocalistic Communication and Perceptions of a Speaker," *Speech Monographs* 38(1971):235–41.

Complementation

Fourth, other nonverbal cues may add to or modify the verbal message with further details, such as to make clearer the speaker's attitude toward the situation, the message, or the other person. This relationship is sometimes referred to as **complementation.** For example, if you want to express yourself so that another person will understand precisely what you mean, you may, during the time you are looking for just the right words, use a particular hand signal in which your index finger and thumb come closer and closer together. When you feel you have expressed yourself precisely and delicately, the index finger and thumb may actually touch.[6]

6. Desmond Morris, *Manwatching: A Field Guide to Human Behavior* (New York: Harry Abrams, 1977), 58–63.

Contradiction

Fifth, the verbal and nonverbal messages may not always agree. Sometimes, in fact, the message sent in the verbal channel is exactly the opposite of the message sent in the nonverbal channel—a **contradiction.** When two messages conflict in this way, they are called a **double-bind message.**[7] The individual who receives the message is put into a double-bind as to which message to believe. A verbal message may be "I am happy to meet you" or "I am delighted you have come," accompanied by the nonverbal message of a non-expressive face, no smile, and a subdued monotone voice. Which message do you believe?

7. Paul Watzlawick, Janet H. Beavin, and Don D. Jackson, *Pragmatics of Human Communication: A Study of Interactional Patterns, Pathologies, and Paradoxes* (New York: W. W. Norton, 1967), 212–14.

When messages in the verbal and nonverbal channels of communication conflict, adults usually perceive the nonverbal message to be the more accurate reflection of the individual's feelings or attitudes, and they will frequently act on the nonverbal messages. Children, on the other hand, tend to perceive the verbal message to be the accurate message and act upon it.[8]

8. H. Wass, "Pupil Evaluation of Teacher Messages in Three Channels of Communication," *Florida Journal of Educational Research* 15 (1973):46–52; D. E. Bugental, J. W. Koswan, L. R. Love, and M. N. Fox, "Child Versus Adult Reception of Evaluative Messages in Verbal, Vocal and Visual Channels," *Developmental Psychology* 2(1970):367–75.

Regulation

The sixth way nonverbal communication relates to verbal communication is through a process in which verbal messages are controlled by nonverbal messages through a process called **regulation.** This regulation occurs when we enter an interaction, as we exchange the roles of speaker and listener during the interaction, and as we leave an interaction. We can signal our desire to enter into an interaction with someone by smiling and engaging in eye contact with the person, especially if the distance between us is no more than twelve feet.[9]

9. E. Goffman, *Behavior in Public Places* (New York: Free Press of Glencoe, 1963), 84.

10. S. Duncan, Jr., "Some Signals and Rules for Taking Speaking Turns in Conversation," *Journal of Personality and Social Psychology* 23(1972):283–92.

Several nonverbal messages or cues also help us to keep the floor while we are speaking. These cues are called turn-suppressing cues because they help to keep others from interrupting us.[10] One of these cues is to use a sustained intonation pattern. Most often when we come to the end of a sentence or are finished speaking, our voice drops if it is a declarative sentence or rises slightly if it is a question. By maintaining, instead, a level intonation pattern, we signal to others that we are not finished. Also, we can signal that we have not completed our train of thought or message by taking a breath, continuing a gesture which we have started as we stopped speaking, and especially by keeping our gaze averted or away from a person. Sometimes individuals learn to make sounds such as "um," "uh," "well" after every few words in a sentence. They have learned to put these sounds in to indicate they are not finished speaking and that the other individual should wait.

When we are finished speaking we signal this to the other person by completing our gesture, raising or lowering our voice, and looking at the person expectantly. This signals that we are ready to take the role of listener so the other person can take the role of speaker.

When we want to leave an interaction, we may smile and nod our head more, reach out and shake hands, begin to edge forward in our chair to put our feet on the floor, and, if we are standing, turn our body to face the door or exit.[11] We may even reach out and offer our hand to the other person to shake as a signal that we would like the interaction to stop. If we are not sensitive to both the sending and receiving of these regulatory cues, the other individual in the interaction is likely to perceive us as being insensitive in our relationships with other people or not as acculturated as we ought to be.

Other nonverbal cues are sent by listeners to signal to the speaker that they are being attentive (head nods, eye gaze, and a facial expression appropriate to the speaker's content), that they agree, or that they are confused and would like the speaker to expand on some remark. Simultaneously with the verbal flow of communication between us, we use our hands, face, posture, eyes, legs, and feet to send messages or cues to one another.

11. M. Knapp, R. Hart, G. Friedrich, and G. Schulman, "The Rhetoric of Goodbye: Verbal and Nonverbal Correlates of Human Leave-Taking," *Speech Monographs* 40(1973):182-98.

HOW NONVERBAL BEHAVIOR FUNCTIONS ALONE

Not all of the functions which nonverbal communication performs, however, are associated with its support of the language system. We also use nonverbal communication to express our emotions, to present our impressions of our personality and self-concept to others, to convey attitudes about our relationships with others (such as dominance/submission, inclusion/exclusion, liking/dislike), and to manipulate and persuade others.[12]

12. Michael Argyle, *Bodily Communication* (New York: International Universities Press, 1975); Judee K. Burgoon and Thomas Saine, *The Unspoken Dialogue: An Introduction to Nonverbal Communication* (Boston: Houghton Mifflin, 1978).

Nonverbal Attributes We Cannot Control

A number of physical characteristics that are unrelated to any specific message intent can have a significant effect on our effectiveness in interpersonal communication. These attributes include a person's height, body shape, gender, skin color, size of nose, eye color, and other physical characteristics. We know these factors affect the outcome of interpersonal communication. We know, for instance, that a premium is placed on height. Males and females who are tall are perceived as more credible than those who are not tall.[13] During the twentieth century the winner of national presidential elections could have been predicted (with astounding success) simply by the height of the candidates.

Studies indicate that higher salaries are paid to taller male and female employees, even when their qualifications are equal to those of shorter employ-

13. C. D. Ward, "Own Height, Sex, and Liking in the Judgement of the Heights of Others," *Journal of Personality* 35(1967):381-401; P. R. Wilson, "Perceptual Distortion of Height as a Function of Ascribed Academic Status," *Journal of Social Psychology* 74(1968):97-102.

Height significantly affects the perception of credibility and attractiveness.

14. S. D. Feldman, "The Presentations of Shortness in Everyday Life — Height and Heightism in American Society: Toward a Sociology of Stature," reported in "Physical Attractiveness," by Ellen Berscheid and Elaine Walster, in Leonard Berkowitz, ed., *Advances in Experimental Social Psychology*, vol. 7 (New York: Academic Press, 1974), 178–79; Barbara Ford, "Prejudice: Society Shuns the Short, Fat and Ugly," *Science Digest*, May 1974, 19–23.

15. E. Aronson and B. W. Golden, "The Effects of Relevant and Irrelevant Aspects of Communicator Credibility on Opinion Change," *Journal of Personality* 30(1962):135–46.

16. Franklyn Haiman, "An Experimental Study of the Effects of Ethos in Public Speaking" (Ph.D. dissertation, Northwestern University, 1948); "The Case Against Chauvinism: A 20-Year Bill of Particulars," staff report in *Human Behavior* 1, no. 3 (May/June 1972):46–49.

ees.[14] Among job applicants who are identical except for a difference in height, the taller applicants are hired more often and receive better salaries. Women as well pay considerable attention to the height of the males they date — they prefer tall men. Height affects our interpersonal effectiveness.

Skin color also appears to have a significant effect upon communication effectiveness. Many studies conducted in the fifties investigated the effect of skin color on communicator credibility. The findings consistently indicated that Caucasians were likely to be perceived as more credible (thus more effective in persuasion attempts) than persons with black skin.[15] Of course, skin color is not related to message intent, but it nevertheless affects the outcome of an interpersonal interaction. The same thing has been true of gender. Even females perceive males as more credible.[16] Whether or not we are born as male or female, black or white, will have a significant effect upon the outcome of our communication attempts. Of course, the studies that have produced these results have been conducted within the context of a university community which is primarily upper-class, WASP, and in America, so these results are culturally biased.

One of the nonverbal attributes that people in America do not generally like to discuss is the influence of physical attractiveness. In this country we like to think that we judge people on their merits. We do not like to think or believe that one person has an inherent advantage over another person merely because of the facial or body structure with which he or she was born. However, some research suggests that while physical attractiveness is a somewhat ambiguous quality, people who are physically attractive are liked more and are considered to be more intelligent, personable, sensitive, warm, responsive, kind, interesting, modest, sociable, and outgoing than people who are not physically attractive.[17] Men and women who are not physically attractive are perceived to have a deficiency of those qualities we have just attributed to attractive people. Some people do have more going for them simply because of the luck of birth, and these people have a head start in interpersonal communication effectiveness. Even after we have interacted a great deal with someone, we respond significantly to the way the person looks. It seems that the physical attractiveness itself continues to have its effect even though we may already have become aware of attitudinal differences and personality deficiencies.[18] We still continue to perceive people more positively if they look nice. These findings have any number of implications. One of the most important is that it is to our advantage to make ourselves as physically attractive as possible, given the limitations with which we have been born and the opportunities available to us (thanks to hairdressers, cosmeticians, plastic surgeons, and clothiers). It is not just a matter of vanity to make ourselves more attractive, it is effective interpersonal communication. The more attractive we are, the more success we are likely to experience in our interactions with other people, other factors being equal. This is probably true in social situations, learning situations, and job situations. Even though these situations may not directly relate to attractiveness, we are frequently judged on the basis of our attractiveness anyway, and this judgment has a significant effect on the way people receive our messages. Thus, it is to our advantage to determine what is perceived as attractive by those with whom we interact and to strive toward that ideal — not because we are trying to conform or because we are vain, but because we wish to become as effective interpersonal communicators as possible.

We need to remember, however, that there are no universal standards of attractiveness. What is attractive in one cultural context or at one time may be repulsive in another. Whereas height may be an important attractiveness ingredient to white Anglo-Saxon Protestants in America, it may be of little importance in some other cultures. Size of a woman's feet was of considerable importance to the Chinese at one time, but its importance was never as great as bust size is to American men. Thus, in trying to be attractive, we must make our attempt in terms of the culture of the person we wish to have perceive us as attractive.

There are many physical characteristics of individuals that affect communication which cannot be changed very much, if at all. It is difficult to make oneself taller once growing has stopped — elevator shoes to the contrary not-

17. K. K. Dion, E. Berscheid, and E. Walster, "What Is Beautiful Is Good," *Journal of Personality and Social Psychology* 24(1972):285–90.

18. Ellen Berscheid and Elaine Walster, "Physical Attractiveness," in Leonard Berkowitz, ed., *Advances in Experimental Social Psychology*, vol. 7 (New York: Academic Press, 1974), 205–6.

withstanding; it is difficult to change one's skin color; and it is difficult to change one's gender. Although such nonverbal attributes cannot be changed, we can be aware that they are factors that influence communication. Then we can be prepared to perform whatever communicative behaviors are necessary to make up for adverse effects of our nonverbal attributes. Likewise, we should be prepared to take advantage of any positive nonverbal attributes that might work for us.

Nonverbal Attributes We Can Control

How we wear our hair, our choice of clothes, how we use cosmetics, whether we smoke and what we smoke, how we use our voice, and how fluent we are — all are nonverbal attributes that we have some control over and that communicate something about us.

Hair

We can intentionally manipulate many of our physical attributes in order to influence others. We can have our hair cut and styled in ways we think will favorably influence other people. The length of our hair and the way we have it combed and styled affects other people's perceptions of us.[19] At one time wearing long hair was a symbol of a particular life-style and political philosophy. For a while the long hair worn by hippies and liberals was adopted by many other people, and it became difficult to stereotype someone with long hair. This phase of behavior has, incidentally, become more ambiguous (and thus less useful for communication) now that the trend is moving back to shorter hair for both males and females. Even with the current changes, hairstyles are used with communicative intent. This is nothing new. In the first letters from Paul to the Corinthians, Paul discussed the desirability of women wearing their hair long. He also was concerned that men should not wear their hair long.[20] Today our concern with hair is every bit as strong as it was at that time, and we continue to worry about how hair is arranged and/or covered.

Facial hair also affects the way people perceive males. For several decades American males did not wear beards and mustaches to any great extent. In recent years many more young men have begun to wear beards, mustaches, and long sideburns. People who wear beards are frequently perceived as more sensitive, more masculine, more intelligent, and warmer than people who do not wear them. It is also true that people who wear beards are perceived as more deviant, more likely to be radical, more independent, and less group oriented.[21] An individual who decides to grow a beard is usually making a conscious decision with the intent of affecting other people's perceptions of him.

19. Jurgen Ruesch and Weblon Kees, *Nonverbal Communication* (Berkley, Calif.: University of California Press, 1956), 41.

20. Roy B. Chamberlin and Herbert Feldman, *The Dartmouth Bible* (Boston; Houghton Mifflin, 1961), 106–7.

21. D. G. Freedman, "The Survival Value of the Beard," *Psychology Today* 3(1969):36–39; Marion E. Starling, "Nonverbal Communication: A Study of the Effects of Men's Hairstyles" (paper, Purdue University, May 1972).

Long hair that was once associated with "liberal" politics has become more ambiguous symbolically.

Clothes

When we wear appropriate clothing for an occasion, we will have a greater influence on those with whom we are interacting. Leonard Bickman pointed out that college students dressed "conventionally" when they were campaigning for Senator Eugene McCarthy in 1968.[22] The tactic was known as the "clean for Gene phenomenon" and has been a strategic weapon ever since. The students knew they were going to be interacting with people to whom "hip" or "college" dress would be unacceptable. Even today knowledgeable young people "dress up" for job interviews in order to be more effective in securing jobs.

Clothing norms usually depend on the communication setting. A student who had a summer job inventorying water supplies in rural Missouri conducted his first interviews with farmers dressed in a suit, white shirt, and tie. He was not getting much cooperation and decided that the way he dressed might have something to do with it. When he began to wear work pants, jeans, and workshirts, the farmers began to respond much more cooperatively. *What is appropriate dress depends on the situation and the people with whom we are interacting.*

22. Leonard Bickman, "Social Role and Uniforms: Clothes Make the Person," *Psychology Today* 7(April 1974):48–51.

Cosmetics

Females employ makeup to influence other people. The cosmetics industry is one of the major industries in America today. Women color their hair, add color to their lips, highlight their cheeks, accentuate their eyes, extend their eyelashes, and do other things to change their appearance. What the effect of all of this is we are not entirely sure, although some uses of makeup may be related to research findings on nonverbal communication. For instance, the use of eye makeup by women may be an attempt to make the eyes look larger. Research indicates that when the pupils of the eye are dilated, a woman is perceived as more sexually attractive to males than when the pupils are not dilated.[23] It may be that for centuries women have recognized that if they could make their eyes appear larger, this might be perceived as more sexually attractive.[24] Of course, women do not talk about it in these terms; they simply talk about being more or less attractive depending on how makeup has been applied.

Smoking

Pipes, cigarettes, and cigars can be aspects of appearance that some people deliberately manipulate to affect others. Young males in college often attempt to learn how to smoke a pipe to create the image of someone who is solid, calm, and thoughtful. The cigarette as a nonverbal behavior begins to interest us when we are in high school, and sometimes earlier. In America, films and television portray people smoking cigarettes as being sophisticated and worldly. Cigarettes, cigars, and pipes are perceived differently when smoked by males and females. For instance, cigars and pipes are not yet accepted as appropriate for females, and thus females who smoke a pipe or a cigar are perceived as radical or "different."

Voice

While some people think voice quality is a totally biological phenomenon, it can be altered by the individual and is used by all of us to influence others. A harsh, cutting nasal voice has one effect on people; a soft, well-modulated voice a completely different effect.[25] Just as we have stereotypes about hair of different lengths, we have stereotypes about different kinds of voices.[26] A deep voice tends to come from a larger man and a high-pitched voice tends to come from a smaller, thinner man. Using vocal characteristics alone, we are pretty accurate in identifying the age, sex, body shape, height, weight, education, and social class of others.[27]

Most of us learn different vocal qualities from the environment in which we are reared. Voice quality of people in the southwestern United States is

23. J. W. Stass and F. N. Willis, Jr., "Eye Contact, Pupil Dilation, and Personal Preference," *Psychonomic Science* 7 (1967):375–76.

24. Richard G. Goss, "Reflections on the Evil Eye," *Human Behavior* 3, no. 10 (October 1974):16–22.

25. J. Sachs, P. Lieberman, and D. Erickson, "Anatomical and Cultural Determinants of Male and Female Speech," in R. W. Shuy and R. W. Fasold, eds., *Language and Attitudes: Current Trends and Prospects* (Washington, D.C.: Georgetown University Press, 1973).

26. Ibid.

27. Burgoon & Saine, *Unspoken Dialogue*, 152, 156.

very different from that of people in the southeastern United States. Still another voice quality characterizes people living in the northeastern United States. In fact, we can find pockets within individual cities in which the voice quality differs markedly from that of most people in the surrounding region. Regional differences are acquired during childhood, but we probably subconsciously develop a voice that enables us to project a desired image. There are limits to how much we can change our voice quality, but singing teachers, voice coaches, and speech teachers throughout the country have considerable success showing people how to change the quality of their voices.

Fluency

Fluency is another vocal characteristic that affects our credibility. People with severe nonfluencies, sometimes called "stuttering," are perceived as less credible,[28] less dynamic, and less qualified; the perception of trust remains unaltered, however. An organization called Toastmasters International is concerned with nonfluencies in speech, among other things. This organization so firmly believes that nonfluencies are detrimental to effective communication that during some of their chapter meetings a person who is called the " 'ah' counter" drops a marble in a coffee can to produce a sharp sound every time a speaker utters a verbalized pause or an "ah." The Toastmasters feel that this kind of nonfluency interferes with effective communication, and thus they try to correct it.

There is evidence to indicate that speech that is too fluent may be perceived negatively also.[29] If we speak too fluently or too glibly we may be perceived as "slick" and possibly untrustworthy. Richard Nixon, for example had been a college debater and had been in public life for many years and acquired an extremely fluent speech pattern and rhythm. His speaking voice and rate were measured and constant, with few nonfluencies and hesitations. As a result he seemed practiced and nonspontaneous at all times. This may have contributed to a public perception of him as untrustworthy and lacking in warmth.

In chapter 4 we mentioned that when we first meet people we develop an implicit personality theory that we use to predict their behavior and to govern our own communication behavior. The aspects of appearance and voice just discussed, and others, determine to a large extent what that implicit personality theory will be. The way we are perceived and our subsequent effectiveness (or lack of it) as communicators are significantly affected by our appearance. Although to some people it may seem like "selling out" when we dress for an occasion and for the people with whom we will be interacting, or spend time in training our voice, it is actually good communication sense.

28. K. K. Sereno and G. J. Hawkins, "Effect of Variation in Speaker's Non-fluency upon Audience Ratings of Attitudes Toward the Speech Topic and Speaker's Credibility," Speech Monographs 34(1967):58–64.

29. John E. Dietrich, "The Relative Effectiveness of Two Modes of Radio Delivery in Influencing Attitudes," Speech Monographs 13(1946):58–65.

Expressing Emotions and Attitudes

When we are in an interaction with another person, a great deal of the meaning we transmit concerning our feelings or emotions and our attitudes is carried by the nonverbal channels of communication. For example, Mehrabian suggests that the amount of liking we have for another person is communicated primarily in this way.[30] Mehrabian's formula indicates that of the total affection or liking that we communicate to another person, only 7 percent is communicated by words; 38 percent is communicated by how we use our voice (rate, pitch, and volume of speech); and 55 percent is the result of facial expressions (smiles, eye contact, and frowns).

More recent research calls into question some of Mehrabian's figures, and attributes to words a greater relative percentage of meaning than does Mehrabian's formula[31]; however, nonverbal communication still accounts for more meaning than do words. Whether we accept Mehrabian's earlier figures or the more recent research, at least we know that nonverbal communication is very important in communicating liking for a person.

Mehrabian's formula (with the same relative importance for words, vocal quality, and facial characteristics) could apply to the communication of any emotion or feeling. Whenever we indicate our liking or disliking of something — our acceptance or rejection of something — we are communicating feelings. Probably most of our communication at home is feeling-oriented — expressing our feelings — and hence nonverbal communication is playing a major role in what we communicate.

Facial Expression

One of the ways we express emotion is through **facial expression.** In fact, the face is probably the most expressive part of our bodies.[32] Because we have so many muscles and organs within the face, it is possible for us to express complex emotions. It is interesting to note that infants respond to faces more readily than they respond to other objects.[33] Likewise, when a "face shot" occurs on television, the attention level goes up considerably. We pay close attention to faces because we learn a great deal from looking at other faces. We can see the eyes, the mouth, and the area around the eyes and mouth with the various muscular positions that can be assumed. The face most often tells us *what* particular emotion the other person is feeling — or what emotion they wish us to think they are feeling.[34]

Not only does the face communicate a great deal, it also appears to be the kind of nonverbal behavior we seem best able to control.[35] It is with the face that we lie the best. While lack of eye contact causes some people to interpret a person's message as insincere, practiced liars find that they can make extremely good use of direct eye contact to appear sincere while they are lying.

30. A. Mehrabian and S. R. Ferris, "Inference of Attitudes from Nonverbal Communication in Two Channels," *Journal of Consulting Psychology* 31 (1967):248-52; A. Mehrabian and M. Wiener, "Decoding of Inconsistent Communications," *Journal of Personality and Social Psychology* 6(1967):109-14.

31. T. G. Hegstrom, "Message Impact: What Percentage Is Nonverbal?" *Western Journal of Speech Communication* 43(1979):134-42.

32. Knapp, *Nonverbal Communication in Human Interacting*, 263.

33. Ruesch and Kees, *Nonverbal Communication*, 18.

34. P. Ekman and W. V. Friesen, *Unmasking the Face* (New Jersey: Prentice Hall, 1975), 137-39.

35. P. Ekman and W. V. Friesen, "Nonverbal Leakage and Clues to Deception," *Psychiatry* 32(1969):88-106.

It is very difficult for people to determine accurately whether a communicator is sincere or not sincere.[36] People learn to make faces very early in childhood — even learning to smile when they are unhappy, so it is not surprising that we become adept at using our faces to conceal our emotions.

36. Knapp, *Nonverbal Communication in Human Interacting*, 268.

Body Movement

While our attention may be drawn to faces, we can gain more accurate information about another person from other parts of his or her body.[37] We can see subconscious communication occurring through the hands, feet, or body posture. Much of our information about the *intensity* of someone's emotions comes from observing tenseness or relaxation in the person's posture and hand and feet movements.[38]

37. Ekman and Friesen, "Nonverbal Leakage."

38. Ekman & Friesen, *Unmasking the Face*.

Vocal Expression

The words *paralanguage* and **vocalics** refer to nonverbal characteristics associated with the production of words through speech, including pitch, voice quality, and rate and rhythm of speech.[39] We employ variations in all these paralinguistic factors to convey emotion. We need only listen to an accomplished actor to recognize at once how the great flexibility of the voice can alter the meaning of words. Pitch alone conveys much. A high-pitched voice can convey excitement or fear. A low-pitched voice can convey seriousness, sadness, and sometimes affection.[40] We use the word *monotone* to describe the voice of a person who does not vary pitch sufficiently to reinforce and strengthen the impact of the words in a message.

39. G. L. Trager, "Paralanguage: A First Approximation," *Studies in Linguistics* 13(1958): 1–12.

40. Knapp, *Nonverbal Communication in Human Interacting*, 340–49.

Touch

Some of our deepest emotions are associated with touching. When we begin our lives as infants we are nursed, held, and bathed, and this touching is the only kind of communication a father or mother has available to influence the child. Desmond Morris in *Intimate Behavior* suggests that we never get over the infant satisfaction with touching.[41] He believes we learn to associate comfort with both touching and the rhythmic beating of a heart. Whenever we share moments with someone we love, we begin to perform very childlike behaviors with each other. We begin to treat the person we love as one would treat a child, and we allow ourselves to be treated as a child by the person we love. This enables us to enjoy some of the caressing and touching we have associated with the satisfying and warm moments of infancy and childhood. The opposite emotions are strongly aroused when someone touches us without our acceptance and approval.

41. Desmond Morris, *Intimate Behavior* (New York: Random House, 1971), 13–34.

Use of space in an office can
"speak" loudly.

Space

Space also can be used as communication. It is possible to communicate a positive evaluation of another person simply by standing close to him or her.[42] We stand closer to people we like and farther from people we dislike. It is as though we will permit people we value to invade our own personal territory but not those we do not like. Robert Ardrey has suggested the existence of what he has termed the **territorial imperative** in animals.[43] According to him, all animals, including humans, have well-defined territories around themselves which they will defend rather than permit to be invaded. This is probably the basis for our use of space in communication. If so, it is possible that the use of space to communicate liking is, in part at least, genetically acquired as well as culturally learned.

The use of space varies from culture to culture, however, and the norms regarding distance between people during interpersonal communication vary considerably from group to group. Hall indicated the existence of at least four different kinds of distance that middle-class Americans in the northeast employ in communication.[44] They are "intimate," "personal," "social," and "public" distance. Table 6.1 shows the close and far phases of each of the four distances and the different interpersonal communication behaviors appropriate in each case.

We use **intimate distance** with persons we like extremely well to express positive evaluation of them. At this distance the smells and feel of each person are available to the other, thus bringing into the communicative process other senses than sight and sound.

Personal distance is a noncontact distance within which we have interactions with our friends and our family. Hall mentions that a wife is permitted within the close phase of personal distance, but for another woman to step that close violates a norm.

Social distance prevails for business and social discourse. In the far phase people can continue to work in the presence of another person without appearing rude, as is observed frequently in many offices in which a number of people work together. Interpersonal communication can occur at this distance, but with increased difficulty.

Although it is possible for interpersonal communication to occur within the **public distance** range, it is rare. At this distance the principles of public communication become operative. We are not usually concerned with public distance in interpersonal communication. But there are interpersonal situations involving all three of the other distances.

We should be aware not merely what these distances are but the kinds of communication behaviors and relationships and situations appropriate for each. We obviously do not use intimate distance for a business discussion with a real estate agent. Likewise, the use of the far phase of social distance when on a date with a member of the opposite sex would seem strained and formal

42. A. Mehrabian, "Some Referent and Measures of Nonverbal Behavior," *Behavior Research Methods and Instrumentation* 1 (1969):203-7.

43. Robert Ardrey, *The Territorial Imperative* (New York: Dell Publishing Co., 1966).

44. Edward T. Hall, *The Hidden Dimension* (New York: Anchor Books, Doubleday, 1966), 111-29.

Table 6.1

Distance		Measurement	Examples
Intimate			
	Close phase	0–6″	Lovers embracing, soft whispering occurs (if anything at all is spoken)
	Far phase	6″–18″	Mother-child looking at book together; close friends discussing secret; audible whispering
Personal			
	Close phase	18″–30″	Husband and wife planning a party; parent-child in friendly conversation; soft voice when indoors; full voice outdoors
	Far phase	30″–4′	Discussion of subjects of personal interest and involvement; social exchange over cup of coffee
Social			
	Close phase	4′–7′	Impersonal business discussions; discussions with fellow workers on the job; conversations during casual social gatherings
	Far phase	7′–12′	More formal business discussions; distance at which we engage in activities where we wish to be alone, such as reading; when talking at this distance the voice is noticeably louder than for the close phase
Public			
	Close phase	12′–25′	Voice is loud but not full volume; one person addressing a small group
	Far phase	25′ or more	Public speeches before very large groups; interpersonal communication probably not possible; this is the minimum distance kept between the public and public figures (such as politicians and movie stars) most of the time

indeed. The important thing to keep in mind is that we must use the appropriate distance for the situation between us and the people with whom we are trying to communicate or our effectiveness will be jeopardized. Sometimes we try to communicate a desire for closeness by moving closer to the other person. But we need to be very careful and sensitive to the other's response if we do this. Using an inappropriate distance will make the other person uncomfortable and perhaps even angry and hostile.

Other Aspects of Emotional Expression

That we use our face, body movement and posture, voice, touch, and even the distances between ourselves and others to communicate emotions to one another is not all we must understand in order to improve our sending and receiving of emotional information in our interpersonal relationships. There are seven important aspects of this expression of feeling through nonverbal communication.

Dimensions of Meaning   First, just as there are dimensions of meaning in language, there appear also to be dimensions of meaning in our interpretation of nonverbal displays of emotion.[45] There is a **dimension of pleasantness,** similar to the evaluative dimension of meaning in language, bordered on one side by pleasant emotions such as happiness and joy and on the other side by unpleasant emotions such as anger or sadness. There is an **intensity dimension,** similar to the activity dimension found in language, which concerns arousal, or how intensely the emotion is displayed. **Control** is another dimension. It is different from the potency dimension found in the language system. In the control dimension of nonverbal cues the receiver is concerned with the degree of intentionality behind the emotional display. Do we think the other person intended to display that particular degree of emotion? Do we think the other person has the emotional display under conscious control? Our judgment of the emotional displays of others is determined mainly by our response to the intensity, or arousal dimension. Without sufficient intensity we may have difficulty perceiving an emotion accurately. Often as senders we concentrate on accurately representing where our emotion is on the pleasantness dimension. Are we happy or sad, angry or approving? We need to become more aware of the intensity of our nonverbal displays if we want others to interpret them accurately.

45. R. P. Abelson and V. Sermat, "Multidimensional Scaling of Facial Expressions," *Journal of Experimental Psychology* 63 (1962):546–54.

Blends of Emotional Expression   Second, while a few emotional displays appear to be almost universally understood, most are not easy to interpret. The universally understood or **primary emotions** appear to be:[46] interest/expectation, joy, surprise, distress/grief, fear, shame/humiliation, contempt/disgust, anger, and acceptance. The other emotions which we express — like love, boredom, nervousness, sympathy, satisfaction, or pride — appear to be combinations or blends of these primary affects. Each of these **blends** is expressed in different ways and degrees of intensity in different cultures and subcultures, and even families. This makes many of our emotional expressions difficult to interpret accurately. We can also feel and display more than one emotion simultaneously. We may be amused and exasperated, respectful and angry, or confused and fearful — and our emotional display may blend these together.

46. Robert Plutchick, "A Language for the Emotions," *Psychology Today,* February 1980, 68–78; S. S. Tomkins, *Affect, Imagery, Consciousness* (New York: Springer, 1962).

Multiplicity of Emotional Expression   Third, there are many different ways to express any particular emotion. If you are sad, you can cry, become very quiet, or look angry. Often it is difficult to interpret the feeling involved in any given emotional display unless we take into account the situation in which it occurs.

Rapidity of Emotional Expression   Fourth, many of our emotional displays are very rapid.[47] Some occur in less than one-fifth of a second. Usually only those which take two-fifths of a second or longer can be clearly identified. This means that many expressions occur so rapidly they are difficult to interpret accurately.

Critical Areas for Display of Emotional Expression   Fifth, only certain critical areas of the face are used in sending or interpreting many emotions.[48] For example, the critical cues for disgust are given in the cheeks and the mouth, while the critical cues for sadness are given in the brows, the forehead, the eyes, and the eyelids. As we scan someone's face, we may miss rapid critical cues that would help us interpret the person's emotional state.

Affect Display Rules of Emotional Expression   Sixth, much of our interpretation of the emotions others display comes from cultural **affect display rules** which we have learned.[49] These rules tell us what emotion is expected at any given time, how long it is appropriately displayed, what degree of intensity ought to occur, and who ought to display that particular emotion. Cultural display rules tell us what emotion is appropriate and expected in any given situation. If both the wife and secretary of a man attend his funeral and the secretary cries loudly and appears to grieve more than the wife, we might make a wrong judgment about the relative amounts of true feeling expressed. We may think the employer had an inappropriate relationship with his secretary. The truth may be that the wife and secretary simply come from different subcultures. One learned one cultural display rule for funerals — "be expressive" and the other learned another — "be very nonexpressive."

Dishonesty of Emotional Expression   The seventh consideration is that we are a culture of double-bind messages because of our display rules. We are expected to tone down our emotions and to express emotions considered appropriate in a situation even though they are not our true emotions. We try to overintensify some emotions, substitute one emotion for another, underintensify others, or neutralize our expressions entirely.[50] For example, suppose your boss is criticizing some work you have done. You are *very* angry and feel the criticism is unjustified. Still you will probably try not to show the full degree of anger — you will underintensify your display. You might try to neutralize your expression by putting on a "blank face," or try to substitute an apologetic face for your angry one.

47. E. A. Haggard and F. S. Isaacs, "Micromomentary Facial Expressions as Indicators of Ego Mechanisms in Psychotherapy," in L. A. Gottschalk and A. H. Auerbach, eds., *Methods of Research in Psychotherapy* (New York: Appleton-Century-Crofts, 1966).

48. J. D. Boucher, "Facial Areas and Emotional Information," *Journal of Communication* 23 (1975):21–29; P. Ekman, W. V. Friesen, and S. S. Tomkins, "Facial Affect Scoring Technique: A First Validity Study," *Semiotica* 3 (1971):37–58.

49. Ekman and Friesen, *Unmasking the Face,* 137–39.

50. Ekman and Friesen, "Nonverbal Leakage."

We have learned to control the expression of emotion in our face more than we have learned to do this in our body, so we can "lie" more easily with our face. Since the face tells *what* emotion is being displayed, while the body often gives more information about *intensity*,[51] we are much better at hiding *what* than *how intensely* we feel about something.

Because the emotions others are feeling are often hard to interpret accurately, we either rely on the cultural display rules, which tell us what we should expect, or we believe that what we would feel is what they must feel. Often we are not responding to the other person's true feelings at all. We need to be aware of this and check our interpretations with the other person if we are to be effective communicators.

51. Burgoon and Saine, *Unspoken Dialogue*, 203.

Combining Nonverbal Behaviors

Warmth and Friendliness   Most often we use different nonverbal behaviors together to express ourselves. For example, if we are feeling warmth and friendliness toward another person, we would gaze at and touch the person more, smile more, stand closer and position our body to face the person more directly, and lower our pitch and speak softly.[52]

Mirroring nonverbal behavior[53] is another cue we use when we are attracted to someone, especially if the person is of higher status. We "mirror" another's nonverbal behavior by imitating the person's nonverbal cues — position of the body, posture, placement of hands and legs — only we do it like a mirror image. If you have ever noticed two people who like one another sitting on a couch having a conversation, they will probably be turned toward one another and, if both of them have their legs crossed, the crossing will be done so that together they form a **V** with their legs, closing out the rest of the world. Or when one person cocks his or her head in one direction, the other person will follow that particular motion.

We might also use quasi-courtship behaviors[54] — that is, a form of the behaviors we perform when we are in a courtship relationship with another person. For example, preening behaviors or "sexy" postures will be performed in a more subtle manner. They are not performed as frequently, for as long, or with the same facial expression as in a courtship situation, but they are performed to a certain degree.

52. Z. Rubin, "Measurement of Romantic Love," *Journal of Personality and Social Psychology* 16 (1970):265-73; Burgoon and Saine, 174-80; A. Mehrabian, *Silent Messages: Implicit Communication of Emotions and Attitudes* (Calif.: Wadsworth, 1981), 22-42.

53. A. Kendon, "Movement Coordination in Social Interaction: Some Examples Described," *Acta Psychologica* 32 (1970):100-125.

54. A. E. Scheflen, "Quasi-Courtship Behavior of Psychotherapy," *Psychiatry* 28 (1965):245-56.

Status and Power   Attitudes concerning our relative status and power can also be communicated to another individual nonverbally.[55] We gaze more at more powerful people, and we are more likely to mirror them, but they initiate the behavior. We use a more formal, and less relaxed posture when we are with someone who is of higher status. The higher status individual is likely to be more relaxed and to take up more territory or space with his or her body by spreading out arms and legs. As the more powerful individual takes up

55. N. M. Henley, *Body Politics: Power, Sex and Nonverbal Communication* (New Jersey: Prentice Hall, 1977); J. S. Efran, "Looking for Approval: Effect on Visual Behavior of Approbation from Persons Differing in Importance," *Journal of Personality and Social Psychology* 10 (1968):21-25.

more territory, we often simply give the person more space. That is, when we come to stand next to them, we stand farther away from people whom we perceive to be more powerful. Powerful individuals also are given the prerogative of interrupting others, of breaking silences with others, of initiating touch, and of controlling the time of others. Also, they demonstrate their power and relative status through the use of more powerful artifacts such as high desks, larger office spaces, and positions at the heads of tables.

CULTURAL AND SUBCULTURAL DIFFERENCES

56. Hall, *The Silent Language*.

Just as word-for-word translations from one language to another seldom convey exactly the same meanings, so also do nonverbal symbols convey different meanings from culture to culture.[56] When we forget that we *infer from* and *interpret* nonverbal behavior, as emphasized before, problems can arise that are significant and deserve discussion.

57. Ibid., 1€

Edward Hall compared middle-class white Americans with people of other cultures in their use of distance during interactions. He discovered significant differences from culture to culture. The interaction distance preferred by Latin Americans in interpersonal communication is considerably less than it is in the United States.[57] The distance comfortable for a Latin American is to a North American so close that it tends to evoke either hostile or sexual feelings. One can easily picture a conversation between a North American and Latin American in which the Latin American is continually advancing toward the North American and the North American is constantly retreating. The result is that the Latin Americans perceive us as cold, withdrawn, and unfriendly, and North Americans perceive Latin Americans as breathing down their necks, crowding them, and spraying their faces.

Sometimes the differences in nonverbal communication between cultures can be subtle indeed. The subtlety itself can cause problems because differences are not immediately obvious to us. For instance, while people from Japanese, Chinese, and Occidental cultures interpret facial expressions similarly, they apparently differ in the degree of emotion they perceive. They may all perceive that one person they are all observing is happy and another is sad, but the *amount* of happiness or sadness perceived — that is, intensity of emotion — will differ considerably from culture to culture.[58]

58. W. Edgar Vinacke, "The Judgments of Facial Expressions by National-Racial Groups," *Journal of Personality* 17(1949):407–29.

59. Andrea Rich, *Interracial Communication* (New York: Harper & Row, 1974), 189–90.

There are also vocalic differences from one culture or subculture to another. Andrea Rich considers "accent" (or what linguists call dialect differences) to be the most relevant element in vocalic communication from one culture or subculture to another.[59] In the United States, for example, black ghetto residents have one kind of "accent," some Jewish Americans have another, Hispanics another, and so on. Each region of the country has its own distinctive accent.

What is the effect of different accents upon interpersonal communication? According to Haines, an individual's accent can significantly affect perception of his or her credibility.[60] We will not go into which accents have how much credibility; it is enough to suggest here that accents help identify a person's culture, and thus a listener's perception of credibility is developed. Messages produced by a person are accepted by recipients to a greater or lesser degree simply because of the accent. Announcers in broadcasting generally strive for the accent that has been termed ''General American Speech.'' People in the fields of speech and speech pathology are able to identify ''General American Speech'' as a fairly ''accent free'' speech form. It is the kind of speech we are used to hearing from people like Dan Rather, Jane Pauley, or Tom Brokaw on news broadcasts. We would suggest that deviations from ''General American Speech'' cause changes in the perception of credibility.

Sometimes cultures or subcultures develop their own specific nonverbal messages for expressing some emotion or thought. A nonverbal behavior of blacks in the United States usually misunderstood by whites is turning one's back to the person with whom one is communicating interpersonally. For many whites this is insulting. Within the black subculture, however, turning one's back to another person during a conversation is a sign of friendship and trust. One of the most friendly greetings that one black can give to another is to walk up to the person, say something warm and friendly, then turn one's back to the person just greeted and walk away a few steps. The nonverbal message is something to the effect: ''Look, I trust you so much that in greeting you I unhesitatingly place myself in a vulnerable position.''[61]

We could consider innumerable nonverbal behaviors relative to cultural differences — handshakes, eye contact, head nods, sitting positions, standing positions, walking, patting on the back, touching behaviors, rate of speaking, volume and many others. All may vary in communicative content from culture to culture. Whenever we are communicating with someone from another culture, it is imperative that we be aware that probably some of the things we are doing nonverbally which are normal and natural within the culture in which we were reared may offend or threaten a person from another culture. Likewise, if we find ourselves being put off, thinking that others are insulting us by their nonverbal behavior, we must be open to the possibility that the behavior has a different meaning in the cultural background of the person with whom we are communicating.

Male-Female Differences

Even within a culture nonverbal behaviors can have different meanings depending on the roles we play and/or our status in those roles. There are some important differences in the nonverbal communication of men and women in our culture which we ought to be aware of.

60. L. S. Haines, ''Listener Judgments of Status Quos in Speech,'' *Quarterly Journal of Speech* 47(1961): 164–68.

61. Kenneth R. Johnson, ''Black Kinesics: Some Nonverbal Communication Patterns in the Black Culture,'' in L. A. Samovar and R. E. Porter, eds., *Intercultural Communication* (Belmont, Calif.: Wadsworth, 1972), 181–89.

Many nonverbal cues are associated almost entirely with one gender — so much so that if someone of the opposite sex performs these behaviors that person will be perceived as unmasculine or unfeminine. For example, there is a perception that a masculine way of crossing one's legs is to rest the ankle of one leg upon the knee of the other; that a feminine way is to rest the back of one knee over the other knee. This is not to suggest that people who cross their legs one way *are* masculine, or that people who cross their legs the other way *are* feminine. We are only pointing out that stereotypes exist in our society, and as such they can certainly affect communication.

We also use the pitch of our voices to say something about masculinity or femininity. Females, upon reaching womanhood, typically experience a lowering of the voice similar to that of males, although not to the same extent. However, some women do not allow their voices to lower; they maintain instead a high-pitched "little-girl voice," which they hope will influence others to continue perceiving them as little girls rather than as women. This then removes the threat of their having to perform as women and to assume responsibilities as women.[62]

Even when males and females have been matched by height and weight with the same anatomical structures, including even larynxes of the same size, male-female voice quality differences are still there.[63] Researchers conducting this type of research suggest that boys and girls form words differently, with girls smiling more when they speak. Since smiling has the effect of shortening the vocal cords, this could also explain the higher pitch of female voices. The smiling behavior, of course, is a culturally learned nonverbal behavior.

Some nonverbal cues are used more often by women than by men — such as the example just mentioned, women smiling more than men; especially when they are interacting with men.[64] If a man smiles at a woman, the woman will smile back at him 93 percent of the time; but if a woman smiles at a man, he will return that smile only 67 percent of the time. If smiling were only a sign of approval, it would mean that men in general receive more approval from women than women receive from men. It is true that both males and females smile at members of the opposite gender more than they smile at members of the same gender. Women smile back at women only 86 percent of the time, and men smile back at men only 58 percent of the time. This greater amount of smiling by women has been interpreted as an appeasement gesture rather than a sign of pleasantness because women smile more during interactions with people they do not know well than with people they do know well. In other words, they smile when they are uncertain and uncomfortable.[65] As women relax and become more comfortable, they smile less!

Women are much more likely to send double-bind messages involving smiling. That is, when a woman smiles, the verbal message may be neutral or even unpleasant. Men, on the other hand, are more likely to be sending a positive message if they smile. Even children perceive a woman's smile as more neutral and less positive than a man's smile.[66]

62. D. W. Addington, "The Relationship of Selected Vocal Characteristics to Personality Perception," *Speech Monographs* 35 (1968):492–503.

63. Sachs, Lieberman, and Erickson, "Anatomical and Cultural Determinants of Male and Female Speech."

64. Henley, *Body Politics,* 176–77.

65. Ibid., 175–76.

66. D. E. Bugental, J. W. Kaswan, and L. R. Love, "Perception of Contradictory Meanings Conveyed by Verbal and Nonverbal Channels," *Journal of Personality and Social Psychology* 16 (1970):647–55; D. E. Bugental, J. W. Kaswan, L. R. Love, and M. N. Fox, "Child Versus Adult Perception of Evaluative Messages in Verbal, Vocal, and Visual Channels," *Developmental Psychology* 2 (1970):367–75.

Women use more eye gaze than men[67] — they are more likely to look for longer periods of time at the other individual. When eye contact is made during opposite-gender interpersonal interactions, it is more often under the control of the man in the interaction — because the woman is looking most of the time. Initiation and termination occur because of the man's eye gaze in the interaction.

We also expect women to be more emotional or expressive of their feelings in interactions with others — often blaming this on their "hormones." In fact, to a certain degree the emotional expression of both men and women is affected by their hormones. For some women the menstrual cycle plays an important part in shaping the feelings they have and express. But men also have a biologically regulated cycle of good spirits followed by depression.[68] In men the cycle is not accompanied by physical changes, so in a sense it is more difficult to pick up a man's emotional cycle than a woman's. The male cycle averages about five weeks but may be as short as sixteen days or as long as two months. The male cycle is associated with an increased level of the male hormone testosterone. As the level rises, so do anxiety, depression, hostility, and tension.[69]

Certainly in our culture the repertoire of behaviors available to appropriately express some emotions is different for men and women.[70] The liking/affection and sadness/despair repertoires that men can use and still be perceived as "masculine" are smaller than the ones women can use and still be perceived as "feminine." Men are unable to cry and to express as wide a range of feelings of love and friendliness and intimacy as women. As they were growing up they learned fewer "masculine" or "manly" nonverbal cues for expressing these emotions. If they use the cues and codes which women use, they are perceived as feminine. Hence men are perceived as "feeling" fewer of these emotions. Men often substitute "play" wrestling, "teasing," or "silence" for these emotions.

Women, on the other hand, have more difficulty in expressing feelings of anger and hostility.[71] They are not taught as many socially acceptable nonverbal cues to express anger and hostility and still be perceived as feminine. When women are angry, they may cry, look sad or hurt, or disappointed and depressed. These are really disguised responses to their feelings of anger. If a woman wishes to express anger and hostility, she has a choice of being either "masculine" or not expressing the emotion accurately to the other individual. Both men and women seem to have to choose between behaviors that are culturally appropriate but not fully expressive of their emotions in order to be perceived as "masculine" or "feminine," or behaviors that are more fully expressive but are perceived as inappropriate to their gender.

Some nonverbal behaviors are performed more by men. Men initiate touch with women about twice as much as women initiate touch with men.[72] Men and women also appear to interpret the meaning of touch differently.[73] Women

67. R. Exline, P. Gray, and D. Schuette, "Visual Behavior in a Dyad as Affected by Interview Content and Sex of Respondent," *Journal of Personality and Social Psychology* 1 (1965):201-9.

68. Gay Gaer Luce, "Trust Your Body Rhythms," *Psychology Today,* April 1975, 52-53.

69. "Front Runners," *Saturday Review,* February 3, 1979, 6.

70. S. Bem, "Probing the Promise of Androgyny," in A. G. Kapland and J. P. Bean, eds., *Beyond Sex Role Stereotypes: Readings Toward a Psychology of Androgyny* (Boston: Little Brown, 1976), 48-62.

71. Ibid.

72. Nancy M. Henley, "Status & Sex: Some Touching Observations," *Bulletin of the Psychonomic Society* 2 (1973):91-93.

73. Tuan Nguyen, Richard Heslin, and Michele L. Nguyen, "The Meanings of Touch: Sex Differences," *Journal of Communication* 25(1975):92-103.

What might be thought of as "normal" touching behavior between female friends is unacceptable to some people when done by males.

in our culture are more likely to dichotomize the meaning of touch into either warmth and friendliness or sexual desire—to interpret the meaning in each touch as one or the other, depending on the part of the body being touched. If the touch is on the hand, the head, the face, the arms, or the back, it is likely to be interpreted as warmth and friendliness. If the touch is to either the breast or the genitals, it is likely to be interpreted as only sexual desire.

Men do not distinguish between warm friendliness and sexual desire in touch as much as women do. Each touch for a man is likely to have elements of both. This leads to a lot of confusion in interpreting touch. A woman who receives a pat on the back from her employer is likely to interpret that touch as strictly warmth and friendliness, a job well done. The man who sends the touch is also likely to have as part of his meaning certain elements of sexual desire. Later when the employer makes a pass at the employee, the woman is likely to be shocked or upset because she did not perceive any sexual overtures to have occurred. On the other hand, the man who receives a very positive smile and a great deal of warmth and friendliness as a response to the pat on the back is likely to perceive that a sexual overture was initiated and positively reinforced from the woman.

Men and women also use space differently. In our culture women are given, and demand, less personal space—even though they would prefer a greater amount of personal space, especially from strangers and from men.[74] When

74. Frank N. Willis, Jr., "Initial Speaking Distance as a Function of the Speaker's Relationship," *Psychonomic Science* 5(1966):221–22; John J. Hartnett, Kent G. Bailey, and Frank W. Gibson, Jr., "Personal Space as Influenced by Sex and Type of Movement," *Journal of Psychology* 76(1970):139–44.

women are given a choice of how far away from another person they will stand, they will choose a farther distance. When other people choose the distance, they will stand closer to the woman than she prefers. However, women are much more tolerant than men if the person moves closer to them. Men in our culture demand and are given much more personal space than women. When there is a spatial conflict between men and women — for example, when a man and a woman are walking down a hallway and one of them needs to move or they will bump into each other — it is generally the woman who will move.[75]

Men and women also use nonverbal regulators differently. For example, the pattern of interruptions which occurs when men talk with women is different from that in same-sex interactions.[76] In conversations between men and women almost 90 percent of the interruptions are made by men. In same-sex interactions there are fewer interruptions and they are performed equally by both members. Men interrupt women as a way to gain control of the verbal flow of communication. Another way men gain and maintain control of the verbal flow of communication is by responding to topics introduced by women with fewer words than women use to respond to topics introduced by men. Men responding to topics introduced by women are more likely to use what is called a minimal response. That is, there is an overlong period of silence after the woman stops speaking and then the man makes a minimal response such as "uhuh" or "yeah" and becomes silent again. When this occurs women are likely to become silent and allow men to introduce topics and take control of the verbal flow of communication.

Most of the differences observed in the nonverbal communication between men and women have also been observed between high and low status individuals in our culture.[77] In general, the nonverbal behaviors of men are identical to those of high status individuals. The nonverbal behaviors of women are identical to those of low status individuals when in the presence of a high status person: a greater amount of appeasement smiling, more formal and closed body positions, use of less space, less initiation of touch, more eye gaze, less speech, and fewer interruptions. The differences observed between males and females may simply reflect the lower status of women in our society. It is interesting to note that some of these behaviors are not consistently a part of women's nonverbal communication — they occur only in the presence of males, not when women are interacting with one another.

In general, women are much more sensitive decoders of nonverbal cues than men.[78] They score more accurately on tests of nonverbal communication. Some men, especially if they are trained in theatre, counseling, psychology, or in some of the other arts score approximately equal to the average woman.[79] Women are also much more adaptive in changing their nonverbal communication to synchronize smoothly in some interactions.[80] Within sixty seconds a woman can adapt her nonverbal communication — becoming dominant and taking charge, for example, or becoming submissive and letting the

75. Denise Polit and Marianne LaFrance, "Sex Differences in Reaction to Spatial Invasion," Journal of Social Psychology 102(1977):59-60.

76. Mary Brown Parlee, "Conversational Politics," Psychology Today, May 1979, 48-56. Don H. Zimmerman and Candace West, "Sex Roles, Interruptions, and Silences in Conversation," in Barrie Thorne and Nancy Henley, eds., Language and Sex: Difference and Dominance (Rowley, Mass.: Newberry House, 1975), 117.

77. Nancy M. Henley, Body Politics.

78. Marianne LaFrance and Clara Mayo, "A Review of Nonverbal Behaviors of Women and Men," Western Journal of Speech Communication 43(Spring 1979):96-107.

79. Lawrence B. Rosenfeld and Jean M. Civikly, With Words Unspoken: The Nonverbal Experience (New York: Holt, Rinehart & Winston, 1976), 90.

80. Shirley Weitz, "Sex Differences in Nonverbal Communication," Sex Roles 2(1976):175-84.

Women display and decode
nonverbal messages more
sensitively than do men.

other individual take charge. However, again it appears that this flexibility is used only when women interact with men. Women do not appear to adapt to other women. Men do not adapt to either men or women but, rather, maintain their habitual pattern of nonverbal communication in interactions with one another or with the opposite sex. This sensitivity and adaptation has also been interpreted as a sign of the lower status of women in our culture. In general we find that individuals of lower status, whether they are male or female, are much more vigilant, adaptive, and observant of the nonverbal cues and codes of communication given off by higher status individuals.

Understanding the differences in the nonverbal behaviors of men and women should help us understand why we sometimes have difficulty communicating with one another. We do not always mean the same thing by the same behavior. It is difficult for a woman to respond to a man's plea for understanding when his nonverbal behavior suggests "I'm dominant here." Nor is it easy for a man to take seriously a woman's message of "I'm angry and you'd better take me seriously!" if it is accompanied by a smile and other submissive nonverbal cues.

A final word of caution is in order. While we can try to change some of our nonverbal behavior, we must remember that most of the people we communicate with will not have read this book or be aware of what we are trying to do. They will only know that our nonverbal behaviors are unexpected. Consequently they may feel uncomfortable with us. The most effective way to change our nonverbal behavior is a little at a time, carefully observing the reactions of others, until we increase our communication effectiveness and yet are comfortable with ourselves and with others.

Summary

We utilize many different behaviors in our nonverbal communication system. Our nonverbal communication system is not always independent of our verbal communication system. Six ways in which our nonverbal communication interacts with our verbal communication are discussed.

Many nonverbal attributes affect how others perceive us and receive our messages. We can intentionally manipulate nonverbal behavior in order to communicate more effectively with others.

Five ways to display emotional expression and seven critical aspects of interpreting and displaying emotions are discussed. Combinations of nonverbal behaviors are often used to convey complex attitudes, such as friendliness/warmth and status/power.

Examples of cross-cultural and subcultural differences in nonverbal communication are given. Extensive attention is paid to how differences between communication of males and females in the general American culture influences how we perceive and understand, or misunderstand, members of the opposite sex.

7

Listening and Feedback

This chapter focuses on two important and related phenomena in communication—listening and feedback. We will discuss the listening process, the various purposes we may have in interpersonal listening, some common problems in listening, and some ways to improve our listening to others.

One of the responsibilities we have as listeners is to deliver effective feedback to others about the messages we are receiving from them. It also helps others to understand our messages if we use effective communication skills. As we pointed out in chapter 1, once an initial message has been responded to in an interpersonal interaction, all subsequent messages are feedback.

Feedback will be defined, sources and types of feedback will be identified, the effects of feedback on listening and on the communication process will be discussed, and suggestions for using the feedback process effectively will be given. A separate discussion on effectively feeding back feelings will be included since the expression of feelings often plays a dominant role in interpersonal communication. We will consider why it is important to express our feelings, why inhibiting feelings and feedback can be harmful to communication and we will give suggestions for constructively expressing feelings.

It is important for us to remember that sending and listening to interpersonal messages are reciprocal and circular processes. The more effective we are at listening to the other person's messages, the more effective and efficient feedback we can send back to them, and the better they will be able to encode their messages to help us achieve understanding. Much of what we discuss here under listening and feedback can be used to increase our effectiveness as senders of messages. The more we do as senders to make the listening process easier for our receivers, the more interpersonally effective we will become.

LISTENING

The Importance of Listening

The evidence is overwhelming that without specific training we do not develop listening skills that are adequate to meet the needs of modern life. The data indicate that most of us are poor listeners. For example, we can accurately recall only 50 percent of lecture information we hear immediately after hearing it.[1] Misinformation and misunderstanding are common products of our communication listening experiences. Effective listening can make the difference between knowledge and ignorance, information and misinformation, involvement and apathy, enjoyment and boredom, understanding and misunderstanding, and sharing and withdrawal in our interpersonal relationships.

What the listener brings to the communication situation is of prime importance to effective communication. The listener needs to be aware of what is at stake in the communication situation, and the sender needs to understand both the listening process and the listener to achieve the response desired. Unfortunately, listening behavior is often overlooked or ignored.

Adults spend about 70 percent of their waking hours engaged in communication activities. About 10 percent of this communication time is spent

1. Ralph G. Nichols, "Do We Know How to Listen? Practical Helps in a Modern Age," *Speech Teacher* 10 (March 1961):119–20.

writing, 15 percent reading, 32 percent talking, and 42 percent listening.[2] Even during working hours listening accounts for the majority of time spent in communication (33 percent listening, 26 percent speaking, 23 percent writing, and 19 percent reading).[3] Many jobs depend even more heavily on listening.

Business has become increasingly concerned with the listening skills of their employees. Sperry, a major business corporation, ran an advertisement in *Fortune* to report that our average listening efficiency is about 25 percent; consequently, when a message reaches its final destination in the organization it may be distorted by as much as 80 percent.[4] The advertisement emphasizes the extensive listening programs at Sperry to train employees to listen better. Most of us fail to realize the importance of the listening process in our interpersonal relationships until our mistakes have created a misunderstanding, caused an argument, lost us a date, or ruined a job or a class assignment.

The Listening Process

At the outset it seems desirable to define listening. Sometimes the term **listening** is restricted to spoken language[5] and sometimes visual and nonverbal vocal communication are included.[6] In a sense, listening is a combination of what we hear, what we understand, and what we remember. Hearing, the first element, is the reception of sound. It is the response of the nervous system of the human body to the stimulation of sound waves. A listener does not receive a word or message instantly, but rather accumulates sounds bit by bit, identifies short sound sequences as words, and then translates these words and groups of words into meaning. It may be helpful to think of the act of listening as comprising three major stages: hearing, identifying and recognizing, and cognitive processing.[7] The diagram in figure 7.1 illustrates these three stages.

The first stage, hearing, is the process by which speech sounds in the form of sound waves are received by the ear. In the second stage, identifying and recognizing, patterns and familiar relationships of sounds are recognized and assimilated. Through analysis, mental reorganization, and association, the sounds and sound sequences are recognized as words. The third stage, cognitive processing, is the translation of the flow of words into meaning. Cognitive processing involves one or more avenues of thought: indexing, comparing, noting sequence, forming sensory impressions, aesthetically appreciating, and interpreting what we have received.

As identified in figure 7.1, **auditory acuity** is the first factor to affect the hearing of sound—the ability of the ear to respond to various frequencies (tones) at various intensities (levels of loudness). Human beings can hear frequencies from 20 to 20,000 hertz, or Hz (cycles per second),[8] although most words fall between 400 and 4,000 Hz—the critical range of auditory acuity.[9]

2. Raul Tory Rankin, "The Measurement of the Ability to Understand Spoken Language," Ph.D. dissertation, University of Michigan, 1962, *Dissertation Abstracts* 12 (1952):847–48.

3. J. Donald Weinrauch and John R. Swanda, Jr., "Examining the Significance of Listening: An Exploratory Study of Contemporary Management," *The Journal of Business Communication* 13 (February 1975):25–32.

4. Sperry Rand advertisement, *Fortune*, vol. 102, no. 8, (October 20, 1980):102–3.

5. Rankin, "Measurement of Ability to Understand," 847; Larry L. Barker, *Listening Behavior* (Englewood Cliffs, N.J.: Prentice Hall, 1971), 17.

6. James I. Brown and G. Robert Carlsen, *Brown-Carlsen Listening Comprehension Test* (New York: Harcourt, Brace & World, 1955), 1.

7. See Andrew D. Wolvin and Carolyn Gwynn Coakley, *Listening* (Dubuque, Iowa: Wm. C. Brown, 1982), 35–50, for an excellent description of the listening process.

8. Robert O. Hirsch, *Listening: A Way to Process Information Aurally* in William E. Arnold, ed., *Comm Comp*, (Dubuque, Iowa: Gorsuch Scarisbrick, 1979), 9.

9. Wolvin and Coakley, *Listening*, 37.

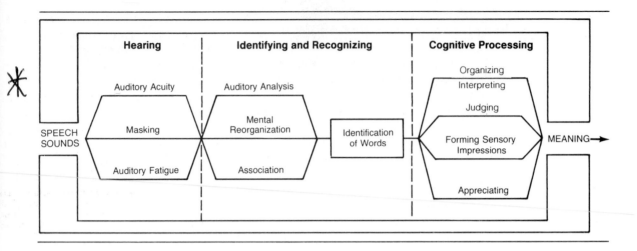

Hearing	Identifying and Recognizing	Cognitive Processing

SPEECH SOUNDS

Auditory Acuity

Masking

Auditory Fatigue

Auditory Analysis

Mental Reorganization

Association

Identification of Words

Organizing

Interpreting

Judging

Forming Sensory Impressions

Appreciating

MEANING →

Figure 7.1 The listening process.

10. Ibid.

11. Ibid., 39.

12. Stephen E. Levinson and Mark Y. Liberman, "Speech Recognition by Computer," *Scientific American,* 244, no. 4 (April 1981):64–76.

The loudness of sound is measured in decibels. Conversational speech is about 60 decibels.[10] A person who requires more than the normal amount of intensity (volume) to hear sounds of certain frequencies is said to have a hearing loss. A requirement of fifteen to twenty decibels over normal would be considered a significant hearing loss. Any loss of this amount in the critical range of 400 to 4,000 Hz is especially serious, since it affects speech perception.

Auditory fatigue can also affect hearing.[11] Continuous exposure to sounds of certain frequencies can cause a temporary hearing loss. A monotonous tone or a droning voice can create auditory fatigue. Studies today are showing that hearing losses, some of an enduring nature, are resulting from prolonged exposure to noise in urban communities. Some researchers suggest that listening to music played at high volume for prolonged periods can also cause a hearing loss.

The second stage in listening — identifying and recognizing sound patterns and relationships — can be affected by the quality of our auditory analysis, by our perceptual processes, by mental reorganization, and by past associations. Auditory analysis refers to an individual's mental process of comparing incoming sounds with familiar sounds. Sounds are recognized in terms of their likenesses and differences.[12]

In the second part of this stage — mental organization — the listener applies some system that will aid retention and will structure the incoming sounds. We may syllabify a word, for example, as we pronounce it to ourselves. If we hear a series of numbers, we may place them in groups of three, or we may repeat the series to ourselves several times. Whether we group, recode, or rehearse, we are engaged in mental reorganization.

Finally, sounds are associated with our prior experiences with those sounds. Words used in speech may be entirely strange to the listener — for example, a foreign language — or they may have become associated with subjective meanings quite different from those the sender had in mind. In any event, the

process of identifying words involves the listener's experience, background, and memory of past associations regarding the incoming sounds.

In the third major stage of listening — cognitive processing — we assimilate the continuous flow of words and respond to them with understanding or feeling.[13] Again, the listener's experiential background is brought into play along with various skills in thinking to make sense of the stream of words being received. As listeners we evaluate information according to its importance to us. We search for main ideas and supporting or secondary ideas; we separate the relevant from the irrelevant; we structure bits and pieces into more meaningful wholes. Some people who are exceptionally skilled in this apparently have an ability to visualize or see an outline of incoming information.

We may also arrange material according to time, space, position, or some other relationship by noting sequences in incoming information. All these functions aid us in creating a framework into which incoming information can be placed and related. Material is easier to process and remember if we note an order of events or a placement of parts of a whole. For example, we may compare and contrast the information we are presently receiving with information we have received in the past. Or we may create a time order such as "what happened first, second, third, . . . and last."

Hearing loss resulting from exposure to loud music is not uncommon among rock musicians.

13. Wolvin and Coakley, 43–50.

Sometimes we react with our other senses to incoming information. Probably the sensory response most frequently used in association with incoming oral information is sight — the ability to add a visual dimension to the hearing/listening dimension. Some people are apparently highly skilled in forming sensory impressions so that they taste words describing tastes, smell descriptions of smells, and generally translate words into sensory images, thus adding to the meaningfulness of the verbal messages they receive.

We may also respond to the aesthetic nature of others' messages. Appreciation can play an important role in listening to messages that are intended to activate the feelings and emotions of the listener.

All these elements and more are used in dynamic relationships to carry out the process of listening — the process by which information is assimilated, ideas are received and reacted to, and interpretations, judgments, and applications are made in order to derive meaning from the messages received.

Purposes of Listening

The development of good listening ability involves recognizing that there are specific purposes in interpersonal listening, each with defined requirements and skills. The four most important interpersonal purposes are (1) listening for enjoyment, (2) listening for information, (3) listening to be empathic or supportive, and (4) listening to evaluate critically. We may listen with all four purposes in mind. We may also enjoy while we learn. However, the most effective listening appears to occur when we know what we are listening for and listen with that specific purpose in mind.

Listening for Enjoyment

14. See Wolvin and Coakley, 61-70, for further discussion.

Appreciative listening[14] can increase our enjoyment of life, enlarge our experience, expand the range of what we enjoy, and decrease the tension of daily life. Much of the daily conversation in which each of us engages serves a social purpose — to share feelings and responses in order to build and maintain positive, supporting relationships. We enjoy listening to someone tell us a "good story" or a joke, make a pun or a humorous comment. In addition, we may listen to satisfy our desire to appreciate and experience art and beauty. Much of our social life involves listening to music, listening to stories or drama on television, engaging in social conversation, and for some persons listening to live drama, oral interpretation, or literature read aloud.

Many people cheat themselves out of pleasant and beneficial listening experiences because they have limited experience in appreciative listening. When we deny ourselves the pleasure of aesthetic listening, we are always the losers. Persons who believe they have to get practical information from everything they listen to condemn themselves to impoverished social and cultural

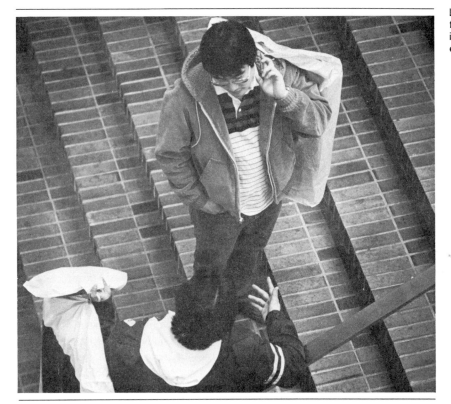

Listening effectively is essential for enjoyment, assimilating information, and making critical evaluations.

experiences. We need to attempt to expand our experiences in appreciative listening—to live more richly, deeply, and pleasantly through expanded appreciation of the richness of our interpersonal interactions.

Listening for Information

Another purpose of listening is to receive information[15]—to acquire an answer to a definite problem or question, to listen for direction, to listen to the news of current interest, and to acquire the opinions and views of others. Through listening we acquire a viable picture of the world and ourselves and how others perceive us.

The information we listen for in interpersonal relationships is more than just the content or topic the other person is discussing. We listen to gain information about the other person's feelings, both toward the topic and toward us. We attempt to understand this information and integrate it with our own perceptions. We need to try to increase the accuracy of our reception as we listen for information.

15. See Wolvin and Coakley, 85-106, for a discussion of comprehensive listening.

Empathic Listening

Sometimes we simply need someone to listen to us. We want to express our needs and concerns, to talk about our problems until we come up with our own solutions.[16]

16. See Wolvin and Coakley, 109–22, for a discussion of therapeutic listening.

In interpersonal relationships we are often asked to provide such supportive listening for others. The listener's role in empathic listening is to provide a climate of trust and supportiveness for the other person. We should not put pressure on the other person to think faster, nor should we interject our own ideas and feelings into the discussion. As we listen empathically, we begin to understand the other person's perceptions, but we must remember that our main purpose in empathic listening is simply to be there for the other person. We must avoid the temptation to begin discussing our own problems and needs, thereby focusing the interaction upon us.

✸ Listening to Make Critical Evaluations

The term *critical* here means careful evaluation,[17] not negativism or aggressive attack or constant challenging. The antagonistic, challenging aspect of being critical can be the antithesis of effective listening. Even critical listening in the positive sense of evaluating carefully can have dire consequences if inappropriate or poorly timed evaluation interferes with receiving information accurately or providing a supportive listening climate. To examine carefully each sentence and idea during a conversation meant to transmit information will seriously decrease the efficiency of listening for information. And if antagonism and negative criticizing interfere with supportive listening, the results are disastrous.

17. See Wolvin and Coakley, 125–48, for a more complete discussion of critical listening.

Critical listening includes evaluating the expertness and trustworthiness of the other; it includes judging the quality of the other person's evidence, support, and reasoning; and it includes analyzing the needs and motivations being aroused in us.

Once again, it should be stressed that the purpose for which we are listening must be considered if we are to listen effectively. We may need to evaluate information in listening, but often the careful evaluative assimilation should be postponed until we fully comprehend the entire message. We are usually well repaid for postponing evaluation.

On the other hand, if the purpose of our listening is to make a decision — a judgment — then we may profit by adopting an evaluative attitude sooner. We may need to evaluate the strength of each main point advanced and carefully test the reasoning and the quality of the evidence used in supporting the point.

Effective critical listening makes us aware of prejudices in ourselves and in others. It forces us to judge on the basis of facts and information rather than on emotions and falsehoods. It calls for patience, objectivity, and the testing of thinking and reasoning.

The important point to keep in mind at this time is that we may have various purposes in mind when listening, and the specific purpose for which we listen ought to determine what skills need to be called into play. A major concern of any listener is to discover the purpose and nature of the interaction and to make adjustment to it.

Problems in Listening

Poor listening can result from false assumptions about listening, from poor listening habits, and from ignorance about good listening techniques. We will consider all these causes of poor listening and their effects on interpersonal communication and suggest some possible solutions.

Misconceptions About Listening

Serious false assumptions about listening are that it is easy, that it is passive, that we relax and merely receive information, and that the listener is not actively involved. Nothing could be further from the truth. Listening — especially empathic, critical, and informational listening — is difficult and fatiguing because it requires active and continuous mental effort.

It is true that in most communication situations listening is voluntary; yet if we listen only when we want to or when it is convenient, we hear only what we want to hear and only what captures our fleeting attention. Productive listening is work. It requires effort and purposeful activity.

These false assumptions often tempt us to use one or more of the following seven poor listening habits described by Barker[18] relative to public communication. We will now consider the ways these poor listening habits also occur during our interpersonal communication.

18. Larry L. Barker, *Listening Behavior*, (Englewood Cliffs, N.J.: Prentice Hall, 1971), 61–65.

Dismissal of a Subject as Uninteresting

Sometimes we find the topic that another person introduces boring. It may be that we have heard some of the content before, or it concerns people we don't know, or we want to discuss something else which seems more important to us at the time. Whatever our reason, the rationalization we use for not listening is that the subject is uninteresting. When we decide that a subject is uninteresting, our listening effectiveness is greatly impaired. But uninteresting subjects are not necessarily without value to us. We may learn something about the other person which will be helpful later in our relationship. To equate interestingness with valuableness is a mistake. It reveals an underlying attitude that says, "If your information interests me and entertains me, it is valuable to me. If you don't succeed, then your information is worthless."

Conveying that nonverbal message to the speaker will have predictable effects. The speaker will feel rejected and the topic may be dropped or the interaction discontinued. Some messages that seem to lack interest may contain highly important and relevant information for the listener or may be very important to the speaker. However, if we decide not to listen, we will not receive that information, or fulfill our responsibility as a listener. When the responsibility for communicating is placed entirely on the speaker, little understanding may occur. The solution to not being originally interested in a subject is for you to take charge and consciously examine the topic's relevance or usefulness to you. Senders do not always point out clearly how information can be useful to you. Sometimes you must purposefully seek out ways the information can benefit you. Sometimes, as a listener, you need to ask yourself, "What is the other person saying that I can use? What worthwhile ideas can I get from this?" Good listeners seem to be interested in whatever they are listening to. Good listeners seldom find topics dull. At the same time, as skilled communicators, our awareness of the potential problems in listening should cause us to help our listeners by identifying the relevance of our topic for them.

The real problem is to determine what you can do when you are not interested to create your own interest. For one thing, we tend to find subjects interesting when they have immediate application for us. Hence, look first for some immediate rewards. If necessary, however, try to discover for yourself how the information could be useful at a later time and place. Ask yourself questions such as, "Why am I here? What initial motive brought me to hear this person?" and "What selfish uses can I find for this material?" This will help you discover genuine interest in the topic.

Effective listening is closely related to our own personal growth, and for selfish and personal reasons it is necessary for us to try to become genuinely interested in receiving ideas from others. Even the most superficial conversation may tell us a great deal about the other person's self-concept, feelings, world view, and attitude toward us and other people.

Avoiding Difficult Listening

A second bad listening habit is to avoid difficult material. Too many of us listen only as long as it is easy, comfortable, and entertaining. If the message becomes difficult or threatening, we just decide not to listen. That habit, of course, deprives us of many opportunities to learn and to acquire new insights and understandings about ourselves and others. Many relationships fail because the individuals involved have seldom been subjected to any discussion of the more complex aspects of their interpersonal relationships. The poorest listeners are inexperienced listeners who are unacquainted with a wide range of interpersonal relationships and who feel threatened when their relationships need more than superficial attention. Good listeners develop an appetite for a wide variety of spoken interpersonal messages. They have even learned to enjoy the challenge of difficult interpersonal subjects. They like the intellectual stimulation and growth which comes from exploring their relationships with others. If you want to become a better listener but feel handicapped by the bad habit of avoiding difficult messages, then you should resolve to eliminate this handicap by participating as a listener in a wide variety of interpersonal communication situations.

Criticizing Delivery and Physical Appearance

A third common problem in listening is focusing on some external aspect of the speaker and listening only if the other person's appearance and delivery are attractive. If the person's appearance is not to our liking, or if the delivery is either vocally or physically distracting, we may become so busily engaged in mentally criticizing the speaker's delivery or appearance that we fail to listen to the message.

A junior in college who was a prospective student teacher was once interviewed by one of us and another person. It was apparent from observation of the other person during the interview that he was not hearing what the student was saying because the student's general appearance had distracted him into being critical. This was even more apparent in our private discussion following the interview, when he confessed that he had heard almost nothing the student had said because the student's appearance was so distracting. This "different" appearance was used by the interviewer to rationalize his poor listening. Many of us have fallen into this habit. If the other person has an annoying mannerism, we focus on that and decide that we cannot listen. We spend the time mentally criticizing either the physical appearance or speech delivery of the other person at the cost of not receiving accurately or beneficially the information sent to us.

This does not happen only when we first meet a person. How many times have you been in an argument with someone and found yourself focusing on the sound of the person's voice, a nervous tapping of the foot, or some facial feature in order to consciously ignore a message you don't want to receive? Our goal should be to listen to the message and not be distracted by the delivery or the appearance of the person. Our aim is to find out what the other person is saying — to find out what knowledge, information, and feelings that person has that we need to know about.

Each of us is sensitive to some particular characteristics or mannerisms which bother us and tend to disrupt our listening effectively to others. If we allow ourselves to be bothered by a droning voice, a shrill pitch, a persistent cough, socially inappropriate dress, and so forth, we will more often than not be led away from concentrating fully on the message. Unfortunately, most people do have some eccentricity as speakers, including ourselves. It may be poor eye contact, an accent, or some distracting bodily activity which makes it difficult for others to listen to us. It is possible, however, for all of us to make the decision as listeners to adjust to those situations — to tell ourselves that it is the message we want to understand and that the idiosyncrasy of the speaker is unimportant. People can be rational. We can learn to control our behavior. Listeners can learn to adjust to speakers, and when we make that adjustment a natural part of our behavior, we will become more effective listeners.

Faking Attention

It is not unusual to observe someone faking attention in a church or in a classroom. Frequently when we use this poor habit the other person is someone in authority and we must listen or we will lose our job, have some reward or privilege taken away, or make other people around us uncomfortable. Faking attention also occurs frequently in interpersonal communication situations. The faker probably thinks, "If I look as though I am listening, the other person will be pleased." The other person may indeed sometimes be deceived, but in most instances the only person deceived is the one faking the listening. We have all tried at one time or another to concentrate on looking interested while we are mentally planning how to get a date with that special someone, find some extra spending money, or finish the homework assignment due tomorrow. On occasion, our faking attention can be exposed by a carefully inserted question from the person we are listening to. Besides suffering the embarrassment of being caught looking like a smiling statue or of failing to respond in the right way at the right time, we cheat ourselves of an opportunity to learn from what is being said to us. In the long run we are the losers. We anger and disappoint the other person because in a way we have broken our social communication contract with them. We have not been listening. We have not been fulfilling our role as a participant in the interaction. Faking attention is very harmful to our interpersonal relationships.

Listening to Only One Part of the Message

Some people listen only for facts. Focusing on "getting the facts" can develop into a bad listening habit. We can become so busily engaged in listening for and trying to remember facts that the other person's ideas and feelings are missed entirely. Memorizing facts is not a way to listen. Facts are useful in constructing and understanding ideas; as such they should be considered secondary to the idea. When people talk, they want us to understand their ideas, and grasping ideas is a skill that is basic to effective listening.

Other people focus on "getting the general idea." They are rarely concerned with the facts, arguments, or evidence which support these ideas. Sometimes this is all we need. But often we need more than a superficial knowledge of the other person's conclusions about themselves, about us, and about our relationship to effectively communicate and understand one another. Still other individuals may focus on understanding the feelings the other person has in the interaction. It doesn't seem important to them to grasp the facts in the situation or the other person's ideas about the facts.

In each case something is missing in the listening process. The other person's message is being only partly received. Good listeners pay attention to all three: feelings, facts, and ideas. They have acquired the ability to discriminate between fact and principle, idea and example, evidence and argument, and inference and observation. Poor listeners tend to be unable to make these distinctions, which require listening to the whole, not just a part of the message. Good listeners know that it is important to get the main idea, to comprehend the underlying structure of the message or the particular argument being given; to recognize the facts, inferences, and observations which underlie the main idea; and to comprehend the other person's feelings about this as well.

This is not to deny that in some listening situations one or more aspects of a message may be more important or critical to our understanding than other aspects. That is why it is also important to determine the purpose for which we are listening and to focus our attention and listening skills so that we achieve this purpose. If the purpose of the message is persuasion, we will be engaged mainly in critical listening. If the message is to inform or instruct, we will be concerned mainly with receiving the ideas and concepts as clearly, accurately, and fully as possible. If the purpose is to provide support and empathy for the other person, we may want to focus mainly on the feelings.

Our objective for improving our listening behavior is to acquire the habit of determining why we are listening so we can focus on the most important aspect of a message while receiving all the other aspects as well. We don't pretend that this is an easy listening skill to achieve. But the more we are aware of the complexity involved in attaining this balance, the more we are likely to become better listeners.

Letting Emotion-Laden Words Arouse Us

Another habit detrimental to listening is allowing our emotions to take control of our listening behavior. When what we are hearing is something we do not want to hear — something that angers or frightens us — we may develop the habit of blocking it out. On the other hand, if the words are "purr words" for us, we are apt to accept everything that is said — truths, half-truths, or pure sham. Our emotions filter what we hear. When we hear something that is opposite to our beliefs, values, attitudes, prejudices, or convictions, we react quickly and emotionally. We become fearful and may begin to argue mentally with the other person. We plan rebuttals to what has been said, and in the meantime have not heard anything else; we think of questions we can ask to "put down" the other person; or we may just turn to thoughts that support our own feelings on the topic. Any of these behaviors may become so habitual that as soon as we hear words, ideas, or arguments that strike our emotions, we react by not listening. Our antagonistic and negative behavior becomes as automatic as if an "antilistening" button were pushed. This may become our habitual response unless we learn to master this behavior and to become good listeners.

An important objective for improving our listening is to learn to hold our fire; to learn not to get too excited about another person's point until we are certain we thoroughly understand it. The aim is always to withhold evaluation until comprehension is complete. Effective listeners keep open minds. They try to identify the words or phrases that are most upsetting emotionally to them and purposely to "cool" their reactions to them; they try to identify the "hidden antagonizers" which impair their ability to perceive accurately and to understand. Hidden antagonizers always touch areas of great sensitivity — our strongest values, convictions, and prejudices. A single emotion-laden word or an argument may trigger our emotional filter, and when this occurs, our listening efficiency drops toward the zero point.

There are some steps we can take to strengthen our behavior control. First, when we hear something that really upsets us, we can extract those words or phrases that are most upsetting to us emotionally and make a list of them. Second, we can analyze why each word influences us as it does. We can ask ourselves what the original basis for our reaction to that word was. Third, we can discuss each of these words with our interpersonal partner. We may discover that these words carry unique and purely personal connotations for us that are without foundation. That is, we may find that the other person does not mean to arouse those particular emotions in us. In any event, getting these words out into the open and identifying them will be of great help in enabling us to cool our reactions to them.

Wasting Advantage of Thought Speed over Speech Speed

The seventh poor listening habit has to do with how we use the extra time available to us as a listener because of the great difference between speech speed and thought speed. The average rate of speaking is about 125 words per minute, but the brain can handle words at a much faster rate. It is not uncommon to find people who can read at rates of 1,200 words per minute and easily understand what they have read. Some individuals have read as rapidly as 10,000 words per minute and then scored over 80 percent on factual tests of the material. Numerous experiments in compressed speech (speech that is speeded up mechanically) have shown that people can listen effectively at speeds four to five times faster than normal speech.[19] Because the brain can handle words at a lightning pace but when we listen it receives words at a snail's pace, there is a lot of time available for our brains to sidetrack us. Our

19. Ibid., 63.

brains can and do work with hundreds of thoughts other than those spoken to us. We use the extra thinking time when we listen, but how do we use it? Sometimes we daydream, fantasize, or think about other activities unrelated to the message we are hearing. According to some studies we spend 30 to 40 percent of the time we are awake daydreaming, with the average daydream only 5 to 14 seconds long, although really complicated daydreams can take as long as 90 seconds.[20] Even if we catch ourselves and come back to what the other person is saying, we have missed something in the speaker's line of thought and it is now more difficult to grasp the ideas expressed. What is being said seems less interesting, and our daydreams beckon us to return.

20. "It's All in a Woman's Day," *Woman's Day*, August 8, 1980, 20.

We need to make the wisest possible use of the spare time created by the difference between speaking rate and thinking rate. The good listener learns to capitalize on thought speed. Most of us can think easily at about four times the average rate of speaking.[21] That is, we have about four hundred words' worth of thinking time to spare during every minute a person talks to us.

21. Barker, *Listening Behavior*, 63.

We can use the spare time purposefully to enhance our understanding of the message we are receiving. We can use the following mental activities to fill this spare time:

1. Anticipate what the other person will say; by comparing our prediction with the other person's actual message, we may discover discrepancies which point to ideas and reasoning we have missed or misunderstood.
2. Note the adequacy with which each point is supported; the kinds of examples the other person chooses; what details are highlighted and what are deemphasized or left out; the reasoning involved.
3. Observe the person's nonverbal behavior: vocal characteristics, gestures, posture, facial expressions, etc.
4. Mentally review what has been said, noting consistencies or inconsistencies that may need to be clarified.
5. Listen "between the lines" for additional meaning—for hidden or unstated meanings; for new meanings (that is, meanings other than those assigned by us initially); for what is not said as well as what is said.

These are some of the ingredients of concentration in listening, which make it apparent that listening is an *active* process that requires our concentration and an enormous amount of energy.

FEEDBACK

Our responsibility as listeners includes sending feedback to the other person. Effective listening occurs only when the cues we send back to the other person allow that person to know we have received the intended message. It is on the basis of this feedback that other people can adjust their messages to improve our understanding. This *corrective function* is the primary purpose of feedback.

Feedback Defined

Weiner, a cybernetics specialist who was one of the first persons to be concerned with the feedback process, defined it as ''the property of being able to adjust future conduct by past performance. Feedback may be as simple as that of the common reflex or it may be a higher order feedback, in which past experience is used not only to regulate specific movements, but also whole policies of behavior.''[22] Communication scholars have generally accepted the essential characteristic of this definition: that the corrective function is the heart of the feedback process. *Feedback, then, enables communicators to correct and adjust messages to adapt to the receiver.* Without feedback from the other person there is no way to monitor or regulate the communication process so that we achieve integration and agreement with the other person. Without feedback we would be left with a haphazard, random, chance system of influencing others. We could send out our messages but we would have no way of knowing if they were received, how accurately they were received, or if the other person agreed or disagreed with us. If the other person disagreed with us or misunderstood us, we would not know it or be able to adjust our message, to clarify it or make it more acceptable.

Since effective communication exists between two persons when the receiver of a message gives it the interpretation intended by the sender, unless we were 100 percent perfect with each initial message, we would never understand one another. Effective communication results solely from the ongoing corrective process made possible by feedback.

One point should be made clear: communicators are both senders and receivers of feedback simultaneously. We have been discussing feedback as though it were going from one person (the receiver) to the other person (the sender) in a linear manner; that is, as though the original message stimulates a feedback response. We must remember that the process is complex and interactive. Feedback flows simultaneously in both directions. It emanates from both speaker and listener and exerts a mutual influence upon both participants.

Sources and Types of Feedback

There are a number of ways of categorizing the different types of feedback we receive. We will look at five of those ways to help explain the complexity of the feedback process.

22. Norbert Wiener, *Cybernetics* (New York: John Wiley & Sons, 1948), 33.

Verbal or Nonverbal Feedback

Feedback may be classified according to the channel used — that is, as either verbal or nonverbal. Verbal feedback can convey complex, abstract messages to others. Nonverbal cues such as facial expression, posture, gestures, sighs, tone of voice, and other bodily movements or physical responses provide important feedback about our feelings and attitudes to the sender. In fact, nonverbal messages are often used as much as or more than verbal messages by police, medical doctors, psychiatrists, therapists, and others in investigative or interviewing situations.

Unfortunately, we are not even consciously aware of or in control of many of our nonverbal behaviors which others may interpret as feedback. In addition, our nonverbal communication is not always interpreted accurately even when we intentionally send it. While our words may not always be interpreted as we mean them, they do seem to serve as a more "concrete" form of feedback that we can both agree has occurred. This means that verbal feedback is often more available for discussion and clarification between us.

Internal or External Feedback

Feedback can be classified as either internal or external.[23] When we monitor our own performance and think about what we are saying as we encode the message, or when we reflect about something we have just said, we are using internal feedback. When we are listening to the verbal response of the other person, or observing that person's nonverbal responses, we are using external feedback. We may also hear what we are saying as we say it (external feedback) and rephrase it to give it added meaning (internal feedback), thus using both sources, external and internal, for self-feedback. Johnson clarified the distinction between internal and external feedback well:

> Put very simply, internal feedback is at play in the speaker who is being reflective about something he has just said, while external feedback is operating when the speaker is being sensitive to the reactions of other people to what he has said. When external feedback is at work it necessarily affects — and is affected by — the internal feedback that is going on at the same time. The two kinds are doubtless even more closely interwoven than this would indicate, however; even if no other persons are present, the reflecting that is done by a speaker or thinker on what he has just said or thought is influenced in some degree by his past experiences — and his contemplations of future experiences — with external feedback. So, when we say that there are two kinds of feedback we do so with the realization, of course, that while they might be distinguished, one from the other, they cannot possibly be disentangled. As his own listener, every speaker attends as best he can as though with the ears of a multitude.[24]

23. Wendell Johnson, *Your Most Enchanted Listener* (New York: Harper & Row, 1956), 174.

24. Ibid.

There are many reasons our internal feedback might not match the external feedback we are receiving. First, our internal feedback is filtered by our field of experience. Our internal feedback process is limited by the expectations we have concerning interpersonal communication — how messages should be encoded to be effective with different types of people in different kinds of interactions. Second, our message may not have been received as we intended it to be. And third, we may not entirely receive or accurately interpret the external feedback we receive from others.

Positive or Negative Feedback

25. Gerald R. Miller, *Speech Communication: A Behavioral Approach* (Indianapolis: Bobbs-Merrill, 1966), 55.

Feedback may be either positive or negative.[25] This category system focuses on the reinforcement aspect of feedback. When we are pleased or approve of a message we reward the other person with positive feedback. The reward may be a smile, a warm glance, a softer voice; or it may be more tangible — words of approval, a date, a sale, or a job offer. Positive feedback tells the other person we are pleased and that we would like the same communication behavior continued.

Negative feedback notifies the other person that we do not agree with or approve of the message we are receiving. It can be as subtle as a lifted eyebrow or as explicit as divorce proceedings. A person receiving positive feedback tends to continue the behavior — to produce the same kind of message, that is, to send more messages similarly encoded and similar in their purposes. A person receiving negative feedback tends to cease or modify the behavior — to change the message.[26]

26. David K. Berlo, *The Process of Communication* (New York: Holt, Rinehart & Winston, 1960), 111–13.

Both kinds of feedback are important to the communication process, since one kind alone — whether negative or positive — provides the source of a message with only partial information.

Negative feedback tells the other person what *not* to do to please us but does not tell which one(s) of all the many possible alternative behaviors the other person could perform would satisfy us. If, when we are pleased, we fail to send positive feedback to the other person, he or she has no way of knowing that one satisfying alternative has been discovered. Consequently the other person is likely to discontinue the unrewarded behavior and try other alternatives until some positive feedback is received.

Indirect or Direct Feedback

27. John W. Keltner, *Interpersonal Communication: Elements and Structures* (Belmont, Calif.: Wadsworth, 1970), 92.

Feedback may also be classified as direct (purposive) or indirect (nonpurposive).[27] In other words, some feedback messages are consciously and purposefully constructed by the receiver and sent directly to the sender. Other responses of the receiver may be beneath the awareness level and are not purposefully constructed, but are simply "given off." Many of these are nonverbal.

Negative feedback by itself provides only partial information to the source of the message.

Purposeful feedback is originated by the receiver and sent directly to the source of a message for the purpose of providing information relative to that message. It is intentional feedback communication. Indirect feedback is not information purposively selected and sent; it is instead nonpurposive and unintentional feedback communication. Let us look at some examples. The employee evaluation interview is an example of purposive feedback. Whenever we say "we need to sit down and discuss this issue" we are preparing to deliver purposive feedback. We can use internal feedback to intentionally rehearse the words and sentences we plan to say to another person as we give them feedback during a conversation.

We have little control over our nonpurposive or indirect feedback. A common example of this is the situation in which we send one feedback message verbally, but also send a nonverbal feedback message that clearly contradicts the verbal. The nonverbal feedback message may be communicated by posture, tension, movement toward or away from the other person, facial expression, breaking and refusing eye contact, tone of voice, rate of speech, or any one of numerous nonverbal ways of communicating. The person responding did not consciously intend to send a contradictory message, but it was "given off" nonetheless as unintentional feedback without the conscious intent of the sender. These unintentional nonverbal behaviors often have to do with feelings, likings, and preferences. Another example of indirect feedback is the "Freudian slip" in which we let slip something verbally which we didn't intend (or want) to say, although it may have been motivated by unconscious intentions.

Immediate or Delayed Feedback

Feedback may be immediate or delayed. In face-to-face interpersonal communication, whether formal or informal, we have access to some immediate feedback. Such feedback gives face-to-face communication great adaptive and corrective potential. Immediate feedback has a more dramatic impact on the interaction because that which is being responded to has occurred recently. We all know of situations, however, when it has been impossible for us to deliver immediate feedback. We needed to wait until we were alone with the other person or until we had calmed down sufficiently to be able to deliver effective feedback to the other person. Our feedback was delayed. In many cases delayed feedback is ineffective because we have forgotten the exact message or behavior we want to respond to or because we cannot recapture the precise feelings we had at the time so that we can clearly explain our reactions to the other person.

Effects of Feedback

Experiments in which feedback was the manipulated variable have demonstrated dramatically that different feedback characteristics have a powerful effect on communication and communicators. Its effect on various dependent variables has been investigated and reported in the journals of several academic areas — communication, education, psychology, business administration, and speech sciences, for example. The following effects have important consequences for interpersonal communication.

Amount of Feedback

As feedback increases, communication is slowed down.[28] The slowest communication occurs when complete verbal and nonverbal messages are used. As we would guess, corrective and adaptive communication takes time. If you want fast communication, then one-way communication is faster than two-way. Of course, you may be misunderstood entirely, but you will at least have fast misunderstanding. In addition, as feedback increases, accuracy of communication increases.[29] With greater amounts of feedback, the receivers feel more confident about the communication outcome. Conversely, as the amount of feedback decreases or, even worse, is absent, accuracy decreases, miscommunication and confusion increase, and receivers become more anxious.[30]

Positive and Negative Feedback

When we receive negative feedback from others our encoding process changes. We speak more slowly and talk less.[31] Our speech also has more unfilled pauses[32] and more nonfluencies (ah, you know, uhm, well, etc.).[33] When we receive negative feedback we also change the content of our messages. We are less likely to state our own opinions clearly and forcefully. Rather, we become more ambiguous about how we feel or we use more neutral statements.[34]

Conversely, when we receive positive feedback from others we are more fluent, speak faster, talk more, and speak louder.[35] We are more likely to state our opinions strongly and forcefully.

We should recognize that when we send negative feedback to another person many of these effects are likely to occur. The other person will appear to be less effective as a communicator to us, will perform more poorly, and will not be as accurate or open with us. The stronger our negative feedback, the more frequently and with greater strength these effects will occur.

28. Harold J. Leavitt and Ronald A. H. Mueller, "Some Effects of Feedback on Communication," in Dean Barnlund, ed., *Interpersonal Communication: Survey and Studies* (Boston: Houghton Mifflin, 1968), 251-59.

29. Ibid.

30. Ibid.

31. J. A. Blubaugh, "Effects of Positive and Negative Audience Feedback on Selected Variables of Speech Behavior," *Speech Monographs* 36 (1969):131-37.

32. W. Stolz and P. H. Tannenbaum, "Effects of Feedback on Oral Encoding Behavior," *Language and Speech* 6 (1963):218-28.

33. J. C. Gardiner, "A Synthesis of Experimental Studies of Speech Communication Feedback," *Journal of Communication* 21 (1971):17-35.

34. W. S. Verplanck, "The Control of the Content of Conversation: Reinforcement of Statements of Opinion," *Journal of Abnormal and Social Psychology* 51 (1955):668-76.

35. Stolz and Tannenbaum, "Effects of Feedback on Oral Encoding Behavior," 218-28.

Creation of an Interpersonal Climate

How the other individual perceives our feedback affects his or her response to our message. Our communication behavior can stimulate defensiveness or trust and openness in the other person. Unless we understand that certain communication behaviors tend to elicit defensiveness, we may find ourselves in situations in which the other person becomes defensive without our understanding why. "As a person becomes more and more defensive, he becomes less and less able to perceive accurately the motives, the values, and the emotions of the sender."[36] The receiver of our feedback is more likely to distort it, to question our motives, and to reject our feedback.

36. Jack R. Gibb, "Defensive Communication," in *Journal of Communication* 11 (1961):141-48.

Gibb has identified several communication behaviors that tend to stimulate defensiveness in the other person and opposite behaviors that tend to create supportive climates and reduce defensiveness. There are six pairs of behaviors in Gibb's category system. Those in the left column, when perceived by a receiver, tend to arouse defensiveness, while those in the right column are interpreted as supportive and tend to reduce defensiveness.[37]

37. Ibid.

Gibb's Defensive and Supportive Behaviors

Defensive Climates	Supportive Climates
1. Evaluation	1. Description
2. Control	2. Problem Orientation
3. Strategy	3. Spontaneity
4. Neutrality	4. Empathy
5. Superiority	5. Equality
6. Certainty	6. Provisionalism

Gibb's categories of behaviors grew out of his analyses of tape-recorded discussions that revealed that defensive behavior increased as the communication characteristics in the left column were perceived and decreased as those in the right column were perceived. Let us consider each pair of behaviors in greater detail.

Evaluation vs. Description   Evaluative communication makes either direct or implied judgment of the other person. We can communicate evaluation of another person verbally by name-calling or labeling them: "you're unfair"; "you're irresponsible"; "you're pretty"; "you're thoughtful," etc. We can also evaluate another person by approving or disapproving of what the other person said: "you're right"; "that's not moral"; "you're a good person"; or by suggesting that our value system is superior. Messages such as "an intelligent decision would be to . . ." or "the right way to do this is . . ." subtly imply that the other person's own choice might be bad. We also evaluate others nonverbally by head nods, tone of voice, our use of space, etc. (see chapter 6).

Alternatively descriptive communication informs the other person of our perceptions—how we feel, what we believe—without evaluating that person. There is a subtle yet important difference between the messages in the preceding paragraph and "I like it when you remember to send me a card on my birthday" or "I feel angry and humiliated when I have to wait for you."

Each of us, of course, makes judgments about others and forms attitudes toward others; but we can attempt to reduce the number of blunt and strong evaluative messages we send others. We use communication to elicit cooperation from others so that we and they can enjoy mutual satisfaction of our needs. Sometimes our communication requires us to talk about the other person to that person, but when we do, we ought to focus on describing our own reactions rather than being evaluative of the other person if we want the other person to perceive us as supportive.

When we complain about another to his or her face, we can predict (providing we have learned this principle of communication) that the other person will become fearful and defensive. Children who are subjected only to evaluative communication by their parents—"you're a good boy, you're a bad girl"—become anxious and defensive about their behavior. A man or woman constantly "put down" by her or his companion acquires defensive communication strategies. Gibb has observed that as we communicate more descriptively about our reactions and the situation as we see it, defensiveness decreases. If we can remove the evaluative labels, a more supportive climate can be fostered between us.

Control vs. Problem Orientation   Controlling feedback contains an attempt to change the other person's mind, to get the other to do something, or in some way to influence the other. We resent being dominated by another person. We want to feel independent and responsible for ourselves and not to feel controlled by another person. When someone tries to control us, we resist; we become defensive. If the other person wants to make our decisions for us, it means that that person believes we are ignorant, unwise, uninformed, or in some way inadequate to live our own lives. Other people feel the same way. Messages such as "what you need to do is . . . ," "if you would only do this my way," or "you simply do not have the experience to make this decision" are open attempts to control others and arouse their defensiveness; attempts at hidden or subtle manipulations increase that defensiveness.[38] Messages such as "if you loved me, you would . . . ," or "I'm sure you wouldn't mind if I . . ." are often perceived correctly as subtle attempts to control others.

On the other hand, when other people perceive us as cooperating to solve our mutual problems, working with them, respecting their ability to work on the problem without having a predetermined solution or answer to shove

38. Ibid., 31.

down their throats, they respond positively. They see problem-oriented behavior as supporting and helpful to themselves and the relationship. Messages such as "we need to decide this together," "we're both responsible," and "I'll do this if you'll do that" engender an open and trusting rather than a defensive climate in a relationship.

Strategy vs. Spontaneity   When we perceive the other person as having a hidden plan or strategy which he or she is trying to work on us, we become defensive. We are suspicious when we think something is concealed, gimmicky, or tricky. Messages such as "it isn't necessary to talk about that," or "you can do it that way if you *really* want to" are often perceived as concealing hidden motives. Gibb has found from his analyses of the tapes of sessions of training groups that persons often perceive what the strategies of their colleagues are[39] and when they do, they become defensive. On the other hand, spontaneous behavior appears to be free of deception and tends to reduce defensiveness in others. Generally other people feel we are spontaneous when we respond to what is presently occurring in the interaction, when our messages are relevant and contain enough self-disclosure so that our feelings and attitudes seem clear, and when our verbal communication is consistent with our nonverbal.

This does not mean, however, that we need to be absolutely frank and totally open in every encounter. Rather, spontaneity and openness should be tempered with consideration for the depth of our relationship with the other person and the ability of all persons involved to accept the responsibility that full frankness and total openness carries with it. The same principle applies to the extent of the spontaneity and openness we should display relative to self-disclosure. There lurks a danger in totally disclosing ourselves to every person encountered; moreover, there can be danger in too much "telling it like we perceive it." Nevertheless, we often err in the opposite direction — not being as open and spontaneous with the other person as the situation warrants. When we are perceived to be engaged in a deceptive strategy, such behavior makes the other person defensive.

Neutrality vs. Empathy   Sometimes when we are unsure of how other people will perceive us we try to keep our communication neutral. Occasionally when the other person is upset we use an intellectual and detached style of communication to "calm things down." Messages such as "I see a real need for us to metacommunicate together in order to further analyze our conflict," or "let's leave our feelings out of this" don't sound empathic. Unfortunately, neutrality sometimes appears to be lack of interest or concern. If other people perceive that we do not care about them, they tend to become more guarded. If, however, we communicate warmth and caring, trust and openness are encouraged. Empathy "indicates that the speaker identifies himself with the lis-

39. Ibid., 33.

tener's problems, shares his feelings, and accepts his emotional reactions at face value."[40]

40. Ibid.

Empathic feedback is especially important in times of personal crisis. There are times in the lives of most of us when we need a person we can turn to — a close friend, husband or wife, or family member — who will listen to us and provide empathic feedback, both verbal and nonverbal.

Also, most of us have had the experience of providing an empathic ear for a close friend. If you recall such an experience, you know that the primary function was to provide supportive feedback. That feedback, undergirded by love and caring, is of great importance in helping people to cope with crisis situations. Certain crisis situations are common to most of us. Death, divorce, retirement, and accidents are examples of common experiences that are traumatic to various degrees.

One of the problems in crisis situations is that the person experiencing the crisis may have no one to whom to turn and is not always aware that intervention assistance is available. He or she may have no knowledge of or contact with intervention services. Many communities have organized crisis centers and hotlines and have undertaken wide educational and publicity campaigns to make these services known. If the individual facing a crisis communicates with empathic, knowledgeable others in an open and clear manner, he or she gains information from the exchange of ideas and emotional strength from the helpfulness and supportiveness of caring people. These elements are necessary components of constructive decision making and of satisfactory crisis resolution. Through communication we adapt to our environment. Facing a crisis and resolving it constructively is adaptation to the environment — adaptation to change; and empathic, supportive feedback is an important component in that process.

Superiority vs. Equality   The communication of superiority of wealth, power, social position, intellectual ability, or whatever arouses defensiveness in the receiver of such messages. Whenever we take the "I'm OK, but you're not OK" position described in chapter 3,[41] we are likely to create defensiveness on the part of the other person.

Communication of equality reduces defensive behavior in the receiver. Absolute equality seldom exists, of course, but when we value others, respect them, and like them, we can communicate with them as equal and respected participants in the interaction. The message we send is "I'm OK, you're OK."[42]

Certainty vs. Provisionalism   The sixth set of communication behaviors identified by Gibb, certainty versus provisionalism, can be equated with dogmatism versus flexibility and openness. One of the most thorough studies of dogmatism is reported by Rokeach in *The Open and Closed Mind.*[43] He defines dogmatism as "(a) a relatively closed cognitive organization of beliefs and disbeliefs about reality, (b) organized around a central set of beliefs about absolute authority which, in turn, (c) provides a framework for patterns of intolerance toward others."[44] When we perceive another individual as dogmatic, it arouses a great deal of defensiveness in us.

Dogmatic people have a closed, rigid view of how the world is and of what is absolutely true and absolutely not true. This orientation affects how they process the information we send them. It also affects how they receive feedback from others and send feedback to others. Table 7.1 is a summary comparison of the information processing of dogmatic individuals compared with open-minded, more provisional individuals.

To the dogmatic individual every message is black or white, absolutely right and true or absolutely wrong and false. There is little ability to discriminate — to see the partly true and partly false, the somewhat-but-not-exactly true. Feedback from a dogmatic person would reflect this all-or-nothing tendency. The dogmatic person also sees a wide discrepancy between his or her beliefs and beliefs outside his or her system. Unless the other person's views tended to closely match the dogmatic person's, the dogmatic person would tend to send the other person a lot of negative or rejecting feedback.

Since dogmatic individuals are source oriented, we could predict that their feedback to the messages of others might contain references to some ultimate source or authority which they feel the other person should not question. Dogmatic individuals often imply that they are connected to that source and are therefore "superior," which arouses defensiveness in others.

When dogmatic individuals receive information or feedback from others, they evaluate that incoming message on the basis of inner drives, inner stan-

41. Thomas A. Harris, *I'm OK — You're OK* (New York: Harper & Row, 1967).

42. Ibid.

43. Milton Rokeach, *The Open and Closed Mind* (New York: Basic Books, 1960).

44. Milton Rokeach, "The Nature and Meaning of Dogmatism," *Psychological Review 61* (1954):194–204.

Table 7.1

Open Minded	Closed Minded
1. Evaluates messages objectively, using data and logical consistency.	1. Evaluates messages on the basis of inner drives.
2. Differentiates easily. Sees shades of gray.	2. Thinks simplistically — i.e., in black-and-white terms.
3. Is content oriented.	3. Relies more on the source of a message than on its content.
4. Seeks information from a wide range of sources.	4. Seeks information about other beliefs from own sources.
5. Is provisional and willing to modify own beliefs.	5. Rigidly maintains and defends own belief system.
6. Seeks comprehension of messages inconsistent with own set of beliefs.	6. Rejects, ignores, distorts, and denies messages inconsistent with own belief system.

dards, and internal pressures rather than on the basis of logical consistency, observations, facts, or scientifically produced data. It would not matter to a closed-minded person how "good" the evidence was or how "compelling" the logic of an argument. The dogmatic person is unable to distinguish easily between incoming information and the source of that information. Who is sending the feedback is more important to a dogmatic person than the content of that message, and will probably determine whether the message is accepted and believed. If you are a believable source, your feedback will be accepted. Also, the dogmatic individual tends to seek information only from his or her particularly trusted "sources." A person who is dogmatic about religion, for example, will get all information about other religions from people of his or her own religion. The dogmatic person would not be likely to accept information from a person of another religion about a religious belief. Only the dogmatic person's own sources can be trusted to "speak the truth." When we are perceived as being "untruthful" we become defensive.

We can also expect the closed-minded person to rigidly defend his or her system of beliefs as if the change of one small belief would cause the whole world to come tumbling down. Because the closed-minded person cannot tolerate inconsistency, dissonance, or contradiction, that person tends (consciously or unconsciously) to reject, ignore, distort, or deny messages inconsistent with his or her own belief system. The dogmatic individual is usually not receptive to disconfirming feedback from others.

The open-minded individual is, on the other hand, content-oriented — able to think in terms of the message with less emphasis on the sender. Open-minded individuals are much more receptive to feedback from others. They hold their beliefs more provisionally and are able to adjust them, or even to discard a belief if that is warranted by the data. The open-minded individual differentiates more easily and is more likely to send and to receive and accept feedback which is "shades of gray." They also are more likely to accept and even seek feedback and information from a wider range of sources. More open-minded people seek clarification and understanding of messages which are inconsistent with or contradictory to their own beliefs, and they can more easily tolerate feedback from others that is discrepant with their own belief system.

The characteristics of dogmatic individuals described above are among the most decisively limiting variables in interpersonal communication. Dogmatism is a personality characteristic and therefore difficult to change. Furthermore, we should realize that if the feedback we send to others or if our pattern of reception of feedback from others resembles that of the dogmatic individual, we are going to arouse defensiveness in the other person.

To maximize the chances of a constructive, productive encounter with a dogmatic individual, we should carefully consider the six characteristics of such a person just discussed. They indicate how that person is likely to interpret our messages and react to us in the communicative encounter.

If we are able to create a supportive climate rather than arouse defensiveness in the recipient of our feedback, the other person will be more accurate in perceiving our feedback, will understand our motives more clearly, and will be more likely to respond positively to our message.

Reciprocity

Whatever type of feedback we send to another person, we are likely to receive the same type of communication in return. "During social interaction it is very common for an act by A to be followed by a similar act from B. This we call response matching. . . . Similar response matching takes place with regard to emotional state, bodily contact, and other elements of social behavior."[45] Numerous studies made between 1955 and 1969 verified this phenomenon. These studies found that length of utterance follows this rule, and also length and frequency of pauses and interruptions. Jokes lead to jokes. Giving opinions leads to the other person giving opinions. Showing solidarity, disagreeing, and asking questions all lead to similar response behavior. Smiling elicits smiling, and self-disclosure leads to self-disclosure.[46] The **reciprocity phenomenon** operates equally well with the feedback of feelings. Feelings expressed (or repressed, for that matter) tend to elicit the same kind of behavior from the other person.

A relationship is a two-way street. For two persons to be friends, they must engage in behaviors that enable mutual liking, trusting, and knowing to develop. We tend to like those persons who like us and to trust those persons who trust us. It is not surprising, then, that feeding back feelings of liking and warmth tends to prompt the other person to express feelings of liking and warmth, or that expressing dislike and coldness causes the other person to feel dislike and coldness. The feelings we express toward another tend to be

45. Michael Argyle, *Social Interaction* (New York: Atherton Press, 1969), 171–72.

46. Ibid.

reciprocated by the other. To know and understand this principle of reciprocity gives us an important insight into the process of interpersonal communication. We can expect the feedback we receive from others to resemble the feedback we are sending. If we find that feedback objectionable, perhaps we should check the characteristics of our own feedback.

Suppressing Feedback

We can suppress our feedback to others not only by failing to send response messages, but also by sending inaccurate, ambiguous, or contradictory messages. One of the consequences of suppressing our feedback is that we experience unmet interpersonal needs. As we pointed out at the beginning of this section, if we do not send feedback to another, the other person cannot adjust messages or behavior to please us. As we discussed in the first part of this book, we communicate to satisfy our needs — needs that go far beyond food and shelter, some being quite complex and psychological in nature. Communication is our primary vehicle for satisfying these needs. Consequently, as our communication is successful in helping us, we are reinforced for communicating to others and we develop confidence in our communication. We view communication positively and we develop positive relationships with others.

However, when we are not able to meet our needs through communication with others, we lose confidence in our coping ability and become less confident of others, even to the point of becoming defensive and guarded in our communication with others. Such behavior, of course, is counterproductive: the more defensive we become, the less effective our communication becomes. Little wonder we then become anxious about getting along in the world, and that a general feeling of anxiety results. Unresolved anxiety then leads to more defensive tactics in interacting with others. Fear, anxiety, doubt — these feed defensive communication behavior. You have probably observed defensive communication in others. You have observed the fear in their posture, eyes, facial expressions, and body movement. You have noticed their withdrawal behavior — turning away from you, avoiding eye contact, shifting their weight backward, stepping backward, or hesitating verbally.

Many people do not recognize that they contribute to the failure of others to meet their needs. They expect others to know, without being told, their needs, values, attitudes, beliefs and feelings. Often they rationalize their inability to express themselves or their reticence to send feedback with the words, "If you loved me you'd be able to understand without my telling you." Unfortunately even the deepest, most caring, and sensitive feelings of love for another person will not make us magically telepathic. We all need to send and receive feedback to meet our interpersonal needs.

Another consequence of suppressing feedback and inhibiting the expression of feelings, according to Johnson, is that the quality of our problem solv-

47. David W. Johnson, *Reaching Out* (Englewood Cliffs, N.J.: Prentice-Hall, 1972), 90.

ing goes down.[47] Some people believe the opposite: that any expression of feelings interferes with problem solving; that when we engage in logical problem solving, feelings should be left out of the process. They are wrong. Actually, the expression of feelings is a valid part of the problem solving process, and when the feelings are ignored and suppressed, our thinking and decisions are poor. Unresolved feelings can contribute to biased decisions. We suspect that almost all of us have, at one time or another, accepted a poor idea because we could not handle or would not express a feeling we had. We could not say to the person suggesting the idea, "I like you very much, but I don't like that particular idea." We may have just suppressed the feeling and acceded to the idea. We may have rejected good ideas for similar reasons. Bales's research has revealed that the quality of problem solving is improved when participants freely give both positive and negative statements. When either is suppressed, communication quality is diminished.[48]

48. Robert F. Bales, "In Conference," *Howard Business Review* 32 (1954):44–50.

Suppressing the feedback of our feelings can also affect our perception of persons, events, and information. Feelings not dealt with can create blind spots of misinterpretation and distortion. The greater the suppression of our feelings, the greater the number of blind spots in our reception of information.

When we suppress affective feedback, we create a relationship between two (or more) unreal and nonauthentic people. People have emotions. Even as we think and observe, so are we happy or unhappy, fearful or secure, depressed or joyful. Feeling is not a once- or twice-a-day experience. Feeling is with us all the time, just as thinking is. In fact, feeling accompanies thinking, and probably certain kinds of feeling go with certain ways of thinking. Thus, to try to suppress feeling in communication is to deny yourself to the other person, for among the things that make you uniquely you are your feelings and emotions.

The psychologically healthy person does not inhibit feelings and suppress feedback. The healthy person is attuned to feelings, accepts them, and integrates them into his or her communication, thinking, and relating to others.

If you are to know the real person you are interacting with, you need to know the feelings that are associated with that person's ideas and decisions. If a person will not share these feelings with you, but suppresses that feedback, or if you will not allow that person to express these feelings, then it is not the real and authentic person with whom you are communicating. Gut-level communication, as well as head communication, is an important aspect of the total person. The dishonesty that results from suppressed feedback of feelings creates artificial persons and superficial relationships. Whether in marriage, organizational committees, or whatever, when persons pervert or destroy their authenticity by suppressing feedback of feelings, their relationships are set on a dangerous and self-destructive path.

In summary, suppressing feedback results in a serious deterioration of interpersonal relationships: unmet interpersonal needs in the quality of problem solving, in information reception, and in creating and sustaining productive relationships.

Guidelines for the Effective Use of Feedback

The following guidelines can be used to help you develop more effective feedback practices. They are commonly cited for effective interpersonal communication in various settings — instruction, transactional analysis, problem-solving discussion, therapeutic interactions, to mention just a few.[49]

1. Effective feedback includes accurate and honest expression of your feelings.

   Before you can feed back feelings easily and constructively, you must develop an awareness of your feelings and emotions and learn to accept them. How have you been behaving toward your feelings as you communicate with others? It might be helpful if the next time you engage in an argument with someone, you intentionally think about your feelings. How are you feeling? Are you afraid? Angry? Jealous? If you can admit your feelings, take a good look at them to identify them, estimate their strength or intensity, and try to discover what caused them or where they came from; then you can know yourself better.

   Johnson has suggested that a person unaware of feelings, unaccepting of feelings, or unskilled in feeding back feelings is likely to express feelings by labeling others, giving commands, asking questions, making accusations, name calling, making sarcastic remarks, and expressing approval or disapproval.[50] In contrast, persons who are aware of their feelings and who understand their emotions usually express them by naming the feeling, reporting what the feeling motivates them to do, or describing the feeling as a simile or metaphor. The first type of feedback of feelings (those more characteristic of persons not accepting or perhaps even unaware of their feelings) is directed toward the other person. The second type of feedback is directed toward the self (''I am afraid,'' ''I feel angry,'' or ''I feel confident''); reporting action you want to take (''I could kiss you!'') or utilizing a figure of speech (''I feel as though a bulldozer ran over me'').

   John Powell has developed five principles to guide you in creating effective feedback for emotions and feelings.[51] They are:

   a. Feeling statements should not imply a judgment of the other person. Become aware of and describe your own feelings and emotions rather than labeling the other person.

   b. Do not judge emotions as moral (good or bad). Do not link emotions to sinfulness. Experiencing fear or anger does not make you or the other a bad person.

   c. Integrate your emotions and feelings with your intellect and reason. Understand that emotions are normal and useful. Accept the fact of their usefulness intellectually. Analyze your emotions. Learn the precipitating causes. Increase your emotional vocabulary so that you can become more expressive.

49. See for a further discussion: Barker, *Listening Behavior*, 123-24; Keltner, *Interpersonal Communication*, 97-99; John Stewart and Gary D'Angelo, ''Responsive Listening'' in Jean M. Civikly, ed., *Messages: A Reader in Human Communication* (New York: Random House, 1977), 189-95.

50. Johnson, *Reaching Out*, 91.

51. John Powell, S.J., *Why Am I Afraid to Tell You Who I Am?* (Niles, Ill.: Argus Communications, 1969), 50-85.

d. Report your emotions and feelings so that others are allowed to know you.

e. With rare exceptions, you must report your emotions at the time they are experienced. Reporting a feeling the following day is not the same as reporting it at the time it is experienced. Emotions are transient and difficult to recapture.

   We express our emotions and feelings nonverbally as well as verbally, and it is important that we learn to express them accurately and honestly. (You may want to review the section in chapter 6 on nonverbal expression of emotions. We need to become more effective in nonverbal expression of our emotional states also.)

2. Effective feedback, used for reinforcement, includes both positive and negative messages. Either one without the other is incomplete.

3. Effective feedback is descriptive rather than evaluative. By describing, the individual is left free either to use feedback or not to use it at all. And descriptive feedback does not elicit as much defensive behavior.

4. Effective feedback takes a problem orientation; is spontaneous and empathic. Avoid attempts to dominate the other person; the use of hidden strategies and expressions of neutrality.

5. Effective feedback recognizes the equality of all members of the interaction. Be provisional.

6. Own your own feedback—"I think, I feel, I will, I am, etc."—rather than attributing the feedback to others—"we feel"—or stating it as an eternal truth—"everyone knows."

7. Immediate feedback is more effective than delayed feedback. Generally, it is most useful if provided at the earliest opportunity.

8. Effective feedback is directed toward the specific behavior you would like changed rather than toward general conclusions you have made about the other person's behavior or underlying attitudes.

9. Effective feedback is directed toward behavior that the sender can do something about rather than toward behavior or circumstances over which the person has no control.

10. Effective feedback is constructive rather than destructive. It is motivated by the desire to help the sender and is given in that spirit. It is directed toward the objectives of increasing fidelity in the exchanges of meaning and of enhancing integration.

11. Effective feedback does not overload the communication channels by imposing all of one's interpretations on the message received. Rather, the objective is to provide only necessary feedback—enough information, but not too much.

12. Effective feedback is not ambiguous or contradictory. Feedback may be ambiguous because of the words used or because of contradictions between verbal and nonverbal messages. Moreover, any single nonverbal cue can be used to express any number of emotions or feelings. A blush, for example, can indicate anger, embarrassment, pleasure, or hostility. There is, consequently, plenty of room for error in our interpretation of verbal and nonverbal feedback. We need to integrate our verbal and nonverbal feedback and send clear and accurate feedback to others.

13. Effective feedback is consistent. If you send one message on one occasion and the opposite on another occasion, no one will believe your feedback.

14. Seek feedback from others. Learn to paraphrase by *saying in your own words how you've interpreted the other person's ideas and feelings.* Practice "parasupporting [in which] *you not only paraphrase the other's comments, but also carry his or her ideas further by providing examples or other data that you believe help to illustrate and clarify those ideas.''*[52] Seek feedback for your paraphrasing and your parasupporting feedback so that you know you are interpreting the other person correctly.

52. Stewart and D'Angelo, "Responsive Listening," 191, 192.

15. Realize that delivering effective feedback is not easy. While your early attempts may seem forced and unnatural, persevere. You will improve.

16. Check your own feedback behavior. How effectively do you follow the preceding guidelines?

Summary

The first part of this chapter emphasizes the importance of the listening process and our need for improved listening skills. Three stages in the listening process are described. Four purposes of listening are explained and the skills needed for each described. Eight specific problems that interfere with listening are discussed and solutions offered.

In the second part of this chapter feedback is defined and its relationship to listening, especially its corrective function, is explained. Five sources and types of feedback are identified to explain the complexity of the feedback process. How feedback influences several characteristics of communication, creates a supportive or defensive climate, and stimulates reciprocity are explained. The consequences of suppressing feedback also were covered. Finally, sixteen guidelines for making feedback more effective are presented including a discussion of the effective expression of feelings.

8

Conflict and Communication

1. To be able to define conflict and describe its three key characteristics.
2. To be able to describe how several characteristics influence the intensity of a conflict, including:
   a. four styles of conflict communication
   b. three perceived and real types of conflict goals
   c. the relative power structure of the participants
   d. the amount of trust in the relationship
3. To be able to describe four levels of conflict intensity and explain how each characteristic influences this intensity.
4. To be able to describe ways to reduce the intensity of a conflict.
5. To be able to explain the importance of seven factors involved in cooperative negotiation of interpersonal conflicts:
   a. a positive and healthy attitude toward conflict
   b. maintaining open communication lines and what behaviors discourage this
   c. accuracy in conflict communication and five ways to make communication more accurate
   d. setting a particular time and place for conflict negotiation
   e. maintaining perspective
   f. six steps to rational problem solving
   g. mediators and arbitrators in conflict resolution

CONFLICT CAN BE CONSTRUCTIVE OR DESTRUCTIVE

Few, if any, of our interpersonal relationships are free of interpersonal conflict. Each of us is a unique individual with our own needs, values, beliefs, feelings, opinions, and preferred (if not habitual) ways of behaving toward other people. It is unlikely that we will ever interact with anyone who will completely match our needs and desires without any adjustment on the part of either one of us.

We experience conflict daily in our interpersonal relationships over many different kinds of issues. Some of our conflicts involve disagreement over what we perceive as major things; some involve issues we are almost embarrassed to admit concern us. Some topics that were identified by a group of college students as things that have caused conflict were: fingernail biting, what one should eat, use of tobacco, use of marijuana, use of alcohol, use of drugs, what we should believe, driving habits, whether or not to get a job, lifetime goals, how to spend leisure time, how clean our living areas should be, who our friends ought to be, how to relate to other persons, how to spend our money, and how high to make the fence. Some of these topics may seem ridiculous or insignificant, but to the people with the conflicts, they were not ridiculous. Often when a conflict is about what we perceive as a "minor issue" or problem, we don't want to define it as a "conflict." The word *conflict* may itself seem threatening to us.

Our interpersonal communication during a conflict may range from subtle disagreement to overt hostility. However, we don't need to yell, slam doors, or turn white (or red) with rage before we recognize that we are engaged in a conflict situation.

One of the reasons we are anxious when we recognize a conflict situation is that we are uncertain about the outcome. Conflict generally means that we would like some change in our lives, or that someone else wants us to change. In addition, we might have to talk about issues which we have previously avoided discussing because they made us uneasy. Even if we are willing to engage in a conflict with another person, we may be unsure that our skills will allow us to both achieve our own goal and simultaneously help the other person achieve his or her goal. Even the simple recognition of a conflict between us may change our feelings about ourselves, about each other, and about the relationship we have even if we never discuss the conflict. If we can effectively resolve our conflict with the other person, however, we will find that the needs of both of us will be met more completely and satisfactorily in our relationship. Successful negotiation of conflict allows us, both as individuals and as partners in a relationship, to grow and change without destroying our relationship. This chapter is designed to help create the last type of change — positive, constructive growth for both the individual and the relationship. Effective conflict resolution is the key to healthy and productive interpersonal relationships.

Although conflict may be a necessary element of growth in our interpersonal relationships — a positive factor — it can also have a destructive effect on us and our relationships. Conflict is a part of all our healthy relationships, but it can also destroy our relationships unless we learn to handle and manage it. Whether conflict is harmful or helpful depends on how it is used and how constructively we cope with it. That is the challenge, and therein lies the objective of this chapter: to learn about conflict and the factors at work in it.

We begin by defining a conflict situation and describing conflict by communication styles, by type of goals involved, by power structure and trust, and by intensity. We then discuss reducing intensity by negotiating interpersonal conflicts cooperatively, thereby helping to produce satisfying interpersonal relationships.

In a world growing smaller via technology, becoming more crowded with people, and experiencing a rapidly increasing rate of interaction, it is increasingly important to effectively resolve interpersonal conflicts. To moderate excessive conflict and make constructive use of conflict, we must understand the interpersonal-conflict phenomenon, and we must understand and acquire skill in communication as it relates to effective conflict resolution. The central

Growing urbanization has increased the rate of interpersonal interactions and the potential for conflict.

Conflict and Communication   **213**

role communication plays in successful conflict management and resolution means that this area of study is one of the most significant in interpersonal communication. But before we delve further into the study of conflict, we need to define it.

Defining a Conflict Situation

Many attempts have been made to distinguish conflict from other concepts. Competition, disagreement, controversy, misunderstanding, problem, combat, antagonistic interests, aggressiveness, hostility, tensions, and rivalry are just a few of the concepts that have been compared with conflict.[1] Frost and Wilmot offer the following definition of **conflict** in their book *Interpersonal Conflict:*

> From a communication perspective, *conflict is an expressed struggle between at least two interdependent parties, who perceive incompatible goals, scarce rewards, and interference from the other party in achieving their goals. They are in a position of opposition in conjunction with cooperation.*[2]

This definition contains three key characteristics found in many definitions of conflict. First, a conflict situation involves something which is either in limited supply or is perceived as being in a limited supply. Neither one of us can have all we want. It may be a material object which we both cannot simultaneously use or possess, or a position of status and power which only one of us will gain. Our time and space are also limited.

Many conflicts concern our attitudes and values.[3] Since each of us would seem entirely independent and quite capable of holding any value or attitude as deeply and firmly as we wish, what is the limiting factor that creates a conflict situation for us? Values and attitudes lead to behaviors; often we cannot perform our valued behavior if the other person is to simultaneously perform his or her valued behavior. In addition, whenever another person holds a belief or value which conflicts with ours, our sense of one hundred percent "rightness" or "trueness" about our values and beliefs is threatened. This perception becomes especially salient when we are interacting with that person about that particular value or belief. We become more aware that both sets of beliefs or values cannot simultaneously be "true" or "right." We have perceptually defined "truth" and "right" as limited resources.

Second, in a conflict situation we must interact with the other person(s) to achieve our goal. If one of us wants to go to a basketball game and the other to a ballet, we are not in a conflict situation unless each of us wants the other to go along. There is no conflict unless we need the other person to cooperate

1. John W. Keltner, *Interpersonal Speech-Communication: Elements and Structures* (Belmont: Wadsworth, 1970), 223–25; Raymond W. Mack and Richard C. Snyder, "The Analysis of Social Conflict — Toward an Overview and Synthesis" in Fred E. Jandt, ed., *Conflict Resolution Through Communication* (New York: Harper & Row, 1973), 25–87; M. Deutsch, "Conflicts: Productive and Destructive," *Journal of Social Issues* 25(1969):7–8.

2. Joyce Hocker Frost and William W. Wilmot, *Interpersonal Conflict* (Dubuque, Iowa: Wm. C. Brown, 1978), 9.

3. Mack and Snyder, "Analysis of Social Conflict," 36–37.

with us to achieve what we desire or need. If we can act independently of the other person to achieve our goal, we are not in a conflict situation.

Third, although we often feel as if we are engaged in a conflict situation as soon as we perceive the first two characteristics, a conflict situation requires that we communicate that realization to the other person. Otherwise we are engaged in intrapersonal or internal conflict of our feelings, opinions, or desires. We may even have an expectation that if we communicate to the other person we will surely be engaged in a conflict situation. But none of these circumstances engages the other person in a mutual, interdependent relationship with us. For that, communication is necessary. An interpersonal conflict situation necessitates the involvement of at least two people.

Conflict Communication Styles

Each of us has our own typical style of communication which we employ when we are engaged in a conflict. We may also choose a style depending upon circumstances. Some **conflict communication styles** are more likely to lead to positive, constructive outcomes for our relationships while others are more likely to be destructive for our relationships. Unfortunately, certain interpersonally destructive behaviors have come to be so closely associated with conflict situations that they are often included as a necessary and integral part of a definition of the term *conflict*.[4] These behaviors are ones "designed to destroy, injure, thwart, or otherwise control another party"[5] so that one person wins and the other loses. Actually, just as there are many types of conflict situations, there are several ways we may choose to respond to a conflict situation. Our definition of conflict neither precludes nor does it necessitate the inclusion of any particular style.

Win/Loss Style

A win/loss style is a highly aggressive approach to a conflict situation. It implies a high concern for the self and relatively little concern for the other person.[6] The attitude underlying this communication style is often "I'm OK, you're not OK," and therefore I need to consider only my ideas, values, needs,[7] etc.

This style is somewhat similar to the "hard" bargaining game described by Fisher and Ury of the Harvard Negotiation Project.[8] If we choose a win/loss conflict style, the other person is our adversary; our goal is to achieve what we desire; our strategies and tactics are to mislead the other person, apply pressure through emotional blackmail, power plays, and unexpectedly confronting the other person with high-intensity messages. The win/loss style includes messages of promise as well as threat messages. In short, people in conflict situations try to get what they want—try to win from the other—often by threatening the other person with punishment or promising rewards

4. Ibid.

5. Ibid.

6. See Frost and Wilmot, *Interpersonal Conflict,* 28–32, for a discussion of communication styles based on the concern for self/concern for others described by Ralph Kilmann and Kenneth Thomas, "Interpersonal Conflict-Handling Behavior as Reflections of Jungian Personality Dimensions," *Psychological Reports* 37(1975):971–80.

7. See Pamela E. Butler, *Self-Assertion for Women: A Guide to Becoming Androgynous* (San Francisco: Harper & Row, 1976), 124–49, for a differentiation of communication styles based on Thomas A. Harris, *I'm OK—You're OK* (New York: Harper & Row, 1967).

8. Roger Fisher and William Ury, *Getting to Yes: Negotiating Agreement Without Giving In* (Boston: Houghton Mifflin, 1981), 13.

if the other person will behave according to the promiser's wishes. Bowers clarifies this distinction:

> Imagine two parties to conflict, Archer and Target. A threat exists when one (say, Archer) predicts that he will impose negative sanctions on the other, these sanctions to be contingent on some behavior of the other. A promise simply changes the sign of the sanction: Archer predicts that he will deliver positive sanctions to Target contingent on some behavior of Target's.[9]

9. John Waite Bowers, "Guest Editor's Introduction: Beyond Threats and Promises," *Speech Monographs* 41(March 1974).

In real life, messages are usually not so simple, or one-sided. Messages may openly express a threat and imply a promise or make a promise with an implied threat. A message can also do both explicitly: "If you . . . I will . . ., and if you don't . . . I'll. . . ." Bowers invented the word *thromise* to describe "messages expressing such a double contingency."

Individuals with a win/loss conflict style often try to exert control over the other person by exploiting the other's weaknesses or humiliating or dominating the other person. The objective of the win/loss strategy is to hurt the other person by limiting or preventing the person from winning his or her goal. Thus this style tends to be destructive. Even in short-term relationships this style will often make the other person defensive and uncooperative.

Yielding Style

Individuals with a high concern for others (You're OK) and a low concern for themselves (I'm not OK) choose yielding, passive, or inhibited responses to the other person in a conflict.[10]

10. Frost and Wilmot, *Interpersonal Conflict*, 31; Butler, *Self-Assertion for Women*.

11. Fisher and Ury, *Getting to Yes*, 13.

The "soft" bargaining game described by Fisher and Ury[11] contains many elements of an accommodating conflict style. The individual is willing to make one-sided concessions to the other, looks for an answer the other person will accept, and yields to pressure from the other person. Individuals with this style often suppress their own feelings and ideas. Frequently because of this their own needs are not met. Yet they are often frustrated and surprised because they have "tried so hard" and have been "more than fair" to the other person.

One rationalization used to justify the choice of a yielding style appears to be greater concern for the relationship than for the conflict situation itself. The individual is more concerned about achieving some agreement which will result in remaining friends with the other person. The long-term effect of a yielding style on a relationship is often one person's submission and the other's dominance, rather than the friendly, loving, caring relationship sought by the individual who chose this style to protect the relationship. Thus this style tends to be more destructive than constructive in maintaining a healthy satisfactory relationship with others.

Avoiding Style

This conflict style is chosen by individuals who have relatively little concern for themselves or the other person, feeling that neither of them is OK.[12] Individuals with this style withdraw physically or psychologically when a conflict occurs. They try to postpone or avoid discussing the problem, distract the other person's attention, smooth over the situation without confronting it directly, or remain silent when the other person tries to discuss the conflict.

While we all at one time or another may avoid a conflict until we feel more prepared to deal with it, overuse of this style is generally destructive for our relationships. Small frequent conflicts are more easily managed effectively than large infrequent ones. When we avoid the small conflicts they often become large ones. When we are finally forced to face the large conflict we may not be able to resolve it constructively.

Cooperative Style

Individuals with a moderate to strong concern for both themselves and the other person choose to work with the other person, by compromise or collaboration.[13] When we compromise with another person both of us win a little and lose a little. If our concern is strong enough, we will try to find or create a solution so that we both achieve what we desire.

Conflict in interpersonal communication can be collaborative.

12. Frost and Wilmot, *Interpersonal Conflict,* 31; Butler, *Self-Assertion for Women,* 125.

13. Frost and Wilmot, *Interpersonal Conflict,* 30.

14. Butler, *Self-Assertion for Women*, 125.

15. Frost and Wilmot, *Interpersonal Conflict*, 30.

16. Fisher and Ury, *Getting to Yes*, 13.

The attitude involved in a cooperative style is "I'm OK, You're OK."[14] Frost and Wilmot suggest that individuals with this attitude are likely to be assertive in their communication style rather than passive or aggressive.[15]

Fisher and Ury suggest "principled" bargaining as a solution to the "hard" or "soft" games. It includes strategies and tactics generally used by those with a cooperative conflict style:[16] a problem-solving orientation, a focus on inventing options, the use of reason, a concern for both participants' needs, and achievement of a mutually satisfactory solution. A cooperative style is the most constructive way to handle conflict. It builds healthy, productive, satisfying relationships with others. In the final main section of this chapter a set of procedures is presented which uses this style to achieve effective solutions of interpersonal conflict situations.

Types of Conflict Goals

There are at least three types of perceived goals or objectives involved in interpersonal conflict: (1) goals or objectives that are nondivisible or nonshareable; (2) goals or objectives that may be divided and shared in various proportions between the parties in conflict; and (3) goals or objectives that may be fully claimed and possessed by both parties in the conflict.

Conflicts with Nondivisible or Nonshareable Goals

Some objects of conflict really are not divisible. Both contestants cannot win. If one wins, the other must lose. There can be no ties and no sharing of the desired objective. If two men are competing to "win the hand" of a girl they each want to marry, both cannot win — at least not under the existing laws of our country. The loser might win "other" objectives but both cannot marry the girl. Marriage is a "winner-take-all" objective. If your boss has an opening for a section manager, either you will win the position or lose it to someone else. Of course some goals are only perceived by one or more of the parties to be nondivisible. However, the more nondivisible the goals of a conflict are perceived to be, the greater the intensity of the conflict. Win-all-or-nothing conflicts can be extremely difficult and dangerous situations. Such conflicts, if carried out fully to the end, result in total loss for one of the adversaries. They demand the use of the win/loss conflict style discussed previously.

Conflicts with Partially Shareable Goals

Sometimes the objectives of the conflict are shareable. Although each participant may desire to win all, it is possible to win some and lose some while the adversary also wins some and loses some. Deutsch, as well as most other scholars who have studied conflict, states that most conflicts are of this type — they have shareable objectives, or can be redefined so as to make sharing possible.[17] For example, if you and your partner have a limited amount of money to spend, and one of you wants to buy tickets to a rock concert and the other wants to buy a plant for your room, you might decide to buy less expensive seats for the concert and a smaller plant. In such conflict situations there can be a cooperative interest in reaching an agreement, since both parties can win some, and that may be preferable to losing all. Partially shareable goals encourage the cooperative style of conflict management and reduce the intensity of a conflict.

One of the difficulties in conflicts of this type is that the goals may not be perceived as partially shareable. Rather, if they are misperceived as win-lose conflicts, black-or-white situations, a shared resolution becomes more difficult. Or, through inappropriate communication behavior of the parties involved, these conflicts may escalate into conflicts whose goals are nonshareable. The win/loss conflict style often encourages this process to occur. The cooperative style of one person can be dominated or destroyed by the win/loss style of the other person.

Conflicts with Fully Shareable Goals

Fully shareable objectives are congruent goals that may be possessed by both parties to the conflict. Such conflicts cease to be conflicts as soon as they are perceived correctly by the persons involved. For example, you might buy the tickets this week with the understanding that you will buy the plant next week. When participants understand that they both can win fully, a natural, cooperative situation is created which fosters the use of the cooperative conflict style.

How we define the goal of a conflict determines to a large extent how we will behave during that conflict. If it is possible for us to change the goal structure itself, or to change our perceptions to a conflict with partially or fully shared goals, it will be easier for us to resolve the conflict.

Power Structure

All interpersonal relationships have a power structure. Power, however, can be derived from many sources. French and Raven suggest five possible sources.[18]

1. *Reward power* is the ability to deliver something of value which the other person wants. It can be material goods, warmth and supportiveness, or access to others who can then deliver the reward.
2. *Coercive power* is the ability to punish the other person. Punishment includes removal of rewards which the person presently enjoys, such as a position of status and power. It includes requiring the person to perform some disliked task, and it may even include corporal punishment.

17. M. Deutsch, "Conflicts: Productive and Destructive," *Journal of Social Issues* 25(1969):7-8.

18. R. P. French and B. Raven, "The Bases of Social Power," in Darwin Cartwright and Alvin Zander, eds., *Group Dynamics* (New York: Harper & Row, 1960), 601-23.

3. *Expert power* is the ability to deliver some special service because you have special knowledge or abilities. One person may type better while the other cooks better.

4. *Legitimate power* is derived from our different roles and positions in the social structure. Sometimes legitimate power is codified in our legal structure, but often it is simply a matter of tradition and the norms which we have been taught. Employers assign tasks to employees. Children obey parents. Whenever people suggest that we ought to obey them because ''that's the way things are,'' they are invoking their perceived legitimate power. Not that we need to agree, of course.

5. *Referent power* is exercised over someone when the other person wants to be like us. We are a model. There may be only one aspect of our personality or ability the other person wants to emulate — such as our ability to get along with children; or the other person may want to be like us in many ways. We have referent power over people because they will do what we do. Also, generally, they will want us to like them.

Each of us derives some power in a conflict situation from the fact that the other person needs us to achieve his or her goal. Depending on our relationship and the situation, both parties will have some mixture of the five power sources just discussed relative to the other person's power mixture. It is important to remember that how much power we have in a relationship is always relative to the other person's power over us.[19] Therefore, our power ratio is different for every relationship in which we participate.

The types of power we have relative to the other person will influence our choice of behaviors in an interpersonal conflict. Individuals with a win/loss style use power as a weapon. They are not interested in yielding or equalizing the power in a relationship. However, they generally have little referent power over us because we dislike their conflict style. Some individuals may choose an avoidance or yielding conflict style because they feel they have little power to influence the other person in the situation. The cooperative conflict style is more likely to be chosen by individuals who feel they are equal in their overall power and influence over one another — even though they may differ in relative power for any single type of power.

Trust

The extent to which we believe we can trust or predict the other person's behavior in a conflict situation will also affect our choice of interpersonal conflict behaviors and the intensity of the conflict. Trust has been defined as ''reliance upon the behavior of a person in order to achieve a desired objective,

19. Frost and Wilmot, *Interpersonal Conflict*, 52.

the achievement of which is uncertain in a risky situation."[20] A conflict situation meets most of the conditions Giffin considers necessary for behavior to be considered trusting:[21] each individual is relying on another individual and risking a potential loss to achieve a desired goal or outcome which is uncertain. Many conflict situations would also meet Giffin's final condition that the individual's "potential loss if his trust is violated is greater than his potential gain if his trust is fulfilled."

Many authors restrict "trust" to those conditions in which the trusting individual expects the other person to act positively so the first person will achieve a desired objective.[22] While *reliance* does mean to depend confidently, confidence is to a large degree based on how predictable we perceive the other person to be.

Several factors have been found to affect the degree of trust or predictability we have concerning the other person. The consistency or reliability of the other person's past behavior is important to us.[23] Unless the person has been consistent in the past we will not have much confidence in our ability to predict his present or future behavior.

We will also trust the person more if we think he or she is an expert concerning the conflict in which we are engaged.[24] Perhaps the person has a special ability, skill, experience, access to important information, or is known for sound judgment. Of course none of these will be of any use to us unless we consider the expertness a dependable, consistent characteristic which we can use to make a confident prediction about the other person's future behavior.

The relative power structure of the relationship will also affect how trust is distributed in the relationship. According to the research of Deutsch and others, a power hold over the other person causes one to trust that other person more.[25] When we hold power over other people we can more easily affect their behavior, and we would predict that they will be more likely to choose alternatives that please us.

Another factor that can affect the degree of trust is the nature and quality of the communication between the persons involved in the conflict. When the communication is open, when intentions and goals are identified, and when expectations and plans for reacting to violations are stated, then trust is encouraged.[26] When those things are kept hidden, trust is more difficult to establish because there is less predictability possible concerning the other person's behaviors.

The stronger our belief in the good intentions of the other person, the more likely we are to choose a cooperative conflict style. The greater our expectations that the other person intends to harm us, the more likely we are to choose a win/loss style ("I'll hurt you first"), a yielding style ("I give up, don't hurt me"), or an avoiding style ("I'll pretend you aren't there").

20. K. Giffin, "Interpersonal Trust in Small Group Communication," *Quarterly Journal of Speech* 53(1967):224-34.

21. Bobby R. Patton and Kim Giffin, *Interpersonal Communication: Basic Text and Readings* (New York: Harper & Row, 1974), 443.

22. See W. Barnett Pearce, "Trust in Interpersonal Communication," *Speech Monographs* 41 (1974):236-44.

23. Patton and Giffin, *Interpersonal Communication*, 444.

24. Ibid.

25. M. A. Deutsch, "Trust and Suspicion," *Journal of Conflict Resolution* 2(1958):265-79.

26. J. Loomis, "Communication and the Development of Trust and Cooperative Behavior," *Human Relations* 12(1959):305-15.

Conflict communication can occur in many situations — important or unimportant.

Intensity of Conflict Situations

The term *conflict situation* is *not* restricted to extremely important issues, intimate relationships, or occasions when one or both participants are highly aroused. In fact, interpersonal conflicts are waged with varying degrees of intensity. Keltner, a communication scholar, suggests that the following characteristics influence the degree of intensity in a conflict:[27] the relationship of the partners to one another, the intentions of the partners or the goals they anticipate achieving, the conflict communication style chosen by each individual, the presence or absence of procedural rules and the degree to which the rules have been agreed upon, the method of decision making which is used, and the actual rewards and outcomes which are possible, including both the distribution of the goal(s) and the relative condition of the participants when the conflict has been resolved. The trust which exists in the relationship and the power structure in the relationship also affect the intensity of a conflict. In the preceding sections we discussed some of these factors separately. Each of these characteristics affects the others to determine the intensity of any conflict. In the following section, we will offer a four-part classification system for conflict intensity.

27. Keltner, *Interpersonal Speech-Communication*, 231.

Levels of Conflict Intensity

We will discuss four levels of conflict intensity originally suggested by Keltner. Many other levels could be created using the characteristics of goals and power structure previously discussed. If a conflict situation has elements of two neighboring categories, it will also probably fall in between those two categories in intensity.

Cooperative Conflict   Keltner suggests that the lowest level of conflict intensity occurs when the participants perceive themselves to be compatible and with complementary or fully shareable goals. The participants are then willing to work together, to discuss the conflict, until they can reach agreement. They trust one another and generally use informal rules of procedure which are often implicit in their communication and never explicitly discussed. Their fully shared goal solution allows both parties to achieve all that was desired from the conflict. Individuals who perceive themselves as having approximately equal power relative to one another, or who perceive existing power differences as legitimate, are more likely to engage in **cooperative conflict.**

Controversy   Keltner suggests that in a **controversy** level of conflict participants perceive themselves as rivals who can both win part of what they desire. They may or may not have equal power over one another, but they generally do not perceive their relative power as highly disparate. They generally have a moderate degree of trust in one another, so that they are willing to establish and follow procedures which are mutually acceptable. They may argue, bargain, or negotiate the outcome of the conflict. In general, the parties in a controversy want the solution to be reasonably satisfactory for all parties involved. The outcome of a controversy may be slightly more beneficial for one party than the other, but neither party desires to harm the other or prevent the other from achieving some of his or her goal.

Competition   According to Keltner, participants in the **competition** level of conflict perceive that only one party will achieve his or her goal; the other must lose. Competitors generally perceive some difference in relative power before they enter a competition. In addition, competitors generally trust ``the rules'' and sanctions for breaking those rules more than they trust one another. Therefore competitors usually appear to follow a set of clear procedural rules which they try to make as explicit as possible. They are also likely to attempt to use force and hidden power manipulations as well as bargaining, negotiation, and persuasion to achieve their goal. In a competition, however, we are satisfied to win our goal. We do not generally want to hurt the opponent any more than is absolutely necessary to achieve our goal. We feel that they have already lost enough when they lose the unshareable goal. Many times the loser and the winner remain friends and even agree to engage in other competitive conflicts.

Combat   Keltner calls the most intense level of conflict combat and suggests that they are waged like wars. Participants perceive themselves as enemies and do not trust one another even to keep to mutually agreed-upon rules for waging the conflict. They often try to use force as well as aggressive communication to overcome and destroy one another. In **combat** the conflict is waged to hurt the opponent as much as to achieve the goal. Often dominance by one partner and submission by the other are a part of the goal each is striving for. Sometimes the less powerful person in a conflict will choose to engage in combat in an attempt to reduce the power of the other.

Reducing the Intensity of a Conflict

It is possible to reduce the intensity of a conflict by changing any of the characteristics discussed previously. For example, when you are engaged in a conflict with someone, ask yourself if it is possible to change from goals that are unshareable (combat and competition) to goals that are partially shareable (controversy) or, even better, to ones that are fully shareable (cooperation). Or ask yourself if you can modify your intentions: ``I have to really get this guy'' (a combat intention) might be changed to ``I'm sorry we both can't win, but I intend to reach my goal'' (a competitive intention).

Sometimes a conflict situation includes a set of rules we have developed or mutually agreed upon, or laws developed by others which we are obligated to follow in achieving our resolution. Ask yourself if some changes in the rules under which you are waging the conflict might reduce its intensity. You could agree not to use certain words, or not to engage in conflict at certain times or in front of other people. You might try to make the procedures which you are implicitly using more explicit so that both of you can discuss them and evaluate their usefulness in resolving the conflict.

One of the most effective ways to reduce conflict intensity is to change your communication conflict style and learn to cooperatively negotiate a conflict resolution.

NEGOTIATING INTERPERSONAL CONFLICT COOPERATIVELY

Interpersonal negotiation is especially important in conflicts with partially shareable goals. Its purpose is to resolve a conflict satisfactorily. The rest of this chapter focuses on the process of interpersonal negotiation by discussing several principles that seem to be helpful in creating a successful interpersonal negotiation.

Developing a Positive and Healthy Attitude Toward Conflict

We need not fear, try to avoid, or cover up conflict. Conflict may be harmful or helpful, bad or good, destructive or facilitative — depending on how we cope with it. We should recognize the inevitability of interpersonal conflict and believe in its potential for helping us productively handle growth and change as individuals and as partners in our interpersonal relationships. Further, we can develop a positive, confident attitude toward understanding conflict and the role played by interpersonal communication in constructive conflict resolution. Coser calls for such a positive and accepting attitude toward conflict.[28] He points out that early sociologists studying conflict looked on it as something totally undesirable, a disruptive force in interpersonal relationships and in society. Their objective was to find ways to completely eliminate conflict — an objective that is now considered counterproductive for developing healthy relationships and an effective society. According to Coser, later sociologists began to recognize that conflict has desirable qualities as well as negative ones. They recognized that conflict helps people create interpersonal relationships by providing a motivation for forming coalitions with other people.[29] Successful negotiation of conflict also provides a means for maintaining relationships in spite of differences and disagreements, and it allows us to adapt

28. Lewis Coser, *The Functions of Social Conflict* (Glencoe, Ill.: Free Press, 1956), 31.

29. Ibid., 26–28.

to change in our relationships. Interpersonal conflict, like organizational and group conflict, is necessary. As Johnson says:

> Every interpersonal relationship contains elements of conflict, disagreement, and opposed interests. . . . It is inevitable that you will become involved in conflicts whenever you have a relationship with another person. A conflict-free relationship may only be a sign that you really have no relationship at all, not that you have a good relationship.[30]

30. David W. Johnson, *Reaching Out* (Englewood Cliffs, N.J.: Prentice-Hall, 1972), 203.

Total and permanent absence of conflict, were it possible, apparently would not be a desirable situation even for our most intimate relationships. It may be that there is a real need for people who are creating an intimate relationship to have some conflict, some disagreement. Bach and Wyden have indicated that closeness is characterized by disagreeing and making up — that the desire to be in harmony with the other person creates a need for conflict just to establish and maintain our notion of harmony and agreement.[31] Many of us have assumed that controversy, confrontation, and conflict are automatically undesirable, to be avoided at all times and at all costs. We may have held the false idea that the primary purpose of learning, or of communication, was to eliminate problems and conflict. Such is not the case. Challenge, questioning, choosing, and testing are necessary elements in growth and in life.

31. George R. Bach and Peter Wyden, *The Intimate Enemy: How to Fight Fair in Love and Marriage* (New York: Avon Books, 1968), 25-26.

Our fear of conflict, of the other person knowing us, or of our knowing ourself may prevent us from engaging in effective conflict negotiations. The price we pay for such fear is in broken or superficial relationships and unnecessary pain in our present relationships. This does not mean that communication can solve all our conflicts to our satisfaction. Some conflicts are, as we have discussed, win/loss situations. One party will win, the other will lose. We also need to remember that interpersonal conflict communication requires a minimum of two people. We cannot force the other person to communicate effectively or to engage in effective conflict negotiations with us. We can, however, attempt to practice the following principles.

Maintaining Open Communication Lines

Unless the communication lines are open and used, conflicts go unresolved. "Communication, the opportunity to exchange information concerning the possibilities of the situation, is necessary; without communication no creative solutions occur."[32] It ought to be apparent, then, that pouting, "clamming up" so as not to communicate, and fleeing from the conflict are counterproductive behaviors. They make about as much sense as does the ostrich's sticking his head in the sand. Rather, one of the most important variables in resolving conflict is willingness and opportunity to engage in full communication. Don't expect the other person to read your mind.

32. Thomas M. Steinfatt, David R. Seibold, and Jerry K. Frye, "Communication in Game Simulated Conflicts: Two Experiments," *Speech Monographs* 41(1974):34.

It is also important to use as many channels of communication as possible. Both verbal and nonverbal communication contribute to the resolution of conflict.[33] A well-known scholar in marital and family communication has pointed out that the use of all channels, verbal and nonverbal, is also a characteristic of successful management and resolution of marital conflict. Her studies show that families successful in the management of conflict exchange information through verbal and nonverbal channels much more frequently than do families that are unsuccessful in managing conflict.[34] An increase in the number of channels used and open face-to-face communication serve to increase cooperative behavior and facilitate interpersonal negotiation.

"Lack of communication" is the number one marital complaint for both men and women who file for divorce.[35] Marriage counselors often discover that a couple has closed all lines of communication. One of the first tasks is to get the channels of communication open, to restore the opportunity for communication, and to get the persons involved to communicate with each other.

Maintaining open communication lines is not easy. It requires a willingness to take the risk of being vulnerable to the other person. Some of the responses we deliver to the other person which close down the line of communication are the following: only negative feedback, evaluative/judgmental responses, an avoiding or a win/loss conflict style, and ineffective expression of our emotions or feelings. Review the section on effective feedback practices in chapter 7.

Fleeing conflict is usually counterproductive.

33. David W. Johnson, "Communication and the Inducement of Cooperative Behavior in Conflicts: A Critical Review," *Speech Monographs* 41(1974):73.

34. V. M. Satir, *Conjoint Family Therapy: A Guide to Theory and Technique* (Palo Alto, Calif.: Science and Behavior Books, 1964).

35. Norman Lobsenz, "Sexes Divided Over Divorce," *Family Weekly*, June 20, 1982, 16.

Conflict and Communication

Working for Accuracy in Your Communication

Be careful about what you say. Just as it is common for individuals in conflict to close down communication channels instead of moving toward fuller and freer communication, so too it is common for individuals in conflict to communicate threats and statements that are not accurate rather than objective and accurate information. When we refuse to communicate with each other, or when we communicate inaccurate or less than honest information in a conflict, there is not much hope for inducing cooperative behavior between us which will help us move toward mutually beneficial conflict resolution. When both parties communicate intentions with integrity, increased cooperative behavior follows; but when one person is deceptive, the other person's trust and cooperative behavior decrease and competitive behavior increases.[36] Unfortunately,

> Duplicity seems to be a constituent of nearly everyone's communicative repertoire. The rudiments of lying are often learned at an early age, by observing the communicative strategies employed by parents and peers and by undergoing punishments for being truthful. From introspection alone, it seems clear that lying is an adaptive behavior first practiced in situations where it is a harbinger of success or, at least, promises to help us avoid negative sanctions.[37]

Whenever we are threatened or in a competitive or win/loss situation, we tend to increase our deceptive tactics — unless the other person's honesty has been demonstrated.[38]

Attention to the following aspects of communication will help you to increase your accuracy:

(1) *Know yourself.* Examine what you want from the conflict. Which needs of yours are involved? Do you want more intimacy or less? Does this affect your self-esteem? How much control do you want in the relationship?

What emotions are involved for you? Anger? Fear? Humiliation? Do you feel too vulnerable even to discuss the way you feel? Often when we cannot explain our fear or anger, some unconscious expectation or hidden agenda we have for the other person has not been met. What did you expect? Why?

What do you want the other person to do? Why? If the other person performs as you wish, will it make you feel a certain way? Would that particular behavior mean *to you* that the other person feels a certain way or holds certain attitudes you want the person to hold? How do you think the other person wants you to feel?

(2) *Avoid ambiguous communication.* Ambiguity leads to misunderstanding and confusion on the part of the other person. What you want is understanding. Ambiguity can result from too little information. It results also from too general information and from contradictory information. These problems have been discussed earlier. They are especially important relative to conflict

36. M. Pilisuk and P. Skolnick, "Inducing Trust: A Test of the Osgood Proposal," *Journal of Personality and Social Psychology* 8(1968): 121–33.

37. Mark L. Knapp, Roderick P. Hart, and Harry S. Dennis, "The Rhetoric of Duplicity: An Exploration of Deception as a Communication Construct." Paper presented at the convention of the Speech Communication Association, New York, November 10, 1973.

38. G. H. Shure, R. J. Meeker, and E. A. Hansford, "The Effectiveness of Pacifist Strategies in Bargaining Games," *Journal of Conflict Resolution* 9(1965): 106–17.

Avoid information overload. An individual can handle only so much information at one time.

situations. The aim is for specific, objective, concrete communication. Again, review of the effective feedback practices discussed in chapter 7 would be a good idea.

(3) *Avoid polarized communication and "allness" statements.* Polarized communication results from oversimplifying. The conflict becomes black and white, right and wrong. Both persons think they are right; each believes the other is wrong; each thinks he or she is the one maligned; and each knows that his or her "answer" is the "solution." "Allness" statements are stereotypical generalizations about yourself and the other person: "You always overreact." "You never pay attention to me." "I'm completely fair." People, ourselves included, are almost never one hundred percent perfect about anything.

(4) *Avoid information overload.* Researchers have discovered that when a person is inundated with information, problems arise.[39] Overload can be in terms of quantity or in terms of the nature of the content. Either way, a person can handle only so much information at one time. You have experienced situations when you felt you had to get away by yourself to "clear your head," not only because of the amount of cognitive data you had been taking in, but also because of the amount of affective data. Emotions get bound up in certain situations, especially in conflict situations. So be sensitive to the amount of information — emotional and intellectual — that you are bombarding the other person with and that you are "taking on." Accuracy is increased if we deliver

39. W. Charles Redding, *Communication Within the Organization* (New York: Industrial Communication Council, 1972), 87.

information in chunks which are neither too big to assimilate nor so small they cannot create understanding between us.

(5) *Keep the content of messages substantive, orientational, and assertive rather than emotional, aggressive, or passive.* How we speak to the other person is as important as what we say. A survey in a popular magazine describes it well:

> We asked readers what they are most likely to do when they are displeased with their husbands and what their husbands are most likely to say — say nothing, brood about it, hint that they're unhappy, express their feelings or start an argument. We also asked how often they and their husbands behave in these different ways when they do argue — leave the room, sulk, sit in silence, swear, shout, hit out, cry or break things.
>
> The most happily married wives are those who say that *both* they and their husbands tell each other when they are displeased and thus try to work out their displeasure together by communicating in a calm and rational way. They also say that they and their husbands rarely or never fight in any of the different ways we listed; that is, they seldom resort either to the active-aggressive fighting (swearing, shouting, hitting out, crying or breaking things) or to passive-aggressive fighting (leaving the room, sulking or staying silent).
>
> The wives who are most unhappily married are in relationships where one or both partners can't talk calmly about what's bothering them.[40]

When the content of our messages is primarily substantive and orientational rather than emotional or affective, we elicit cooperative behavior from the other person, and agreement or consensus is more likely to be reached.[41]

Substantive messages clarify our previous statements, make suggestions, give information, present our opinions, analyze, reason, and express our feelings in a rational, calm fashion. High-orientation verbal behavior includes statements of procedural suggestions, relevant facts, and conciliation or willingness to consider other alternatives and ideas, and it identifies the rules we abide by and the sanctions we are prepared to deliver. The latter type of statements are helpful in inducing cooperative behavior if they are objective, accurate, honest, and related procedurally. That is, we openly and honestly tell the other person what we are prepared to do or not to do for them in the present situation. Cooperative behavior is increased as the content of bargaining communication increasingly allows for honest and unambiguous expression of intentions, expectations, conditions of retaliation, and conditions of reconciliation, and as it encourages messages that emphasize reciprocity of choice and the desirability of cooperative choice, or that threaten penalties for noncooperation.[42]

Assertive messages express respect for the rights of the person sending the message as well as the rights of the person receiving the message. We have the right to express our own wants, needs, desires, opinions, and feelings. We

40. Carol Tarvis and Toby T. Jayaratne, "How Happy Is Your Marriage?" *Redbook*, vol. 147, no. 2 (June 1976), 92.

41. Robert F. Bales, *Personality and Interpersonal Behavior* (New York: Holt, Rinehart & Winston, 1970); Morton Deutsch and Robert M. Krauss, "The Effect of Threat upon Interpersonal Bargaining," *Journal of Abnormal and Social Psychology* 51(1960):181–89.

42. Johnson, "Communication and Inducement of Cooperative Behavior," 73; Loomis, "Communication and Development of Trust," 305–15; G. Evans, "Effect of Unilateral Promise and Value of Rewards upon Cooperation and Trust," *Journal of Abnormal and Social Psychology* 69(1964):587–90; Shure et al., "Effectiveness of Pacifist Strategies"; R. Radlow and M. F. Weidner, "Unenforced Commitments in 'Cooperative' and 'Noncooperative' Non-Constant-Sum Games," *Journal of Conflict Resolution* 10(1966):497–505; and P. G. Swingle and A. Santi, "Communication in Non-Zero-Sum Games," *Journal of Personality and Social Psychology* 23(1972):54–63; K. W. Terhune, "Motives, Situation, and Interpersonal Conflict Within Prisoner's Dilemma," *Journal of Personality and Social Psychology*, Monograph Supplement 8 (1968).

also need to respect the right of the other person to do the same. One of the ways we do this is by using "I" rather than "you" messages so that we take responsibility for our messages.[43] "I" messages arouse less defensiveness in the other person because the other person's psychological space has not been invaded and they have not been held responsible for or made the cause of our feelings. They are free to describe the situation from their perspective, to agree or disagree with us.

43. Butler, *Self-Assertion for Women,* 133–38; Thomas Gordon, *Parent Effectiveness Training* (New York: Wyden, 1970).

Emotional, aggressive, or passive messages are not effective as a communication strategy if we are cooperatively negotiating a conflict. Emotions expressed through overuse of high-intensity messages or through violent and hostile action stimulate hostility and defensiveness in the other person.

Affective threat statements are charged with negative emotionality — anger, antagonism, and hostility against the other person. High-threat verbal behavior is characterized by a large number of statements reflecting antagonism toward that person. Most often the other person knows that we do not mean to carry out these threats, or that we are not able to carry them out. The other person does not believe us, and we accomplish very little except make ourselves look hostile, foolish, and irrational. Undercommunication in the form of silence, sulking, and leaving also expresses our hostility and uncooperativeness to the other person. If you remember the principle of reciprocity of feedback discussed in chapter 7, you know that hostility begets hostility.

Aggressive messages deprecate others, label the other negatively, and make one-sided demands. Aggressive messages are typical of the win/loss conflict style we discussed earlier.

Passive messages — especially silence and sulking — are typical of the avoiding and yielding conflict style. The yielding style is associated with avoiding any personal responsibility for the conflict or for negotiating its solution. The responsibility rests entirely on the other person. The person using this style claims to be hurt, anxious, and willing to please. The yielding style is often accompanied by attempts to subtly manipulate the other person.

Setting Aside a Time and Place to Discuss the Conflict

When we are careful to choose a time when we will be rested and prepared to talk calmly, we facilitate the negotiation process. Making an appointment to discuss the conflict also lets the other person know that we are serious in our desire to solve it.

Choose carefully the place where the discussion is to occur. Ideally it should be private, free from distractions such as the telephone, moderately comfortable, and equally familiar to both participants. Avoid the use of space which is "owned" or used more often by one of the participants. We come to have strong territorial feelings about such spaces. Within them we are more willing to attack others, defend ourselves, and less willing to compromise.

When discussing a conflict, try to choose a time and neutral place where interruption is unlikely.

Maintaining Your Perspective

If you or the other person feels that the conflict situation or your reaction to it seems unusually strong, either for you or for "people in general," check your perspective. Go back and answer the questions again in the section under "knowing yourself." Have you missed a hidden agenda or expectation? Is this a recurrent theme of many of your conflicts? If so, it may represent some hidden dynamic in your relationship with this person or with people in general. Ask yourself if the outcome of this particular conflict is critical to your relationship with the other person. Answer the question "Why?" Do you feel this will be important one year from now? Five years? Ten years from now?

Try to keep your sense of humor. Laughter eases tension in a relationship. Remember also that a joke or witty comment is one way of introducing a topic which the other person may feel uncomfortable talking about openly. If you react strongly, the topic will probably not be brought out into the open. On the other hand, you do not need to accept offensive jokes in a "spirit of co-operation." Simply state assertively, "I don't think that's funny or that it contributes to a solution to our problem."

Using a Rational, Problem-Solving Approach to the Conflict

A rational, problem-solving approach is the best procedure for handling conflict constructively. We suggest including the following steps:

Gather Information

In any communication setting, and especially in conflict situations, we communicate best when we are informed. There is no substitute for data. Therefore, in conflict situations we need to practice saying, "Whoa! First, I must get my facts straight! I must make sure I have accurate data!" If you are lucky enough to be in conflict with a person who is operating from data too, interpersonal negotiation is considerably easier.

Unless the other person has chosen a cooperative conflict style, you may not get information easily from that person. Remember that someone who has information about someone else has power over that person, so be prepared to share your information to gain information from the other person.

Reword and ask the other person the same questions you were told to ask yourself in the paragraph about "know yourself."

Do not try to read the other person's mind, and don't make inferences about the other person's motives. In trying to prepare for the "worst" you will probably suspect the other person of wanting to hurt you. You may also overestimate the other person's desire to help you. "People draw from comments on substance unfounded inferences which they then treat as facts about that person's intentions and attitudes toward them."[44] We need to be careful to distinguish observation from inference. The other person may not mean what we are inferring from his or her behavior. The only way to know for sure is to request the information from the other person. (If we think the response is dishonest, we will probably go to a win/loss conflict style.)

44. Fisher and Ury, *Getting to Yes*, 20.

Try to Create a Mutual Definition of the Conflict

What is its cause? What type of conflict is it? What events led up to the conflict? What event(s) triggered it? What is the true size of this conflict? The smaller it is and the more specific it is, the greater the probability of resolving it satisfactorily. The larger it is and the more vague we are in explaining it, the greater the difficulty of resolving it. Include in the discussion why each one of you cares about the conflict. Try to be open about your needs and feelings about the conflict.

Generate All Possible Solutions

Flexibility in considering possible solutions and awareness of alternatives in this situation are important to the problem-solving approach. Both parties should work cooperatively in doing this. At this stage try not to be critical of the suggestions either of you makes. A solution that seems worthless and impossible may, when combined with another idea, or creatively revised, end up being the final choice which satisfies the needs of both of you.

Consider Trades and Compromises

Remember, "one wins relative to his own goals and value system: satisfaction with the bargaining outcome does not necessarily imply crushing one's opponent."[45] A person gives up one thing wanted by the other person, and the other person gives up another thing wanted by the first person. Each of us may find it advantageous to win some rather than attempt to win all but risk losing everything.

45. Nancy A. Reiches and Harriet B. Harral, "Argument in Negotiation: A Theoretical and Empirical Approach," *Speech Monographs* 41(1974):37.

In compromise each of the parties to the conflict is willing to give up some goals or values to preserve or win other goals or values of higher priority. Each party settles for something less than what was wanted. Very often, if not always, parties who resolve conflict via compromise are able to do so because they possess a common goal of higher priority. Each gives up lesser goals so that both can have part of the important goal — the shared value. The tragedy is that often, even when the conditions for compromise exist, as when there is a basic agreement on the important goal, agreement may be destroyed or ignored because of negative interpersonal relationships — lack of trust, hostility, closed-mindedness, and poor interpersonal conflict communication skills.

Decide How to Evaluate Solution

Whatever plan is selected to resolve the conflict, how and where the plan will be checked to see if it has solved the problem should also be discussed. There needs to be some way of discovering whether or not the solution is mutually satisfying. The more objective and specific the criteria we can generate for this step, the more likely we are to choose a satisfactory solution. Establish a definite time limit at the end of which a formal evaluation of the solution will take place.

Turning to a Mediator/Arbitrator

Mediation refers to allowing a third party, an outside party, to assist in solving a conflict.[46] The mediator chosen must be someone trusted and respected by all parties to the conflict. We must recognize that a mediator — whether friend, relative, clergy, or marriage counselor — will not make our decision for us. A mediator serves as a catalyst.[47] He or she gathers information, reasons, persuades, provides data, and attempts to facilitate a resolution to the conflict.

46. Keltner, *Interpersonal Speech-Communication*, 246-51.

47. Ibid., 247.

As a final resort, we can consider using an arbitrator, although this is rarely done in interpersonal relationships unless some legitimate higher authority is perceived to have the right to make a final judgment. **Arbitration,** unlike mediation, gives the power of decision to the "outsider," the arbitrator. The parties to the conflict give up their right to make decisions in the resolution of the conflict. The arbitrator as a judge and jury, hears the arguments, considers the evidence and the cases presented, and decides how the goal sought by the contestants[48] is to be awarded. "Let Mom (the teacher, the manager) decide" is an appeal for arbitration.

48. Ibid., 251-52.

Summary

Dealing with conflict is a necessary part of our interpersonal relationships. Constructive resolution of interpersonal conflict allows our interpersonal relationships to meet our needs and to adapt to change. In this chapter interpersonal conflict is defined and its three key characteristics described. The intensity of a conflict is influenced by the intentions and goals of the participants, the communication styles which the participants may choose, the relative power structure of the participants, and the amount of trust in the relationship. Four levels of conflict intensity are defined and some suggestions for reducing the intensity in a conflict are given. Seven principles for the cooperative negotiation of interpersonal conflicts were described: (1) developing a positive attitude toward conflict; (2) maintaining open communication lines; (3) increasing accuracy in communication; (4) choosing a time and place for discussion; (5) keeping a perspective; (6) using a rational problem-solving approach; and (7) using a mediator or arbitrator.

Interpersonal Communication Contexts

9

Dyadic Communication

---

1. To be able to define dyadic communication and indicate two important reasons for examining it.
2. To be able to give two reasons why dyadic communication cannot be explained from the perspective of the individual's messages alone.
3. To be able to describe how communication functions and changes throughout the life of a relationship:
   a. during the initiation of a relationship
   b. during the acquaintance process
   c. during the formation of a stabilized relationship
   d. during the termination of a relationship
4. To be able to explain the concept of "equilibrium" and its importance for maintaining satisfactory relationships.
5. To be able to explain two criteria for judging satisfactoriness of equilibrium in a relationship.
6. To be able to list six types of rewards which can be exchanged in a relationship.
7. To be able to describe four areas in which it is important to establish and maintain satisfactory equilibrium in our relationships.
8. To be able to explain the factors which determine an "appropriate" equilibrium.

Daily we are involved in numerous situations in which we are interacting with just one other person — **dyadic communication** situations. Sometimes we seek information; sometimes we attempt to secure someone's agreement or approval; sometimes we make a new acquaintance; sometimes we just enjoy visiting with a friend or acquaintance; and sometimes we engage in intimate talk, disclosing and sharing with another our deepest feelings and concerns. Dyadic situations are virtually numberless.

We usually think of dyadic communication as an informal interpersonal situation involving two-way face-to-face verbal and nonverbal interaction. In dyadic communication two persons initiate messages and responses as they mutually influence each other. Each person simultaneously sends and receives information so as to create shared meanings. This free interchange gives to dyadic communication a high potential for information sharing and effective integration. It is not surprising, then, that some of the most influential and satisfying communication experiences for each of us are dyadic situations.

DYADIC COMMUNICATION: FOUNDATION OF OTHER FORMS OF COMMUNICATION

1. William W. Wilmot, *Dyadic Communication,* 2d ed. (Reading, Mass.: Addison-Wesley, 1979), 18–32.

2. Paul H. Fischer, "An Analysis of the Primary Group," *Sociometry* 16(1953):272–76.

3. R. D. Laing, H. Phillipson, and A. Russell Lee, *Interpersonal Perception: A Theory and a Method of Research* (London: Tavistock Publications, 1966).

Dyadic communication represents the basic, or "foundation," phenomenon in interpersonal communication.[1] All other forms of interpersonal communication rest on the ability to establish and maintain a one-to-one interaction with another person. We spend more time in dyadic communication than we spend in groups, whether of three or more.[2] For these two reasons it is important to take a close look at the dynamics of dyadic communication.

It is not possible to understand dyadic communication by considering one person at a time. No matter how intensely and thoroughly we look at one person alone and then at the other person alone, we cannot fully understand either person in the dyadic situation. To understand the dyadic situation, we have to study the two personalities as they interact.

First, as discussed in chapter 3, since our self-disclosure is different for each and every person with whom we interact, every one of our dyadic partners knows only a part of us. We are not the same person to the stranger in an elevator as we are to a classmate, to a boss, or to any other person with whom we establish a relationship. Each person knows us as a unique personality, and each relationship we establish with another person is a unique relationship.

Second, in dyadic communication, each of us creates the other half of the dyad, the person to whom we are responding, as the transaction process occurs.[3] We respond not only to the other person, but to the person we perceive the other to be. (You may want to review the material in chapter 4.) The behavior of each of us toward the other is mediated by our experiencing of the other, and the experiencing of each of us is mediated by our behavior and the behavior of the other person. This is the transaction process, the process of each of us creating, together, the meaning we have for each other in the relationship. Each dyad as an entity constitutes a social system in which each person is simultaneously influencing and being influenced by the other.

In this chapter we examine the communication life of dyadic relationships: how relationships are initiated, formed, and how some relationships are terminated through interpersonal communication. We also examine the four areas that must be agreed on in order for a relationship to be maintained.

THE LIFE OF A RELATIONSHIP

In a way a relationship has a life. It is born, it grows, and it ends. Some relationships last a lifetime while others are short-lived. Some relationships grow strong and deep while others are transient and shallow. Whether it is now old or young, long-lived or short-lived, deep or shallow, each dyadic relationship of which you are presently a part had a beginning. There was a period of becoming acquainted with that person and of forming the relationship.

The Entry Phase

The "entry phase"[4] or "initiating stage"[5] of an interpersonal relationship occurs in the first few minutes.[6] This formative period begins even before we begin to talk with each other. Each of us forms an immediate general "image" of the other which provides an almost instantaneous "definition" of who the other person is. In research studies, two-second glimpses have been found to be sufficient for individuals to develop an image and a set of general expectations of the person glanced at. As discussed in chapter 4, the immediate perception of a stranger is as a unit, as a whole.

Although the almost instantaneous general impression is formed from a combination of specific traits, a single dominant or striking factor may heavily influence that general impression.[7] A smile, frown, icy glance, bright color, and so on may be especially influential in the assignment of psychological and personality traits.

Some of the traits we perceive are especially influential in our perception of other traits. If the person is perceived as "warm," then he or she is likely to be perceived as also being sincere, honest, generous, wise, and happy.[8] (You might want to refer back to the discussion of implicit personality theories in chapter 4.)

Our perceptions of physical traits influence our perceptions of psychological traits, and vice versa — our perceptions of psychological traits influence our perceptions of physical traits. First impressions are extremely important which means that things first noticed are of special significance. Many of these are described in chapter 6. The physical appearance we first present and what we first say and do are important determiners of the other person's image of us. Some of these determiners are our gestures, posture, and rate of speech. Similarly, some unusual or especially prominent physical appearance factor — such as unusual or inappropriate clothes — may be a powerful determiner of the first image another person forms of us.

4. Charles R. Berger, "The Acquaintance Process Revisited: Explorations in Initial Interaction" (unpublished manuscript, Northwestern University, 1973), 1; Irwin Altman and Dalmas A. Taylor, *Social Penetration: The Development of Interpersonal Relationships* (New York: Holt, Rinehart & Winston, 1973).

5. Mark L. Knapp, *Social Intercourse: From Greeting to Goodbye* (Boston: Allyn & Bacon, 1978), 17–18.

6. Leonard Zunin, *Contact: The First Four Minutes* (Los Angeles: Nash Publishing Co., 1972).

7. See S. E. Asch, "Forming Impressions of Personality," *Journal of Abnormal and Social Psychology* 41(1946):258–90. Also, see the discussion of person perception and the trait theory of impression formation in chapter 4 of this book.

8. H. C. Smith, "Sensitivity to People," in Hans Toch and H. C. Clay, eds., *Social Perception* (New York: Van Nostrand Reinhold, 1968), 14.

First impressions are important and can significantly affect an interpersonal interaction.

This first impression is an important determiner of the interaction that follows; and the verbal interactions or "opening lines" we use during the first few minutes influence our subsequent interaction leading to the establishment of a unique dyadic relationship.

A getting-acquainted, second, stage of this entry phase of an interpersonal relationship has been called the "experimenting stage."[9] At this point the encounter is extremely unstable. Either member of the dyad can terminate the interaction without upsetting or offending the other person very much — each holds a virtual veto. This stage is usually characterized by verbal fencing during which we "size up" and try to find out who this other person is. If we discover that the other person has attitudes, values, and beliefs like our own, and if we feel "safe" with the other person, we will tend to reveal ourselves more freely. If, however, we feel threatened or insecure with this stranger, we will reveal as little of ourselves as possible.

Research indicates[10] that the most common material discussed during the first four to five minutes of an interaction is demographic information — such as where you are from, what kind of high school you went to, how many members you have in your family, in what year of school you are, your job, etc. In fact, relatively little other information is exchanged until after the first four or five minutes. The pattern then shifts to expressing attitudes and opinions about activities, objects, or things and discussing people who are not involved in the interaction but who might be common acquaintances.

9. Knapp, *Social Intercourse*, 18–19.

10. Berger, "Acquaintance Process Revisited," 14.

The disclosures we make about ourselves in this stage are relatively shallow, safe, and conservative.[11] Nevertheless, these data serve as a basis for inferences each person makes about the other person.

11. Altman and Taylor, *Social Penetration*, 11.

By knowing a person's age, one might be able to accurately infer the person's musical preferences. The kinds of topics covered in initial interaction do help to generate a network of propositions about the persons revealing the information. The propositions or predictions generated from the initial data may be in error; however, the fact that such "theories" are generated on the basis of "superficial" interaction is indeed significant. For if the inferences made on the basis of data obtained in the first few minutes of the encounter suggest that persons may be dissimilar on other, more salient, attributes, the probability that they will continue to interact might well be lowered. By contrast, if the inference pattern suggests a high level of similarity on attributes not yet sampled, the probability that the interaction will continue will be increased. Thus, inferences based on "superficial" interaction may well determine whether persons will continue their relationship.[12]

12. Berger, "Acquaintance Process Revisited," 4.

One of the prime functions served by this exchange of demographic information is to reduce the uncertainty we have about the other person in the interaction.[13] By exchanging demographic information, we gain clues as to the possible attitudes and opinions the other person is likely to hold. We begin to make inferences about that person's attitudes and opinions without directly asking for them. This aids us in predicting areas where our opinion would probably differ so that we can avoid bringing up topics which might cause unpleasantness between us. We rarely discuss personal topics such as future plans, our personalities, or the specific reasons we have for our past, present, or future behavior.[14] Generally, we don't feel prepared to disclose that much about ourselves so soon in a relationship because we do not know the other person well enough to be able to predict how he or she will react to the disclosure.

13. Ibid., 15.

14. Ibid., 14.

Sometimes we meet someone under special circumstances which suggest to us that we can predict some of the person's attitudes and opinions immediately.[15] We expect, for example, that individuals attending a wedding will be friends of either the bride or groom. Under these circumstances we may discuss this topic first and exchange demographic information a little later.

15. Ibid., 14–15.

Newcomb describes this process as a kind of "reciprocal scanning" of one another which is "a crucial part of the interactional behavior that goes on between persons who are getting acquainted. . . . Following any opportunity for reciprocal scanning — even a brief one on early acquaintance — there is apt to be some delineation on the part of the interacting persons of the area of mutually shared orientations — of at least some small sector about which they [will be able to] agree that they agree or disagree."[16]

The first four or five minutes of an interaction function to reduce our uncertainty in the situation and to enable us to make a judgment about what we

16. Theodore M. Newcomb, *The Acquaintance Process* (New York: Holt, Rinehart & Winston, 1961), 261.

17. Berger, "Acquaintance Process Revisited," 15.

share with the other person.[17] From such initial encounters fledgling relationships are born. During subsequent encounters each person becomes more fully acquainted with the other and the relationship is clarified and becomes established.

The Acquaintance Process

Our communication pattern changes during the second stage of an interpersonal relationship. At the beginning of the **acquaintance process**[18] we generally are still engaged mostly in small talk. These pastimes include talking about the weather, the gas shortage, the flowers in bloom, cars, hobbies, clothes, travel, sports, and other chitchat topics. Such dyadic communication provides opportunity for meeting our social needs at a relatively shallow and safe level and helps us to get to know the other person better.

18. Theodore M. Newcomb, *The Acquaintance Process* (New York: Holt, Rinehart & Winston, 1961); Donn Byrne, *The Attraction Paradigm* (New York: Academic Press, 1971); Sidney M. Jourard, *Self-Disclosure: An Experimental Analysis of the Transparent Self* (New York: John Wiley & Sons, 1971).

At the beginning of this stage we do not perceive the other person entirely as a unique individual. Our communication tends to be formal and based on cultural norms for interacting with people who are playing a particular role.[19] We don't need much, if any, personal information about our doctor to spend a few minutes each visit in pleasant conversation which is not related to medical matters.

19. Gerald R. Miller and Mark Steinberg, *Between People: A New Analysis of Interpersonal Communication* (Chicago: Science Research Associates, 1975).

Over time, and many interactions, our communication may gradually change. The topics we choose and what we say concerning those topics may become more intimate.[20] This has been referred to as an "intensifying stage" as we begin to explore our personalities, attitudes, beliefs, values, needs, and motivations in greater depth.[21] Some individuals are impatient with the earlier part of this process. As one student put it, "I want to get to important conversation right away and not have to play silly chitchat games at the beginning." Even if we feel the same way, it is important for us to realize that small talk helps us develop trust in the other person. We are better able to predict the reactions of others because we have a greater number of past experiences with them to draw on for information. Also, those past experiences generally will have been positive or we would not be interested in continuing the relationship. This results in increased trust between us. We need to feel sufficient trust in the other person before we begin intimate self-disclosure to them.[22]

20. Altman and Taylor, *Social Penetration*, 15–20.

21. Knapp, *Social Intercourse*, 19–20.

22. Lawrence R. Wheeless and Janis Grotz, "The Measurement of Trust and Its Relationship to Self-Disclosure," *Human Communication Research* 3(1977):250–57.

23. Sidney M. Jourard, "Self-Disclosure and Other-cathexis," *Journal of Abnormal and Social Psychology* 59(1959):428–31.

24. A. W. Gouldner, "The Norm of Reciprocity: A Preliminary Statement," *American Sociological Review* 25(1960):161–78.

Individuals who are willing to disclose personal information to others in an initial contact tend to induce others to engage in greater self-disclosure. This tendency for disclosure to beget disclosure has been called the "dyadic effect"[23] or the reciprocity phenomenon. During this phase of the acquaintance process there is a very strong "norm of reciprocity."[24] If we tell someone something intimate about ourselves, we expect the person to reciprocate with something about himself or herself which is at about the same level of intimacy. If the message we send to a new acquaintance is "I don't like the way my boyfriend is always late; it makes me feel he doesn't care," we don't expect the other person to respond with "Yeah, but I think he's a neat dresser"; or "True, but I think your real problems are your masochistic personality and deep-rooted feeling of inferiority."

This does not mean that the other person must reveal himself or herself only on the same topic or at exactly the same level of intimacy. The matching process is not that exact.[25] However, if the other person reciprocates with a much *less* intimate disclosure, we will probably think that he or she is not interested in developing a relationship with us. If the disclosure is much *more* intimate, we may feel that the other person is "going too fast," putting pressure on us to be more intimate than would make us feel comfortable. We may even feel that our "personal territory" or our "privacy" is being invaded.

As the acquaintance process continues and we reciprocate self-disclosures, we begin to perceive similarities between ourselves and the other person in attitudes, personality characteristics, interests, values, and beliefs. We begin to establish rapport with the other person which facilitates the use of less formal language.[26] We may even develop idiosyncratic ways of behaving with one another which we would not use with other people. Certainly we begin to interact with the other person as a *unique* individual with needs, values, attitudes and a personality which are different from all the other people we know.[27]

Forming a Stabilized Relationship

Establishing a more structured relationship begins with an "integrating stage."[28] As we begin this process of integrating with another person, we start to take on roles relative to each other.[29] One of us may do most of the organizing of when and where we meet; the other person may initiate or introduce most of the topics we finally discuss with each other.

We begin to perceive ourselves as belonging together, as a "couple."[30] As we spend more time communicating with one another, we find characteristics which we think set us apart from other people, which make our relationship "unique" and important. We begin to speak for one another: "Well, Sue and I feel . . ."; or "Sure, Tom and I can come Friday night." We each expect our other friends to become friends of our new partner and to include him or her in all our shared activities. Often we drop or begin to see less frequently "old friends" we don't both get along with well.

We may even merge our living or working quarters, purchase belongings in common, and go through a public ceremony as a form of commitment to our relationship. Sometimes this public ceremony is just an exchange of pins for "going steady." Sometimes it is a legal ceremony like marriage. This public legitimizing of a relationship has been referred to as a "bonding stage" because the simple act of going through a public ceremony can change the way we feel about our relationship, if for no other reason than that other people

25. D. A. Taylor, "Motivational Bases," in Gordon J. Chelune and Associates, eds., *Self-Disclosure: Origins, Patterns, and Implications of Openness in Interpersonal Relationships* (San Francisco: Jossey-Bass, 1979), 134.

26. Robert A. Lewis, "A Longitudinal Test of a Developmental Framework for Premarital Dyadic Formation," *Journal of Marriage and the Family* 35(1973):16–25.

27. Miller and Steinberg, *Between People.*

28. Knapp, *Social Intercourse,* 21–22.

29. Lewis, "A Longitudinal Test."

30. Wilmot, *Dyadic Communication,* 150; Knapp, *Social Intercourse,* 21.

31. Knapp, *Social Intercourse*, 21-23.

are now aware of our mutual commitment.[31] And, if the law itself prescribes or determines certain aspects of the relationship, the ceremony itself may change the relationship.

As a relationship progresses in intimacy, each of us becomes more concerned with maintaining our own identity within that relationship. At any time during the initiation and formation of a relationship we may become concerned because we are "getting too close" or "too involved" with the other person. We may feel we need to separate ourselves from the other person a little in order to reestablish our feeling of being an independent person. This need may be especially strong after the intense integration phase which leads to a bonding ceremony. In an attempt to establish a balance between closeness as a couple and separateness as individuals, we may begin a process of

32. Ibid., 23-24.

"differentiating" in which each of us begins to establish individual territories.[32] A certain chair or corner of a room becomes "my place to work." Or, we might sometimes feel a need to talk to an old friend without our partner being present. Maybe we just feel like having a little "individual attention" from someone for a change, or we want to discuss an interest we share with the friend but not the partner. No matter how close we are to another human being, there will be some interests, values, and attitudes we do not share.

Some people feel threatened when this natural "moving apart" begins because it can seem like the "beginning of the end" of perfect "coupleness." Healthy long-term relationships, however, often cycle back and forth between this stage and the integration stage. We should not be frightened or angry when we or our partner suggest that in some ways we have different needs or interests. If we accept this and use healthy conflict negotiation procedures to establish a new and more satisfactory relationship with the other person, our reintegration as a "couple" will be even stronger.

Of course, this process can also signal the beginning of the end if we find we are happier not being close to the other person.

Terminating a Relationship

There are several indications that a relationship has become sufficiently unsatisfactory for one or both of the individuals to contemplate terminating it. First, communication becomes restricted — certain topics are no longer discussed, self-disclosure decreases in intimacy, and even the amount of com-

33. Ibid., 24-25.

munication may decrease. This "circumscribing"[33] of the communication in an interaction can lead to the alienation and unwillingness to communicate discussed in chapter 3.

As this unwillingness to communicate increases, the individuals may turn to the highly ritualized communication patterns which are typical of interactions between strangers. The relationship is "stagnating"[34] in much the same sense

34. Ibid.

a pond becomes stagnant. The two individuals may watch television together

Relationships can stagnate if we don't put forth an effort to maintain them.

or even participate in other shared activities, but they no longer feel much hope about any constructive, positive sharing developing through their communication.

Another indication of a deteriorating relationship is physically "avoiding"[35] the other person. We can avoid someone by developing a busy work schedule; by taking up a sport which our partner can't share; by making commitments to other people or organizations; or simply by ignoring the other person's communication — being slow to speak when the other person asks us a question, using nonverbal communication which shows a lack of interest in the other person, "forgetting" when an interaction is supposed to take place, and being vague about plans for future interactions.

There are many reasons why a relationship can become unsatisfactory.[36] (1) We may blame the personality or some behaviors of our partner for making the relationship difficult for us. (2) We may feel that our partner no longer cares about us or loves us and therefore is not willing to compromise with us and make a fair contribution to the relationship. (3) We may feel that the other person is putting pressure on us to become more intimate and involved than we want to be in the relationship. The other person may want to spend more time with us than we feel comfortable with, to know where we are and what we are doing whenever we are not present. (4) We may feel that the criterion of **distributive justice** is being violated in our relationship: either we are not receiving our fair share, which makes us angry, or we seem to be taking advantage of the other person, which makes us feel guilty.[37] (5) We may no longer feel the satisfaction we previously received from the relationship because the

35. Ibid.

36. Michael J. Cody, "A Typology of Disengagement Strategies and an Examination of the Role Intimacy, Reactions to Inequity and Relational Problems Play in Strategy Selections," paper presented at annual Speech Communication Association Convention, Anaheim, Calif., 1981, 19.

37. Elaine Walster, G. William Walster, and Ellen Berscheid, *Equity: Theory and Research* (Boston: Allyn & Bacon, 1978).

other person has changed. He or she is no longer slim and sexually attractive, does not make as much money as before, is not as warm and affectionate now, or no longer shares our interests. We may also have changed so that behaviors which used to satisfy our needs no longer do so. As people change, sometimes they can satisfactorily adapt to one another and sometimes they cannot change to meet each other's needs and still have their own needs met in the relationship.

Whether or not we decide to partially or completely terminate a relationship depends on our **comparison level for alternatives**.[38] That is, do we think that the potential alternatives to our present relationship are likely to be better and more satisfying? If we think they are, then we are likely to terminate the relationship. If we think they are not likely to be more acceptable, then we may stay in a very unsatisfactory relationship, one in which our communication is circumscribed and where the relationship is stagnating, simply because we do not feel that we "deserve" anything better. Since these beliefs are really perceptions about our self and the world, our self-concept has a strong influence on the decision to terminate a relationship.

Five Strategies for Terminating a Relationship

There appear to be five common communication strategies which we may use in terminating a relationship.[39] Most of us use more than one.[40] The particular strategies we choose to use are affected by the reasons we have for terminating the relationship, how intimate the relationship has been,[41] and whether we wish to partially or completely terminate the relationship.[42]

The most commonly used strategies deescalate the relationship.[43] Using strategy one, we openly, firmly, but considerately confront the other person and discuss our desire to interact less or "just be friends" with the other person. If we want to avoid an open confrontation, we can use strategy two, withdrawal (as described previously in the discussion of circumscribed and stagnating relationships). This is the most common way people terminate a relationship.[44] If we are angry because we feel the relationship has not been "fair," we are more likely to choose an avoiding strategy. We are also more likely to choose this strategy when the relationship has not been an intimate one.[45] We are less likely to choose this strategy if we wish to remain friends and only partially terminate the relationship.[46]

We are more likely to choose an open, honest confrontation where the relationship has been intimate, where the other person has made us feel pressured, or where we feel our partner has failed to compromise and contribute to the relationship.[47] If we feel that events outside the relationship are the cause of the breakup, we are also more likely to choose an open, honest confrontation.[48]

38. J. W. Thibaut and H. H. Kelley, *The Social Psychology of Groups* (New York: John Wiley & Sons, 1959), 21.

39. Cody, "Typology of Disengagement Strategies," 11; Leslie A. Baxter, "Self-reported Disengagement Strategies in Friendship Relationships," paper presented at annual Western Speech Communication Association convention, Portland, 1979; Leslie A. Baxter, "Relational Closeness, Relational Intention, and Disengagement Strategies," paper presented to annual Speech Communication Association convention, San Antonio, 1979; Michael T. Perras and Myron W. Lustig, "The Effects of Intimacy Level and Intent to Disengage on the Selection of Relationship Disengagement Strategies," paper presented at the annual Western Speech Communication Association convention, Denver, 1982.

40. Cody, "Typology of Disengagement Strategies," 20.

41. Ibid.

42. Perras and Lustig, "Effects of Intimacy Level," 10.

43. Cody, "Typology of Disengagement Strategies," 10, 20.

44. Baxter, "Relational Closeness."

45. Cody, "Typology of Disengagement Strategies," 21, 24.

46. Perras and Lustig, "Effects of Intimacy Level," 10.

47. Cody, "Typology of Disengagement Strategies," 23.

48. Perras and Lustig, "Effects of Intimacy Level," 3.

When we terminate a relationship using strategy three, we may express our sorrow that the relationship has ended and try to be considerate of the other person's feelings. Sometimes we would like to keep the other person for a friend, only partially terminating the relationship.[49] We are also more likely to use a communication strategy which shows a positive regard for the other person if our relationship has been intimate and if we feel that the cause of the breakup is that the other person is putting pressure on us to be closer than we wish.[50] If we feel it is our partner's fault that the relationship has failed, we are not likely to use this strategy.[51]

With strategy four, we may decide to explain our reasons for terminating the relationship, to justify our actions to the other person. If we feel the relationship was unfair to us, we are more likely to justify our leaving to the other person than if we feel we benefited more than the other person.[52] If we feel the breakup was our partner's behavior, personality, declining affection, or failure to compromise, we are also more likely to give reasons for our decision.[53] More justifications also occur if the relationship has been an intimate one.[54]

The fifth strategy is trying to manipulate the other person into breaking off the relationship.[55] One person may behave in ways which make the other person angry and then inquire, "What's bothering you?" When the other person explains how he or she feels, the manipulator points out how beneficial the end of the relationship would be for both of them. Or the manipulator may simply communicate that he or she is terminating the relationship and refuse to discuss it any further. This strategy is often chosen when one person feels pressured by the other's desire for a more intimate relationship.[56]

How we exit our relationships is an important problem with which we ought to be concerned. In fact, it is the inability of persons to handle this problem that has led, in part, to shallow relationships, even to the avoidance of meaningful relationships and to consequent alienation.[57] The point we wish to make at this time, however, is that exiting relationships is as much a part of the real world as is initiating and maintaining interpersonal relationships.

There are a few commonsense principles that might make our communication more effective during this difficult time in a relationship. First, we must learn to accept the relational nature of our interactions. As we pointed out in chapter 7, on listening and feedback, we may send a message, but the other person responds to the message which he or she has created. We are never alone in an interpersonal relationship, never solely responsible for what occurs between us. This means that we are not entirely in control of the other person. The relationship is created together, and problems in the relationship are a function of behaviors of both people.

Second, we can choose the communication strategies we will use in terminating a relationship instead of simply "allowing" it to happen. We suggest that the most effective strategies use open, honest, direct communication; that

49. Perras and Lustig, "Effects of Intimacy Level," 10.

50. Cody, "Typology of Disengagement Strategies," 23.

51. Ibid.

52. Ibid., 21.

53. Ibid., 23.

54. Ibid., 24.

55. Ibid., 20.

56. Ibid., 23.

57. Alvin Toffler, *Future Shock* (New York: Random House, 1970), 96–98.

they include respect and care for the other person's feelings and give a reasonable justification for the demise of the relationship. This does not mean that both parties will agree, or even that the relationship will end pleasantly. People feel better about themselves, however, if, when they end relationships, they do so as effectively as they initiate and maintain them.

MAINTAINING SATISFACTORY RELATIONSHIPS

58. Michael Argyle, *Social Interaction* (New York: Atherton Press, 1969), 199–202.

Once a relationship has been established at any of the stages we have discussed, the task of communication is to maintain and sustain it. The key word in maintaining satisfactory dyadic relationships, used by many scholars, seems to be **equilibrium.**[58] An equilibrium is a state of balance. A relationship in equilibrium is stable, harmonious, and satisfactory for both parties. These balance points, or equilibrium, that we achieve or develop with another person are never the same in any two relationships. We might think that once a relationship is worked out all problems are forever solved. However, if we view life as a process, virtually nothing is static. Change is the one thing we can count on, which means that we will have to take specific action to maintain our equilibrium; we will have to make adjustments and perform certain behaviors that maintain the relationship as mutually satisfying to both participants. In some relationships goals, role-relations, and communication remain almost static. We may know Mr. Hendricks down the street for years (mow his grass, babysit his children, and wash his car), and our relationship and communication will not vary very much. In other relationships the goals and role-relations will probably be redefined many times as the relationship changes if a balanced relationship is to be maintained.

59. J. W. Thibaut and H. H. Kelly, *The Social Psychology of Groups* (New York: Wiley, 1959), 81.

We often use the following two criteria in determining our satisfaction with the equilibrium we have achieved in a particular relationship. The first criterion is a **comparison level** against which we "measure" the relationship.[59] It is an expectation of the minimum we deserve in any relationship that we have derived from past experiences with other people. For example, if Mary is warmer and more responsive than any other friend we have had, we will be satisfied. But if Mary, behaving just the same, is not as warm and responsive to us as we have come to expect in the past from friendships with Louise and Sam, then we will not be satisfied. In other words, our satisfaction is not determined by Mary's behavior alone.

This is also one of the reasons our communication behavior alone does not determine how others react to us. When we think we are being fair by treating two friends alike, one of our friends may be happy and the other one unhappy with us. We may want to have lunch with each of them alone once a week so that we can talk just together. One friend will be happy with this and appreciate our interest while the other will feel left out and lonely because we don't want to lunch together every day.

The second criterion is called **distributive justice.**[60] We expect to be rewarded for the time and effort we put into a relationship. Furthermore, we expect that the rewards available in a relationship will be distributed in such a way that the person who brings the most to the relationship will get the most from it. You are more likely to ask for the loan of a car from someone you helped study for a test for five hours, than from someone for whom you only answered a quick question. The husband who, when asked why his working wife continued to do most of the housework, replied "I make more money than she does" is using the criterion of distributive justice to rationalize that aspect of the equilibrium point in their relationship: the person who brings more financial resources to the relationship is rewarded with more leisure time, or more control, or more affection.

The following six resources have been suggested as interpersonal rewards which we can exchange in a relationship: (1) love or affection, warmth, and comfort; (2) esteem and status or prestige; (3) personal services related to our body or our possessions; (4) information, such as expert advice or knowledge; (5) goods, such as objects and materials, and (6) money.[61] The first four can be expressed through our communication to others. How we weigh each of these and how satisfactory we find their distribution in our relationship will determine how we will judge the equilibriums we establish in our relationships.

Four areas appear to be of particular importance in establishing satisfactory balances in our interpersonal relationships: responsiveness; dominance; affection; change.[62] Many of the messages we send are designed to create and maintain a balance in one of these areas in our relationships.

No matter what stage of a relationship we have reached, we need to achieve equilibrium for each of these four areas if we are to maintain the relationship at that stage. These equilibriums will be different for any two relationships, even for two relationships which seem to be at approximately the same stage of development. There are also many norms we have learned for what constitutes an "appropriate" equilibrium at different stages of a relationship with people of different status; people of the opposite sex; people of the same sex. Achieving an equilibrium that is satisfactory and easy to maintain for both people in a relationship is not a simple process.

Appropriate Responsiveness

The first[63] area in which two people need to develop a relational equilibrium concerns how they will define what is to be considered **appropriate responsiveness**[64] to each other. That is, in their messages what kinds of responses seem reasonable and responsive to each other? If one person asks a question, how soon and in what manner is the other expected to answer? Do we have to laugh at jokes we don't think are funny? Will sarcasm be perceived as appropriate, or will it hurt the other person and make him or her feel excluded or rejected? What guidelines will be established for satisfying

60. G. C. Homans, *Social Behavior: Its Elementary Forms* (New York: Harcourt, Brace, 1961), 75.

61. Uriel G. Foa and Edna B. Foa, "Resource Exchange: Toward a Theory of Interpersonal Communication," in A. W. Siegman and B. Pope, eds., *Studies in Dyadic Communication* (New York: Pergamon Press, 1972), 293.

62. Judee K. Burgoon and Jerold L. Hale, "Dimensions of Relational Messages," paper presented at Speech Communication Association Convention, Anaheim, Calif., November 1981.

63. W. C. Schutz, *FIRO: A Three Dimensional Theory of Interpersonal Behavior* (New York: Rinehart & Company, 1958), 168.

64. Argyle, *Social Interaction*, 202; Burgoon and Hale, "Dimensions of Relational Messages."

needs for inclusion when two people are not in identical emotional states? If one person is angry and wants to talk about his or her job upon arriving home at night and the other person wants to relax and listen to music, how do they respond to each other?

One area in which it may be difficult to achieve a balance is nonverbal expressiveness. How much attentiveness do we have to show in our facial expression before the other person accepts that we are "listening"? How loud does our voice have to be before the other person knows we are "serious" about something? What do we feel is the appropriate amount of time to spend together rather than alone as individuals?

How responsive we feel we ought to be to the other person will depend on the stage of the relationship. For example, if you are just becoming acquainted with someone who is fighting with a roommate, you will feel right about listening empathically for a short time. After a while you may begin to feel that the other person is asking you to be too responsive to what is, after all, "not your problem." If, however, you are a close friend of the other person, you might listen empathically for days or even weeks before you reached that point.

The relative "appropriate" responsiveness of each person to the other will also depend upon the sex of each and their relative status. Individuals of lower status are expected to be relatively more responsive to the other than those of higher status. Women are expected to be more responsive than men. (You may want to review the sections on sex and status differences in chapter 6 on nonverbal communication.)

How we feel about one another will also affect our responsiveness. John M. Gottman, a psychologist and author of *Marital Interaction: Experimental Investigations,* studied 487 couples over nine years and suggested that withdrawing responsiveness to another person is one way we express our feelings:

> In one experiment, Gottman and his colleagues paired happily and unhappily married men and showed them videotapes of their own and one another's wives sending verbal messages pregnant with nonverbal content, such as pleading or playfulness. The happily married men had little difficulty interpreting the intended nonverbal messages, whether sent by their own wives or by the others' wives. The unhappily married men could often interpret the messages of other men's wives, but when it came to their own, they often drew a blank.[65]

65. John M. Gottman, *Marital Interaction: Experimental Investigations* (New York: Academic Press, 1979); Anthony Brandt, "Avoiding Couple Karate: Lessons in the Marital Arts," *Psychology Today,* October 1982, 43.

When we respond appropriately to the other person, that individual feels "included" in our relationship. Two types of communication that are especially important for making others feel included, social communication and stroking, will be discussed next. They both serve this important function even in long-term intimate relationships (although other types of communication may also serve to let the other person know that he or she is being responded to appropriately).

Social Communication

Social communication is a characteristic behavior which satisfies our need for inclusion. It can be distinguished from other communication because it is **consummatory** (of primary value at the moment only) and quite different from **instrumental communication** (used to accomplish a specific goal or to solve a specific problem). In **social communication** the talk is its own purpose. This does not mean that any kind of talk satisfies. There is a science and art of conversation with rules of its own; the identifying characteristic of social conversation is its sociability — its existence for its own sake. Other forms of communication via talk — the quarrel, debate, gossip, confessional, interrogation, public speech, interview, and so on — are instrumental, used to obtain practical ends. The purpose of social conversation is to give pleasure; thus no content, idea, or theme need be dominant. As soon as the talk becomes objective (instrumental) its purpose changes and it ceases to be social communication. In social conversation we seek to achieve harmony, a consciousness of being together, and enjoyment of one another. We reject conversation that is "too intimate" and "too individual" because it cannot be shared by others. Topics which are appropriate in intimate interaction situations, such as talk with a close friend or between husband and wife, are not appropriate in social conversation. That is why stories and jokes are common at parties — they provide a content that can be shared by the group.

Stroking

Stroking also satisfies our need for inclusion. Berne, a psychologist, defines a "stroke" as "a unit of recognition."[66] He elaborates by stating:

> "Stroking" may be used as a general term for intimate physical contact; in practice it may take various forms. Some people literally stroke an infant; others hug or pat it, while some people pinch it playfully or flip it with a fingertip. These all have their analogues in conversation, so that it seems one might predict how an individual would handle a baby by listening to him talk. By an extension of meaning, "stroking" may be employed colloquially to denote any act implying recognition of another's presence. Hence a *stroke* may be used as the fundamental unit of social action. An exchange of strokes constitutes a *transaction*, which is the unit of social intercourse.[67]

66. Eric Berne, *What Do You Say After You Say Hello?* (New York: Grove Press, 1972), 447.

67. Eric Berne, *Games People Play* (New York: Grove Press, 1964), 15.

68. George A. Borden and John D. Stone, *Human Communication: The Process of Relating* (Menlo Park, Calif.: Cummings Publishing Co., 1976), 82.

Stroking is sometimes considered the "basic unit of social communication."[68] We appear to be very social beings. We require social stimulation. Some persons require more stroking or responsiveness than others, but all persons need it sometimes. Stroking may be positive or negative, verbal or nonverbal.

Most stroking is done nonverbally. We trust the nonverbal strokes more than the verbal ones. It's easy to say "I love you" because it is a conscious behavior, but the way you say it (the vocal-nonverbal part) is usually unconscious and thus more to be trusted.

The eyes rather than the voice, are the most active strokers we have. RECOGNITION is shown there first. (That is why we have the term "poker face.") If you show no emotions in your eyes, people do not know where you are in relation to them. This can be very disconcerting. The reverse is also true. If you are able to control the expressiveness of your eyes so you can stroke without meaning it, then you set up all kinds of false perceptions in others. If you were to smile at us with your eyes, we might think you were recognizing us approvingly when really you were faking it and hate us both (which may be the case if you don't like what you are reading). The only way we can find out is to have a session of strokes to see if our first perceptions were correct. This constitutes communication, or as Berne states it, "social intercourse." . . . If we engage someone in conversation, the very fact that we are talking to him or her is a positive stroke. What we say, as well as the way we say it, may add some more strokes. Sometimes these two types of strokes cancel each other out, but we are always left with the initial stroke, that of contact.[69]

69. Ibid., 82–83.

In fact, the types of feedback discussed in chapter 7 can be thought of as stroking without much difficulty. Whatever the type, it confirms our existence among others in a social world.

Once an equilibrium of responsiveness is established in any dyadic relationship — that is, the level necessary for satisfaction of the needs of both individuals for inclusion and recognition with respect to each other — both people will try to maintain it in their relationship.

Dominance or Control

70. Schutz, *FIRO*, 168.

The second[70] area to be balanced in a dyadic relationship concerns dominance or control: who will control whom, and when. If the two people have different ideas about who will make a decision, who will talk most, or who will give commands, they will have to reach some agreement or compromise. Throughout the life of the relationship it will be necessary to maintain or negotiate "agreed-on" dominance behaviors.

71. Argyle, *Social Interaction*, 201.

"The commonest source of conflict in dyadic interaction is where each wants to dominate."[71] It is also common to find the converse — conflict occurring because each individual wants the other person to make decisions and take the responsibility for directing some aspect of the relationship.

Men appear to desire more control over the other person in their dyadic relationships and rate this ability to influence the other person as one of the positive outcomes they look for in a love relationship.[72] This greater need for dominance in a relationship appears to have two adverse effects. First, men disclose less about themselves to their partner,[73] and this failure of self-disclosure is directly related to fear of losing control over the partner.[74] But without self-disclosure it is more difficult for the partner to meet the person's needs.

Second, where a dominance pattern is established in a marital relationship with one spouse clearly dominant, both spouses are less likely to understand and know what they can expect from the partner in the relationship.[75] When we send many messages which reflect an attempt to control the other person and the situation, the total communication which occurs between partners appears to be significantly reduced, and this decreases understanding of each other and the relationship.

How control is communicated in a relationship varies from the very subtle — a lifted eyebrow — to the obvious use of physical force. How much control we feel is appropriate from the other person depends on the stage of our relationship, our relative status, whether we are the same or opposite sex, and the norms we have learned. If we are a little too loud in a restaurant, we may find even the waitress's raised eyebrow offensive. But we would probably listen very respectfully to a request to lower the noise at our party from the police officer our neighbors have called at three o'clock in the morning. Most young women we have spoken to would still find it difficult to ask an unknown young man for a first date. They would feel more comfortable, however, if they had known him for some time. If they had been dating him for a while, they would think almost nothing about asking him to accompany them to some social occasion.

We may feel very uncomfortable thinking of all the ways we exert control over others, and others exert control over us. Nevertheless, we need to establish the equilibrium for control in our relationships. This balance point must reflect the desires of *both* parties for control in the relationship if we are to be successful in maintaining a satisfactory long-term interaction.

Affection, Attraction, Intimacy, and Trust

The third area where two people need to work out an agreement that fulfills their needs is love and intimacy,[76] whether they are husband and wife, mother and daughter, boss and secretary, teacher and student, and so on. When we ask the question "Should we kiss on a first date or not?" we are attempting to establish some norms for a beginning equilibrium for affection in a relationship. The need for this equilibrium does not exist only in "love" relationships or in long-term intimate friendships. It exists in all our relationships. When

72. Letitia Ann Peplau, "What Homosexuals Want in Relationships," *Psychology Today*, March 1981, 28–38.

73. Lawrence B. Rosenfeld, Jean M. Civikly, and Jane R. Herron, "Anatomical and Psychological Sex Differences," in Gordon L. Chelune and Associates, eds., *Self-Disclosure*, 80–109.

74. Lawrence B. Rosenfeld, "Self-Disclosure Avoidance: Why I am Afraid to Tell You Who I Am," *Communication Monographs* 46(1979):63–74.

75. Frank E. Miller, L. Edna Rogers-Millar, and John A. Courtright, "Relational Control and Dyadic Understanding: An Exploratory Predictive Regression Model," in Dan Nimmo, ed., *Communication Yearbook* 3 (New Brunswick: International Communication Association, 1979), 213–24.

76. Schutz, *FIRO*, 168.

Risk-taking — a part of everyday life, even game-playing — is an especially important element in building trust and intimacy in a relationship.

we meet someone we think we would like to know better, we try to guess how attractive that person finds us. From the beginning of our acquaintance, we will need to discuss or reach an agreement on the following topics: How much self-disclosure about out attitudes, values, beliefs, and feelings do we expect from one another? What constitutes "trust" between the two of us? What are our mutual requirements for "listening" to one another? How much "rapport" is desirable for both of us? What degree of warmth, friendliness, and attraction should there be between us to make the relationship "right" for both of us? As we come to know each other better, the balance point for affection, attraction, intimacy, and trust in our relationship will change.

Trust, for example, is established through disclosure to a loving, caring, re-sponding person coupled with reciprocal disclosure by that person. Getting to know each other well and building an intimate relationship depends on both persons being self-disclosing. When each discloses to the other, trust is built as the other responds with acceptance and support. Trust is destroyed when the risk-taking disclosure behavior of one is rejected, ridiculed, or be-trayed. Two elements, then, are especially important in intimate communi-cation: risk-taking through self-disclosure, and the acceptance and support of the responding person. We cannot expect to be able to engage in satisfying intimate communication if we are unwilling or too fearful to take the risk of making disclosures to the other person. We cannot hide behind masks or pro-tect ourselves by being tight-lipped and closed to everyone. Rather, we must learn to open ourselves to others — to take intelligent risks through self-disclosure. We must become aware of the responsibility placed on us when another discloses himself or herself to us. Can we be supportive and accepting? We find trust as we demonstrate our trustworthiness.

To be cared for or loved for "oneself," one must disclose oneself. If we want to care for or love someone, that someone must permit us to know him (or her). That seems so obvious, doesn't it? But apparently it is one of the most common difficulties in intimate communication. Jourard and Whitman, psychologists and marital counselors, say:

> We discovered that even with those they cared most about, people shared little of their true feelings or their most profound longings and beliefs; revealed little of what they really thought on such touchy subjects as sex, self-image, religion. . . . As a therapist and research psychologist I often meet people who believe that their troubles are caused by things outside themselves — by another person, bad luck or some obscure malaise — when in fact they are in trouble because they are trying to be loved and seeking human response without letting others know them. . . . Even in families — good families — people wear masks a great deal of the time. Children don't know parents; parents don't know their children. Husbands and wives are often strangers to each other.[77]

77. Sidney M. Jourard and Ardis Whitman, "The Fear That Cheats Us of Love," *Redbook*, October 1971, 83.

Each of us probably has been guilty of unnecessary closedness and concealment. We say that we feel things we really do not feel, and that we believe things we really do not believe. We try to present our best selves, sometimes false selves, to be loved. Also, we hide to protect ourselves from change, because change is so frightening. But often these behaviors are counterproductive. They produce an effect exactly the opposite of what we really intend. (See the discussion in chapter 3 concerning dropping the false masks we wear.)

Although disclosure of feelings, attitudes, and beliefs is a necessary characteristic of intimate and satisfying dyadic relationships, we want to emphasize that it must be intelligent and benign disclosure. We are not suggesting that you can be or should be brutally open about every feeling, attitude, and thought. McCroskey, Larson, and Knapp, communication scholars, make this point:

> Disclosure is a particularly important concept in our discussion of interpersonal communication in marriage. Much writing in the popular literature suggests that open communication on all aspects of marital life leads to greater understanding and adjustment. However, there are serious limitations that one should place on that generalization. We have all encountered situations in which individuals in particularly playful or rueful moods give in to momentary impulses to make intense personal disclosures. We sometimes regret these disclosures, even beyond the point where we can derive any comfort from the convenient cop-out, "I'm telling you this for your own good." From the marital situation, the

Self-disclosure is necessary for the development of intimate and satisfying dyadic communication.

effects of such intense disclosures are long-range and cumulative and may even be destructive. The intensity of the involvement and the commitment which characterizes the marital situation are such that the married couple experimenting with "truth sessions" may discover that their momentary experimentation will have consequences that go far beyond their expectations. The critical questions which should be asked are, "Is the disclosure necessary or likely to have productive consequences? Can the other person handle it?" The second question implies an almost moralistic assertion. The assertion is that when we disclose personal information to another, we are in effect "messing with his mind." If what we say has deep personal implications for the other, then the responsibility for the consequences clearly lies with the person who is doing the disclosing.[78]

78. James C. McCroskey, Carl E. Larson, and Mark L. Knapp, *An Introduction to Interpersonal Communication* (Englewood Cliffs, N.J.: Prentice-Hall, 1971), 175, 176.

Despite the acknowledgment that one cannot always be totally open, we stress the need for disclosure and honesty when they meet the criteria identified by McCroskey, Larson, and Knapp. Otherwise friendship communication, courtship communication, and marital communication fail in their purposes; the acquaintance process, rather than being a time of mutual exposure of the self and acquaintance with the other, is a period of mutual deception, a period in which people construct false images, one of the other. The result may be that each develops a friendship with or marries a stranger. It is difficult to establish a satisfying relationship if each person's concept of the other is inaccurate. How can a person who selects someone he or she does not know or understand behave in loving ways and reciprocate in fulfilling needs?

Failure to disclose and to be open is especially dangerous to the development of a close and meaningful sexual relationship. Jourard and Whitman state:

Given a reasonable lack of prudery, a lusty sex life grows best out of a relationship between two persons who can disclose themselves to each other in all areas of their lives without fear of being hurt. . . . Sex deteriorates when a couple cannot establish a close, mutually revealing, *nonsexual* relationship; the very defenses one uses to keep from being known and possibly hurt by the spouse one cannot understand are the same defenses that impede spontaneity in sex.[79]

79. Jourard and Whitman, "Fear That Cheats Us," 157.

So important is the fulfillment of needs of affection and intimacy at the dyadic level that

if two people seek different degrees of intimacy there will be incongruity and awkwardness. . . . If A uses social techniques such as standing nearer, looking more, and smiling to a greater extent than B, B will feel that A is intrusive and overfamiliar, while A will feel that B is cold and standoffish. Clearly A is seeking an affiliative response from B; it is not enough for him to be able to look B in the eye — B must look back and with the right kind of facial expression.[80]

80. Argyle, *Social Interaction*, 201.

If we are to maintain a satisfactory dyadic relationship, then the affection and intimacy needs of both of us must be met at the level we define as appropriate or necessary for us at that stage of our relationship. Sometimes this means that one of us will need to be more open or affectionate than we want to be. At other times we may wish our partner would be more expressive but realize that it is not possible. We will need to negotiate with one another until a comfortable balance point has been achieved for us both.

Change and Separateness

We also need to consider the freedom to grow, the freedom to adapt to change, and the freedom to change or to retain one's individuality in a relationship. "Once we have formed our image of who and what we are, we proceed to behave as if that were all we ever could be. We 'freeze' as though we had taken a pledge to ourselves that even if we did change, we'd try not to notice it. And we don't want the other person to change either."[81] In fact, sometimes one person tends to smother the other, to absorb the other person so as to destroy his or her individuality, and to deny the other person the freedom to grow and to change in response to an ever-changing world.

> Freedom and the right to grow are a difficult and painful gift for a couple to give each other, but there is no alternative. People outgrow the roles in which they have been cast by their partners, and when they have grown and changed, each must be able to let the fact be known so that the partner he or she loves can take it into account. . . . Husbands and wives need tough and candid talk aimed at dispelling misunderstandings. They need to understand how they differ, what they respect and love in each other, what they hold in common — yes, and what enrages them in each other. If we speak honestly, we must be able to say, "What you are doing right now makes me angry."[82]

Too often the members of intimate dyads become locked in such strong mutual habitual behavior patterns[83] that change is virtually impossible without outside interaction or help. When one partner responds to change by simply dismissing the other as unreasonable, messed up, unintelligent, or even in need of professional help of some kind, or by a persuasive campaign designed to "correct" the faulty thinking of the other, the other person is likely to become very defensive or angry. These courses of action are likely to be unproductive. They are not likely to change the other individual "back," and they make the open and honest communication and negotiation that might improve the situation very difficult, if not impossible.

"Ownership" of the other is an even more counterproductive characteristic that can occur in an intimate or marital relationship and adversely affect a couple's ability to deal with change in the relationship. It is understandable, of course, how this characteristic might develop. As other people begin to

81. Jourard and Whitman, "Fear That Cheats Us," 157.

82. Ibid., 158.

83. McCroskey et al., *An Introduction to Interpersonal Communication*, 170–71.

perceive the two as a couple, even if they are just roommates in a college dormitory, one begins to feel that the partner ought to ''recognize'' the coupleness, think as the other does, spend more time with him or her, and begin to make the relationship ''a higher priority'' than other interests or relationships.

The effect is even stronger when such a relationship is publicly legitimized. The marriage liturgy, either religious or civil, urges the couple to become one; and, indeed, there is a ''oneness'' in an integration as deep and close as marriage. However, a seductiveness about this phenomenon is that one or both members of the dyad may be tempted to try to force a personal definition of the relationship on the other person by designing a persuasive campaign to ''make us one like we used to be.'' As mentioned in chapter 8, even the desire for a harmonious relationship can engender conflict as each tries to convince the other that his or her own idea of harmony is better than the other person's idea of harmony. When ''oneness'' is the only perception either or both members of the marriage dyad have, then undue and unhealthy attempts at control can result. One person, the controller, begins to determine all of the outcomes of the couple's interaction. This ''ownership'' has a stifling effect on the marriage or on any other intimate dyadic relationship in which that phenomenon exists. In such a situation there is no freedom for the ''owned'' to grow and to respond to an ever-changing world. Or, the growth occurs but is not handled in small, manageable increments; so the relationship is damaged or destroyed when it is finally forced to adapt to a large change which is nothing more than the sum of many little changes which had not been previously adapted to.

We do want to emphasize that observing principles of communication so as to communicate smoothly and effectively does not of itself guarantee a satisfactory long-term dyadic interpersonal relationship. It may mean only that two persons agree to disagree easily, smoothly, and clearly — that each member of the dyad has his or her own identity, goals, values, needs, and the like. Genuine incompatibility in these areas cannot be compensated for by more ''talk.'' Substantive differences must be resolved as they relate directly to the specific dyadic relationship, or the relationship will have no reason to exist. Our ability to negotiate and maintain a balance between stability and change, between ''oneness'' and ''separateness'' in our relationship is very important.

A Harmonious Balance

When our needs are satisfactorily met in the areas just identified, we have an effective dyadic relationship. Rather than acting independently or in conflict, we interact compatibly as a smoothly working social system and enjoy a satisfying dyadic relationship. It may take some time to establish this state. Once it has been established, we will meet any attempt to deviate from it with com-

84. Argyle, *Social Interaction*, 203.

munication which will restore it to normal.[84] We have discussed how individuals can use effective listening, responding, and negotiating behaviors (recall chapters 7 and 8) to become more effective in establishing and maintaining a harmonious balance in their relationships.

It should be apparent during the formative stage of a dyadic relationship whether or not two people can develop a harmonious balance that will provide a mutually satisfying relationship. Often, however, it is not. As we discussed in chapter 3, and elsewhere, much of our early relationships with others is based on our pleasing but "false" masks. That is why many of our relationships do not seem to fulfill our expectations — we based these expectations on early, superficial interactions with the other person. If we continue to fail to disclose our expectations to our partner, we will not be able to achieve a harmonious state with the other person.

If, however, we work out our roles and relationships satisfactorily over a period of time, then we can maintain the relationship by maintaining the balanced reciprocal behavior by which each of us responds to the needs of the other so that the needs of both are met. When harmonious, mutually agreed-on, and mutually satisfying interaction occurs relative to affection or intimacy, control, inclusion, change, separateness, and all our other needs, then relationships are maintained.

Summary

We spend more time in dyadic communication than in groups. Such two-person communication is the foundation of other interpersonal communication. We explain why examining the communication of individuals will not explain dyadic interaction. Communication changes and fulfills different functions during the successive stages of a dyadic relationship: the initiation of a relationship; the acquaintance process; the formation of a stabilized relationship; and the termination of a relationship.

The importance of establishing equilibrium, or states of harmony, for maintaining relationships is explained. Two criteria — the comparison level and distributive justice — affect how satisfactory we will judge any equilibrium to be for us as a member of a relationship. Six rewards which we can exchange in a relationship were described. The four areas in which equilibrium must be established are: appropriate responsiveness; dominance or control; affection, attraction, intimacy, and trust; and change and separateness. The factors which determine what we consider to be an "appropriate" balance in a relationship were explained. The development of a harmonious balance in these four areas as the foundation of satisfactory interpersonal relationships is stressed.

10

Small Group Communication

---

1. To be able to identify the important characteristics that define a small group.
2. To be able to discriminate between tasks that are more effectively performed through small group communication and those that are more effectively performed by an individual.
3. To be able to explain the four communication phases that consistently occur in problem-solving groups.
4. To be able to discuss the factors that affect conformity in small groups.
5. To be able to explain the role of the deviate in the small group and the group's response to the deviate.
6. To be able to explain why groups often make riskier decisions than do individuals.
7. To be able to discuss the role of small group communication as a technique for persuading people to support decisions.
8. To be able to discuss the effects of status and leadership on communication patterns in groups.
9. To be able to explain the relationship of small group communication networks to individual satisfaction and group efficiency.
10. To be able to discuss the "leader" in small group communication.

Objectives for the Reader

Americans like to form committees. We have committees to plan picnics, dances, automobiles, and even committees to investigate committees. We like to work on problems in small groups.

With so many small groups about us at work, in government, at church, and at school, it must be apparent that understanding how communication functions in small groups is necessary if we are to operate effectively at work and at play.

What are the characteristics of a leader, and how does a person assume leadership in a small group? Are decisions made by small groups as good as decisions made by individuals? Can an individual working alone solve a problem better than a group of people working on it together? Are several heads better than one, or do too many cooks spoil the broth? What is the effect on an individual of being in a small group? Does the small group cause us to be less or more conservative? All of these are legitimate questions about small group communication. We answer some in this chapter and point out directions of thought regarding others.

Communication in a small group context has probably been studied as extensively as almost any other communication phenomenon. As far back as the 1940s there was intense interest in what was then called "group dynamics."[1] The concern was with making people into better group participants and with what made a good leader. Countless studies investigated correlations between personality and leadership. Subsequent empirical research has focused on small group behavior, ranging from leadership to seating arrangements to conformity behavior to group cohesiveness. Interest in the small group as such has become so great that today we can find dozens of texts on small group behavior in several different fields — communication, education, political science, psychology, and sociology.

THE NATURE OF SMALL GROUP COMMUNICATION

Before we can discuss small group communication it is necessary to explain what we mean by *small group* in this context. Small groups can be a three-person committee, a family, a jury in a court trial, or a group of five people planning a party. Just as those examples obviously seem to be small groups, it is equally obvious that the U.S. Senate, the United Nations General Assembly, the Republican or Democratic national conventions, and all the people at any given moment in Times Square in New York City are not examples of small groups.

While the primary characteristic that differentiates small groups from other groups of people is not size, most small groups range in size from three members to twenty.[2] Groups of two, dyads, are covered separately in chapter 9. In this chapter we operationally define **small group communication** as *including from three to twenty people who can interact with one another face-to-face, who are not inhibited from interacting because of group size, and who share some need or needs that can be satisfied through participation in the group's activities.* Actually, this definition of small group communication is an outgrowth of the definition of interpersonal communication in chapter 1. There

1. Fred L. Strodtbeck, "Communication in Small Groups," in Ithiel de Sola Pool et al., eds., *Handbook of Communication* (Chicago: Rand McNally, 1973), 658–60.

2. Michael Burgoon, Judee K. Heston, and James McCroskey, *Small Group Communication: A Functional Approach* (New York: Holt, Rinehart & Winston, 1974), 2–3; Marvin E. Shaw, *Group Dynamics* (New York: McGraw-Hill, 1971), 4.

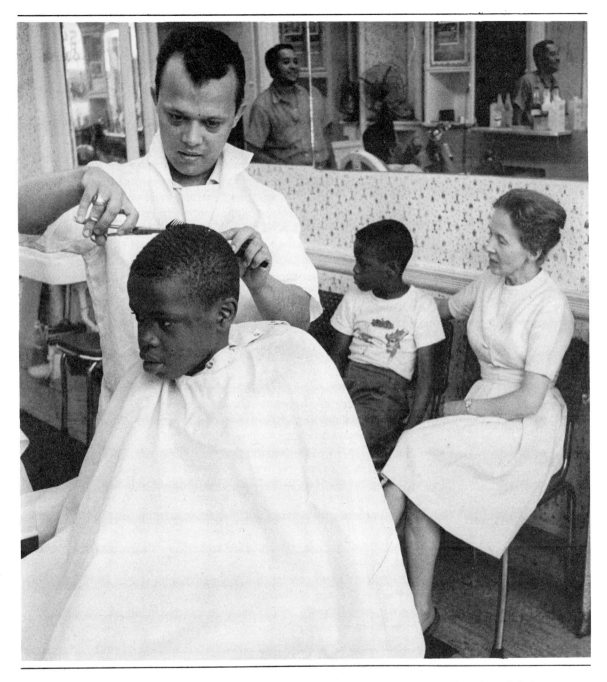

Several people in the same room do not necessarily constitute a ``small group.''

we defined interpersonal communication as a process in which individuals attempt to influence one another through the use of a common symbol system in a situation that permits equal opportunity for all persons involved in the process to influence one another.

The people at any given moment in Times Square are surely too numerous to interact with one another face-to-face, each having an equal interaction opportunity uninhibited by the size of the group. In addition, they do not share a need or needs that can be satisfied by their interacting in the group. If we consider a group of five people planning a party, we begin to see that the characteristics of a small group are evident. Five people are few enough to permit free interaction in an uninhibited manner. And people who have volunteered to be on a committee to plan a party — the group's common goal — probably have social or ego needs that planning the party can satisfy.

Much research has examined communication in groups, especially groups of two to six people. However, enough research has been done with groups larger than that to warrant the range used in our definition of a small group.[3] Robert Ardrey speculated that eleven or twelve may be some sort of "natural size" for a group.[4] Alex Osborn, in his *Applied Imagination,* suggested that the ideal size for a brainstorming group is about twelve.[5] These suggestions indicate that "ideal group size" is greater than has usually been studied in experimental situations. However, once there are additional people in a group, size itself begins to inhibit contributions from members of the group.[6] Within a specified amount of time, as the number of people within a group increases, the opportunity for talking decreases, because the amount of time available for discussion must be shared by more persons. Our own experience in the course of teaching has been that when class size gets beyond fifteen or twenty people, the character of interaction of teacher and students changes significantly. Somewhere in that fuzzy range of fifteen to twenty members, groups cease being small groups and begin to take on the characteristics of a public communication situation in which one person is predominantly in charge of talking to other people.[7]

So it is apparent that number of people is a limiting but not the primary distinguishing characteristic of small groups. Setting the range for small groups from three to twenty is more related to equal opportunity for all group members to influence one another.[8] Although it is not the identifying characteristic, size is nevertheless fairly consistently within that range because as groups surpass this range the size itself inhibits interaction. This can then prevent group members from reciprocally influencing one another and satisfying shared needs.

Probably more important than size of the group is a *commonality of goals of the members*[9] — that they have needs in common that can be satisfied through membership and participation in the group. We cannot stress this too much. When members of clubs and organizations find they no longer want to attend meetings and participate in activities, the group probably no longer

3. Edwin J. Thomas and Clinton F. Fink, "Effects of Group Size," *Psychological Bulletin* 60(1963):371–84.

4. Robert Ardrey, *The Social Contract* (New York: Atheneum, 1970), 368.

5. Alex Osborn, *Applied Imagination* (New York: Charles Scribner's Sons, 1957), 234.

6. L. Richard Hoffman, "Group Problem Solving," in Leonard Berkowitz, ed., *Advances in Experimental Social Psychology* (New York: Academic Press, 1965), 107.

7. Burgoon, Heston, and McCroskey, *Small Group Communication* 2–3; Shaw, *Group Dynamics,* 4.

8. B. Aubrey Fisher, *Small Group Decision Making: Communication and the Group Process* (New York: McGraw-Hill, 1974), 16–24; Gerald M. Philips and Eugene C. Erickson, *Interpersonal Dynamics in the Small Group* (New York: Random House, 1970), 171–74.

9. Philips and Erickson, *Interpersonal Dynamics,* 40.

satisfies the needs of those people. Then the group begins to disintegrate, since it no longer has a reason for survival. Participating in the group goal no longer satisfies the various needs of individuals in the group.

Effectiveness of Small Group Communication

How effective is the small group? Have you ever had the feeling that you might have been able to solve a problem better by yourself than did a committee that attempted to solve it? That question has been examined in several experiments. The conclusions are that it depends on the kind of task to be accomplished. Generally speaking, tasks that are somewhat repetitive or mechanical are better handled by individuals than by groups.[10] For example, it makes very little sense to have a committee formed within an organization to make regular purchases of paper supplies.

What seems best suited to group work is a task of some degree of complexity and/or a problem that requires creativity for solution.[11] It is true that sometimes an extremely bright, capable, and creative individual can produce a better solution than can a group of average individuals working together; however, since an extremely bright, creative person is not always available, the probabilities of solving complex tasks and problems demanding creativity are greater when handled by a group than by an individual, providing certain conditions are met.

First, the problem must be dividable in some way[12] so the labor can be divided among the various members of the group. It should be possible for one person to gather information about one aspect of the problem, another person to gather information about another aspect, and so on. The group should be able to make maximum use of the total resources available to it.

Second, there should be an atmosphere of acceptance within the group so as to encourage free and uninhibited contributions by all members.[13] This is especially true when solutions are being suggested. All members should feel free to contribute whatever ideas they have without fear of criticism from other members of the group. If this is possible, more ideas relevant to solving the problem can be elicited. Therein lies the advantage of several heads being better than one, for out of several different heads a good solution to the problem is more likely to come. Also, if members of the group are aware of effective small group behavior, they may be able to build on ideas, synthesize ideas from different persons, and thus produce a group solution superior to any that could be offered by any one individual.

Finally, problems that require recall of information seem particularly well suited to small groups rather than to individuals.[14] With more people in a group, there is a greater probability that a given piece of information will be recalled by at least one group member. Also, the total information remembered by a group will be more than any one individual will recall.

10. J. Tuckman and I. Lorge, "Individual Ability as a Determinant of Group Superiority," *Human Relations* 15(1962):45–51; R. W. Husband, "Cooperative Very Solitary Problem Solution," *Journal of Social Psychology* 11(1940): 405–9; and Fisher, *Small Group Decision Making* 39–42.

11. Ibid.

12. Barry E. Collins and Harold Guetzkow, *A Social Psychology of Group Processes for Decision-Making* (New York: John Wiley & Sons, 1964), 18–27.

13. Osborn, *Applied Imagination*, 84.

14. R. A. Hoppe, "Memorizing By Individuals and Groups: A Test of the Pooling-of-ability Model," *Journal of Abnormal and Social Psychology* 65(1962):64–71.

15. J. H. Davis and F. Restle, "The Analysis of Problems and Prediction of Group Problem Solving," *Journal of Abnormal and Social Psychology* 66(1963):103–16; D. W. Taylor and W. L. Faust, "Twenty Questions: Efficiency in Problem Solving as a Function of Size of Group," *Journal of Experimental Psychology* 44(1952):360–68.

One possibly negative aspect of small group effectiveness in problem-solving situations is the total time taken whenever a group interacts.[15] If one person alone can solve a problem in one hour and five persons can solve the problem in a half-hour, it may appear that the small group is better than the individual because the group takes less time. However, if we put a per-"man-hour" value on the time, the small group would cost more in the situation just described because it used two and a half hours and the individual only one hour. In other words, what is the "best" way of solving a problem at any given time may have to be defined in relation to cost instead of or in addition to time — and perhaps even other factors. This is a very real consideration that we should keep in mind at all times, especially in our jobs.

If small groups are not a suitable tool to tackle some problems, and if they use a large number of total hours, then why do so many organizations turn to small groups for solutions to problems? The answer to this question must go beyond the suitability of tasks and the cost-effectiveness of small groups. We must examine the effects of small groups on the individual. And to do that we must first understand patterns of interaction in small groups.

INTERACTION IN SMALL GROUPS

Many students are disturbed at attempts made to classify them and to generalize about their behavior. We have often heard students complain in class, "But I am not at all that way," "I do not at all act that way," and "I am different." It is true that individuals deviate from some of the patterns that have been observed in empirical research; however, the similarity of how most individuals behave is striking. Among these striking consistencies that have been observed over time are the phases of interaction of small groups. Different observers have labeled these phases differently, but the consistencies of the observations become apparent as we consider them.

Interaction Phases—a Description

16. Lawrence B. Rosenfeld, *Human Interaction in the Small Group Setting* (Columbus, Ohio: Charles E. Merrill Publishing Co., 1973), 39–62; T. M. Mills, *The Sociology of Small Groups* (Englewood Cliffs, N.J.: Prentice-Hall, 1967); B. W. Tuckman, "Developmental Sequence in Small Groups," *Psychological Bulletin* 63(1965):384–99.

17. B. Aubrey Fisher, "Decision Emergence: Phase in Group Decision-Making," *Speech Monographs* 37(1970):53–66.

Since the phases of small group interaction have been covered by other writers,[16] we will focus on the four main phases that crop up consistently within the many different studies that have been conducted. Fisher[17] labeled the four phases *orientation, conflict, emergence,* and *reinforcement.* We will use his terminology.

In the first phase, **orientation,** group members try to get to know one another, feel one another out, discover roles and status, and get to know the lay of the land, so to speak. They become oriented toward one another and the problem that faces the group.

During the second phase, **conflict,** there are increasing instances of disagreement among group members and a tendency to maintain positions indicating disagreement. There is a mounting atmosphere of polarization and controversy.

In contrast to the negative comments and behaviors in the conflict phase, there is a greater tendency toward positive, favorable comments and interpretation in the third phase, **emergence.** Group members use more ambiguous language and make more ambiguous statements to indicate disagreement without appearing quite so disagreeable in phase three. Comments are made that indicate a more favorable attitude toward the position that is emerging from within the group. This phase serves an important function for group members who have opposed the group's decision. It enables them to make their position more ambiguous and to become one of the group again. It is important that members in the majority allow minority members to "save face" during this phase.

The fourth phase, **reinforcement,** is readily apparent to anyone who has ever participated in a group decision. During reinforcement everyone makes comments about how well the group worked together and how good a solution was reached. Essentially, people say things that they feel reinforces the decision and the decision-making process. Statements are made that are very positive and that enable people to view the decision, the decision-making process, and themselves positively.

This last phase is probably an example of dissonance reduction. Recall the discussion in chapter 1 of our need for consistency. Phase four is an excellent example of this need. Typically, if we have been through an arduous decision-making situation that involved conflict and took up our time, it is probably important for us to perceive that experience positively. To think that we may have wasted our time is inconsistent with that need. Thus, during the reinforcement phase we spend much time telling ourselves and others what a good job we did. Whatever mental pain or time loss we experienced is at least justified or rationalized in our minds.

These stages of interaction are primarily related to problem-solving groups. However, most groups, whether they be problem-solving groups or not, very likely go through similar stages. These phases probably are not peculiar to problem-solving groups but could be expected in a group of any kind.

By paying close attention to the kinds of comments being made by people in small group communication, it is possible to determine the stage a group is in and to use that knowledge to guide one's own comments and behavior. If we begin to perceive that a group has gone into the emergence stage, we should adapt to that and not continue conflict behavior lest we be rejected by the group as deviates. This is, in essence, a suggestion that, when you are a member of a group, you try to proceed according to whatever stage the group is in. To use an older cliché, slightly modified, "When in conflict phase, conflict, but when in reinforcement phase, reinforce."

Keep in mind that these four phases are **descriptive** of how group members actually interact — that is, what normally happens in small groups. The description does not represent any kind of ideal **prescription** of how groups should try to interact.

Problem-Solving Phases—a Prescription

We are now going to discuss a *prescriptive* approach to stages in small group problem solving. Our orientation changes from a consideration of what *does* happen in small group problem solving to what *should* happen.

The approach we consider is widely accepted by people who teach small group communication. It was originally developed by John Dewey as an attempt to prescribe an ideal set of steps for individual problem solving based on "the scientific method."[18] Writers in small group communication and discussion texts have employed the approach as an ideal set of steps that groups should go through to discuss and solve problems. There are six steps in Dewey's model:

1. *A felt need.* Before a problem can be solved, a difficulty, problem, or need must be expressed. For instance, in a fraternity or a sorority, if pledging has not been successful in past years, a committee may be formed called a membership committee. The "felt need" facing this small group is to increase the low membership and recruit more pledges. At this stage of problem solving, the group must be able to agree that there is a need. At this point the need is vague and generally stated and serves the function of providing the reason and motivation for group formation and effort.

2. *Problem definition.* Unfortunately, many groups are content to proceed from a vague awareness. Using Dewey's approach, however, the membership committee should proceed from the general statement of low membership to a more specifically defined problem. This could include anything from determining that the fraternity or sorority house looks shabby, to "we don't get out and meet people and ask them to join the group," or "our rush activities during rush week are too unorganized to give us credibility among potential pledges." In other words, during this stage of problem solving, the group must examine the general need in order to determine the *specific* reasons for it so they can move to the next step of the problem-solving sequence.

3. *Problem analysis.* It is necessary next to analyze the problem in terms of causes, history, component parts, and the like. The membership committee might focus on the appearance of the house. This could result in a statement that the sorority or fraternity lacks an approach to maintenance and cleaning, which results in the shabby appearance perceived by prospective pledges. Likewise, an analysis of why people do not get out to meet prospective pledges may result in a conclusion that members are shy. The analysis might also suggest that the type of social gathering organized to meet prospective pledges

18. J. Dewey, *How We Think* (Boston: D. C. Heath, 1910).

during rush week is not attractive to prospective pledges. Thus they do not come to the house, and the members do not have a chance to meet them. Whatever is decided during this step of problem solving, the group should try to explore all the possible causes of the problem as well as implications of the problem for the future. This kind of analytical approach can frequently be surprising to groups if they go through it conscientiously. It can result in previously unrecognized components of the problem being noticed.

4. *Solution proposals.* Having defined and analyzed the problem, the group members should propose solutions. During this stage of problem solving there should be no critical comments. People should be encouraged to suggest answers to the problem, no matter how bizarre they may seem. In our example, if someone suggests that the fraternity or sorority should have a party at which classical music is played and everyone dresses formally, it is not appropriate *during this step of problem solving* for another committee member to comment that nobody would come or that such a party would be dull. During this stage everyone on the committee should provide encouragement for people to give ideas, no matter how wild they may sound.

5. *Solution testing and comparison.* During this phase of problem solving the solutions are criticized and their practicality discussed. Different proposals are compared with one another so that the better alternatives can be selected from among all the solutions proposed in step 4. The previous suggestion regarding the classical music at a rush party might be torn to shreds by members who feel strongly that it would not work. It is also possible they might decide that it is a good idea. At this point solutions may be criticized on the basis of their cost, the time involved, the number of people required, available materials, and the like. It is also quite appropriate during this stage for ideas to be combined. It may well be that one part of idea A and one part of idea B are workable, and therefore the group may decide to combine the workable parts of ideas A and B and discard what are considered to be the unworkable parts.

6. *Solution/implementation.* The logical final step in the problem-solving sequence would seem to be that the solution/solutions to the problem is/are selected and put into action. Some people in public speaking have referred to this as an *action step.*

Although this sixth step concludes Dewey's model, it is our feeling that a seventh step should be added — an *evaluation process.* The group should meet after the solution to the problem has been implemented to evaluate its success or lack of it. But first the group should determine the criteria by which they will evaluate the solution. For instance, in the example discussed, the criterion might be the number of pledges actually recruited into the fraternity or sorority. Or the group might decide that in addition to the number, the quality of pledges is equally important. Whatever the criteria agreed on, the group should employ them in their evaluation of the success or failure of the group's solution. If the solution has been successful according to the group's standards, it should be continued into the future. On the other hand, if the group in our example decides that the rushing procedures did not work, as evaluated against the group's criteria, then they should go back to step one of the problem-solving process and begin all over again. The group cannot know for sure where they went wrong in trying to solve the problem and what caused their solution not to work unless they go back to the beginning in the problem-solving sequence. This is a circular process: groups solve problems, put solutions into effect, evaluate them, and then try to solve them all over again. It is a continuing process, but one based on the assumption that people can solve problems rationally.

Dewey's model has considerable appeal for many scholars. We have used the method in small group discussion courses and have found it to have great utility. It works. Groups that conscientiously and intelligently follow this model solve problems rather efficiently. It is important to follow the steps in this model in the order indicated, and also to keep in mind that there are other dynamics in any group process in addition to the problem-solving steps. As discussed shortly, group pressures and other factors also affect the outcome of problem solving in a group. It is not always possible to proceed through a group discussion in as orderly a fashion as this ideal model would suggest, but we present it with the hope that you will keep it in mind as you take part in problem-solving discussions. At the very least, you can strive for this ideal, fully realizing that it may never be completely attainable.

Group Influence

Conformity

It is exceedingly important to recognize how much influence a group has over us. Many of us have been with a group of people who were smoking and drinking. While with the group, because everyone else is smoking and drinking, we often find ourselves doing the same thing, even though we may never have smoked or drunk previously. This is the result of pressure for **conformity.** It is common for us to conform to group pressures.[19] For instance, it is not unusual to see a group of teenagers all dressing alike or wearing their hair the same way. Sometimes a group will go so far as to dictate the kind of socks members may have on their feet (or decree no socks). Group power to cause conformity is observable all around us in untold numbers of situations. It is important for us to understand how and why this happens and what conditions seem to cause greater conformity than others.

Some personality characteristics cause a person to be more conforming in behavior than do other characteristics. Rosenfeld suggests drawing the conclusion that personality affects conformity in the following ways:[20] When a person is somewhat submissive, or if a person's self-concept is low, he or she is more likely to conform to the wishes of a group. The higher a person's intelligence, the less likely he or she will conform to the wishes of the group.

19. R. S. Crutchfield, "Conformity and Character," *American Psychologist* 10(1955):191–98.

20. Rosenfeld, *Human Interaction,* 70.

We cannot totally change our personality, but we can be aware of how these personality characteristics affect our conforming behavior and, just as important, how they affect other people's tendency to conform.

These characteristics relate to some of the needs we discussed in chapter 1. For instance, if a person has very high social needs and these needs can be satisfied by the group, that person is more likely to conform to the group's wishes. Likewise, a person with great ego needs is very likely to conform to the group's wishes if the person perceives that the group can satisfy his or her ego needs. Furthermore, we would suggest this rule of thumb: the more the individual believes his or her needs can be satisfied through membership in a group, the more likely that person is to conform to the group's wishes. As a group becomes more important to you, the group's influence over you increases.[21] Of course, the reverse is true also.

Another factor that apparently increases the amount of conformity is the size of a group. As size increases up to about four people, conformity increases.[22] However, as the group increases beyond that size, there is a possibility for deviates from the group's norms to find support, and thus there

Friendship groups frequently cause us to conform, even in matters of dress.

21. J. N. Jackson and H. D. Saltzstein, "The Effect of Person-Group Relationships on Conformity Processes," *Journal of Abnormal and Social Psychology* 57(1958):17–24; E. J. Thomas, "Effects of Facilitative Role Interdependence on Group Functioning," *Human Relations* 10(1957):347–66.

22. S. E. Asch, "Effects of Group Pressure Upon the Modification and Distortion of Judgments," in Harold Guetzkow, ed., *Groups, Leadership, and Man* (Pittsburgh: Carnegie Press, 1951), 177–90.

23. H. Cantril, "The Invasion from Mars," in E. E. Maccoby and T. M. Newcomb, eds., *Readings in Social Psychology* (New York: Holt, Rinehart & Winston, 1958), 291–99.

will not be as much group conformity. Other factors that appear to increase conformity in groups are the existence of a crisis,[23] the perception by the group that a task is important, or the existence of competition. We are willing to conform to expedite matters. This tendency toward conformity for the sake of expediency may have been one of the factors that led to the Watergate cover-up during the administration of President Nixon. It may have been that a crisis atmosphere inhibited persons from taking positions deviant from the group. This, in turn, may have caused several people to conform to a position taken by the group although they were not wholly in agreement.

24. Jackson and Saltzstein, "The Effect of Person-Group Relations"; E. J. Thomas, "Effects of Facilitative Role Interdependence," in Collins and Guetzkow, eds., *A Social Psychology of Group Processes*, 143–45.

Perception of a common fate[24] also increases our tendency to conform. If we perceive that the rewards we are going to receive will depend on the result of a group decision as opposed to our own individual decision, we develop a greater tendency to go along with the group — toward conformity. As we perceive that we will all share in the same reward or punishment, we are more likely to accept whatever decisions and behaviors the group decides on. You have, no doubt, experienced this kind of occurrence in a class in which the teacher assigned group projects with the understanding that each group would receive one grade, and everyone in the group would receive that grade. As you perceived that everyone in the group was going to receive the same reward, or share a common fate, you were more likely to conform to the wishes of the group.

Conformity is a word that has negative connotations for many people. We do not like to hear someone say that we are likely to conform. It is important for us to recognize, however, that conformity serves an essential function within groups. Members of groups choose to share behavior patterns because it helps them satisfy their own needs. If people did not develop and conform to norms in groups, it would be almost impossible to predict behavior. Unpredictability would keep the group from functioning effectively as a group because members need to be able to predict what a fellow member is going to do. Try to imagine how groups would function if members could not predict one another's behavior. The more we can predict the behaviors of other members of the group, the more we are able to predict their responses to our messages.

Individual Deviation

25. Michael Argyle, *Social Interaction* (New York: Atherton Press, 1969), 226–27.

While it is true that the group has considerable power over individuals and that most of us tend to conform to group wishes, it is also true that groups do have deviates. A deviate is someone whose behavior is significantly different from that of most of the members of the group. This deviation serves at least three functions.[25] First, deviates frequently contribute new ideas that others of the group do not have. Second, when a deviate engages in behavior contrary to the norms of the group, that points up those norms, making them far more explicit. Third, the presence of deviates also makes apparent what happens to those who break the norms. The net outcome of a deviate's punishment, or of the norms being made more explicit, is probably that other members who are having their needs satisfied through membership in the group are likely to adhere to those norms more than ever.

Why does an individual become a deviate? Once we are members of a group, why should we want to become deviates and run the risk of being outcasts? There are four reasons we may become deviates.[26] First, we may simply be more influenced by norms of another group than by the norms of the group we are in. This may occur because another group is more likely to satisfy our needs (or at least we think it will). Second, it is possible that we may have personality characteristics that prevent us from accepting a norm. For example, there are some people whose personalities are extremely argumentative and aggressive and who, if placed in a group where the norm is one of nonconflict and compromise, may find it impossible to accept that norm. Third, a member of the group may think of something nobody else in the group has thought of, and this can turn him or her into a deviate. When this occurs, it is important for the individual first to make himself or herself a valuable member of the group and then try to persuade the group to accept the new idea or point of view. Otherwise the person will simply remain a deviate in the eyes of the members. The fourth reason a person will sometimes deviate within a group is simply for the purpose of challenging the leader. No doubt you have experienced a situation in which you watched someone challenge the ideas, evidence, or facts a leader was proposing when seemingly there was no good reason for the challenge. If you examined this phenomenon closely, you may have observed that what was being challenged was not really the ideas being expressed but rather the position of leadership occupied by the leader. Sometimes it is possible to challenge leadership through taking a deviate position.

What happens to the person who deviates? The first response of a group to a deviate is to increase the amount of communication directed toward that person.[27] Group members attempt to persuade the person to adopt the norms of the group and "come back into the fold." If this does not work, the group cuts off communication with the deviate. The person is literally isolated from the group's communication. The third and most extreme response occurs when the deviate is radical in his or her view and the group is totally unable to change the person back to the norms — it is to expel the deviate,[28] physically rejecting the person and not allowing him or her to be in the group at all. This possibility is what has necessitated clauses in fraternity charters explaining how members can be expelled from the brotherhood. Likewise, some churches have procedures for expelling deviates from the fold.

26. Ibid.

27. S. Schachter, "Deviation, Rejection and Communication," *Journal of Abnormal and Social Psychology* 46(1951):190–207.

28. Collins and Guetzkow, *A Social Psychology of Group Processes*, 180–82.

The Risky Shift

29. Kenneth L. Dion, Robert S. Baron, and Norman Miller, "Why do Groups Make Riskier Decisions than Individuals?" in Leonard Berkowitz, ed., *Advances in Experimental Social Psychology* (New York: Academic Press, 1970), 305–11.

Another effect of the group on the individual is the **risky shift** phenomenon: an individual becomes more radical as a result of being in a group.[29] It is not unusual for individuals who would develop a conservative solution to a problem when working alone to become radical with their solutions and more willing to take risks while part of a group. Groups seem to produce more risky solutions to problems than individuals do. Almost a "mob psychology" begins to occur, even though within a small group. We have often observed faculty as well as student groups adopting actions that later perplexed the individual members of the groups because they were so radical or "off the wall." You have probably experienced similar events yourself.

30. M. A. Wallach, N. Kogan, and D. J. Bern, "Diffusion of Responsibility and Level of Risk Taking in Groups," *Journal of Abnormal and Social Psychology* 68(1964):263–74.

There are several suggestions why this is so. First, there apparently is a *diffusion of responsibility* in a group.[30] If you are working alone to solve a problem, you personally take full responsibility for the solution you suggest. However, if you are part of a five-member committee, the solution produced by the committee is only partly your responsibility. As professors, we have frequently observed that students in a class who know they are going to be called on are usually prepared, since they know they are going to have to confront the teacher on a one-to-one basis. However, if the entire class is going to discuss a reading, it is not unusual for some students to skip the reading. We believe this to be a good example of diffusion of responsibility. When the entire group is involved, everyone is more willing to take a risk because the responsibility for having read the material is diffused over more people. On a one-to-one basis, the individual feels full responsibility and is less willing to take risks.

31. Roger Brown, *Social Psychology* (New York: Free Press, 1965), 698–70.

32. Y. Rim, "Machiavellianism and Decisions Involving Risk," *British Journal of Social and Clinical Psychology* 5(1966):30–36.

33. M. A. Wallach and J. Marli, "Information Versus Conformity in the Effects of Group Discussion on Risk Taking," *Journal of Personality and Social Psychology* 14(1970): 149–56; E. Burnstein and A. Vinokur, "Testing Two Classes of Theories about Group-Induced Shifts in Individual Choice," *Journal of Experimental Social Psychology* 9(1973):123–37.

Second, it has also been suggested that *people take greater risks in groups because that is a norm in our society.*[31] This explanation is based on the assumption that in our society a conservative individual is not as valued as a risk-taking individual. Because they are more highly valued, the risk-takers have more influence on the group than do the more conservative members. Third, a *more risky position is a more dramatic position,* more exciting, and easier to present in a graphic manner. Fourth, *risk-oriented members are more extroverted,* which may enable them to interact more effectively.[32] It is apparent that the group can cause both conformity and risk-taking in individuals.

Finally, during group discussions the more conservative members become aware of their position relative to others in the group. As they discover that others in the group are more risk-taking, they too may become more risk-taking. This information function of the group contributes to the risky shift. Both information regarding the position of others and the arguments supporting those positions influence people to become more risk-taking.[33]

Support for Decision

A fourth influence of a group is that individual members accept more readily a decision if they have taken part in the group discussion leading to it. For example, if a person hears a lecture or receives an order to do a particular thing, there is frequently a tendency to resist doing what is asked. However, if the same person participates in a group discussion about the same topic and the group reaches the same decision as that advocated in the lecture or in the order, the person is more likely to accept and act on that position, inasmuch as it is based on a group decision he or she took part in.[34] This probably is one of the reasons classroom teaching has changed so much in recent years in colleges and universities. The classroom lecture used to be the primary mode of presentation of material for students. Today it is much more common for the professor to sit down and discuss the material with the students. Students generally reach the same conclusions whether the teacher is presenting the material in a lecture or in classroom discussion (sometimes teachers guide these discussions in a rather heavy-handed manner to have the students reach the desired conclusions). The reason for this change in teaching procedure is an awareness on the part of many college professors that students are more likely to accept the material if they themselves participated in a discussion of it and if they arrived at the conclusions themselves rather than received them through a lecture.

The use of the small group as a persuasive device was recognized by the late President John F. Kennedy in some of his political campaigns. During his congressional campaigns Kennedy organized, with the aid of his family (and especially the women of his family), a number of "teas." These tea-and-cookie hours took place in the homes of private citizens throughout his state of Massachusetts. The objective was to get people in the neighborhood to come together and participate in small group discussions about the candidate and to meet the candidate. By doing these things, the people participating became publicly committed to the candidate and, of course, were more likely to support the group's conclusion that the candidate was the person to vote for. This was far more effective than a series of speeches or television advertisements in which the candidate told them they should vote for him. Many other candidates have since followed Kennedy's example in such effective use of small group communication.

Small groups are frequently used for problem solving for the same reason, even when they may be less efficient than an individual making the decision alone and then communicating it to other people. If employees take part in a decision through small group discussion, they are likely to support the decision with far greater enthusiasm than if the same conclusion was reached otherwise and passed on to them through an order. True, small group communication may not be the most efficient means of problem solving in terms of hours expended, yet it may nevertheless prove more effective because it results in greater acceptance of decisions reached.

34. J. R. P. French, Jr., I. C. Ross, S. Kirby, J. R. Nelson, and P. Smith, "Employee Participation in a Program of Industrial Change," *Personnel* 35(1958):16–29.

Communication Patterns

Whenever you have been in a small group discussion, you have probably noticed that everyone in the group does not spend the same amount of time talking. Some talk more than others. You may also have noticed that these differences follow fairly predictable patterns. For example, messages flow according to the status, or power, held by individual group members: high-status and high-power individuals initiating more messages than low-status and low-power persons.[35] Likewise, once power and status are well established within a group, group members direct more of their messages toward the person or persons with high power and high status.[36] One of the high-power/high-status persons acts as the ``hub'' of the small group, giving and receiving more messages than anyone else in the group.

The pattern just described is true primarily after the power structure of the group has been developed. Before the power structure is established, it is more common for people who aspire to high status/power to direct more of their messages to potentially low-status persons than to other aspiring high-status persons. Group members who aspire to high status see the potentially low-status members as people on whom they can build their power base. They therefore direct many of their messages toward these individuals in a bid to develop support for their desired high status/power.

One of the results of differences in status and power within the small groups is demonstrated by **communication networks** — the pattern of message flow among the members — that form within such groups. After a group has functioned for a while, a specific pattern evolves in which certain members repeatedly talk with one another, thus forming a ``network.'' Of importance in communication networks within small groups is the factor of **centrality.** This is the degree to which a small group is more or less centralized in its message flow and decision making. As a small group is more centralized, the communication pattern is one in which messages are funneled primarily to one or possibly two people with high status/power and then emanate from the same one or two people.[37] Also, the decisions tend to be made by the same one or two people who are central to the communication patterns of the group.

Studies that have created these communication networks artificially include the classic studies of Leavitt[38] and Bavelas,[39] which established that the *more decentralized communication networks are faster whenever complex problems are being solved. For less complex problems the centralized networks are more efficient.* The relative efficiency of networks is, thus, dependent on the complexity of the problem to be solved. As problems are more simple, solutions are reached faster and with fewer errors in centralized communication networks.[40] As problems become more complex, the decentralized networks are more efficient and the problems are solved faster with fewer errors. Whether the problems are complex or simple, however, centralized networks bring about solutions with the fewest messages.

35. Collins and Guetzkow, *A Social Psychology of Group Processes,* 170–77.

36. Ibid.

37. Marvin E. Shaw, ``Communication Networks,'' in Leonard Berkowitz, ed., *Advances in Experimental Social Psychology,* vol. 1 (New York: Academic Press, 1964), 111–47.

38. H. J. Leavitt, ``Some Effects of Certain Communication Patterns on Group Performance,'' *Journal of Abnormal and Social Psychology* 465(1951):38–50.

39. Alex Bavelas,``Communication Patterns in Task-oriented Groups,'' *Journal of the Acoustical Society of America* 22(1950):725–30.

40. Shaw, ``Communication Networks,'' 122–24.

The degree of member satisfaction present within both the decentralized and the centralized networks is also important. Members of small groups with decentralized communication networks experience greater satisfaction from their participation in the small groups.[41] In the centralized network the position of the individual within that network greatly affects satisfaction. As we occupy a more central role (a position through which more messages are directed and from which more decisions flow), we experience a higher degree of satisfaction. On the other hand, the more peripheral positions within any communication network, whether centralized or decentralized, cause and reflect greater member dissatisfaction.

41. Leavitt, "Some Effects of Certain Communication Patterns," 38–50.

Leadership

Researchers in the area of small group communication have paid a great deal of attention to the subject of leadership. Perhaps this is so because many people are intensely concerned with obtaining leadership positions and being leaders. Whatever the reason, the results of research on leadership have been very mixed. Early attempts to examine the subject through empirical research were directed toward determining the personality factors that caused leadership. Just about everything anyone could think of was correlated with leadership. The one conclusion we can safely draw from this research is that it is impossible to say with any certainty which particular personality characteristics lead to leadership positions within small groups.[42] At one time it was suggested that honest, trustworthy persons are good leaders. Research has indicated that this is not necessarily so.

42. Fisher, Small Group Decision Making, 74–76.

A communication-based factor that results in a person being chosen as leader is the *quantity* of verbal interaction of that person.[43] The more a group member interacts verbally, the greater the likelihood that he or she will be chosen as leader of the group. In groups that exist for a short time, the quality of verbal interaction is probably not as important as the quantity, although this may not be true of groups that function over longer time periods. People who interact a lot are perceived as having greater motivation and interest in the group. This perception often leads to their selection as group leaders. The quantity of verbal interaction is not the only factor related to leadership, however.

43. R. M. Sorrentino and R. G. Boutilier, "The Effect of Quantity and Quality of Verbal Interaction on Ratings of Leadership Ability," Journal of Experimental Social Psychology 11(1975):403–11.

The factor most closely associated with leadership is the situation itself. The demands of a group's task, along with the needs of the group and its members, dictate the kind of person who will be chosen as a leader for that group.[44] The person who evolves as a leader in a street gang in a large city is not likely to become the leader of an academic department in a university. The personality characteristics and personal qualities demanded in each of those two situations are poles apart: whereas honesty may be demanded of the person

44. Shaw, Group Dynamics, 278.

chosen to lead a university academic department, dishonesty may be a highly valued characteristic for a person who is going to lead an urban street gang — the leader of a street gang may be the person who can steal the most cars.

The most effective leadership provided by an individual is that which grows out of the situation itself.[45] If the situation calls for aggressiveness, then an aggressive person will be the most effective leader. If a situation calls for patience and calm, a person who is patient and calm will be the most effective leader. This approach to leadership suggests that at any given time any member within a group may be a potential leader, depending on the demands of the situation. This is not to say that all members of a group will become leaders. Rather, it suggests that no qualities we know of will absolutely guarantee effective leadership for all situations. In fact, short courses and mail-order classes that purport to teach you how to be a leader and focus on the development of certain qualities in an individual are undoubtedly misleading at best.

The primary prerequisites for effective leadership — if any can be stated — would probably be *intelligence and sensitivity to the needs of the group*. For a person to be able to cope with the many tasks that confront a leader, intelligence (not necessarily super intelligence) is probably a necessity. Sensitivity is necessary for enabling the individual to perceive the needs of the group and know how to respond to them. It would be nice if we could unequivocally name the qualities that will make a person into a leader. Unfortunately, that does not seem to be possible. The situation will determine the qualities necessary, and since there are any number of situations facing groups, it is apparent that we cannot list qualities that will be appropriate to each and every situation.

Intelligence and sensitivity as such are probably related to two kinds of leadership roles that have been discovered through empirical studies. These are the *task and social-emotional leadership roles*.[46] Groups have both task needs and social-emotional needs. The task needs of a group are those which are related to a problem external to the group. A task leader would have special qualifications for fulfilling the task needs of the group.

The social-emotional leader is someone who can respond to the interpersonal needs internal to the group. Within every group there are personality conflicts and behaviors of members that interfere with the interaction of the group. It helps to have someone who can be a social-emotional specialist in the group. This person can help "pour oil over troubled waters" and help group members work together despite their differences. This person is what we might call a *people specialist* or a *people leader* as opposed to a task leader, although the terminology most commonly used is *social-emotional leader*. This person coordinates and facilitates the efforts of the other members of the group, despite the fact that he or she may not have much expertise in the area relating to the group's task. The social-emotional leader stimulates the members of the group and urges them to get along and work together so that they can make use of the task expertise in their midst.

45. Fred E. Fiedler, *A Theory of Leadership Effectiveness* (New York: McGraw-Hill, 1967), 133–80.

46. Collins and Guetzkow, *A Social Psychology of Group Processes*, 210–22.

Probably the best example of a person with whom we are all familiar who is more a social-emotional leader than a task leader is the president of the United States, though to be sure he is not leader of a small group. Most often, people of the United States elect someone as president who is a social-emotional leader. The reason for this is obvious: there are so many different kinds of tasks facing a president at any given time that it is impossible to elect someone to that office who qualifies as an expert in all of the task areas that will confront the White House. Electing someone who is an expert in economic affairs may be fine as long as the president is dealing only with economic affairs. Unfortunately, the president also has to deal with military problems, foreign relations, and ecological problems. All of these demand task expertise of many different sorts, far too many for any one individual to possess. Therefore, we tend to elect as president a person who is able to manipulate and work with people — a person who has the social-emotional expertise that facilitates the finding of task experts for each individual problem facing the coun-

Teachers can be thought of as both task leaders and social-emotional leaders. Their role varies with the situation.

try. Then the president can coordinate the efforts of all these people, thus enabling them to work together, just as a social-emotional leader would do in a small group. It seems to us that this is the mark of a good administrative leader: a person who can help other people work together.

It is important to point out that the task leader and the social-emotional leader can be one and the same person in a group. It is possible for one individual to have expertise in both areas. It is not unusual, however, to find that if the formally designated leader of a small group is a task leader, there will be an "informal leader" in the group who is a social-emotional leader — and vice versa. Thus, in many groups we find two leaders, one of them formally, the other informally fulfilling the group needs.

One final comment regarding leadership has to do with whether a leader actually leads or follows. It is our impression that leaders never really lead their groups but instead manage to be a mere half step ahead of them at best. From our earlier discussion of needs, it should be obvious that people do not knowingly do something contrary to their own needs. The person who is chosen as a leader, and the person who is most effective as leader, is someone who responds to the needs of the group. A would-be "leader" takes positions and says things that are acceptable to the group, as a result of which the group members perceive that that person should lead them where they want to go. Historians have long debated whether great persons make great events happen or whether events make the person great. Implications of our discussion here would be that there really is no such thing as a leader who causes a small group to go off in a direction the group does not wish to go inasmuch as people cannot accept a position they are not prepared to accept.[47] Rather, the likelihood is that the leader is simply someone who is sensitive to the group and is willing to go in the direction the group is ready to go, and who simply coordinates and helps its members toward a goal they already have.

47. Carolyn W. Sherif, Muzater Sherif, and Roger E. Nebergall, *Attitude and Attitude Change* (Philadelphia: W. B. Saunders Company, 1965), 18–59.

WHERE SMALL GROUPS OCCUR

Up to this point our discussion of principles of communication behavior in small groups has been largely theoretical and to a certain extent abstract. One of the questions that might be running through your mind at this point is: "That's all well and good, but how often is this going to affect me and be of importance to me? When am I going to be in a small group and have to know about these principles of small group communication?" To which we reply that there are at least three different small groups in which you are likely to participate and communicate: the family, work groups, and friendship groups.

The Family

The family is the first small group one is a part of. Small group characteristics of the family are easily observable. Its size is usually within the range we suggested as appropriate for a small group. The influence on its members is so strong that probably the best criterion for predicting someone's political or religious philosophy is the political or religious philosophy of that person's family.[48] In other words, group influence is significant in the family.

It is also apparent that the family has a division of leadership roles very comparable to those discussed earlier. The task role in American society is usually filled by the father, who most often earns money for the family and makes the task decisions regarding houses, money, and cars.[49] The social-emotional leadership role is most often filled by the mother. She is concerned about the children — when they are ill, when tempers flare, when feelings are hurt — and looks after the social relationships within the family and even those with other small groups. We should add that these leadership roles have been undergoing considerable change in recent years in America. Fathers are beginning to respond to the social-emotional needs of families to a greater extent, while mothers are also acting in response to the task needs of the family. The family in this country may be evolving into a group in which two leaders share both leadership roles.

One might expect that communication patterns of small groups would have effects on members of the family similar to the effects they have on other small groups. The highly centralized communication pattern in which the leadership is autocratic would, as in earlier times, very likely be the most efficient yet would probably produce the least member satisfaction. If the family were to become more centralized in its communication patterns, those not in authority would very likely experience dissatisfaction. On the other hand, a decentralized pattern within the family would very likely produce a great deal of satisfaction for members of the family. Inclusion in discussion of affairs and decision making for the family would probably be satisfying for all members of the family.

Work Groups

Work groups are another kind of small group that most of us find ourselves part of. We have been discussing, up to this point, the problem-solving group primarily because it has been the focal point for most of the research in small group communication, and also because it is the kind of work group with which the majority of us have most frequent contact. Whether at work or in a club (or even sometimes in the family), we find ourselves engaged in problem-solving situations with three or four other people. This is a common occurrence, and all of the principles we have discussed up to this point are certainly applicable.

48. Theodore M. Newcomb, "Attitude Development as a Function of Reference Groups: The Bennington Study," in Eleanor E. Maccoby, Theodore M. Newcomb, and Eugene L. Hartley, eds., *Readings in Social Psychology,* 3d ed. (New York: Holt, Rinehart & Winston, 1958), 265–75.

49. T. Parsons and R. F. Bales, *Family Socialization and Interaction Processes* (Glencoe, Ill.: Free Press, 1965).

Small group communication is an essential part of most work situations.

Therapeutic Groups

A particular kind of work group is the therapeutic group. Group therapy has become a common approach to handling personal problems by psychologists and counselors. Likewise, for people who are not mentally disturbed, functioning with an encounter group, a T-group, or a sensitivity group has become a common means of working out interpersonal problems.[50] These groups, while not at first glance work groups, do have a specific task set for them: to improve the members of the group or help them to improve themselves. These groups typically follow the patterns of other small groups in that they have a task leader (trainer) and generally a social-emotional leader or leaders as well. Frequently the same person fulfills both roles. The groups go through phases comparable to those already discussed, and people are usually enthusiastic about their membership in these groups.[51]

We are frequently asked in classes how effective encounter groups, sensitivity groups, and T-groups are but almost always hesitant to answer that question. We have had experience in sensitivity groups, and that experience has been positive. It has resulted in changes in behavior patterns that seem to have improved interactions with other people. For many people, however, a sensitivity group has little effect in the long run.[52] There is no question that

50. C. Argyris, "On the Future of Laboratory Education," *Journal of Applied Behavioral Science* 3(1967):153–83.

51. Warren G. Bennis, "Patterns and Vicissitudes in T-Group Development," in Leland P. Bradford and Kenneth D. Benne, ed., *T-Group Theory and Laboratory Method* (New York: John Wiley & Sons, 1964), 248–78.

52. Phillips and Erickson, *Interpersonal Dynamics,* 19.

there is an immediate effect, which lasts through the next day or couple of days after the sessions. However, in the long run, over several weeks or months, it appears that the effect of being in a sensitivity group is negligible. Participation in such a group is an intensely dramatic occurrence; indeed, it is very difficult to have gone through the experience of being told that you are too aggressive or that you are too passive without feeling that the experience has been an intense one. The impact of a session seems to be somewhat short-lived, however, because after completion of an encounter session people return to their original environments and regress to their original behavior patterns. This is one of the problems that many mental patients experience after treatment. They go back into the original environment that caused the difficulty, and the likelihood is that that environment will cause the difficulty all over again. Likewise, after leaving an encounter group and returning to the original environment that created the behavior patterns we have, it appears that we tend to resume our old ways.[53]

53. Ibid.

There has been some question about the harm of encounter groups. The rate of breakdown as a result of these experiences is very small, and the likelihood is that the people who have experienced problems in encounter groups probably would have experienced them anyway.[54] We could go a little further and say that experiencing one's problems in encounter groups is probably better than experiencing them out in the real world, where people would be far less sympathetic.

54. Martin Lakin, *Interpersonal Encounter: Theory and Practice in Sensitivity Training* (New York: McGraw-Hill, 1972), 140–41.

Coacting Groups

Another kind of working group is simply a group of people who work together—for instance, four or five people who work side by side in an office. They are really more coacting than interacting, so one could question our referring to these people as a small group. Although they do not have a common goal, they can interact with one another in an uninhibited manner. There are indications that working together in a group appears to facilitate getting work done.[55] Simply being aware of the presence of other people causes us to work more effectively at some kinds of tasks. Of course, it is also true that if we are in a work group in which the interpersonal attraction is considerable and the social-emotional structure is very positive, people may interact with one another so well and to such an extent on a personal basis that the work may not get done the way it should.[56]

55. R. B. Zajonc and S. M. Sales, "Social Facilitation of Dominant and Subordinate Responses," *Journal of Experimental Social Psychology* 2(1966):160–68.

56. R. H. Van Zelst, "Validation of a Sociometric Regrouping Procedure," *Journal of Abnormal and Social Psychology* 47(1952):299–301.

Friendship Groups

One of the best examples of the principle of group influence is the adolescent friendship group, ranging from the early teens to somewhere in the midtwenties. These groups exert an exceptionally strong influence on the individual member. The norms developed regarding clothing, eating habits, and other

57. M. Sherif and C. W. Sherif, *Reference Groups* (New York: Harper & Row, 1964).

58. Argyle, *Social Interaction*, 246–49.

59. Sherif and Sherif, *Reference Groups*.

behavior patterns are very strong.[57] It is of special interest to note that the norms for all groups, conservative and liberal alike, are strongly enforced. At this stage in our lives we have very high ego and social needs, and our peer group seems to be the group most able to satisfy them. We are trying to break away from another small group, the family; consequently we seek out another group, our peer group, to which we can relate and which will accept us.[58] Because we desire this acceptance so much and because our needs are so thoroughly satisfied through group recognition, we are willing to conform to the wishes of the group. These groups have powerful influence over their members and can cause individual members to do things they would never ordinarily even consider doing as individuals.[59] Lest you begin to feel that this is true only of adolescent groups, bear in mind that the same thing is true of any friendship group, so long as the group is satisfying the needs of the individual members. Through friendship the group possesses a powerful hold on the individual.

Of course, we should also indicate that most friendship groups do not have a task external to the group that a work group would have. These groups are primarily socially-emotionally oriented. The leaders in these groups are social-emotional leaders who facilitate interaction among members of the group. Occasionally a friendship group will be faced with a specific task; in that case a task leader will probably be developed or called on. However, it is more usual for the groups to remain primarily social-emotional.

Summary

Small groups play a very important role in our lives, whether in government, industry, family, church, or school. Interaction among members is what distinguishes a small group along with commonality of goals and needs of members that can be fulfilled in the group. While size of group alone does not determine interaction, the practicable range is probably from three to fifteen or twenty people. Routine decisions are often better made by an individual; complex decisions that require creativity often are better made by a small group (a committee). Individuals who deviate from group norms have a special function. Persuading people to support a decision (such as choice of political candidate) can be especially effective through small group communication. The power of the small group over the individual member not only demands conformity, it even causes the "risky shift." The group selects leaders relative to the group's needs.

11

Interviewing

Objectives for the Reader

1. To be able to define interviewing.
2. To be able to explain the three most common objectives of interviews.
3. To be able to discuss the ten characteristics of an interview proposed by Donaghy.
4. To be able to explain the alternating nature of the roles of the participants in an interview.
5. To be able to discuss purposes of the initiation, operation, and termination stages of interviews.
6. To be able to explain and use the different types of interview questions.
7. To be able to discuss the types of information a prospective employer will seek during an employment interview.
8. To be able to describe the verbal and nonverbal behaviors which are effective in an interview.
9. To be able to prepare an appropriate resumé.
10. To be able to discuss the criteria for developing a successful persuasive conference.
11. To be able to explain the advantages of a persuasive conference over other forms of persuasion.
12. To be able to explain the seven steps to develop, structure, and evaluate a persuasive conference.

We are including this separate chapter on interviewing because, of all the forms of interpersonal communication covered in this book, probably none will have a greater effect on your career than this specific form of dyadic communication. It may improve your understanding of the interviewing process to review chapter 9 to refresh your memory regarding the principles of dyadic communication. These principles apply fully to the interviewing setting.

If you are planning to go to medical school, law school, or any other professional school, you will probably be interviewed by someone from that school prior to being accepted. During that interview you will be evaluated, and it is likely that the way you interact during that interview will have a significant effect on the decision whether to accept you at that professional school. If you are planning to apply for employment immediately after graduation from college, you will probably have to submit a written application and should expect to be interviewed by your prospective employer or someone from a personnel department of that employer. The results of that interview will determine whether or not you get the job, what your salary will be, and even some of your future prospects in that company or organization. Even after you have been out of college for several years and have been working in an organization, if you elect to remain in that organization you will frequently have to go through interviews to be considered for higher positions in the organization. Likewise, if you decide to leave the organization in the hope of advancing your career, you will need to submit to further interviews in other organizations when you apply for new positions. Also, there will be other kinds of interviews to go through as a part of your regular job responsibilities.

In other words, interviewing is one of the most pervasive forms of interpersonal communication found in the business world today. We get our jobs through interviewing, we perform our jobs through many interviewing situations, we leave our jobs through an interview frequently, and we get new jobs through interviews. It is, therefore, important for you to consider the material in this chapter, the material presented by your instructor in the classroom, and any other material you can find relative to the interviewing process. When one of us began as a student in the field of communication, interviewing did not exist as a course on a university campus. For that matter, it didn't exist as a part of most communication courses. Today colleges and universities are offering not only interpersonal communication courses with sections devoted to interviewing, but also courses wholly devoted to interviewing. As recently as five or ten years ago it was difficult to find a chapter on interviewing in an interpersonal communication book (or any other kind of communication book), much less a whole book devoted to interviewing. Today most communication books devote a chapter to interviewing, and there certainly are numerous books devoted to interviewing practices and skills.

Interviewing has become an important part of American business and governmental life. The journalist could not obtain information for stories, the television or radio reporter could not secure material for news broadcasts, the public opinion pollster could not get data for the polls, the doctor could not get the information necessary to make diagnoses, the lawyer could not get enough information to defend a client, and teachers could not help students without the interview. Interviewing is a communication activity encountered in most walks of life. We probably could carry on but a fraction of our activities without some form of interviewing occurring. It is our hope that you will apply the information covered in chapters one through ten to any interviewing situation you find yourself in. This additional chapter provides further information and specific, practical suggestions to help you whenever you are in an interview situation.

WHAT IS INTERVIEWING?

Donaghy has defined interviewing as a "planned, oral, face-to-face dyadic interaction utilizing inquiries and responses to gain objective and subjective information with differentiated and alternating participant roles, a serious purpose, and multiple measures of success."[1] This definition is one of the most complete we have found.

1. W. C. Donaghy, *The Interview: Concepts and Skills* (Glenview, Ill.: Scott, Foresman, in press).

The three most common objectives of interviews are to obtain information, to provide information, and to persuade. Informational interviews aim either to obtain beliefs, attitudes, feelings, or objective data from the interviewee, or to explain to, instruct, or appraise the interviewee. Public opinion polls and research surveys use the "information-getting" interview; explaining to a new employee the procedures and policies of an organization is an "information-giving" interview. Also in the informational category are counseling, reprimand, and appraisal interviews; problem-solving conferences; police and insurance investigations; the receiving of complaints; and interviews of celebrities or experts for newspapers, radio, or television.

A person who wishes to modify the beliefs or attitudes of another person may attempt to do so through a conference — a persuasive interview. The sales interview is an example: the interviewer (the salesperson) is attempting to sway the interviewee (the customer) to a point of view. Other examples would be a subordinate attempting to persuade a superior to accept a proposal; or trying to secure a bank loan. Throughout life each of us engages in interviews in which we try to persuade another person to agree with us. Persuasive interviews are discussed later in this chapter.

Following on his definition of interviewing quoted earlier, Donaghy outlines ten characteristics that define and describe an interview:

(1) a serious purpose, (2) planned interaction, (3) oral interaction, (4) face-to-face interaction, (5) dyadic interaction, (6) inquiry and response, (7) objective and subjective information, (8) role differentiation, (9) alternating roles, and (10) multiple measures of success.[2]

2. Ibid.

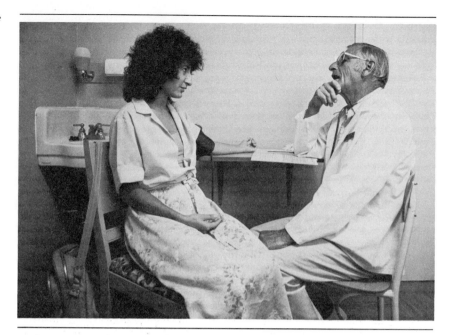

Medical interviews are but one type of interview.

It is apparent that not just any dyadic interaction constitutes an interview. For dyadic interaction to become something more than social interaction between two people, it must have *a serious purpose* — that is, one or both participants must have in mind some serious goal to be gained through the interaction. For a doctor, this goal could be securing information about physical symptoms from a patient in order to make a diagnosis; for an employer, it could be getting enough information about someone to determine whether or not to hire that person.

The serious intent on the part of one or both parties in an interview is related to the second characteristic of an interview: *planned interaction*. If a doctor wishes to gain enough information from a patient to make a good diagnosis, the doctor must have planned some sort of strategy of questioning to get the necessary information. The doctor does not spend all of the time with a patient talking about the weather or a sports event or something they saw on television the previous night. Rather, the doctor probably has certain questions to elicit the information needed to make a diagnosis, and also a strategy for determining temperature, blood pressure, heart rate, location of pains, and the like. In other words, the doctor must have planned the interaction in order for an interview to accomplish its serious purpose. The same is true of an employer in a job interview.

Oral interaction would ordinarily be a characteristic of an interview. It is possible that if one or both people were deaf, they might use sign language in an interview, and thus no oral interaction would occur; but in such a case the sign language is a substitute for oral language. Under normal circumstances, an interview is an interpersonal communication process in which the parties talk and listen to each other. The *face-to-face interaction* could conceivably include an interview conducted over the phone, or via a video connection. The latter would more completely satisfy this characteristic because nonverbal communication behaviors would not be excluded. As discussed in chapter 6, nonverbal communication behaviors are extremely important for understanding feelings and catching subtle nuances of meaning when we are talking with another person. Both parties in an interview need to see as well as hear each other.

The *dyadic interaction* characteristic implies that the two-party nature would hold even though more than two people might be involved. For example, if three people were involved — A, B_1, and B_2 — there would simply be two dyads: A and B_1 would be one; A and B_2 would be the other.

The *inquiry and response* characteristic means that parties in an interview tend to ask questions and respond to questions. A common assumption by many people who write about interviewing is that the questioning is done by someone who is most often labeled an "interviewer" and the answering is most often done by someone called an "interviewee." It is our feeling, however, that because the nature of interpersonal communication is such that both parties mutually influence each other, we are probably misleading ourselves to label one person as the controller of the situation and the other as one who is "helplessly" responding. It probably would be more appropriate to suggest that both parties in an interview are asking questions, and both parties are responding to questions. It is our feeling that interviewing, as a form of interpersonal communication, exemplifies the notion of mutual influence. As will be seen later when we discuss different types of interviews, who is the "interviewer" and who the "interviewee" is frequently difficult to discern in actual interview settings.

Through the pattern of inquiry and response followed in an interview, both parties seek *objective and subjective information*. Both parties seek information such as the salary for a job, years of education completed, prior work experience, and so on (objective). Also, both parties seek information such as the attitude a person may have toward a job, the orientation someone has toward other people, the overall climate in an organization, and so forth (subjective). The face-to-face setting of the interview permits both parties to observe nonverbal behaviors, which, in turn, permit inferences about such subjective things.

Because the inquiry and response pattern works in both directions in an interview — it is not possible to say that one person is the controller and the other person the controlled — we agree with Donaghy that in every interview there are both *role differentiation* and *alternating roles*. Certainly at any given instant in an interview it would be possible to suggest that roles are differentiated by one person asking for information and the other person giving

If both participants in an interview are of equal status, roles sometimes alternate so much that it is difficult to determine who is "in charge."

information. However, at a later instant these roles may be reversed. In other words, the traditional view of interviewing in which one person consistently maintains the questioning role and the other person consistently maintains the answering role is not valid. Both participants seek and give information throughout the interview. To be sure, role differentiation could be defined by what kinds of information are sought and what kinds of information are given. For instance, the kind of information sought by a personnel officer for a corporation would be different from the kind of information the job applicant would seek in an interview. Nevertheless, we feel that there will be both role differentiation and alternating roles in every interviewing context.

The last of the ten characteristics of an interview is that there are *multiple measures of success*. It is not always easy to determine whether or not you have been successful in any interview. There are, of course, behavioral outcomes of any interview which can be assessed. Did you or did you not get the job? If you hired someone you interviewed did the person work out or not? If you conducted a public opinion poll, did the people respond to the questions about a political candidate or didn't they? If an interview is designed to change a behavior of somebody already on the job, did that person actually change the behavior after the interview? Notice that the ways of assessing success or failure depend on the specific goals of the interview. The last of the ten characteristics of an interview is most closely related to the first, the specific serious purpose of the interview. It is important for both parties to determine prior to the interview what their objectives are and what the measures of success will be.

The roles of the communicators in dyadic communication constantly vary. We could simply say that both persons involved in dyadic interpersonal interaction are communicators; one does not serve one function and the other another function. This is true in interviewing also. The person doing the questioning at one moment may at another moment be the person doing the answering, as indicated earlier in the discussion of Donaghy's suggestion that alternating roles are a characteristic of an interview.

Very likely the designation of an "interviewer" role and an "interviewee" role is derived from the thought that one person is more "in charge" of the interview than the other person. For instance, in a job interview the perception of most people is that the person from the company is the one in charge of the interview. We think it is unfortunate that this perception has developed because in any job interview the job applicant is just as likely to be "in charge" of the outcome of the interview as the person who is doing the hiring. The applicant and the hirer have equal opportunity to influence each other, if only because of the nature of interpersonal communication as we have discussed it throughout this book.

If who should be in charge of the interview were based on who has the most at stake in the interview, it would be a difficult matter to say that one person has any more at stake than the other. Whether or not the applicant gets the job is certainly of great importance to the applicant. And certainly whether the hirer hires someone who is inappropriate for the job is of considerable importance as well. Both persons involved in a job interview have much at stake.

Since your first contact with the job interview will very likely be as a job applicant, it is important for you to realize that although the person doing the hiring may be referred to as an "inteviewer" (implying that this person is in charge of the interview), you have considerable potential for control in the interview as well. You should attempt to control the structure and content of the interview just as much as the person doing the hiring. You should not be heavy-handed at this, nor should you be obvious. Rather, we are simply suggesting that your perception of the job interview process should not be that you are "at the mercy" of the "interviewer"; rather, it should be that both of you have something at stake and, therefore, both of you should be contributing, controlling, and developing the interview. Remember, in interpersonal communication we look for mutual influence of all parties concerned. This is true in the interview as in other situations.

We feel that because both participants in an interview should alternately have a responding, then an initiating role, it follows that both parties should be responsible for preparing for the interview so there is a high probability of successful outcome for both parties. Most people talk of the interviewer as the only one who should prepare for the interview and devise questions and strategies for eliciting information from the "interviewee." It is important for the "interviewee" to prepare for the interview as well.

How should you prepare for an interview? If you are applying for a job, you should, of course, research the company and the job; and you should also try to find out as much as possible about the person who will do the hiring so you can have questions about that person and how you may expect to interact with that person in the future.

STAGES OF THE INTERVIEW

Traditionally, authors have written about the stages of the interview as *the opening, the body,* and *the closing.* To be sure, these stages do correspond to the actual behaviors people engage in in an interview. However, it is our feeling that the terms "opening," "body," and "closing" are too parallel to those in an essay, as discussed in a composition course. This makes the interview sound like a "set piece." We prefer the terminology that Emmert and Donaghy used to refer to all communication systems: an *initiation stage,* an *operation stage,* and a *termination stage.*[3]

3. P. Emmert and W. C. Donaghy, *Human Communication* (Reading, Mass.: Addison-Wesley, 1981), 224-37.

Initiation Stage

The *initiation stage* of any interview is the beginning of the interaction between the two parties, during which the relationship between the participants is established. The objectives of this stage are to establish confidence and trust, clarify the purpose of the interview, and identify mutual goals. Rapport, an important element throughout the interview, is largely established in the initiation stage. Some preinterview factors also relate to the establishment of rapport. The request for an interview should not be made in terms that will alarm or threaten either party. The place selected for the interview should be private, comfortable, and conducive to a smooth and satisfactory interviewing operation.

All the concerns of verbal and nonverbal communication discussed in chapters 5 and 6 should be kept in mind during the initiation stage. For instance, the smile is important for a perception of trust and warmth. It helps establish rapport between the participants in the interview. A firm handshake — not excessively strong, but certainly not weak and limp — also contributes to a perception of trust and warmth.

Comments that establish a perception of common ground and mutual interests are important. This is **phatic communication** (communication which appears to have no "real" purpose). When people talk about the town they are in, or about sports or entertainment they both like, these comments which seemingly have "no purpose" help to establish common ground for them.

Discovering or affirming similar likes and dislikes helps them achieve trust in each other, as discussed in chapter 9. It is important to understand this function of these early comments during the initiation stage of an interview.

During the initiation stage both participants should try to put the other party at ease, because no one goes into an interview without some degree of nervousness, heightened expectation, or sometimes even fear. Trying to do your best and make correct decisions always creates pressure. Some people experience something parallel to stage fright as they are about to enter an interview. Remember that this is very likely not so much fright as it is heightened excitement and being ``up.'' It is also something to take advantage of. With the increased adrenalin level and rate of heartbeat, we probably are experiencing a higher energy level. It is possible to use that heightened energy level to speak, gesture, and sit more confidently and thus be perceived more positively.

Operation Stage

Following the initiation stage of an interview is the *operation stage*. This is what most people consider the substantive part of the interview. It relies heavily on the question-answer process, which is discussed later in the chapter. The operation stage can be structured in different ways.

Interview Structure

The structure can be thought of as the organizational plan or strategy used to guide the question-answer process within the body of the interview. The interview can be structured in terms of questions used and in terms of the general pattern of questions as directive or nondirective.

Although roles alternate in most interviews, we can think of interviews in which an ``interviewer'' controls the interaction as more directive and interviews in which the ``interviewee'' controls the interaction as nondirective. In the directive structure, the ``interviewer'' decides what questions will be asked, what topics will be covered, the sequence of the topics and questions, and the overall procedure that will be followed in the interview. In the nondirective approach, the ``interviewer'' allows the ``interviewee'' to make almost all of these decisions. The ``interviewee'' is reinforced and encouraged to talk about whatever he or she wishes. Interviews used for research purposes may require a standardized procedure so there can be a basis for response comparisons. But if the purpose is to get information from an ``interviewee'' in a nonresearch situation, then a flexible approach may be profitably used.

A directive interview may have different degrees of directiveness. The most directive would be the standardized interview: each question precisely worded; each question carefully ordered in the sequence of questions. In other words, every question is asked in exactly the same words and at the same place in the interview for every person interviewed. Both the verbal content for the "interviewer" and the sequence of the content are rigidly controlled. Such an interview structure is most frequently used in research interviewing because "interviewee" responses are compared to common or standardized stimuli.

Some directive interviews are not rigidly standardized. They may have a directive structure to cover a specified number of areas, but the "interviewer" is free to move into one area or another as the situation seems to warrant. The "interviewer" is also free to add questions, to probe on a given topic, or to shorten investigation of a given topic. Although the structure is basically directive rather than nondirective, it allows a great amount of flexibility and adjustment to the "interviewee."

The different structures vary in value and efficiency according to the purpose of the interview. Counseling and therapy interviews are often nondirective since it is desirable to reduce threat to the "interviewee," to give the "interviewee" control over his or her information sharing, and to make the "interviewee" responsible for information acquisition and for growth. On the other hand, the employment interview is often directive, but with considerable flexibility built into it. Research interviews are normally structured so as to be standardized.

Termination Stage

Some interviews come to a natural close as the result of the nature of the progress of the discussion or as a result of the inclination of the participants. Other interviews really need to be continued, but circumstances dictate that they be closed. Still other interviews could be continued profitably because things are going so well, but time dictates that they be ended. Regardless of the reasons or conditions, the interview termination ought to contain a short summary by at least one participant and an opportunity for the other person to make additions or corrections to the summary and an indication of the next steps, or "where we go from here."

This stage of the interview is comparable to the last stage of a dyadic social interaction. To be sure, the termination stage in an interview, which has a serious purpose, is different, but some of the same things occur. For instance, in both cases the parties involved must say "goodbye" and acknowledge that the interaction is over, that the relationship will not exist any longer. They usually feel a need to reduce dissonance and to assure each other that the interaction went well. In the case of an interview, they need to reassure themselves that it was a good interview in which both parties learned a lot and achieved goals. This is why it is so important in an interview for both participants to indicate agreement on what went on in the interview and to indicate the degree to which the goals of the interview had been reached.

Just as a small group or a dyad proceeds through stages of interaction, so also does an interview, as a subset of the dyad, proceed through stages of interaction. The three stages of initiation, operation, and termination must occur or the interview may not be satisfactory for either participant. Without an initiation stage, which permits the development of a relationship, it may be impossible for the participants to function effectively during the operation stage; and this may lead to an unsatisfactory termination.

PREPARING FOR THE INTERVIEW

Preparing to Ask Questions

We have already stated that although most people think of interviews as interactions in which it is primarily the "interviewer" who asks questions, we feel that both parties in the interview should ask questions and respond to questions. One of the first steps in developing interviewing skills consists of becoming acquainted with the various types of questions and/or applications in interviews.

Types of Questions

Two main types of questions are *open questions* and *closed questions*. Both types can be used by either party in an interview. They achieve very different results. **Open questions** call for a response of more than just a few words. For instance, one type of open question, the *open-ended question*, is extremely vague in that it may do nothing more than specify a topic and ask the respondent to talk. For example, someone might ask during an interview, "What do you think about the company's working conditions?" Another open-ended question might be, "Tell me a little bit about yourself." A second kind of open question is more direct in that it identifies a more restricted topic area and asks for a reply on that restricted topic. In some classification systems this type is classified separately from open questions and is known as the **direct question**. For example, a person might ask, "What did you do on your weekends last winter?" You can see that in all of these open questions the person who is responding is fairly unrestricted in what he or she may say. One of the reasons we use the open question is to enable a person to tell us more about themselves than simply "objective information." A person responding to open questions such as the previous examples, will in essence be telling about themselves as well as about the company or whatever.

Closed questions, the second main category of questions, call for a specific response of a few words. The most obvious examples of closed questions are those which call for a yes or no — a bipolar response. An example might be, "Does your company have dental benefits in their health plan?" The likelihood is that the person who is responding to this question will say either "yes" or "no" (although it might be possible to answer "I don't know"). Another kind of closed question would be, "What two courses did you like most and what two courses did you like least in college?" The respondent is not going to be able to say much more than to name four courses. Closed questions are useful for eliciting comparable responses among people to be used for making comparisons among those people. For instance, if you are applying for several different jobs and interviewing with several different companies, you may want to ask them all the same closed questions concerning health benefits or retirement plans or vacation and the like so you can get responses you will be able to compare. Likewise, people doing interviews for companies may want to do something similar so they can compare responses from various applicants.

Both open and closed questions tend to influence the length of the respondent's responses. Open questions encourage the respondent to talk at greater length; closed questions inhibit participation by the respondent.[4] Since one of the problems in most interviews is getting the respondent to become freely involved and to participate in the interview, it is unwise to use only closed questions. Open questions used in the early part of the interview or at the introduction of each new topic are more likely to "open up" the other person. Closed questions are useful as follow-ups for the responses to open questions when more specific information is needed.

Three other kinds of questions that are useful for achieving different responses in an interview are mirror questions, probing questions, and leading questions.

Mirror questions are nondirective. They are useful to encourage the respondent to expand on a response that you believe is incomplete. Mirror questions are usually restatements of what the respondent has just said. If he or she has said, "I don't approve of legal abortion," a mirror question might be, "You say that abortion should not be legal?"

Probing questions are useful to inquire more deeply into the reasons for an attitude or belief or to elicit more specific information. Not all probes are *why* or *how* questions, although these are the most common probing question words. A variety of other vocalizations act effectively as probes and encouragements: "Uh-huh," "I see," "That's interesting," "Oh?" "Good," "I understand," "Go on" — all have the effect of requesting further comment from the respondent. Probes and encouragements are introduced at any time — during pauses, or while the other person is speaking. They indicate careful attention and interest and are intended to encourage the speaker to "tell more" without the listener directing in a closed way the further response. It is important to avoid habitual use of only one probing word.

Silence is fully as important as direct probing questions and sounds. As indicated in chapter 6, the discussion of nonverbal communication, silences can communicate. The inexperienced interview participant is often afraid of pauses and silences. He or she tends to fill every silence, and by so doing rushes through

4. S. A. Richardson, S. B. Dohrenwend, and D. Klein, *Interviewing: Its Forms and Functions* (New York: Basic Books, 1965), 147.

the interview. Sometimes if the respondent is slow in answering a question, the inexperienced person may rush in to rephrase the question or to ask a new question. With experience, we can learn when to use silence as a means of communication — as a probe. Research findings indicate that silences of three to six seconds are most effective in getting the respondent to provide more information.[5] Hence, when we use silence as a probe, we should be prepared to terminate the silence within six seconds or when silence seems destined to fail as a probing technique.

Leading questions strongly imply or encourage a specific answer. They "lead" the respondent to an answer we expect. The leading question can be detrimental when used for the wrong reasons. If we want straightforward, valid, and reliable information from the respondent, we should avoid using leading questions. Cannell and Kahn state: "Questions should be phrased so that they contain no suggestion as to the most appropriate response."[6] Bingham, Moore, and Gustad state: "Avoid implying the answer to your own question."[7] If, however, we wish to test the respondent to see if he or she really understands or is genuinely committed, then a leading question may be useful. For example, if the speech therapist asks the parent of a stuttering boy, "You *are* slapping his hands every time he starts to stutter, aren't you?" the therapist is leading the parent to an incorrect answer to see whether the parent clearly understands that slapping the child for stuttering is inappropriate behavior.

One type of leading question is the tag question, which calls for a *yes-response* or a *no-response*. "Naturally, you agreed with the decision, didn't you?" is an example of a yes-response question. One of the components of leading questions is expectation. If we ask, "Are you twenty-one years old?" it is a direct, closed question but it is not a leading question. If, however, we ask, "Of course, you are twenty-one years old, aren't you?" this indicates an expectation. Expectations can be identified by the syntax and logic of the question, but, as noted in chapter 6, intonation can also communicate expectation. Through intonation and emphasis we could imply surprise and incredulity at anything other than the expected answer, thus making the question "Did you agree with that decision?" into a leading question.

Another form of the leading question is the **loaded question,** which uses loaded words and has highly emotional connotations. It reaches touchy spots and strikes strong feelings. It may present a dilemma from which it is difficult for the respondent to escape. Questions that are not stated objectively are considered loaded. Various techniques are used to indicate the bias or expectation. Prestige may be used. "The president of the United States believes that the problem is serious; don't you agree?" is an example of using prestige to indicate the bias. The interviewer may also associate positive stereotypes with responses that are desired or negative stereotypes with responses that are not desired.

5. See R. L. Gordon, "An Interaction Analysis of the Depth-Interview," Ph.D. dissertation, University of Chicago, 1954; G. Saslow et al., "Test-Retest Stability of Interaction Patterns During Interviews Conducted One Week Apart," *Journal of Abnormal and Social Psychology* 54(1957): 295–302.

6. C. F. Cannell and R. L. Kahn, "The Collection of Data by Interviewing," in L. Festinger and D. Katz, eds., *Research Methods in the Behavioral Sciences* (New York: Dryden Press, 1953), 346.

7. W. V. D. Bingham, B. V. Moore, and J. W. Gustad, *How to Interview* (New York: Harper Brothers, 1959), 74.

To gain an understanding of the question-answer process, you need to become familiar with and be able to recognize the various types of questions that may be used. Through guided practice, you can develop skill in using questions.

Preparing to Answer Questions

Most of us would never think of taking an exam or quiz without some preparation. How do you go about this? Try to think of the way you study for exams and you will very likely be able to teach yourself a lot about how to prepare to answer questions in an interview. In both cases one thing we need to do is think about questions we might be asked. Obviously we cannot anticipate every question someone will ask during an interview, but we can surely anticipate some. If you are a job applicant, you should certainly expect a potential employer to ask you:

What did you study while in college?

What did you learn in the courses you took?

What kinds of skills do these different courses provide for you?

What kinds of job experience have you had that might make you well suited to the job you are applying for?

Do you have any hobbies or interests that would make you better than other applicants for this job?

Why are you interested in this job?

Why do you think you should be hired for this job rather than anyone else?

What do you think you have to contribute to our firm?

What goals do you have for yourself in the coming year?

What goals do you have for yourself over the next five years?

What goals do you have for yourself throughout your entire lifetime?

How willing would you be to move in order to get a promotion?

These questions could go on and on and on; as a job applicant you should try to anticipate as many as you can.

Likewise, the person who is hiring in a job situation should try to anticipate your questions. It is not unusual for a job applicant to ask some of the following questions:

What is the company's vacation policy?

How much autonomy will I have in my job?

What are the possibilities for advancement in this company?

What benefits does the company offer?

Arrange for as many interviews as possible to get a "feel" for the job interviewing process.

A company official should expect to be asked these and many more questions during an interview and should be prepared with information to respond to them.

If you have been good at anticipating the questions an instructor would ask, you probably do better on quizzes or exams than if you are not good at this — and the way you get good at anticipating questions is through practice. We have observed that the more practice people have at interviewing, the better they get at anticipating questions. Thus, we recommend that you sign up for as many interviews as you can when you are looking for a job, whether or not the company is one you are seriously interested in, in order to get practice interviewing. Likewise, many schools have courses in interviewing and/ or special training programs put together by placement services which permit you to have practice interviewing. These are all useful, and we encourage you to take advantage of them.

Preparation Through Research

Another way to prepare for asking and answering questions is through research. You can learn a good deal about a company if you put your mind to it. Check the indexes of business journals, newspapers such as *The Wall Street Journal*, and periodicals such as *Forbes* and *Fortune* for recent news stories or feature articles about the corporation to which you are applying.

If it is not a large company that would be written about in publications such as those mentioned, and if it is a local firm, you could interview people who have dealt with the company, people who know something about how the company functions, and people who work there. Ask questions about how the firm is run and how they treat their employees.

Keep in mind that everything you learn about the company will help you answer as well as ask questions relative to the job and your possible affiliation with that company.

You might also keep in mind that if you are applying for a specific job, you ought to do some research about that particular job.

Likewise, someone conducting interviews should do research about the people being considered for hiring. This certainly includes reading available resumés or personal data sheets. It could also include learning about the college an applicant has been or is about to be graduated from, or the company where an applicant is currently employed.

Both parties to any interview should have done as much research as they can about each other, about the subject matter of the interview, and about the organizations concerned.

Verbal Preparation

Many people don't think about preparing to speak in an interview. If you have ever taken a course in public communication, that training will help you during an interview. Your fluency will be one of the most important factors in an interview for creating a perception of your competence. People who are fluent are perceived to be more competent or more qualified than people who are not fluent.[8] Nonfluency will probably not adversely affect a perception of your trustworthiness, however.

How do you develop fluency? There is an old story about the person who stopped a man carrying a violin case on a street in New York City and asked, "How do you get to Carnegie Hall?" — to which the musician responded, "Practice, practice, practice." Practice helps our speaking, too. The more practice we get speaking, the more fluency we achieve. We can practice by talking into a tape recorder and then playing it back. If you hear some nonfluencies in your speech, don't be too disturbed — everyone has some. If the nonfluencies are excessive, you need to practice more.

If you still have some years left in college, sign up for a public communication course and get practice speaking. Sign up for an interviewing course if your school offers one and get practice speaking in the interviewing context. Other things you could do to improve your oral competency would be to work at your college radio station; or appear in some dramatic productions at your school; or take part in campus politics. We have noticed that most campus politicians become more fluent the longer they participate in campus

8. J. G. Hollandsworth, M. E. Dressel, and J. Stevens, "Use of Behavioral Versus Traditional Procedures for Increasing Job Interview Skills," *Journal of Counseling Psychology* 24(1977):503–10; J. G. Hollandsworth, R. C. Glazeski; J. Stevens, and M. E. Dressel, "Relative Contributions of Verbal, Articulative, and Nonverbal Communication to Employment Decisions in the Job Interview Setting," *Personnel Psychology* 32(1979):359–67; J. G. Hollandsworth, R. C. Glazeski, and M. E. Dressel, "Use of Social-skills Training in the Treatment of Extreme Anxiety and Deficient Verbal Skills in the Job Interview Setting," *Journal of Applied Behavioral Analysis* 11(1978):259–69.

politics. We also suggest that you participate in fraternity or dormitory government or, if you wish, in church activities that require you to speak; volunteer for charities; volunteer to speak on behalf of political candidates. We strongly suspect that the more students have to speak to other students or speak in groups, the more this improves their ability to speak fluently.

To prepare for interviews you should practice out loud. It is not enough to dream up questions you might want to ask or that you might anticipate for possible responses. Practice delivering these questions and these responses.

Especially, beware of any words you may have seen on paper but not heard pronounced, or words whose meaning you are not absolutely sure of. Look up pronunciations and definitions. Misusing or mispronouncing a word during an interview would surely diminish the perception of your competence or qualification.

Nonverbal Preparation

Just as it is important to prepare answers and improve verbal fluency for an interview, it is equally important to prepare ourselves to make a good impression nonverbally. There are things we can do to make ourselves appear more credible in business interviews. First, we should pay attention to our clothing. The clothes we wear do make a difference when we meet someone in a business setting. Both males and females should wear suits when going to job interviews. Females should probably wear suits with skirts rather than pants suits. Both males and females are most credible when wearing dark blue suits, black suits, gray suits, tan/beige suits, and/or some of the dark pinstripes.[9] All of these colors cause the person we are meeting to perceive us as competent.

Women should avoid frilly or lacy blouses and should wear fairly plain white or cream colored blouses with simple ties or scarves.[10] This standard women's substitute for the man's shirt and tie seems to be very much accepted in the business world for women executives, we have noticed in recent days. Men should wear white, blue, or light tan shirts with coordinated ties.[11] Both males and females should avoid trendy clothing. For an interview, dress conservatively.

It should be immediately apparent that the type of clothing acceptable on a college campus among fellow students and professors is not the type of clothing that will produce the best impression during an interview. Jeans, sweatshirts, cut-offs, T-shirts, flannel shirts, and the like do not produce a favorable image during an interview.

Hairstyle also should probably be conservative. Extremely long hair for either men or women is not as credible as moderate length hair. Crew cuts and flat-tops are not as credible for males as a moderate length haircut. Today women appear to be most credible in a business setting and in interviews when their hair is worn moderately short because this is associated with age and age is associated with experience, which in turn suggests greater qualification.[12]

9. J. T. Molloy, *Dress for Success* (New York: Warner Books, 1975), 30–50; J. T. Molloy, *The Woman's Dress for Success Book* (New York: Warner Books, 1977), 49–61.

10. Molloy, *The Woman's Dress for Success Book*, 54–56.

11. Molloy, *Dress for Success*, 51–68.

12. Molloy, *The Woman's Dress for Success Book*, 83–85.

If we are concerned about our success in a job interview we should take care about our visual presentation of self.

These suggestions about nonverbal preparation do not represent value judgments. Rather, they present what research and our own experience show to be most effective in interviewing situations.

Your nonverbal presentation also encompasses such elements as makeup and jewelry. Probably the best rule of thumb about makeup is that if somebody notices it, you have too much on. For a business interview, conservative light makeup for women is probably in order, but false eyelashes and extreme eye makeup are not. Both males and females should be careful not to wear too much jewelry. Wristwatches, wedding rings, and engagement rings are certainly acceptable, but to go much beyond that begins to look excessive. A stickpin or sometimes a simple necklace will not detract from a woman's credibility, but such things as bracelets that jangle or earrings that are noticeable can detract from credibility in an interview.[13]

Again, refer back to the discussion of eye contact, posture, and other nonverbal behaviors in chapter 6. Remember that during an interview you are trying to project a confident, self-assured image. This should suggest that you would not use closed postures but, rather, open and confident postures. Likewise, the smile is in order, but excessive smiling may cause you to be perceived as weak, whether you are male or female. Remember that males and females differ in the amount of eye contact they like. Thus, if the person you are talking with is female, you should probably try to engage in greater eye contact; if male, use less eye contact — for all the reasons stated in chapter 6.

13. Ibid., 89–92.

Review of the material in chapter 6 will remind you that how you fare in an interview will not depend just on what you say, it will also depend on how you say it, how you look, and the nonverbal behaviors that accompany what you say. Try to control these as much as possible so that your nonverbal behaviors will cause people to perceive you as a credible, confident, self-assured person.

SELECTION/EMPLOYMENT INTERVIEWS

Because one of your primary concerns after graduation (or before) will likely be to secure employment, the most important type of interview for you is the *employment* interview. Out of this interaction both parties make a decision: that you should or should not work for that concern. Both parties in an employment interview are attempting to elicit information from the other as well as influence the decision of the other. Unfortunately job applicants too often assume that the sole objective in this type of interview is to get hired. This is unfortunate because you cannot be suited for all jobs; therefore, you probably will not be happy in all jobs; neither will you be able to do your best in all jobs. A major goal for you as an applicant should be to determine if this job is right for you (and you for it), just as the other person's goal is to determine if you are right for the job. Square pegs are neither as successful nor as happy in round holes as are round pegs.

Keep these mutual objectives in mind as you consider the following lists of suggestions. They are general guidelines for the two parties in the employment interview.[14]

14. Adapted from Robert S. Goyer, W. Charles Redding, and John T. Rickey, *Interviewing: Principles and Techniques* (Dubuque, Iowa: Kendall/Hunt, 1968), 23–25.

Suggestions for the applicant:

1. Clarify the job requirements.
2. State why you are applying for this job with this company.
3. Present your qualifications in terms of having something of value to offer the company. Deal as much as possible in specific details and examples — job experiences, avocations, travel, activities, offices held, organizations, and schoolwork.
4. Do not hesitate to admit potential weaknesses. Under no circumstances should you attempt to bluff or fake on these, but wherever possible, make a transition from a weakness to a strength; at least, when the facts justify it, show some good extenuating circumstance for the "weakness." (This does *not* mean supplying alibis or excuses!)
5. Do not depend merely on a "smooth front" (appearance and smile) to "sell yourself." Provide full information to the prospective employer.
6. Get as much information as possible on such sensitive matters as salary (usually in terms of a range, or of the "going average").

7. Let the employer set the "tone" or atmosphere of the interview. Be a little more formal than usual—but don't be too rigid! Be cautious about jokes, wisecracks, sarcastic asides, and so forth!

8. Watch the opening moments of the interview. Avoid making remarks that create a "negative set" for the rest of the interview. Avoid starting the interview with a remark such as "I'm really not sure that my background will be appropriate for your company or for this job," or "I'm sorry to say I haven't had any experience along these lines."

9. Be informed on the company: its history, geographical locations, general methods of doing business, reputation, and so forth.

10. Try never to have an interview concluded without some sort of understanding about where you stand, what is to happen next, who is to contact whom. This does *not* mean you are to push the employer against the wall and force a definite commitment!

Suggestions for the employer:

1. Take the initiative in getting the interview under way; don't sit back and stare at the applicant. Offer your hand first. Ask the applicant to be seated. Establish rapport *before* probing for information.

2. Make an easy, casual, smooth transition from opening greetings to the first serious topic of the interview.

3. Start off with "easy" materials and aspects in the applicant's background that are not sensitive areas. Encourage the applicant to talk freely about something which the information on the application blank suggests should be easy for the applicant to discuss with specific details and examples.

4. Don't give a "sales pitch."

5. Do more listening than talking. Encourage the applicant to "open up." Listen carefully—including "between the lines." Insert brief prompters to encourage more talk; use "mirror" techniques.

6. Don't exaggerate the benefits of the company or the job! Create confidence and trust by being honest about potential or actual drawbacks.

7. Avoid evaluative comments on the applicant's answers such as, "That's too bad," or "I'm certainly glad you said that!"

8. Without being mechanical about it, try to cover topics in a systematic order. Your objective is not only to avoid hit-and-miss jumping around but also to avoid giving the impression of engaging in an oral examination!

9. Be alert to cues in the applicant's answers and behavior. Adapt immediately to what is said so that you can follow up a promising lead. Probe suspected weaknesses.

10. Ask questions that will reveal the applicant's attitudes and personality in relation to the job's total requirements.

The employment interview is a give-and-take process, highly dynamic and rich in its informational and persuasive potential. The person who desires to improve his or her behavior as an interviewer or interviewee must learn to be extremely perceptive and accurate in observation and understanding of other persons.

Presenting What Employers Are Looking For

A major question to consider as you contemplate applying for a job would certainly be, "What are the people who do the hiring looking for?" Although we have touched on some of this previously, we want to emphasize the order of importance of the elements that company representatives in employment interviews consider in deciding to hire a person. Some research shows the order of importance to be: (1) communication skills, (2) grade point average, (3) work experience, (4) appearance, (5) extracurricular activities, (6) location preference, and (7) academic accomplishments.[15]

Notice that items 1 and 4 are interpersonal communication factors over which you have control — and which constitute the subject matter of this entire book.

15. H. D. Tschirgi, "What Do Recruiters Really Look For in Candidates?" *Journal of College Placement*, January 1973, 75–79.

Your Resumé

You have an opportunity to demonstrate communication skill in writing prior to or at the beginning of the interview, and thereby cover items 2, 3, 5, and 7 just mentioned. By presenting a resumé, or vita as it is sometimes called, you enable the other person to learn about you quickly, and perhaps more easily do some research on you ahead of time. So you may want to include this important data sheet with your letter of application. With your resumé in hand, that person can ask more questions that are appropriate to you as an individual rather than rely entirely on "standard" questions. Your providing this information in writing, as well as orally during the interview, makes it much more likely that the other person will remember that information about you.

Also, it is easier for you to fill out an organization's own personnel information sheet when you apply for a position at its office if you have already assembled the data about yourself. If you had not already prepared a careful inventory of yourself before seeking an interview, to do so would be one more good way to prepare yourself for the interview.

A resumé should have at least three general categories: personal history, educational history, and work experience. In addition, you will want a list of possible references — people who are able and willing to furnish recommendations for you. The following is an outline you could use to prepare a resumé.

I. General information
   A. Your name
   B. Address
   C. Telephone number
   D. Date of birth
   E. Marital status
II. Education
   A. Schools attended
   B. Honors earned
   C. Grade point average
   D. Major
   E. Minors
   F. Activities
III. Experience
   A. Prior work
   B. Experience-related activities
IV. References
   In addition to listing an individual's name, address, and phone number, you can give a brief sentence that summarizes the particular qualities or abilities he or she could comment on.

The following suggestions for preparing an effective resumé are based on guidelines presented by Downs, Smeyak, and Martin.[16]

16. C. W. Downs, G. P. Smeyak, and E. Martin, *Professional Interviewing* (New York: Harper & Row, 1980), 148–49.

1. Arrange the information on the page so that there is a lot of white space. The less cluttered the resumé, the easier it is to read. Also, judicious use of white space makes the appearance of the resumé more attractive.

2. Arrange the information you are presenting in "chunks," with headings that correspond to the four major categories listed previously. These can be arranged in whatever sequence you consider most appropriate for the job you are seeking, but the information should be "chunked" so it is easier to digest.

3. Whenever you are listing things chronologically (such as education and work experience), list them in REVERSE chronological order, the most recent accomplishment first. Your most recent educational degree and your most recent work experience probably are most indicative of your abilities, so highlight them by presenting them first.

Figure 11.1

```
                    SEAN PHILLIPS

2332 Baker Street            Height:  5'8"
Maranack, Wisconsin 24810    Weight:  140
Telephone:  517-374-9685     Marital Status:  Single
                             Birthdate:  April 23, 1960


EDUCATION:

     1979-83  University of Missouri, Columbia, Missouri
              B.S. Major:  General Business;
                   Minor:  Communication
              Grade Point Average:  3.21 ( A=4, B=3, C=2,
              D=1)

              Activities:  Debate, Chess Club, and Acacia
              Fraternity

     1976-79  Maranack High School
              National Honor Society:  Junior and Senior
              Years

              Activities:  Band, Debate, Computer Club,
              and Student Council


WORK EXPERIENCE:

     1979-83  Part-time employment as radio announcer at
              WCCC, Maranack, Wisconsin and KNMF,
              Columbia, Missouri

     1978-79  Part-time employment as a clerk at J.C.
              Penney, Maranack, Wisconsin


REFERENCES:

     Furnished on request either from Sean Phillips or
     from University of Missouri Placement Service,
     University of Missouri, Columbia, Missouri, 63302
```

4. Conciseness is a virtue in resumés, as in many things. Your resumé should provide a QUICK understanding of your background for anyone who reads it. Downs, Smeyak, and Martin suggest that usually it should be two pages long or less.

5. Do not omit any time periods. Whenever we see years missing from a resumé, either in work experience or education, we become suspicious, or at least concerned.

6. Consider writing more than one resumé. Remember that you may be legitimately applying for more than one type of job, each of which calls for different qualifications to be emphasized. A different resumé for each type of job with the appropriate qualifications highlighted is worth considering.

7. Be sure to list references, with addresses and phone numbers, or indicate that references are available on request. Especially if you want to use a single resumé for different jobs, for which you would use different references, you may wish to have references available on request. Be sure to check with the people you are using as references before listing them; they might be offended to be listed without their agreement.

Figure 11.1 shows what a resumé might look like.

The employment interview is an experience we usually have many times throughout our careers. We hope it is evident that it is an experience you should spend time preparing for. It is not prudent to simply show up and "wing it."

PERSUASIVE INTERVIEWS

Persuasive interviews are seldom called persuasive interviews. They are called conferences, sales presentations, or other things. But whatever they are called, they are situations in which one person attempts to persuade or influence another person. In some conference situations, each person has a proposal or persuasive goal in mind to present. Most organizations make extensive use of conferences to initiate action and to solve problems.

The possibility of success in these persuasive conference situations is increased when the following criteria are met:

1. The proposal satisfies a need or desire of the person to be persuaded.
2. The persuader and persuadee have similar beliefs, attitudes, values, cultural background, and moral standards.
3. The proposal is shown to be workable and practical.
4. Objections to the proposal can be shown to be outweighed by benefits and advantages.
5. No better alternative is available.

Of these five criteria, the creation of a need or desire in the person to be persuaded is perhaps the most important. In any event, the smart persuader in the conference situation is concerned with all of these factors and organizes his or her efforts in the conference around these objectives.

There are good reasons why the persuasive conference is used extensively. It is far superior to memos, brochures, meetings of several persons, news-

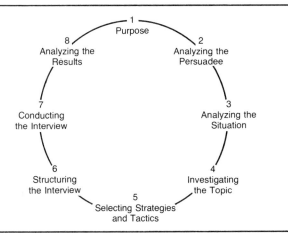

Figure 11.2 This figure is based on one in Robert L. Kahn and Charles F. Cannell, *The Dynamics of Interviewing*, (New York: John Wiley & Sons, 1964), 103.

papers, the publication of the organization, or direct orders given orally. The advantages of the conference or interview situation are:

1. The persuasive message can be adapted to the specific person.
2. One can get immediate feedback, verbal and nonverbal.
3. The persuadee can participate in the process.
4. Strategies can be changed because the process is open, alive, and defined at the time.

There is no form of communication so open and so adaptable as the face-to-face conference or interview situation.

To prepare well for a persuasive interview or conference, you need to consider several factors in a systematic way. Kahn and Cannell's illustration of those factors is shown in figure 11.2.

The first step is to determine the *purpose* of the interview: the goal the persuader has in mind; the action, attitude, or belief the persuader wants the persuadee to accept. It is essential for the persuader to know clearly and precisely what he or she wants the outcome of the conference to be.

The second step in the process is to *analyze the persuadee* carefully. The conference needs to be adapted to that particular person. Age, sex, race, intelligence, group memberships, hobbies, superior and subordinate relationships, work experience, attitudes relative to the goal or proposed action, temperament, personality, interaction history with others — these and other factors that seem to be relevant to the persuasive encounter ought to be considered. The persuadee's values, beliefs, and motives as they relate to the proposal are essential factors to consider. The effective persuader does not plunge blindly into interactions. Rather, he or she attempts to discover as much as possible about the persuadee so that messages and interactions can be adapted specifically to that person.

The third step is to *analyze the situation*. Where will this conference take place? Can you obtain privacy and be free of interruptions? Is it a formal or informal setting? Will it be on your ground, the persuadee's ground, or neutral ground? What will be the likely atmosphere? Trust? Suspicion? Apathy?

The fourth step is to *do your homework* – i.e., the investigating and research necessary to thorough knowledge and understanding of the problem under consideration.

The fifth step is to *select the strategies and tactics* you will use in the interview or conference. You will want to use a different strategy for a hostile person from that you would use for a cooperative person, for example. Some strategies are: (1) the common-ground approach, (2) the yes-yes approach, (3) the implicative approach, (4) the climax-order approach, (5) the anticlimax-order approach, (6) the one-sided approach, and (7) the both-sides approach.

The **common-ground approach** is one in which beliefs, attitudes, feelings, and goals that are held in common by the persuader and the persuadee are identified and used to achieve the acceptance of the proposal. The **yes-yes approach** leads logically via an inductive process from small agreements progressively to acceptance of the major proposition or action. The **implicative approach** is an indirect approach in which the goal is argued for by implication but *not directly*. It is not explicitly stated. This approach is often used when the proposal will be met with hostility or negative response, or when the persuadee is so insecure or defensive that he or she has to "have the idea first." Reasons, arguments, and data congruent with the desired proposition are given, but the solution or conclusion is not stated. The persuadee is left to discover that. Only by implication is the proposition made known.

The **climax-order** strategy simply means that the strongest argument is given last. **Anticlimax order** means that the strongest argument is given first. **One side** of the argument is given when the persuadee is apt to be in partial agreement already, is not resistant or hostile, and is not accustomed to verbal interpersonal interaction in decision-making situations. On the other hand, when the persuadee is opposed to the proposition, even hostile to it, and is accustomed to verbal argument and decision making, it may be better to present **both sides** of the issue.

The sixth step in preparing for the conference or persuasive interview is *structuring the interview*. The strategies and tactics just discussed are fitted into an overall structure or pattern of organization for the interview or conference. The standard pattern of organization has been identified as follows:[17]

I. Opening
  A. Establish rapport
  B. Give a clear, concise statement of purpose, need, or problem
II. Body
  A. Problem or need
      1. Point-by-point development of the reasons, causes, or aspects of the need or problem

17. Adapted from Charles J. Stewart and William B. Cash, Jr., *Interviewing: Principles and Practices* (Dubuque, Iowa: Wm. C. Brown, 1982), 57–72.

a. Always point out how the reason, cause, or aspect concerns the persuadee

b. Employ a variety of evidence and appeals to motives, beliefs, values, and frames of reference

c. Summarize and get agreement (at least tentative) before moving to a new reason, cause, or aspect of the need or problem

2. Summarize the need or problem and get overt agreement from the persuadee before proceeding further

B. Criteria: standards, requirements, norms the solution should meet

1. Present the criteria

2. Discuss briefly why each criterion is important in evaluating solutions to this need or problem

3. Encourage the persuadee to add criteria to the list

4. Summarize and get agreement on all criteria to be used

C. Evaluation of solutions

1. Deal with one solution at a time

2. Explain the solution in detail

3. Evaluate the solution criterion by criterion

4. Handle objections before they arise, if possible

5. Get agreement on how well the solution meets the criteria

6. Move to the next solution, if more than one is to be considered

III. Closing

A. Summarize what has been discussed in the interview and the agreements reached

B. Obtain a commitment from the persuadee if at all possible

C. Arrange for the next interview or for the first step in implementing the solution

The seventh step is to *conduct the interview*, and the final step is to *analyze the conference or interview*. While the interaction is fresh in the persuader's mind, he or she should take stock. Is the persuasion completed? Will it require more research? Will it require another meeting or two? Is a new strategy called for? What is the next action?

SUMMARY

The focus of this chapter has been on a specialized application of dyadic communication, the interview. The interview, like other forms of dyadic communication, is a situation in which both parties can mutually influence each other. It is important that we never assume that either party should sit passively and answer questions; both parties in an interview should take an active part.

Because each party can control as well as be controlled in an interview, it is important for both to plan and prepare accordingly.

Glossary

abstraction process
Verbal process of placing objects, persons, and concepts into categories based on the similarities among members of the categories, while the differences among category members are overlooked.

acquaintance process
When persons come to know each other.

affect display rules
Cultural norms for appropriately expressing emotions.

affection messages
Responses to the need for affection.
overpersonal messages
An excessive response to the need for affection.
personal messages
A moderate response to the need for affection.
underpersonal messages
A deficient response to the need for affection.

alienation
Being estranged, separated from, or alone and withdrawn from others.

anomia-alienation
A general unwillingness to communicate with others.

anticlimax-order approach
Persuasive technique in which the strongest argument is given first.

appropriate responsiveness
What is judged to be reasonable in amount and quality of interaction with another person.

arbitration
Process of resolving a conflict by using an unbiased outsider, who is given the power to dictate a resolution.

articulation
The precision of our pronunciation.

attitudes
Inferred mental state in which a person evaluates a person, object, or concept as either positive or negative. Attitudes are usually inferred from behaviors that can be observed.

auditory acuity
Sensitivity to sounds.

auxiliary behaviors
Behaviors that are unrelated to our original need to communicate but which affect other people's perceptions of our messages.

balance theory
Theoretical explanation of the need for consistency developed by Fritz Heider.

blends
Emotional displays which are (1) combinations of primary affects or (2) expressions of multiple emotions; most emotional displays are blends.

body image
Physical self; size, attractiveness, and socially admired physical characteristics.

both-sides approach
See *two-sided approach.*

categorization
Process of grouping the phenomena in our environment into categories according to their similarities.

centrality
The amount of centralization in communication network of a small group or organization.

central traits
Characteristics that other persons perceive as a controlling and primary personality characteristic of the individual.

circular view of communication
Implies that communication proceeds from one person to another and back to the first person.

climate
The prevailing communication mood, tone, or atmosphere in an interaction.
defensive climate
A prevailing mood of suspicion, nonreceptivity, and mistrust in an interaction in which the participants feel compelled to protect themselves.
supportive climate
A prevailing mood of openness and acceptance in an interaction.

climax-order approach
Persuasive technique in which the strongest argument is given last.

closed-mindedness
Opposite of open-mindedness; evaluates on the basis of inner drives and needs; thinks in black and white, either-or categories; focuses on the source; seeks information to reinforce beliefs; and rejects, ignores, or distorts information inconsistent with own belief system.

closed questions
Have an expected and predictable answer, i.e., *yes* or *no* or some specific and short answer.

cognitive processing
The part of the listening process in which meaning occurs; the continuous flow of words is responded to with understanding and feeling.

combat
Conflict in which the participants desire to hurt one another as much as they desire to achieve their goals.

common ground approach
Persuasive technique in which establishment of ''common ground'' (beliefs, attitudes, desires, theoretic base, assumptions, or premise are agreed to by the persuader and persuadee) is used as foundation for the persuasive strategy.

communication apprehension
Anxiety associated with speaking situations, either formal or informal.

communication context
Combination of the number of people, their relationships, their goals, and the communication phases they evolve through that are used to distinguish among dyadic, small group, and organizational communication.

communication network
Pattern of message flow among the members of a small group or organization.
centralized communication network
A pattern of message flow in a small group or an organization in which most messages are funneled to and received from one or two persons.
decentralized communication network
A pattern of message flow in a small group or an organization in which messages emanate from all members approximately equally and are sent approximately equally to all members.

communicative cues/behaviors
Nonverbal behaviors used as intended messages to influence others.

comparison level
The minimum we feel we deserve from a relationship in order to be satisfied with the relationship.

comparison level for alternatives
The criterion we use to decide whether to stay in a relationship; determined by comparing our possible relationships to see if our present relationship is the best of all alternatives.

competition
Conflict in which the participants perceive that only one individual or group can achieve its goal and the other must lose.

complementary stimulus message
Supplementary message transmitted for the purpose of reinforcing the primary stimulus message.

complementation
Nonverbal communication that adds detail to or modifies the verbal message but is consistent with the verbal message.

compromise
Process of each party to the conflict giving up some goals or values to resolve the conflict and to win some goals and values.

conflict
An expressed struggle between at least two interdependent parties who perceive incompatible goals, scarce rewards, and interference from the other party in achieving their goals.

conflict communication style
The typical pattern of communication behavior used by an individual in a conflict situation.
avoiding conflict style
A style of engaging in conflict situations in which the individual psychologically or physically withdraws from the other person.
cooperative conflict style
A style of engaging in conflict situations in which the individual is willing to compromise and collaborate with the other if the other will also compromise and collaborate.
win/loss conflict style
A style of engaging in conflict situations in which the individual perceives that he/she can only win or lose objectives
yielding conflict style
A style of engaging in conflict situations in which the individual unilaterally gives concessions to the other.

conflict phase
The second phase of small group interaction in which members engage in disagreement.

conformity
Compliance to group pressure or norms.

congruity theory
Theoretical explanation of the need for consistency developed by Charles E. Osgood and Percy H. Tannenbaum.

connotative meaning
Subjective, emotional associations, unique to the individual that affect responses to words.

consummatory interpersonal communication
That directed toward immediate satisfaction of needs by the communication process itself.

contradiction
When nonverbal communication and verbal communication disagree or oppose one another.

control messages
Responses to the need for control.
abdicratic messages
A deficient response to the need for control.
autocratic messages
An excessive response to the need for control.
democratic messages
A moderate response to the need for control.

controversy
Disagreement that is perceived as being controllable and resolvable since both parties can gain part of what they desire.

cooperative conflict
Conflict in which the individuals perceive that both can achieve their goals.

culture
Combined effects of knowledge, experience, meanings, beliefs, bias, attitudes, religion, concepts of the self, the universe and self-universe relationships, hierarchies of status, role expectations, spatial relations, and time concepts shared by large groups of people across generations.

dating
Process of mentally placing a date beside the words for persons, objects, and concepts to remind us that they change over time.

defensiveness
Opposite of trusting another; fear of another and protecting oneself from another.

demographic exchanges
Reciprocal giving of "demographic data" — i.e., age, education, where one lives, occupation, etc.

denotative meaning
Common dictionary meaning of words that includes properties of concepts, but no emotional responses.

descriptive approach
An approach to small group communication in which what normally happens in small groups is described.

deviation (in small groups)
Practice of an individual not conforming to the norms or wishes of the group.

direct perspective
What each person in an interaction really thinks; a comparison of two direct perspectives determines agreement or disagreement.

direct question
A type of open question that identifies a somewhat restricted topic and requires a somewhat restricted answer.

dissonance
Anxiety and pressure toward consistency experienced by individuals when they perceive inconsistency among attitudes, values, beliefs, and/or behavior.

dissonance theory
Theoretical explanation of the need for consistency suggested by Leon Festinger.

distance
  intimate distance
  Distance from 0–18 inches used by intimate friends when communicating about intimate topics.
  personal distance
  Distance from 18 inches to 4 feet used for interactions with our friends and families about personal topics.
  social distance
  Distance from 4 feet to 12 feet used for social interactions and business discussions.
  public distance
  Distance of 12 feet and more used in public presentations to groups.

distributive justice
The expectation that the rewards available in a relationship will be distributed fairly with the individual who provides more to the relationship getting more of the rewards.

double-bind message
When one aspect of a message sent by an individual is the opposite of another aspect of the same message; it is called a double-bind because the receiver cannot respond appropriately to both of the contradictory aspects but must choose to respond appropriately to only one and ignore or respond inappropriately to the other.

dyadic communication
Two-person or two-party communication.

emergence phase
The third phase of small group interaction in which group members come to realize that a decision has emerged from the discussion.

emphasis
When nonverbal communication stresses some aspect of the verbal message.

encounter groups
Small groups formed for the purpose of self-improvement of the participants.

encouragements
Short vocalizations which have the effect of requesting a speaker to continue, such as, "I see," "that's interesting," or "uh huh."

environment
Environment of any communication system includes all the factors outside the system which influence the system.

equilibrium
A state of balance in a relationship; a relatively stable state of adjustment to one another achieved by the participants.

facial communication
All the nonverbal messages produced by the use of facial muscles and organs.

feedback
Receiving information relative to a message sent for the purpose of correcting or adjusting that message if needed.
  delayed feedback
  Feedback delivered sometime after the original message occurred.
  direct feedback
  Feedback which is intentionally sent.

external feedback
Feedback we receive from others.
immediate feedback
Feedback delivered at or near the time the original message occurred.
indirect feedback
Feedback that is performed unintentionally or simply "given off."
internal feedback
Monitoring our own performance and delivering feedback to ourselves.
nonverbal feedback
Uses the nonverbal codes or channels of communication.
positive feedback
The use of positive or pleasurable messages to reinforce another's behavior.
verbal feedback
Uses the verbal channel of communication.

field of experience
The sum of all our past experiences; individuals must have some overlap in their fields of experience to be able to communicate with one another.

friendship groups
Small groups formed for the purpose of satisfying the social needs of group members.

generation gap
Misunderstanding between older and younger people that results from different communication behaviors based on differences in experiences.

gestalt approach to perception
The approach to perception that suggests we perceive perceptual wholes.

gestalt principles of perception
Fundamental rules we use in organizing incoming stimuli.
  good form principle
  Recurring or common forms in our environment are perceived as completed even if we receive only part of the form; symmetry in the form encourages us to perform this closure and perceive the form as complete.
  proximity principle
  Things, people, messages, etc. which are grouped together are perceived as belonging together.

search for order principle
Predictability in incoming stimuli encourages us to look for underlying structure and order.

grammar
The rules for combining words into meaningful units; one of the subsystems of language.

hearing
The part of the listening process in which speech sounds in the form of sound waves are received by the ear.

hidden antagonizers
Words perceived negatively by the recipient of a message when the originator of the message is unaware of any negative connotations.

ideal self-concept
The self we would like to be.

identifying and recognizing
The part of the listening process in which sounds are mentally reorganized into words.

identity crisis
Unintegrated self; one who is in a state of being unsure of who he or she is; one who is doubtful of his or her acceptability.

implicative approach
Persuasive technique in which the persuader argues by using inductive reasoning until the persuadee forms the appropriate solution or conclusion.

implicit personality theory
Set of inferences privately developed by one person about another person at an initial meeting.

inclusion messages
Responses to the need for inclusion.
  oversocial messages
  An excessive response to the need for inclusion.
  social messages
  A moderate response to the need for inclusion.
  undersocial messages
  A deficient response to the need for inclusion.

indexing
General semantic practice to help people mentally remind themselves that all objects, persons, or concepts referred to by a word are not the same. In listening, indexing refers to the ranking of information according to importance and relationship to other information.

informative behaviors/cues
Nonverbal behaviors that provide information to an observer even though the observed one does not intend them to do so.

input subsystem
The reception processes in a human being.

instrumental interpersonal communication
That directed toward the accomplishment of a task.

intentional approach to communication
A speaker-oriented perspective toward defining communication in which only behaviors with the intent to influence another are considered communication.

interactive behavior
Nonverbal behavior that can affect interactions between people whether or not the communicators intend to do so.

interference
Stimuli in the environment that alter or distort messages.

interfering messages
Messages in the environment not produced by the participants in the interaction which alter or distort the messages produced by the participants.

interpersonal attraction
Liking of each other. (See also **perceived attractiveness.**)

interpersonal communication
Process of from two to twenty persons mutually attempting to influence one another through use of a common symbol system, in a situation permitting equal opportunity for all persons involved in the process to influence each other.

interpersonal conflict
See **conflict.**

interpersonal negotiation
Process of participants in a conflict situation attempting to resolve the situation through communication.

interpersonal trust
See **trust.**

interviewing
Planned, oral, face-to-face, dyadic interaction utilizing inquiries and responses to gain objective and subjective information with differentiated and alternating participant roles, a serious purpose, and multiple measures of success.

Johari window
A self-disclosure model representing what is both known and unknown about you to others and to yourself.

language
Processing system composed of two subsystems, vocabulary and grammar, both interacting to produce meaning.

leadership
Situationally based communication behaviors that permit a leader to influence group members relative to social-emotional and task needs of the group.

leading question
Question that is designed to "lead" the respondent to an expected or desired response.

linear view of communication
Implies that communication proceeds from one person to another, that communication is something one person does to another.

listening
Processing of hearing, identifying and analyzing, and assigning meaning to incoming aural stimuli.

loaded question
Leading question that is designed to trap the respondent by using highly emotional connotations.

macromeaning
Process of categorizing the relationships among various stimuli and structures.

meaning
Responses people have to words, resulting from a complex process of association.

nonverbal dimensions of meaning:
control dimension
One of the dimensions of meaning for nonverbal emotional expressiveness, bordered on one end by emotional displays we feel are intentional and under the control of the sender, and on the other by emotional displays we feel are unintentional and/or unconscious.

intensity dimension
One of the dimensions of meaning for nonverbal emotional expressiveness bordered on one end by low-intensity nonverbal expression, and on the other by high-intensity nonverbal expression; accounts for most of our response to nonverbal emotional expression.

pleasantness dimension
One of the dimensions of meaning for nonverbal emotional expressiveness bordered on one end of the continuum by pleasant emotions and on the other by unpleasant emotions.

verbal dimensions of meaning:
activity component
One of the dimensions of meaning for verbal communication, bordered on one end of the continuum by active and on the other by passive.

evaluative component
One of the dimensions of meaning for verbal communication, bordered on one end of the continuum by good/valuable and on the other by bad/worthless; this dimension accounts for most of our responses to words.

potency component
One of the dimensions of meaning for verbal communication, bordered on one end of the continuum by strong and on the other by weak.

mediation
Using a third party in conflict resolution with the third party having no power to dictate a resolution.

message
Symbolic behavior intended to influence another.

message characteristics
Attributes of messages which affect an interaction.

certainty or dogmatic messages
Suggest that the sender is correct and any and all alternative positions are wrong.

controlling messages
Designed to influence or dominate the other person.

descriptive messages
Depict objective behavior, represent or portray our perspective without labeling the other person.

empathic messages
Indicate sharing, caring, understanding of, and identification with the receiver.

equality messages
Imply that the other person is as highly valued and respected as the self.

evaluative messages
Label the other person and/or his or her behavior; directly or indirectly judge the other person.

neutral messages
Intellectual and/or detached messages which demonstrate a lack of concern for the other.

problem orientation messages
Recognize the mutuality of the interaction and the cooperative nature of any solutions that are proposed.

provisional messages
Suggest that the sender is receptive to opposing points of view and willing to change.

spontaneous messages
Appear relevant to the present interaction, are internally consistent, and sufficiently revealing that nothing appears hidden.

strategy messages
Generally contain hidden agenda — surreptitious manipulations that are recognized and perceived by the receiver as unfair.

superior messages
Indicate a feeling of being better than the other person.

metacommunication
Employing language to talk about language; communicating about communication.

meta-metaperspective
Each individual's perception in an interaction of the other person's metaperspective; comparison of the two meta-metaperspectives determines if the individuals in the interaction share a mutual realization of the understanding or misunderstanding with the other person.

metaperspective
Each individual's perception in an interaction of the other person's direct perspective; comparison of the two metaperspectives determines understanding or misunderstanding.

micromeaning
Process of categorizing individual stimuli.

mirror question
Nondirective interviewing technique in which a statement of the interviewee is repeated as a statement or question by the interviewer.

mirroring
The duplication of another's nonverbal communication/behavior in a mirror image (where the right side of one individual's body imitates the left side of the other's body, and vice versa).

moratorium technique
A technique in which the individual delays creating a stable self-image and instead experiments with several self-images to see which one will "fit."

need hierarchy
The arrangement of needs into an order from the most basic physical needs to the highest order ego needs; needs lower in the order must be satisfied before those higher in the order can motivate an individual.

needs
Motivational states people respond to in survival-oriented behavior.

consistency need
Need to have our ideas, values, perceptions, behaviors, and attitudes all be consistent among themselves.

ego need-identity needs:
self-actualization needs
The need to achieve at the highest level that we are capable of achieving.

self-esteem needs
The need to think well of oneself.

physical need
Need to maintain oneself physically over both a long-term and short-term basis:

physiological needs
The basic physical needs of hunger, thirst, etc.

safety or security needs
The need to make long-term plans for the satisfaction of basic physiological needs.

social need
Need to have positive relationships with other people.

affection needs
The need to be warm and intimate with others.

control needs
The need to control and be controlled by others; dominance and power needs.

inclusion needs
The need to interact and associate with others.

nonsharable goals
Winner-take-all situations in which one participant in the conflict situation wins all and the other participant loses all.

nonverbal communication
Behaviors produced to influence others in ways other than words, such as gestures, eye behavior, facial expressions, and posture.

norms
A pattern of behavior, considered "appropriate," which is expected in a culture.

one-sided approach
Persuasive technique in which only one side of an issue is presented.

open-mindedness
Processing information in ways characterized by objective evaluation, use of data, easy differentiation, focus on content, acceptance of and even seeking of information; toleration of ambiguity and dissonant information; and willingness to modify beliefs.

open question
No specific answer is expected; any answer is appropriate; may only specify a general topic of discussion.

orientation phase
The first phase of small group interaction in which people try to get to know one another, discover roles and status, and decide on the group's task.

output subsystem
Includes all the encoding processes for producing messages and behaviors.

paraphrasing
Repeating the other person's message in your own words.

parasupporting
Paraphrasing the other's message and adding examples and data to illustrate and clarify those ideas.

perceived attractiveness
The amount of liking we have for another; derived from three components.

social-liking
The degree to which we would like the other as a friend.

task-respect
The degree to which we would like the other as a work partner.

physical appearance
The degree to which we like the other person's body characteristics.

perception
Mental process of selecting, organizing, and interpreting the many stimuli that impinge upon us at any given moment.

person perception
Mental process of selecting, organizing, and interpreting the available stimuli related to a person we have met.

personal network
Each person's network of personal, trusted friends.

phatic communication
Chitchat or social communication which seemingly appears to have no "real" purpose but which is important to establish shared perceptions of mutual interests, attitudes, values, etc.

pitch range
The height and depth of the sound tones in our vocal repertoire.

power
Dominance, authority, or control in a relationship.

power sources
Where power is derived from.

coercive power
The ability to punish another individual.

expert power
The ability to deliver some special service to another person because of special knowledge or abilities.

legitimate power
Power derived from law or tradition and invested in roles and positions in the social structure.

referent power
The power to influence others to like us or to want to model themselves after us.

reward power
The ability to deliver something of positive value to another individual.

prescriptive approach
An approach to small-group communication in which ideal steps are given to the individual to follow which should lead to more effective small-group communication.

primary affects
Emotional displays which appear to have a unique physiological expression; these are understood across cultures and appear to be universal.

primary stimulus message
Messages produced in response to our original need to communicate, communicated by whatever means seems most effective.

probing question
Question that is designed to elicit more information on that topic.

processing subsystem
Includes all thought processes.

propinquity
Close distance between persons; proximity.

purr words
Words that most people perceive openly indicate affection and warmth; they do not describe the object or person as much as they describe the attitude of the sender toward the other.

quasi-courtship behaviors
The use of nonverbal courtship postures and gestures in an attenuated form to show attraction toward another.

reciprocal scanning
Process of "sizing each other up" in the acquaintance time, especially during the initial or entry phase.

reciprocity phenomenon
Tendency for one behavior to elicit the same behavior in another; in the acquaintance process, it is the tendency to give information about oneself to cause the other person to give information about himself or herself.

reference process
Mental process by which we connect things symbolized with the symbols themselves.

regulation
The process by which nonverbal communication controls verbal communication exchanges.

regulatory function
Feedback serves a regulatory function in interpersonal communication systems when information is sent or received which helps one or more individuals in the interaction correct or adjust communication/behavior to increase reciprocal integration and satisfaction of needs.

reinforcement phase
The fourth phase of small group interaction in which group members positively reinforce one another for their participation and decision making.

repetition
When the nonverbal communication system reproduces some aspect of the verbal message; functions to produce redundancy.

rhythm
The pattern of strong and weak sounds; the way we phrase our words when we speak.

risky shift
Phenomenon of an individual becoming more radical and less conservative as a result of taking part in small group communication.

ritual response
Communication response that is automatic and predictable rather than spontaneous and dynamic.

roles
Culturally prescribed behaviors and powers that exist for an individual as he/she relates to another individual in a particular relationship.

Sapir-Whorf hypothesis
The language we learn facilitates our thinking about some things and makes other things more difficult.

self-acceptance
Having a positive and constructive attitude toward oneself.

self-actualization
Bringing one's ideal self into existence as the real or actual self; fulfilling one's highest need, i.e., to become what one wants to be.

self-awareness
Knowing "who one is."

self-concept/self-image
Physical, social, and psychological perceptions of oneself.

self-consciousness
Extent to which a person is shy, embarrassed, anxious, and overly concerned with himself or herself when in the presence of or watched by others; the opposite of social confidence and poise.

self-disclosure
Making known information about oneself to another.

self-esteem
Liking, valuing, and regarding one's self highly for high self-esteem and assigning unfavorable and negative attitudes toward one's self for low self-esteem.

self-fulfilling prophecy
Bringing into fruition a predicted behavior; the living up to or down to a label. Process by which our expectations regarding ourselves or others cause us to engage in behaviors that result in ourselves and/or others behaving according to our expectations.

self-image
The picture or image we have of ourselves; the categories we use to describe ourselves.

self-monitors
Individuals who focus upon internal attitudes, inner states, and personal dispositions in order to create their self-perception.

situation-monitors
Individuals who focus upon the situation and the appropriateness of the role they are playing in order to create their self-perception.

small group communication
Communication that occurs in a group of three or more people who can interact with each other face-to-face, who are not inhibited from interacting because of group size, and who have common needs that can be satisfied through participation in the group's activities.

snarl words
Words that most people perceive as openly indicated hostility; they do not describe the object or person as much as they describe the attitude of the sender toward the other.

social communication
Talk which serves to establish social harmony in an interaction; talk for the purpose of present social satisfaction rather than long-term needs.

social-emotional needs and leadership
Leadership based upon a response to the interpersonal needs of the group.

stereotype
Abstraction process by which we include all persons from a group in a category and expect them all to be identical.

stroking communication
Unit of recognition; communication to another so as to meet his or her social, affective, or psychological needs.

structuralist approach to perception
Position that perception is the process of combining all sensations additively into a single perception.

substitution
Communication using nonverbal channels or codes as identical replacements for the verbal message.

symbol
The use of something to represent something else; the use may be arbitrary (such as the sounds "mama" to represent a female parent) or natural (such as a raised fist to represent power or anger).

systems view of communication
Implies that communication is a process in which all persons are mutually and simultaneously involved in influencing one another through messages.

tactile communication
Form of nonverbal communication based on touching behavior.

task needs and leadership
Leadership based on a response to a problem external to the group.

tempo
The speed at which we speak.

territorial imperative
The biological need of all animals to control and defend a certain amount of living space.

time binding
Using communication to pass information from generation to generation.

trait theory
Approach to person perception in which we develop perception of personality traits and either add them together or combine them holistically into a perception of those we meet.

trust
The reliance upon the behavior of another person in order to achieve a desired objective, the achievement of which is uncertain in a risky situation.

two-sided approach
Persuasive technique in which both sides of an issue are presented although both may not be equally defended.

unintentional approach to communication
A receiver-oriented perspective toward defining communication in which all behavior in an interactional situation is considered potential communication.

value hierarchy
The continuum of preference or importance of our values; we value those things most highly which reinforce our self-concept.

value system
An enduring organization of beliefs concerning preferable modes of conduct or end states of existence along a continuum of relative importance.
　instrumental values
　Preferred modes of conduct.
　terminal values
　Preferred end states of existence.

vocabulary
Words; one of the subsystems of language.

vocalics (paralanguage)
Nonverbal characteristics associated with the production of words by speech: pitch, voice quality, rate and rhythm of speech.

volume
The loudness of our voice.

words
Units of meaning; arbitrary symbols that are learned through a complex process of association.

work groups
Small groups that respond primarily to task needs.

yes-yes approach
Technique of eliciting agreement from the persuadee, from minor points to the critical decision point.

Credits

Photographs

Chapter 1
Rick Smolan: *2;* Carole Dugan: *7;* American Museum of Natural History: *9;* Wayne Miller/Magnum Photos: *12;* used with permission of Ann Landers and Field Newspaper Syndicate, 1982: *15;* Dennis Brack/Black Star: *23;* Robert Eckert/EKM-Nepenthe: *28;* Jean-Claude Lejeune/EKM-Nepenthe: *29.*

Chapter 2
Robert Eckert/EKM-Nepenthe: *34;* Peter G. Aiken: *37;* United Press International: *41;* Karen Collidge/Taurus Photos: *50.*

Chapter 3
Jean-Claude Lejeune: *56;* Carole Dugan: *60, 66;* Richard Younker: *78.*

Chapter 4
James L. Shaffer: *86;* Carole Dugan: *89;* Bob Coyle: *94;* American Stock Photos/Tom Stack & Associates: *105.*

Chapter 5
Jean-Claude Lejeune: *118;* courtesy of The Coca-Cola Company: *124;* Carole Dugan: *137;* Wide World Photos: *143.*

Chapter 6
Bob Coyle: *146, 151;* Historical Pictures Service, Chicago: *154;* Rick Smolan: *157;* United Press International: *162;* James L. Shaffer: *172;* Allen Ruid: *174.*

Chapter 7
Jon Jacobson: *176;* Rick Smolan: *181;* James L. Shaffer: *183;* United Press International: *195;* Carole Dugan: *201.*

Chapter 8
John Maher/EKM-Nepenthe: *210;* Bill Stanton/Magnum Photos: *213;* Jean-Claude Lejeune: *217;* United Press International: *222;* Carole Dugan: *227;* Robert Eckert/EKM-Nepenthe: *229.*

Chapter 9
Frank Siteman/EKM-Nepenthe: *238;* Bob Coyle: *242, 256;* Robert Eckert/EKM-Nepenthe: *247;* Ron Seymour: *258.*

Chapter 10
Chris Grajczyk: *264;* United Press International: *267;* A. Devaney, Inc., New York: *275;* Bruce Quist: *283;* © Eric Kroll 1979/Taurus Photos: *286.*

Chapter 11
James L. Shaffer: *290;* Robert Eckert/EKM-Nepenthe: *294;* Robert George Gaylord/EKM-Nepenthe: *296;* Allen Ruid: *305;* Bob Coyle: *308.*

Illustrations

Chapter 1
Figure 1.1: used with permission of Ann Landers, 1982.

Chapter 2
Figure 2.2: from W. Schramm, *The Process and Effects of Mass Communication* (Urbana: University of Illinois Press, 1955), *p. 6.* By permission of the publisher.

Chapter 3
Cartoon *(p. 73):* © 1966, L. Lorenz. Reprinted with permission from *The Saturday Evening Post.* Figure 3.2: reprinted from Joseph Luft, *Group Processes: An Introduction to Group Dynamics* (Palo Alto, Calif.: Mayfield Publishing Co., 1970). *Of Human Interaction,* by Joseph Luft, published in 1969, also contains the Johari Window.

Chapter 11
Figure 11.2: based on Robert L. Kahn and Charles F. Cannell, *The Dynamics of Interviewing* (New York: John Wiley & Sons, Inc., 1964), *p. 103.*

Index

Buss, A. H., 108n
Butler, Pamela E., 215n, 216n, 231n
Butter, Charles M., 88n, 90n
Byrne, D., 108n, 110n, 244n

Cannell, Charles F., 303n, 315n
Cantril, H., 276n
Career survival, role of interpersonal
  communication in, 14–15
Carlsen, G. Robert, 179n
Carroll, John B., 39n, 127n
Carroll, Lewis, 123n, 143n
Cash, William B., Jr., 316n
Categorization, process of, 94–95, 136
Centrality, 280
Central traits, 103
Chamberlin, Roy B., 156n
Chimpanzees, and communication, 7
Chomsky, Noam, 125n
Circular communication, 36
Civikly, Jean M., 173n, 255n
Clamming up, 226
Clark, W., 110n
"Clean for Gene phenomenon," 157
Cleaver, Eldridge, 59
Cleveland, S. S., 63n
Climax-order strategy, to persuasive
  interview, 316
Closed questions, 301–2
Closure, phenomenon of, 92–93
Clothes, role of, in nonverbal
  communication, 157
Coacating groups, communication in,
  287
Coakley, Carolyn Gwynn, 179n, 180n
Cody, Michael J., 247n, 248n
Coercive power, 219
Cognitive processing, 180, 181
Collings, M. E., 109n
Collins, Barry E., 23n, 269n, 277n
Combat, 224
Committees, communication in. See
  Small group communication
Common-ground approach, to
  persuasive interview, 316
Communication. See also Interpersonal
  communication
  avoiding ambiguous, 228–29
  avoiding information overload in,
    229–30
  avoiding polarized, 229
  importance of openness in, 114–15
  lack of, as problem, 227
  need for open, 226–27
  working for accuracy in, 228–31
Communication anxiety, 71
Communication contexts, 16–17

Communication networks, 280
Comparison level for alternatives, 248,
  250
Competition level of conflict
  participants, 224
Complementary stimulus message, 49
Complementation, and nonverbal
  communication, 151–52
Compressed speech, 190
Compromise, role of, 234
Condon, John C., Jr., 69n
Conferences, 314–17
Conflict. See also Conflict resolution
  communication styles, 215
    avoiding, 217, 221
    cooperative, 217–18
    win/loss, 215–16, 221, 227, 231,
      233
    yielding, 216, 221, 231
  constructive vs. destructive nature
    of, 212–25
  cooperative negotiation of
    interpersonal, 225–35
  definition of, 214–15
  in dyadic relationships, 254–55
  with fully shareable goals, 219
  intensity of, 223–25
  and maintenance of perspective,
    232
  with nondivisible or nonshareable
    goals, 218
  with partially shareable goals,
    218–19
  as phase of small group interaction,
    270–71
  and power structure, 219–20
  and trust, 220–22
Conflict intensity, 223
  levels of, 223–24
  reducing, 224–25
Conflict resolution, 213–14
  developing positive attitude in,
    225–26
  maintaining perspective, 232
  maintenance of open
    communication in, 226–27
  setting aside time and place for, 231
  use of mediator/arbitrator in,
    234–35
  using rational, problem-solving
    approach to, 232–34
  working for accuracy in
    communication, 228–31
Conformity, 274–76
Congruity theory, 24
Conklin, F., 151n
Connotative meaning, 128
Consistency needs, 23–24

Consummatory communication, 253
Continuous reception, in interpersonal
  communication, 90
Contradiction, and nonverbal
  communication, 152
Control, 18
  dimension of, 165
  of feedback, 199–200
  need for, 19–20
Controversy level of conflict
  participants, 223–24
Conversational speech, loudness of,
  180
Cool Cos: The Story of Bill Cosby, 59
Cooperative communication style,
  217–18
Cooperative conflict, 223
Corrective function of feedback, 192
Coser, Lewis, 225n
Cosmetics, role of, in nonverbal
  communication, 158, 308
Costello, Daniel E., 16n
Counseling, 300
Courtright, John A., 255n
Crisis
  importance of empathic feedback
    in, 201
  role of, in increasing conformity,
    276
Crisis centers, 201
Critical listening, 184–85
Cross-cultural communication, 48
Crutchfield, R. S., 274n
Culture
  effect of, on nonverbal
    communication, 168–75
  effect of, on perception, 113–14
  and language, 122–23, 134
  and multidimensionality and word
    meaning, 131
  and use of hidden antagonizers,
    140–41
  and words, 134–36

Dance, E. X., 7n
D'Angelo, Gary, 207n, 209n
Darley, J. M., 109n
Darnell, Donald K., 128n, 130n
Darwin's theory of evolution, 25
Dating, device of, 139
Davidson, J., 108n
Davis, J. H., 270n
Davis, K. E., 108n
Daydreaming, and listening, 191
Decibels, use of, to measure loudness
  of sound, 180
Decoder, 43